Cryptography and
Public Key Infrastructu
on the Internet

Cryptography and Public Key Infrastructure on the Internet

Klaus Schmeh

Gesellsschaft für IT-Sicherheit AG
Bochum, Germany

WILEY

Copyright © 2001 by dpunkt.verlag GmbH, Heidelberg, Germany.
Title of the German original: *Kryptografie und Publik-Key-Infrastrukturen im Internet*. ISBN: 3 932588 90 8

English translation Copyright 2003 by John Wiley & Sons Ltd,
The Atrium, Southern Gate, Chichester,
West Sussex PO19 8SQ, England. All rights reserved

National   01243 779777
International (+44) 1243 779777
e-mail (for orders and customer service enquiries): cs-books@wiley.co.uk
Visit our Home Page on http://www.wileyeurope.com or http://www.wiley.com

Library of Congress Cataloging-in-Publication Data

(to follow)

British Library Cataloguing in Publication Data

A catalogue record for this book is available from the British Library

ISBN 0 470 84745 X
Translated and typeset by Cybertechnics Ltd, Sheffield
Printed and bound in Great Britain by Biddles Ltd., Guildford and Kings Lynn
This book is printed on acid-free paper responsibly manufactured from sustainable forestry
for which at least two trees are planted for each one used for paper production.

Contents

Foreword by Carl Ellison

Cryptography is variously a hobby, a pastime for children, a branch of mathematics, a tool for personal privacy, a hindrance for law enforcement or the salvation of media companies. It is also an area that has seen much conflict, often reported in the press. In the latter half of the 1990s, when the first edition of this book was published in Germany, the conflict was between law enforcement agencies and citizens who wanted to use cryptography for protecting their own privacy. More recently, the conflict has been between video, audio and software copyright holders, on the one hand, and cryptographers who choose to do research in the area of content protection, on the other. One would think they would work together, but part of research into cryptography is the breaking of cryptographic schemes of others, and legislative efforts in copyright protection try to make it illegal to perform and publish such breaks, threatening to bring research to a stop. We do not know yet how that conflict will be resolved, but when it is, we would be guilty of excessive optimism to assume that there will be no more conflicts over cryptography.

To some of us, cryptography is all in a day's work. To others it is a personal passion. To my average friend, cryptography is something intensely complex, somehow associated with spies and diplomats and clearly something impossible to understand.

Someday, strong cryptography may be so invisibly incorporated into everyday products that the average user would not need or want to understand it. Computer file system internals, networking protocols, SCSI bus commands, etc., are already in that category. They are details that the average user need never address. Even the average computer developer needs only a rudimentary understanding of such details.

That day is not yet at hand for cryptography. The US export rules have been relaxed and more engineers are using strong cryptography (although not always properly), but we are still at the beginnings of making the actual use of cryptography understandable and comfortable for the man in the street. If the end user of a computer system wants to use cryptography intelligently, then he or she will need to understand some of the details of this field.

To the student of cryptography, the field is no longer in its infancy, but neither is it in old age. Most likely it is in its adolescence: a time of growth spurts, identity crises, agonies over acceptance and a struggle to find its place in the mature world. This makes the present a time of real excitement for those of us developing and using cryptography and runs the risk of making it a time of great confusion for the average computer user.

Childhood

Cryptography's childhood was very long. David Kahn's history of cryptology [Kahn] follows its development for millennia. There was the potter 3500 years ago in Mesopotamia who invented and used a cipher in order to protect the secrecy of a new formula for glaze. There were the Hebrew scribes of the book of Jeremiah who used a cipher to hide various names. Medieval alchemists used ciphers to protect their secret formulas. Perhaps from association with the alchemists, cryptography in Europe acquired an aura of magic or even the occult. In India, on the other hand, the Kama Sutra listed cryptography among the 64 arts necessary for a well-rounded individual.

As David Kahn noted, 'It must be that as soon as a culture has reached a certain level, probably measured largely by its literacy, cryptography appears spontaneously – as its parents, language and writing-probably also did. The multiple human needs and desires that demand privacy among two or more people in the midst of social life must inevitably lead to cryptology wherever men thrive and wherever they write. Cultural diffusion seems a less likely explanation for its occurrence in so many areas, many of them distant and isolated' [Kahn, p. 84].

The examples over the years of uses of cryptography tend to be dictated by need. Those who needed to communicate securely at a distance, under the threat of interception, used cryptography for communications. These tended to be military and diplomatic personnel, tracing back to the ancient Greeks and Julius Caesar. Those, such as the Mesopotamian potter, who needed secure storage of information but who lacked the wealth to erect fortified buildings and hire guards, gave us examples of cryptography for storage. International bankers gave us examples of cryptography for authentication. These three areas continue to be relevant today and should be considered separately to be well understood.

Over the years, various inventions spurred rapid developments in cryptography. For the most part, these were the inventions that made communications easier and at the same time more easily intercepted: the telegraph, the radio and now the Internet.

One non-communication invention of the twentieth century has also spurred cryptographic developments, and appropriately so because it grew out of cryptography. That invention is the digital computer. The first digital computers were built to perform cryptanalysis during World War II. Now, of course, the computer is the enabling technology for the Internet, so it has crossed over into communications, but the biggest reason that it spurs development of cryptography is that cryptographic operations are inherently complex. Cryptographic operations are designed to be intolerant of even the smallest mistake. Therefore, these complex operations must be executed perfectly. In the days before the computer, cipher clerks were hired to perform these mind-numbing tasks. Those clerks needed not only to be precise in their work; they also needed to be extremely trustworthy. This is clearly a job begging for a computer. A computer is not always flawless, but it easily beats a human in precision. A computer is not always trustworthy (if it is infected by a virus or plagued with bugs, for example), but it can be the total property of its user and the user is free to make his computer as trustworthy as it is humanly possible to do by locking it in a safe when it isn't being used, for example – something you would not do to a cipher clerk.

Adolescence

The knowledge of cryptography has always been generally available. With the invention of the personal computer, the cipher clerk is now also generally available. This opens up wonderful possibilities. Now, common everyday products can take advantage of the characteristics of cryptography, especially in the areas of authentication, fault tolerance, virus protection and privacy.

With all these possibilities has come public notice. Various law enforcement agencies expressed alarm over the possibility of widespread cryptography. Everyday communications of normal citizens had been laid bare by advances in technology (for example, the cellular telephone), and these agencies had taken advantage of their increased ability to eavesdrop. This ability amounts to power and an agency will preserve its power at all costs. A citizen needs to be aware of the realities of cryptography and its uses in order to be an informed voter and citizen when dealing with the issues of cryptography policy introduced by such agencies.

Another kind of notice has come from organizations and individuals pursuing money. Cryptography looks like a sure thing: something everyone will need, since everyone wants privacy. So, the number of product offerings and patents in cryptography is quite large. Here a citizen needs to be aware of cryptography just to be an informed buyer. Cryptographic products are especially prone to being described with inflated claims.

Today's uses

Today one uses cryptography to exchange 'secure' e-mail, to connect to a 'secure' web page, to use a virtual private network. There are new developments in the use of cryptography to permit a consumer to protect his or her personal data and resources, and hopefully to do so in a way that is simple to understand and easy to use correctly. We see developments using cryptography for Digital Rights Management and a corresponding policy debate over copyright law [Lessig]. There might also be legal actions involving cryptography – suing someone over a digitally signed message, backed by an open PKI – although that possibility looks more remote now than it did in 1998 because of the decline of PKI.

We don't know what will finally develop out of cryptography, but today's two principal classes of use are certain to remain: confidentiality and authentication. Confidentiality allows someone to encipher a message so that an intended recipient(s) can decipher it but no one else can. An intended recipient can be some other person, in which case we are dealing with communications, or it can be oneself at some time in the future, in which case we are dealing with enciphered storage. Authentication allows someone to prepare a message signature or MAC (message authentication code) by which to determine that the message has not been changed and that it originated with someone possessing the secret needed to make that signature or MAC.

Each of these areas of cryptography has witnessed a pitched battle in recent years.

Confidentiality

The battle over confidentiality generated much press coverage and inflamed deep passions. Does a citizen have the right to use cryptography to attempt to keep a secret from the government? If some government is to be permitted to overrule that citizen's right, then which government(s)? ... Germany, the USA, France, Russia, China? At the moment almost all governments have concluded that the citizens' needs for confidentiality are important for national security. However, in light of continual danger from terrorism, whose perpetrators are not localized in one physical country, there continues to be a desire to put entire populations under surveillance and confidentiality via cryptography might interfere with that surveillance.

As long as there are personal computers, compilers and cryptography books, the citizen will continue to have the ability to use cryptography no matter what controls are attempted. Will they continue to have the right?

This needs to be decided in appropriate political fora.

Authentication and authorization

The battle over authentication and authorization is different. There are battles of wills over privacy rights and over property rights. There is also a contest of definitions.

With regard to privacy, there rage debates between those who believe that all cryptographically authenticated remote operations should be backed up by a digital certificate revealing the user's identity and those who believe that one can authorize actions anonymously [Brands].

With regard to property rights, Digital Rights Management allows someone to attempt to enforce property rights in a way that was not available before, and from that ability comes unexpected consequences. Some DRM policies that can be and sometimes are specified violate provisions of copyright law (for example, 'fair use' provisions). Imagine a car that could read the current speed limit from the road, digitally, and absolutely enforced it. Our existing copyright law permits people to use personal judgment and have the result adjudicated later. With DRM, rules are enforced by a mechanism with which one is not able to argue and which offers no room for personal judgment.

Perhaps more interesting is the contest over definitions.

Prior to the invention of public key cryptography, two people who wanted to communicate in secret had to have a secret key that only they knew. Given that shared key, not only would the two parties be able to communicate without fear of eavesdroppers, each party would know that an incoming encrypted message was from the other party. This provided a kind of authentication. For cases when privacy wasn't desired, there was developed a cryptographic operation yielding a MAC (message authentication code), in which the shared secret key was used with the message contents to produce a check value that could be made (or checked) only by someone having the secret key.

Since keys can be betrayed, these secret keys would have to be replaced by fresh ones periodically. Typically this was accomplished by use of a trusted courier, bringing keys from one party to the other. Then in 1976, Diffie and Hellman published the first practical public key cryptosystem, capable of securely delivering keys at a distance, over a non-confidential channel (although one that had to have integrity). In that paper, Diffie and Hellman proposed that one could replace trusted couriers with a kind of telephone book – except this telephone book would have a name and public key for each listed person. This telephone book would be a networked directory rather than a paper book, although one such paper book was actually printed [RJA Global Trust Directory]. To make it possible to operate when that directory was not available, Loren Kohnfelder proposed in 1978 that the line items from this directory be digitally signed and carried by the people who care about these entries. He called such a digitally signed line item a **certificate**.

The claim made by Diffie and Hellman was that if my key was in that directory, anyone could go to the directory and find my public key (via my name) and use my key to send me a message for my eyes only. What they overlooked was that names do not specify people uniquely. Granted, there may be some person who has a globally unique name, but John Smith is not one of those. A security system that works only for people who have globally unique names isn't very interesting. Nevertheless, there are digital signature laws in some countries and in some states of the United States that specify the legal meaning of digital signatures backed up by such certificates, and those laws assume that when a certificate binds a public key to a name, it is binding that key to a person.

Even though the names that serve us so well in our small communities in the physical world fall short for us on the net, we still need authentication and authorization. We need to know things about the people with whom we deal. However, the original assumption was wrong. We need more than just to trust the binding of a name to that other person. We need to know things about that person – usually not a name – and need to learn those facts from authorities on those facts. For example, the SET cardholder certificate provides a fact about a keyholder (permission to use a specific credit card), issued by the authority on that fact (the bank issuing that credit card) without referring to the person's name. That certificate is used in the process of authorization (deciding if the keyholder is allowed to do something), not merely in establishing the name of that keyholder.

SET is just one example, from one limited (but important) area of daily life. SET looks unlikely to become ubiquitous but as more of our daily life moves to the Internet we will need to develop more such certificates and authorization procedures. These procedures in the physical world developed over centuries, by evolution in small steps. On the Internet, operating at 'web speed', the invention is likely to be in much larger steps and to have flaws with larger impacts. This calls for more people who can intelligently review such inventions.

The Internet is exciting. Relationships form, people fall in love, business is transacted, warfare is waged, and life in this world is just beginning to be developed. It is a new frontier for us, now that we have run out of dry land to explore. It is a land with its own rules. Some of those rules are disarmingly familiar while others are radically different. One thing we do know, however, is that cryptography will play a key role in many of these new rules and behaviors.

Happy exploring.

Carl Ellison
Portland, OR

Carl M. Ellison is a Senior Security Architect with the Corporate Technology Group of Intel Corporation. His current research is devoted to delegatable, distributed, public-key authorization. His concentration on security has been a side-effect of a more general career focus on the design of distributed and fault-tolerant systems.

Part 1

Why cryptography on the Internet?

Encryption machine HX-63, 1963 Model
(from the IT-Security Teaching & Study Collection of the BSI)

Introduction

1

If the automobile had followed the same development as the computer, a Rolls-Royce would today cost $100, get a million miles per gallon, and explode once a year killing everyone inside.
ROBERT CRINGELY

Key experience no. 1
In the mid-1990s, network-pioneer Bob Metcalf was one of the more important Internet-pessimists. When, during a lecture, he once again forecast the early collapse of the Internet, he let himself be drawn into making a bet: should his forecast not come true, then he would eat the manuscript of his lecture. Since no such collapse occurred in the meantime, Metcalf finally had to admit defeat. However, he dispensed with the pleasure of eating paper. Instead, while at a WWW Conference, he ate his words in the form of icing-sugar words piped on a cake.

1.1 If the Internet were a car …

The development of the car was unlike that of the computer

A car for 100 US dollars, that needs filling up only once in its lifetime? According to Robert Cringely, such a super-car would have been a reality long since if the development of the automobile had proceeded at anything like the speed of computer development. Each new car model would have had twice the top speed of its predecessor, and even small cars would have a luggage compartment the size of a gymnasium. The glove compartment of a medium -class limousine would swallow the baggage for a two-week holiday without even a hiccup. Naturally, such developments would bring concomitant disadvantages. In the latter years, baggage size would have increased enormously and correspondingly. A simple shopping bag would long ago have reached the size of a single family house. Naturally, it would be especially annoying if pieces of luggage went missing as the result of a 'baggage compartment crash' before we had made a 'baggage compartment backup'. Equally exasperating would be the mandatory requirement to change the engine and all interior furnishings and fittings at frequent intervals.

The development of the car also differed from that of the Internet

In view of the scenario just described, it is perhaps just as well that car development did not parallel that of the computer. But does this conclusion also follow for the Internet ? If car development had followed that of the Internet then we would today have 60 mph motorways with 10-lane 3000 mph access roads. There would be no way of knowing whether the quickest way from London to Bristol was via Bath or via New York! The disappearance of a car without trace would be just as much an everyday event as an unpredictable change in the car's content. One of the worst consequences, however would be that someone could burgle a car travelling at full tilt down the motorway without the driver even noticing.

1.2 Security on the Internet

The Internet displays a considerable lack of security

The comparison with a car that can be burgled while travelling at top speed demonstrates at least one thing quite clearly: the Internet exhibits a substantial array of security failings. Naturally these stand in the way of serious commercial use. How is a bank supposed to offer online banking on the Internet if hackers cannot be prevented from gaining access to the accounts of others? How can business be conducted on an insecure Internet?

Such a lack of security is incomprehensible at first glance. Studying the history of the Internet, however, makes some things clear. The gaps in security are not unrelated to the fact that, for a long time, commercial use of the Internet was not even considered. For a few years the Internet was just a scientists' toy to which scarcely anyone gave a thought. Hardly anyone thought of making money on the network of networks. The Internet continued its cloistered existence until just a few years ago, when the monastery gates were flung wide open.

The Internet was not created for commercial use

What happened then astonished everyone. User numbers increased with explosive speed and the Internet became a mass medium. The '@' generation was born – honest citizens became 'netizens' and the verb 'to surf' gained a completely new meaning. However, not only home users were impressed by the Internet. Business enterprises also profited enormously from the new opportunities. A 'net' or 'com' in the company name was often the only necessary requirement to become a rising star on the Stock Exchange. In just a few years, firms such as Netscape and Amazon achieved growth that would have taken generations in other branches of industry. Internet euphoria was such that one might easily have imagined that the entire world would soon be completely carpeted with Internet cables.

The first Internet boom years are over

Today, some five years after the start of the big boom, we are again a bit further on. Rumours that years would soon be termed 'before the Internet' and 'after the Internet' have not been confirmed. In the industry, the euphoria of some enthusiasts has been replaced by the cool consideration of corporate enterprise decision takers, who ask themselves if, and how, cash can be wrested from the Internet. The investment favourites of the early days have become (pro tem?) the whipping boys of Stock Exchange investors. Internet users are no longer a progressive elite, but people like you and me – even bowling clubs and local league football clubs have their own home page these days. Already, the first Internet Luddites have appeared, and hold themselves to be especially progressive because they want to know nothing more of this new technology. Meanwhile, the younger brother of the Internet, the intranet, has reached school age. But it is rumoured that the intranet is not the solution to all problems, but 'only' a useful tool.

The gold-rush mood on the Internet has calmed down

The gold-rush mood has thus cooled down. However, the boom is still not long past – on the contrary, the Internet is only at the start of its triumphal procession through our everyday life. A procession that will see online shopping, online banking, online apparatus control, and much more, taken for granted.

During the rapid development of the Internet from a scientists' toy to a mass communication medium, it is no wonder that security came a poor second. I have already mentioned that this is a disadvantage, in light of new applications like online trading and online banking. Security had therefore to be added later. Hackers and spies had to be prevented from playing their little games on the network.

Such a belated change in the design naturally comes with problems. Even after adding wings and enlarging it ten-fold, a car is still a car and not a jet-plane. Just as little can the Internet, which was not even designed to be a secure system, be transformed by some patchwork design measures into a suitable medium for confidential business letters, financial transactions or contract closures.

Security had to be built into the Internet belatedly

What therefore was to be done? Since the Internet could not be reinvented from scratch, the existing technology had to be amended. And so people tried to furnish the existing Internet with the corresponding additions and changes that would put a stop to the games of criminally-minded users. This process has now been going on for some years. It is still not finished by far, and will probably never be finished completely. Nevertheless, there has been progress, which has led to an increasing acceptance of the Internet for applications where security is critical.

It is possible to eavesdrop on the Internet

One of the largest dangers on the Internet arises from the fact that it is quite simple to tap into the data that flows through the network. The only way to counter these security gaps reliably is provided by a thousand-year-old science which, because of the present lack of security in computer networks, is experiencing an unforeseen boom: the science of data encryption, known also as 'cryptography'.

Cryptographic procedures were built into the Internet as an afterthought

In recent years, great efforts have been made to introduce cryptographic processes into the existing Internet. These efforts have given rise to so many methods that it is difficult to keep abreast of them. To enable you to find your way around the gigantic field of cryptography on the Internet, I have written this book, which describes the means that modern cryptography makes available, and how these are used on the Internet to confound hackers and snoopers. You will also learn why e-mails are encoded differently from Web pages, how money is transferred over the Internet, and at which points on the network encryption can apply. Naturally, I also tell you about encryption products – about those that have taken the Internet by storm, about others that flopped despite immense effort, and yet others that still have their future before them. Finally, mention must be made of government activities in the field, which often have the unfortunate goal of limiting the application of cryptography.

1.3   The second edition

The present book is a
second edition

The book you hold in your hands is the second edition of this work. The first edition appeared in October 1998 under the name *Safer Net – Kryptografie im Internet und Intranet* (*Safer Net – Cryptography in the Internet and intranet*) [Schm98/1]. After the first edition sold encouragingly well, in mid-1999 I undertook a complete revision, which is now finished. As in the first edition, it has been my goal to write more than a dry reference book. Attractive presentation and reading enjoyment seem to me just as important as the factual content.

The first edition of
the book evoked
many positive
comments

Reactions to the first edition were mostly positive. Again and again it was confirmed that a book about the practical side of cryptography on the Internet – and in particular a description of the numerous standards on the market – had been missing, and that my book closed this gap. Also, the idea of imparting technical knowledge through attractive presentation and readability was well received, as I was often informed. 'That Klaus Schmeh in his book *Safer Net – Cryptography in the Internet and intranet* actually succeeds in keeping boredom at bay for the reader lies in his easy writing style and the personal case examples', wrote *Card Forum* magazine. The magazine *Internet Professionell* rated *Safer Net* as a 'profound, well written and entertaining work covering all aspects of encryption'.

Critical comments, though happily rare, were naturally also in evidence. Most points of criticism concerned various themes that had been covered in insufficient detail, or even not at all. In some cases (such as S/MIME) criticism was surely justified; basically, however, a book such as this is always incomplete. Still, I have done my best to cover everything of importance in the new edition. Apart from the errors of omission in the first edition, there were naturally also some factual errors (for example, there actually is an Internet AG), numerous misprints, and various inconsistencies, mostly brought to my attention by attentive readers. Everyone who advised me on such failings is included in the list of acknowledgements at the end of the chapter.

This book covers a
complex subject

Naturally, the task of writing a cryptology book has not become easier over the past two years. Much has happened since the deadline for the first edition, and an already complex theme has become even more complex.

In this second edition, I hope I can impart to you some of the fascination that cryptography can engender. This centuries-old art, to hide information from prying eyes, has become through the computer an even more fascinating science than it already was. It is waiting for you to discover. This book should be your gateway to it.

1.4   Why yet another cryptography book?

There are numerous
other cryptography
books on the market

Two years before the first edition of this book appeared, there were already numerous books about cryptography on the market. Naturally, others have appeared in the meantime. One could long ago have filled a whole library with books on this subject. Many may ask: is not the present book superfluous? Weren't there already more than enough other works that treat everything of interest in the field of cryptography? My answer to this is 'no'. While the quality and quantity of the presently available books on cryptography leave a little to be desired (see Section 31.2), I still think that this book has its place in cryptographic literature.

This book should fill a gap

About three years ago I noted that there was still a gap in the cryptography book market. At that time there was no book that covered both cryptographic processes and their comprehensive practical application in computer networks. I felt that this was a big cap, for from my experience it was exactly this practical application that was of interest. To close this gap, I wrote the first edition of my book.

Two years after the appearance of the first edition, the gap in the market has become smaller (not only because of my book). Many aspects that I missed three years ago have been covered by other authors in the meantime. Thus, *Safer Net* appeared almost simultaneously with the book *Internet Cryptography* by Richard Smith, which likewise was concerned mainly with the application of cryptography on the Internet. Despite everything, numerous aspects are to be found in my book that readers will look for in vain in most other crypto books. Here is a selection:

The central theme of this book is the integration of cryptography in the Internet

- The central theme of the book, the integration of cryptography in the Internet, is treated here more comprehensively than in any other book I know. Terms like SSL, IPSec, PGPS, S/MIME, SET, HBCIS, DNSSec and many others are covered.

- Other cryptography books are concerned mostly with solutions. The problem – namely the susceptibility to hacking of the Internet and other networks – is mostly treated only peripherally.

- How cryptography can be integrated into the different OSI layers, and whether hardware or software is the right means to achieve it, is described in this book in detail.

- Smart cards are ideal for the implementation of cryptographic processes. Their importance is growing all the time. Nevertheless, smart cards are treated shabbily in most cryptography books – but not in this one.

Even biometrics is a subject in this book

- Biometrics is of course not part of cryptography, but there are numerous points of contact. These are described in this book.

- The theme of public key infrastructures (PKI) and Trust Centres continues to gain in importance, and is therefore treated especially comprehensively.

- Additionally, in this book you find a survey of the more important crypto publishers.

- I have placed particular value on readability and attractive presentation. So you certainly have anything but a dry reference book in your hands.

Reading enjoyment and attractive layout play an important role in this book

Long on words, short on content: I have tried not to write a book for the ivory tower. Instead, practical usability, easy intelligibility and, not least, readability have been given priority. By contrast, in other books you will find more cryptographic processes and more theory.

1.5   My regrets, my requests and my thanks

Despite all our efforts, errors, inaccuracies or other defects will have crept into my book. This was true of the first edition and the second can hardly be different. This regrettable, but unavoidable, fact should be no reason for frustration, but rather an incentive: phone, write or e-mail your comments to me. I am grateful for each *Constructive* pointer, just as for any inspiration or criticism. Since there will surely be a third *criticism of this book* edition of this book, your communications will not land in the waste bin (and *is welcome* certainly not before I have read them conscientiously). Please send your comments to Wiley, or better still via e-mail to schmeh@wiley.com. In this way I gained dozens of valuable hints on the first edition, which have helped me greatly with the new version. Errata and additional information on the book are always available on the World Wide Web under the address www.dpunkt.de/buch/krypto.html.

Besides the author, many others have contributed to the success of a book such as this. At this point I would like to thank all those people most cordially, even if I cannot mention all of them by name. I offer particular thanks to the following people:

My thanks to   • Dr Michael Barabas of dpunkt.verlag for his support in the realisation of this
numerous people   book.

• Carl Ellison for his remarks on the themes of SDSI and SPKI, as well as for his outstanding foreword.

• Gerald Volkmann, Kai-Uwe Konrad, Susanne Gehlen, Marco Breitenstein, Matthias Niesing and Bernhard Esslinger for their comprehensive comments.

• Fred Fischer for his support in connection with the encoding machine photos.

I would also like to thank the following for their support: Jacques Basmaji, Dr Rainer Baumgart, Hans Joachim Bickenbach, H. Bork, Marco Breitenstein, Dr Jörg Cordsen, Dr Jean-Christophe Curtillet, Dr Frank Damm, Bernd Degel, Karsten Dewitz, Manja Diering, Hans Peter Dittler, Prof. Hans Dobbertin, Peter Ehrmann, Oliver Ferreau, Helge Fischer, Carsten Gäbler, Thomas Garnatz, Thomas Gawlick, Stefan Haferbecker, Dirk Heuzeroth, Frank Hoherz, Detlef Hühnlein, Robert Joop, Markus Jünemann, Robert Jung, Dr Wolfgang Kahnert, Paul Knab-Rieger, Andreas Knöpfle, Stephanie Kopf, Andreas Krügel, Willi Mannheims, Stefan Milner, Ilja Ohliger, Prof. Christof Paar, Peter Pahl, Sachar Paulus, Gunnar Porada, Holger Reif, Prof. Dr Helmut Reimer, Stefan Reuter, Thomas Rolf, Prof. Christoph Ruland, Matthias Sakowski, Tahar Schaa, Patrick Schäfer, Christoph Schlenker, Volker Schmeh, Dr Michael Sobirey, Jochen Stein, Malte Sussdorf, Dr Uwe Tafelmeier, Dr Hubert Uebelacker, Boris Ulrich, Rüdiger Weis, Dominik Witte, Reinhard Wobst, Oliver Wolf, Zeljko Zelic, Dr Volker Zeuner, Stephanie Zeutschler, Ursula Zimpfer.

2

What is cryptography and why is it so important?

There is no security, only more or less insecurity.
JOSEF MAIER

Key experience no: 2
One of the oldest known examples of the use of cryptography stems from 1500 BC. About that time a Mesopotamian potter used secret characters to record the formula for a glaze on clay tablets. Even as long as 3500 years ago, there were industrial secrets that had to be hidden from competitors.

2.1 The name of the game

This book is not just (but also) aimed at the expert

'What is cryptography?' Perhaps you asked yourself this as you read the title of this book. Or are you someone who already knows about it? This does not matter; my book is addressed to both groups and I think even the professionals will find something here for them. If you have already worked with a computer, if you know how many bits make a byte, and have already heard something about the Internet, you need not find this book too much of a challenge. As you will see, a little mathematics cannot be avoided, but I have tried to make that part as easy to follow as possible. If you are a professional cryptographer you can certainly bypass the first chapters, but when we come to standards, protocols and products you will hopefully find things that engage your interest. But enough of the preamble, let's get straight to the point and begin answering the question contained in the title: what is cryptography and why is it so important?

2.1.1 What is cryptography?

There are has two answers: one short and one long.

The short answer

Cryptography is the science of data encryption

Cryptography is the science of data encryption.

The long answer

Cryptography is the science concerned with methods of data protection through encryption and related processes. Given that mathematics is an important aid in cryptography, then only through mathematical knowledge and mathematical thought processes can it be possible to develop the procedures necessary for secure data encryption. The other important aid is the computer. It performs the encryption procedures and renders another important service by testing for weaknesses in cryptographic methods.

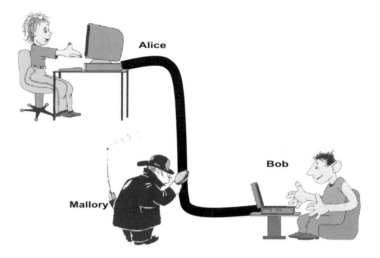

Figure 2.1   Alice and Bob exchange messages that Mallory can read and manipulate. This simple theme forms the basis of this book.

Alice and Bob are the main characters in this book

In cryptography in general, and in this book in particular, we start with a model that is as simple as possible: two people (let's call them **Alice** and **Bob**) exchange data over a channel that can be intercepted. In this book, the channel is usually the Internet, but sometimes it can be a phone line, a wireless radio connection, or a floppy disk being transported in someone's trouser pocket. What matters is that it should be technically possible to intercept the transmitted data, whether by tapping a phone line or stealing the floppy disk. In this book, 'intercept' should always be understood in a general sense. It can mean 'listen in on', 'read', or even 'analyse'.

The villain in this book is called Mallory

To keep our model as simple as possible, we will start from the worst-case assumption, that a villain (let's call him **Mallory**) can intercept and control the transmission channel at will. In our case then, Mallory can intercept, manipulate and retransmit the data that Alice and Bob exchange over the Internet in any way he likes. On the basis of this model, the use of cryptographic encryption and similar measures can preclude that

- Mallory can affect the intercepted data

- Mallory can change the transmitted data without it being detected

- Mallory might pretend to Alice that he is really Bob (and vice versa)

- Without being detected, Alice can claim that a message from her might in reality be a forgery by Mallory.

Mallory can intercept communications between Alice and Bob

Of course, Mallory can also do things that cannot be prevented by cryptographic means. Such things include that

- Mallory can change messages (only he cannot avoid detection)

- Mallory might intercept data (only it will be to little avail if the message is well encrypted)

- Mallory might block the line, bring down a router, or blow up a data processing centre (in which case he would scarcely be able to access any data).

Mallory is always more dangerous than you might think

You may well think that the prerequisites for this model are not always realistic. That someone might have the same possibilities as Mallory is, however, far more frequently the case on the Internet than you might suppose. Above all, it is mostly very difficult to estimate correctly the danger of eavesdropping. Therefore it has proven wiser to take Mallory into consideration from the start and to rate him as a very dangerous opponent, just to be on the safe side. If the dangers seem rather exaggerated to you, just wait until Chapter 3. There I will examine the danger of interception and manipulation more closely and show that it is actually a formidable problem. From the outset, therefore, we will bear in mind Murphy's first law of cryptography: Mallory is always more dangerous than you think (see also Section 32.5).

At this point I will take this early opportunity to throw the first definitions in this book at you. I have just described in detail what cryptography is. The word comes from the Greek, where *kryptein* means 'hide' and *gráphein* means write. Along with cryptography there is also **cryptanalysis**. This is concerned, not with the encryption, but with the decryption of data already encrypted.

Cryptology covers both cryptography and cryptanalysis

Both cryptography and cryptanalysis are contained within the term **cryptology**, which is thus the more commonly used term in the field. As so often happens, the use of such terminology is not uniform in this case either. Since cryptography is worthless without cryptanalysis, one does not normally distinguish between cryptology and cryptography. In this book also, cryptography includes cryptanalysis, and I am speaking here not about cryptology but about cryptography.

2.1.2   Cryptography – an important branch

Cryptography is a branch of computer security

Cryptography belongs to a branch of information technology called **computer security** or **IT security** (in this book usually termed **security**). Cryptography is hence widely connected since computer security is a very large field that embraces many branches. The theme of computer safety is closely connected with that of computer security. The two terms have the following meaning:

- Computer safety is concerned with the guarding against accidental damage. This covers technical defects, accidental deletion, transmission errors, hard disk crashes, lightning strikes, floods, bad servicing, faulty diskettes, and the like.

- Computer security is concerned with guarding against intentional damage. This includes hardware sabotage, hacker intrusion, peeking at secret data, and the like.

Networked computers present dangerous security problems

This book deals exclusively with security. Security can be further divided: first there is the area of the security of individual computers (regarded as isolated units or systems) and, secondly, the security of networked computers (this area is also termed **network security**). Naturally, the former are not in as much danger as the latter. Therefore, and because this is a book about the Internet, I will not go into isolated computers in any detail. We are much more interested in computers connected to a network (namely the Internet), which give rise to two security questions in particular:

- How can a networked computer be protected against an unauthorised person gaining access via the network (i.e. against **hacking** or **cracking**)?

- How can messages that leave the computer be protected against an eavesdropper or manipulator (Mallory in our case) (i.e. **communications security**)?

Cryptography can be regarded as a branch of network security

Now we have finally got to where we actually wanted to be: cryptography. This is of course the science of encryption and consequently an important tool in communications security. Suitable methods of encryption can be used to prevent Mallory from understanding or changing the data he intercepts. Of course, encryption also gives protection against hackers and crackers, if only as a last line of defence when other security measures have failed and an intruder has already gained unauthorised access to sensitive data. However, since this is much less important in practice than the protection of data during transmission, we shall treat cryptography in this book as a branch of communications security. Of course, at the back of your mind you should always keep the idea that encryption can be applicable to other areas.

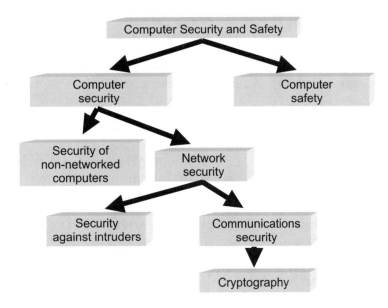

Figure 2.2 Cryptography is a branch of a branch of a branch of a branch of computer security. Cryptography is still an important science.

2.2 Why is cryptography so important?

It pays to be conversant with cryptography

Maybe you are now thinking: why do I need to read a whole book in order to understand what is itself only a branch of a branch of a branch of a branch of computer security? The answer is simple: there are areas of computer security which are not so important that it is worth while either writing or reading a book about them. Cryptography is not one of these, however. As we shall see in the next chapter, the Alice–Bob–Mallory scenario described, in which Mallory can intercept all messages, is simply too valid to be included under 'Other Items'. This is not true just for the Internet alone, but is of general significance. Every e-mail, each Telnet command and each WWW message that you send over the Internet can fall into the wrong hands, with unforeseen consequences. You will learn about those who might be interested in playing Mallory's role in the following sections.

2.2.1 Industrial espionage

Cryptography helps to counter industrial espionage

The most important reason why cryptography is currently experiencing an enormous boom on the Internet is not because of the e-mails that Alice sends to her friend Bob, and which Mallory can read. It is much more to do with concrete industrial interests: a great danger is presented by the former political espionage agencies who, since the end of the cold war, have been concentrating more and more on industrial espionage. According to [Karkow], both East and West are equally involved. Public data networks are increasingly important Section 3.3).

The NSA is a secret service agency of the USA

What is most terrifying of all is the degree of effort the secret services put into the matter. The undisputed world champion of snooping is the American NSA (National Security Agency). You should take note of this name, because this organisation will be mentioned again several times in this book (among others in Section 30.3.6). The NSA is the largest employer of mathematicians in the world and the biggest buyer of hardware worldwide. Wondrous tales are told about their code-cracking abilities and automatic evaluation of intercepted information, even though all NSA activities are executed under the strictest secrecy.

Industrial espionage costs billions

Of course, industrial espionage can be pursued without the help of secret services. Hiring hackers to spy on the competition is not unknown. According to some estimates, the cost per year to German industry alone amounts to billions of euros. Even if only a fraction of this is lost on public networks such as the Internet, the damage from that source alone is considerable. The big problem is that awareness of espionage on computer networks is in many cases not acute enough. The danger in all this can be considerably reduced by suitable measures. One of those measures is cryptography.

2.2.2 Commerce on the Net

Cryptography makes online payment possible

To counter industrial espionage is not the only justification for the existence of cryptography. Equally important as the driving force behind the increasing use of cryptography is the fact that there is big money to be made on an Internet that is free from spying and manipulation. Online payment, for example: it is to be expected that, in the long term, the Internet shopping mall will put pressure on today's mail-order catalogue companies. It is fortunate that, thanks to cryptographic techniques, it is possible to pay securely over the Internet. Another example is online banking: it is undoubtably convenient to call up one's account balance or effect transfer payments from the comfort of one's own desk. However, this is scarcely conceivable without cryptographic security provisions against eavesdroppers and manipulators. In this case, Mallory need not be sought in secret service circles, but in the hacker or criminal world. As we shall see, this has repercussions on the cryptological methods used: while only the best is good enough to protect against the secret services, cryptological processing in the field of finance need not be uncrackable, as a rule. After all, nobody is going to spend a million breaking into the Internet just to interfere with the payment for a pair of socks, or to find out his neighbour's bank balance. The converse of this is that cryptography should be approached with a sense of proportion, and this will be borne in mind throughout this book. For the present, it is enough to know that, thanks to cryptography, payment procedures and similarly sensitive transactions can be protected, which means more convenience for us and more profit for many companies. So, everybody wins.

2.2.3 The private sphere

Cryptography can be used for protection in the private sphere

Luckily, there are also reasons for using cryptography that, in contrast to e-commerce and industrial espionage, have nothing to do with lovely money. Or perhaps you would be happy for an e-mailed love letter or some other private message to be read by a third person, whether you know them or not. With the help of cryptography, this kind of thing can be prevented.

Cryptography is as necessary as an envelope

Perhaps you would say that as a private person you are not interested in industrial espionage and likewise are none too keen on this new-fangled online shopping and banking rubbish. You might also add that, generally speaking, you have nothing to hide, and who would want to read or alter the e-mails you send anyway, even if they had the opportunity? You ask: why use cryptography? Then you have to ask yourself why you send a letter in an envelope instead of sending a postcard. Don't you trust the postman? Does the letter have to pass through too many strange hands? Or is it just a routine measure that takes very little effort? No matter what the reason, it can be taken as grounds for using cryptography. On this basis alone, the justification for the use of cryptography on the Internet cannot be denied, especially as on the Internet it is quite easy to analyse intercepted data, while snooping in the postal service needs a lot of personal effort.

Data protection can so quickly become a farce. Also, there can be no disputing that secret services and investigative authorities also spy on private individuals on the Net – who knows how many strangers probably know everything about them, and whether that information has been gained in a legal manner or not? Cryptography has a further social dimension here: it enables individuals to provide their own protection for their private affairs. The option of using cryptography lets you decide for yourself whether to provide a degree of protection for your correspondence. In a totalitarian society, such a privilege is not to be underestimated. Phil Zimmermann, programmer of the popular encryption software PGP (Pretty Good Privacy), purposely points out that for a long time he has been in a position to paper his walls with thank-you letters from resistance groups in oppressed countries. It is precisely the totalitarian regimes that are most opposed to the use of cryptography.

Cryptography carries hidden dangers

Among all its advantages, it should not be forgotten that cryptography has hidden dangers: using suitable cryptographic procedures, criminals can exchange information at will. Phone tapping and similar eavesdropping measures are as good as useless in the face of sophisticated use of cryptography – and an important tool for fighting criminals goes by the board.

This book offers neutral information on cryptography

What is valid for every technical development is also valid for cryptography: where there is light, there is also shade. In this book, the disadvantages of cryptography will not be glossed over any more than the political and legal aspects of the science. With this book it is not my intention to push your assessment of cryptography in any particular direction. Information will be presented in a neutral manner.

2.3 Uses of cryptography

What can cryptography be used for in practice on the Internet? The following list offers several possibilities but makes no claim to be complete:

- E-mail: the classical field of application. Up to now, encoded e-mails have been of interest mainly on the Internet, but are gradually also gaining importance on intranets.

WWW-connections can be secured using cryptography

- World Wide Web: the WWW has long been more than just a playground for surfers. It is being used more and more as a user tool for database access, for the administration of computer systems, and of course as a shopping centre. Not least, the Web is the main component of most intranets, in which it is used for the exchange of inter-company information. In each case, encryption is necessary.

- Client–server connections: widespread computer systems lead to increased communication, and a greater flow of sensitive information.

- Virtual private networks: companies with several branches like to couple their local networks over wideband connections such as ISDN. It pays to encode all data as it leaves a company network and then decode it as it returns to company territory. This technique is known as VPN (virtual private network).

- Payment systems: scarcely anything has been so keenly awaited as the facility to transfer money easily via the Internet. Thanks to cryptography, such facilities now exist. They are as manifold as their names: Cybermoney, Digital Cash, Electronic Money. In general, I am talking about payment systems for the Internet.

Internet banking can work with cryptography

- Internet banking: why go to the bank if you have an Internet connection? But only with encryption, please.

- Remote access: access to remote computers over the Internet is possible using services such as Telnet or rsh. Programs such as PC Anywhere include similar functionality.

There are many uses for cryptography on the Internet

You can see that there is plenty for cryptography to do on the Internet. However, because each of the named uses has its own special requirements, the subject is rather complicated – but extremely interesting as a result.

2.4 And who the devil is Alice?

Once again, a word about our friends Alice and Bob: as already mentioned, they are in a bit of a pickle because they want to exchange data, but they only have the Mallory-infested Internet available to them. Still, this arrangement does have one advantage for us: we can demonstrate the principles of cryptography using Alice, Bob and Mallory.

Alice and Bob were not invented in this book

Incidentally, without Alice and Bob, cryptographers would be in a fine fix. An attempt to describe an encryption process without them would sound something like: 'A encodes a message to B that C cannot decode because he does not know either A's or B's key ...'. This alphabet soup does not appeal to most cryptographers. To demonstrate cryptographic procedures, Alice and Bob as well as the villain Mallory and, where needed, Carol and others came on the scene ages ago. Alice and company are to be found everywhere in cryptographic literature nowadays – they have been around for some time, even in academic works.

Alice, Bob and Mallory live in Cryptoland

With this book, I decided to breathe a little more life into Alice, Bob and Mallory and to introduce several other characters. As a start, I gave the three of them full names and a homeland: Alice Onliner, Bob Offliner and Mallory Cracker live in the little-known country Cryptoland (Internet-Domain 'cl'). Alice works for the firm Crypt and Co., one of the leading firms in Cryptoland. Her friend Bob studies at Cryptoland University. To communicate with one another, Alice and Bob use the Internet which, in accordance with our model, can be tapped by the villain Mallory. Of course, Mallory is up to all the dodges and leaves no trick untried to intercept or affect the messages passing between Alice and Bob. In this book, good always triumphs and so, thanks to cryptography, Alice and Bob succeed time and time again in putting one over on Mallory. Through these stories you will learn a great deal about cryptography and its application on the Internet – which is exactly the point of the exercise.

Other characters appear in this book along with Alice and Bob

In addition to Alice, Bob and Mallory, other characters appear in this book, such as Alice's friend Carol, online shop owner Oliver and, completely unknown to Alice and Bob, an Internet user called Zak and his friend Zeus. They all play a role in the explanations of cryptographic procedures that will be explored in detail in due time and place.

2.5 Summary

Hopefully, reading this second chapter will have answered some of the more important questions. You know the part cryptography plays in computer security and you have met our friends Alice and Bob from Cryptoland. The main lesson is, however: cryptography is neither a mathematical puzzle nor a plaything for secret services. It is much more an indispensable building block of the information society. We must use it if we are to protect ourselves against espionage and surveillance.

How is it possible to eavesdrop on the Internet?

If someone is paranoid, that doesn't mean no one is stalking him.
AMOS OZ

Key experience no. 3
Diana, Princess of Wales who died in 1997, experienced not only intrusive photographers, but also uninvited eavesdroppers. In addition to journalists listening-in to her mobile phone, the NSA also took an interest in the British royal princess. In 1988, a British tabloid reported on a 1000-page surveillance file that the NSA was supposed to have put together about Princess Diana. Its contents were not known.

You already know that Mallory can intercept any message sent between Alice and Bob. We have assumed the worst. However, before we carry this scenario forward throughout the book we ought to ask ourselves the question of whether the scenario is actually realistic. So the question reads: do we really have to assume that there is an unknown third party with each e-mail, each Web site, each remote access and every chat?

The danger of eavesdropping on the Internet is a real one

The answer to this question quite clearly is 'no'. So in reality, the situation is not quite as bad as we have painted it to be in the case of Alice, Bob and Mallory. On the other hand, the danger is great enough for us to choose our Alice–Bob–Mallory model as the basis for our conjectures. The reason why the danger is so large will be examined rather more closely in the next section. We will take a look at how it is possible to eavesdrop on the Internet and how messages can be manipulated.

Incidentally, you are unlikely to find such a chapter in other books on cryptography. Astonishingly, there is very little literature on the subject of how it is possible to eavesdrop on the Internet. Obviously, the solution (i.e. cryptography) is an easier topic than the problem (i.e. susceptibility to hacking). For this very reason I have written this chapter in my book and ask your forbearance for not having further recourse here to inside knowledge of the secret services and the military. I can only write about what I have found in the literature available to me, and what has been related to me personally at some time or other. With one eye on a third edition of this book, I will be grateful for any additional information that comes my way.

3.1   The structure of the Internet

The Internet cannot be pigeonholed

To understand the danger of eavesdropping on the Internet we must first examine its structure. This is admittedly not at all easy because the Internet is difficult to pigeonhole. There is no Mr Inter that the network is named after, and also no shining genius to be celebrated as its inventor. A date of birth for the Internet is as impossible to find as an Internet governing body or an Internet operational organisation.

The Internet is also difficult to grasp at a technical level. There is no single medium of transmission to which the Internet is connected – from cable to radio to laser, all are permitted and used in practice.

3.1.1   TCP/IP

The Internet is so difficult to delineate because of the fact that it was not put together according to a specific plan. It simply just grew with time. The term 'Internet' first arose after the network it designated had long been in existence. Its

The Internet began in the 1960s

modest beginnings can be traced back to the 1960swhen the American US Defense Department wanted to create a communications network that would have no centre and therefore be difficult to attack militarily. The idea of a network only for military use was happily soon abandoned. Over the years, an ever-wider computer network developed that was used almost exclusively by universities. Growth was mainly the result of already existing computer networks being connected to each other. This is why the Internet is known today, not misleadingly, as the 'network of networks'.

The Internet is defined by its working protocols

That anything at all useful came about from such a chaotic network of computer networks springs from practically the only thing all computers have in common: they speak the same language. The term 'language' is not to be taken literally here, rather it covers the exact rules that computers must follow when exchanging data, the so-called (communications) protocols (see Chapter 12).

TCP/IP is the language of the Internet

The protocols used in the Internet have been brought together under the collective name **TCP/IP** (Transmission Control Protocol/Internet Protocol), even if the designation is not categorically a happy one. TCP and IP are actually only two of the many protocols contained in TCP/IP. There are dozens more, all having their own specific purpose and, in their totality, enabling a standardised communication over the Internet. It would be more exact to speak of the TCP/IP suite of protocols if one wants to be absolutely clear that it is the collection of protocols that one is talking about. Familiar members of the TCP/IP suite of protocols along with TCP and IP are, for example, HTTP, FTP and Telnet, which will be discussed later. Thus the Internet is a worldwide computer network with only one specific attribute: all connected computers use the **TCP/IP suite** of protocols for communication. A comprehensive survey of the TCP/IP suite of protocols is available, for example, in [Lien00] and [Lien01].

All TCP/IP protocols are independent of the physical realisation of the means of data transport. Other protocols, outside TCP/IP, must contend with electric current, light waves, radio waves or laser beams transmitted by cables or through the air. However, there are precisely defined interfaces between these and TCP/IP protocols that enable them to work smoothly together. The advantage is obvious: practically all kinds of communications media can be used on the Internet.

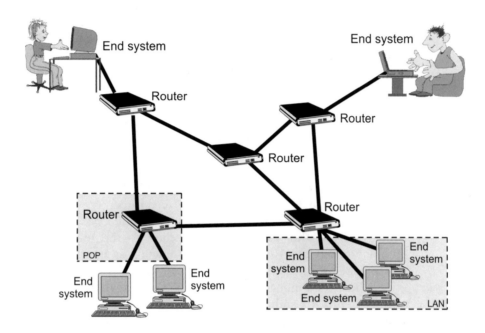

Figure 3.1 The Internet is a network comprising routers and end systems. All components use TCP/IP suite protocols for communication.

3.1.2 Routers and packets

Since the Internet is such a chaotic place, its structure is not easy to describe. Figure 3.1 is a schematic representation which, although somewhat simplified, will meet our purposes.

The Internet is a network of routers and end systems

The Internet should be pictured as a worldwide network whose nodes are individual computers. The so-called **routers** are nodes that accept incoming data over a line and pass it on over another line. Routers serve the transport of data over the Internet. An **end system** is a network node that sends data over the Internet or accepts it from the Net. If the Internet is compared to the telephone system, then an end system corresponds to a telephone, while a router fulfils the function of a telephone exchange.

Each end system on the Internet has an IP address

From the illustrated structure it is possible to send messages from any end system to any other end system. The prerequisite for this, however, is that each end system has an address (the **IP address**), which clearly identifies it. IP addresses correspond to the telephone numbers in a telephone system. An IP address comprises a 32-bit number that is written in the form '123.213.45.111'. However, since such a sequence of numbers is difficult to remember, the TCP/IP protocol suite offers the possibility of using addresses in the style 'caesar.uni-kryptoland' (so-called **text addresses**), which are derived from the IP address by a special process (see Section 3.2.7).

Routers often connect small (e.g. intra-company) computer networks with the rest of the Internet. Such a small, local network is called a **LAN** (Local Area Network), while the bigger parts of the Internet belong to the family of Wide Area Networks (**WAN**). A router between a LAN and a WAN consequently constitutes the connection of a company (or other organisation) to the Internet. Often LANs are not purposely assembled for the Internet, but already existing LANs may be connected to it. The LAN then becomes part of the Internet.

Bob can join the Internet via a PoP

If Bob wants to use the Internet without being connected to a LAN, he can use a **Point of Presence (PoP)**, which is normally achieved over the telephone line (with a modem or an ISDN card). For his access to the Internet over a PoP Bob pays its operator (the so-called **Internet service provider**). In return, the Internet service provider connects Bob with the Internet via a router. Among the Internet service providers there are online services such as CompuServe, T-Online and America Online (AOL), who, as well as connection to the Internet, offer their own information services. Universities often function as Internet providers and offer access to their students free of charge.

Data is transmitted over the Internet in packets

Whether over a modem, ISDN, LAN, WAN or anything else, if a message from Alice to Bob is transmitted via the Internet, then the aforesaid TCP/IP protocol suite is used. All data that Alice sends (e.g. by e-mail) is bundled by her computer into blocks of variable length (so-called **packets**). Each packet contains the actual data, the IP addresses of the sender and recipient and other details. With this information, the router decides to which other router or to which end system it will forward each packet it receives. Each packet travels via different routers from sender Alice to recipient Bob. Forwarding a packet is known as **routing**.

Packets are routed

How a packet is routed depends on the individual case, of course. The factors affecting the destination of a routed packet are the recipient's address, the capacity and loading of the connections to other routers, and configuration settings. It is also possible that during routing, a packet will be split into smaller parts for sending via different routes. It can happen that, because of overloading of the network, a packet goes missing or is intentionally 'thrown away'. Such losses are noted by TCP/IP, however, and (if necessary) remedied by a repeat transmission. When Bob's computer finally receives the packet it then extracts its contents and reassembles the original message. Alice and Bob know nothing about these packets and TCP/IP communication since their software takes care of it all. Alice only sees the transmitted data before it is split into packets, and Bob only sees the reassembled message on his screen.

3.1.3 Security only came later

The original
TCP/IP protocols
were very
elementary
Like the Internet itself, TCP/IP didn't fall out of the sky overnight. The protocols of this suite were created mostly during the 1970s and 1980s to provide a common language for the existing networks. Whereas TCP and IP were relatively coherent, the original versions of most other protocols of this suite were mostly the product of a quick hack, and had numerous shortcomings that only became apparent in practice. Unfortunately, it is anything but simple to replace protocols that are used by thousands, or even millions, of computers without creating chaos and a new Tower of Babel. For this reason, practically all TCP/IP protocols still have shortcomings that can be remedied only in part by new versions. This is a long-drawn-out procedure in itself. While I am on this subject, it is fair to remark that problems often arise in the computer world because it is not appreciated that compatibility is even more important than quality.

The lack of security

Security played no
part in TCP/IP
protocols at
the start
Among the numerous deficiencies of TCP/IP at the start was a complete lack of security. The original developers cannot be blamed for this because the early TCP/IP protocols emerged at a time when the Internet (or its precursor) was used mainly by scientists. There was no talk of hackers and spies at the time, so TCP/IP presented them with a gratefully received playing field. Looked at in this way, it is one of fate's ironies that in 1995 the Internet, of all things, though still lacking security, suddenly became a medium of mass communication that was to be used for banking and shopping. It is little wonder that the subject of security on the Internet suddenly became hot news – after all, there hadn't been any up to then.

The weak spots in security

Let's take a closer look at the TCP/IP security functions, whose absence is blinding:

TCP/IP has
numerous security
deficiencies
- In TCP/IP nothing is encrypted. This is even the case for passwords.

- The sender's address of a message can be falsified with ease (IP spoofing, mail spoofing, see Section 3.2.7).

- The messages that routers send to each other for information purposes can be falsified. In this way routers can be controlled almost at will.

- The conversion of text addresses into IP addresses can be manipulated (DNS spoofing).

- Many implementations of TCP/IP protocols contain errors that cause gaps in security.

Of these points, the first four are of interest in this book. They convey the message that cryptography had no role to play in the development of TCP/IP protocols. During 1995, as this became more and more evident, programmers had to retrospectively equip the already existing TCP/IP protocols with cryptographic mechanisms, or alternatively develop new protocols that already contained them. This process is still under way, with all the problems usually associated with changes and new developments in protocols. These cryptological improvements are the subjects of Chapters 21 to 28 in this book, where they will be discussed in detail.

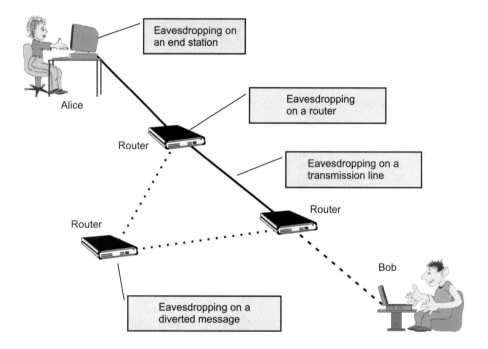

Figure 3.2 Mallory can intercept communications between Alice and Bob at various locations. Encryption cannot protect against eavesdropping on an end station.

3.2 How is it possible to eavesdrop on the Internet?

The methods Mallory can use to eavesdrop on the Internet can be divided into the following classes:

- Eavesdropping on end stations: Mallory extracts the data directly from the computer at which Alice is sitting.

- Eavesdropping on internal network nodes: Mallory works at tapping into the routers, etc.

Mallory has numerous toeholds for his intrusive activities

- Eavesdropping on transmission channels: Mallory has aimed his attack at the transmission channel connecting two network nodes.

- Eavesdropping by diverting messages: Mallory diverts data to a part of the network that is accessible to him.

It is clear that encryption is of little use against eavesdropping on end stations because the data has to be stored unencrypted (at least while Alice is reading it). Luckily, Alice's end station is a part of the Internet that is least accessible to Mallory and easiest for Alice to control. On the other hand, routers and transmission lines are easier for Mallory to access and are largely outside Alice's control. Therefore, Mallory will mostly try to eavesdrop on the internal parts of the network.

3.2.1 The technicalities of eavesdropping

Any transmission line can be tapped

If Mallory wants to intercept a transmission channel, he must first resolve some technical matters. What these are depends on the transmission medium – a copper wire having different properties from a directional radio beam. So let's look at the various possibilities.

Copper cable

Twisted-pair copper cable is hardly the most modern technology, but is still widely used because the matching lines are already installed. If Mallory can only gain access to a copper cable, then, with a metal clamp and simple equipment, he can intercept the data stream, provided it is a low-frequency signal (e.g. telephone communications).

Copper cable is not secure against eavesdropping

A disadvantage for Mallory is that his wire-tapping can be detected by electrical-resistance measurements (this is done, say, in the case of automatic cash dispensers). Using a method known as **inductive coupling**, however, copper cable can be tapped without the resistance being altered. This is also the only way to intercept high-frequency signals, such as are used in computer networks, for example.

Coaxial cables make eavesdropping no less easy: with thick-wire coaxial cable suitable clamps can be attached without breaking the circuit. With thin-wire cabling a short break is necessary, provided no self-bridging sockets are installed [Weck].

Fibre-optics

Fibre-optic cables also can be tapped using suitable tools

Fibre-optic cables are currently the most efficient transmission medium. According to [Weck] they allow the same access as twisted-pair cabling; however, rather different tools are needed.

Wireless communication

Electromagnetic waves, directional radio and lasers belong in the field of wireless communication and can therefore be intercepted easily using suitable receivers. Of course, this is especially the case for satellite broadcasts.

3.2.2 Eavesdropping risks in LANs

LANs are especially open to eavesdropping

Local area networks (LANs) are typical computer networks that serve company buildings or a university campus. Nowadays, many LANs are linked to the Internet and utilise protocols of the TCP/IP suite, thus themselves becoming part of the Internet. Usually they are installed on the basis of IEEE (Institute of Electrical and Electronics Engineers) technology, known under the name IEEE 802. IEEE 802 contains standards for the transmission media to be used (e.g. twisted-pair copper cable or coaxial cable), together with the protocols necessary for simple data exchange. These protocols do not belong to TCP/IP; however, they are frequently from the same suite.

Ethernet and CSMA/CD

IEEE 802.3 is usually described as Ethernet

Of the IEEE 802 standards, IEEE 802.3 is very popular. The best-known commercial product that follows this standard extensively (but is not compatible) is Ethernet from the firm Xerox. This exceptionally successful product is the reason that computer networks standardised to IEEE 802.3 are most generally described as Ethernet, a practice I will adopt in this book. Ethernet is a prime example of the cavalier manner in which security matters were treated during the conception of new standards. It also exemplifies that it is frequently difficult to build security mechanisms into an existing system retrospectively.

We can see where the problem lies if we take a look at the protocol used to communicate over an Ethernet circuit. Let's assume that Alice's and Bob's computers are connected to an Ethernet, along with many others. If Bob now wants to send a message to Alice, he generates a data packet that contains the sender and recipient addresses (Ethernet technology makes special Ethernet addresses available). Bob sends this data packet on to the transfer medium, from where it reaches all other linked computers. Each of the linked computers accepts the packet and checks the recipient address. If this address is not its own, then the packet is not processed further. If it is its own, however (which is the case in our example for Alice), the contents of the packet are read in.

IEEE 802.3 works according to the CSMA/CD principle

The principle of the described protocol is called CSMA/CD. CSMA/CD stands for Carrier Sense Multiple Access with Collision Detection and is so closely associated with the term Ethernet that Ethernets are also called CSMA/CD networks. The term CSMA/CD is explained from the way of working: on an Ethernet several computers are connected to a transmission channel (hence Multiple Access). Each of these computers continually tests the transmission channel (Carrier Sense) to check for data packets addressed to itself. This process is also necessary in order to avoid packet collisions. Only one packet can be on its way via the transmission channel at any one time. Therefore, each computer only sends when the transmission channel is free. If a collision of packages does occur, this is noted by the sending computers and they abort the sending process (Collision Detection).

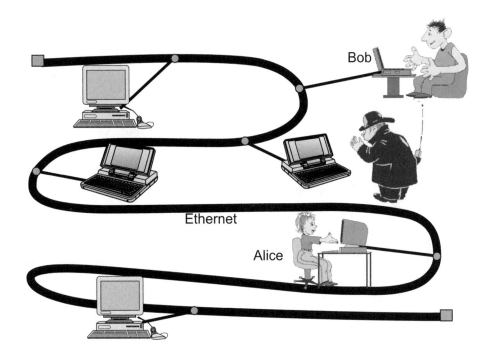

Bob

Ethernet

Alice

Figure 3.3 In an Ethernet, several computers are connected to the same transmission channel. This makes things much easier for Mallory.

Security problems with CSMA/CD

CSMA/CD works by eavesdropping

If CSMA/CD is looked at from a security viewpoint, Alice and Bob can only tear their hair out, while Mallory rubs his hands with glee (see for example [Weck] or [Schläg]). The reason is that 'eavesdropping on the transmission channel' is part of the Ethernet system of working. It even turns up in the network name as 'Carrier Sense'.

Eavesdropping attacks are made much easier by this carrier sensing: when a computer is connected to an Ethernet, Mallory only needs suitable software (a so-called **sniffer**), and not only packets addressed to Mallory are accepted, but all packets flowing through the bus. With a sniffer, Mallory can easily examine the contents of data packets. It must be remarked however, that a sniffer is not only useful to villains like Mallory – it is also needed for legitimate test and control purposes.

New forms of Ethernet reduce access to the medium of transmission

The moral of this story: the scenario of a ubiquitous Mallory is very realistic in an 802.3 network. One small comfort is that new forms of Ethernet reduce access to the medium of transmission. This works by the computers being linked to the network in star formation via a so-called hub or switch. In the hub, it is possible to filter data packets so that they only reach the correct receiver in readable form. This removes a large part of the danger of eavesdropping.

Other LANs

*Other LANs are also
liable to
eavesdropping*

With the other IEEE-802 LANs, such as Token Ring, Token Bus or DQDB, the situation looks scarcely better than with 802.3. In all cases, a medium of transmission used by several stations in common is an unshakeable pillar of the system, and makes good sense financially. The main eavesdropping threat on a LAN is an internal attack, when, for example, a worker wants to spy on his colleagues' data. Because of the common medium of transmission, many LAN security problems can be resolved in only one way: through the use of cryptography.

3.2.3 Eavesdropping on analog telephone lines

Like many other Internet users, Bob connects to his provider, as before, via an analog modem and the telephone network. Therefore, for Mallory it is worth trying his luck by tapping Bob's phone line. The copper cable between Bob's connection and the local exchange provides opportunities for this. For example, [BaHaJK] reports on bugs hidden in or on a telephone that record conversations or transmit them via a sender to the eavesdropper. In principle, it is of course conceivable that the modem could be attacked in this way. It would be much easier, however, for Mallory to snoop around in Bob's cellar (Bob lives in a large block of flats). In this

*In the local area,
mostly copper cable
is used*

block of flats, it is highly likely that there is a switch cupboard hanging on the wall in which Mallory (with minimum technical effort) can latch on to the line leading to Bob. Since copper cable is used in local areas, tapping-in is very simple, just as soon as one has gained access (see Section 3.2.1). In theory, Mallory can also climb a mast or dig up the earth in order to get at a line. An easier method would be to find the local distribution box and intercept Bob's data traffic there. Of course, it is easier to eavesdrop on telephone conversations in this way (only clamps, wire and a loudspeaker are needed) than to analyse the data exchange between two modems. For the latter Mallory will need a protocol analyser that converts the intercepted streams into data. Apparatus of this type can be purchased quite legally from various suppliers (for test and maintenance purposes only, of course).

*From the local
exchange data is
transmitted in fibre-
optic cables or radio*

When it leaves the local exchange, the data flow is digital and is transmitted mostly via fibre-optic cables or directional radio beam. According to [Zimmer], the latter technique is used by the NSA to monitor German phone conversations. In any event, with the help of the relevant telephone companies, snooping on phone conversations is no problem anyway. They are actually not only bound to allow investigation authorities and secret services to eavesdrop, they even have to place expensive monitoring equipment at their disposal. In principle then, it is possible to eavesdrop on conversations and intercept modem connections at will from any location. Since, in a paranoid fashion we not only suppose Mallory to be a hacker, but also to be an employee of the (especially foreign) secret service, and neither do we trust our phone company, we should not overlook this possibility.

3.2.4 ISDN security problems

New technology is applied only slowly over the last mile

The onward transmission of a phone conversation from one exchange to another in industrialised countries has been digital for some time. The changeover to digital technology in this field was relatively free from problems. This is because there are comparatively few lines between the exchanges, and these were so overloaded that investment in improved technology quickly paid off. Things look completely different for the lines between the local exchanges and the end users (the so-called last mile). New improvements can be implemented only slowly here since it is very expensive to equip millions of households with new lines and phones. For this reason, an analog connection is still used between most end-user connection boxes and local exchanges today. For the same reason, copper cable is still used, even today, to cover the last mile, and not modern fibre-optic cable.

ISDN offers digital data transmission for the last mile

A clear step forward is ISDN (Integrated Services Digital Network). This technology provides for the digitalisation of the last mile but uses the existing copper cables between the local exchange and the end user. This would close the last analog holes in telephone transmission without new cables having to be laid. ISDN has enormous advantages: new facilities in ISDN make possible such things as conference switching, call diversion and the like. The sound quality is improved, and the time taken for a connection to be established is reduced. ISDN connections also enable faster data transmission that is less prone to interruption than is the case with analog modems. In many cases, therefore, ISDN is the ideal way to connect to the Internet. Numerous companies are connected to the Internet only by an ISDN link. ISDN has, however, appreciable disadvantages: the rates of transmission fall far below what is technically possible today (even with copper cables). ISDN is also very prone to eavesdropping.

ISDN can be eavesdropped on

Firstly, the same dangers exist when telephoning with ISDN as with a normal connection: Mallory can attach himself to the phone line near Alice's house and subsequently intercept all her calls with ease. With ISDN, eavesdropping with the cooperation of the telephone company can still happen in the ways that have already been described.

Secondly, horror stories are told about the security attributes of ISDN (for a serious overview refer to [Luck99]). Of course, these tales are often an amalgamation of fact and guesswork. Very little is known about actual occasions where gaps in ISDN security were exploited. Nevertheless, it must be accepted that ISDN provides the eavesdropping experts with a very welcome tool for their handiwork. The Office for Security in Information Technology in Germany (Bundesamt für Sicherheit in der Informationstechnik) does not warn about security failings in ISDN for nothing.

An ISDN telephone is a small computer

If numerous reports about gaps in ISDN security are to be believed, they are the result of a synergetic blend of different factors: for one thing, an ISDN telephone is nothing more than a computer in a telephone casing. An ISDN installation can therefore be programed. ISDN also offers a large number of new features that, on the one hand, make phoning more enjoyable, but on the other hand can easily be misused. On top of this, via the ISDN-D channel or remote maintenance access, an

ISDN installation can be reprogramed externally. What could be better for Mallory than to be able to reprogram an ISDN installation externally so that he can use the ISDN features to his advantage? For example, in [Zimmer] there is a report about a hacker who misused the call forwarding feature to have his calls charged to another ISDN user. It is even possible to eavesdrop from any ISDN connection into a room in which an ISDN phone is installed. This is achieved by misuse of the direct response feature to activate the microphone in the telephone unit. Everything that is said near the telephone unit will be transmitted via the ISDN to the eavesdropper. But it gets even better: hackers report that it might even be possible to control a telephone exchange in a similar fashion (especially with an accomplice in the telephone company). This would let an accomplished hacker bring the telephone traffic of a whole region under his or her control.

A lot of know-how is needed to attack ISDN

Of course, all these attacks need a lot of know-how, assuming that they are at all practical. It is also clear that cryptography is no remedy. The reprogramming of ISDN features has to be countered at the root. Nevertheless, encryption can at least help us to cure some of the symptoms. There is also the fact that the three-way conversation feature can be misused to overhear any such conversation from any connection in secret – this eavesdropping by diverting calls is a gift from heaven for Mallory. Supposedly, there are units with which this kind of eavesdropping can be used from any connection without special hacker skills. Such apparatus should be classed as criminally illegal. If an eavesdropper should succeed, as described above, in gaining control of an exchange, then it is possible to divert any phone conversation.

ISDN has several dangerous facilities

Interestingly, there are facilities called Witness and Monitor. These facilities are banned in many countries (in other countries they are permitted), although this doesn't mean that they are not available in Germany. Most manufacturers do not take the trouble to offer different versions of their equipment. Instead, they omit any mention of the forbidden facilities in their documentation. Obviously, there are more than enough ways to eavesdrop on ISDN. Plenty for cryptography to do here, then.

3.2.5 Mobile radio transmission

Mobile phone networks can also be used for data transmission

Dedicated Internet user Alice is not satisfied with only being able to access the Net from her desk. She wants to enjoy e-mail and the Web while travelling – not a problem with a laptop and a suitable mobile phone. Here, the connection to the Internet is achieved by means of a mobile network. These networks are used mainly for telephone conversations with mobile phones, but are also used for data transmission. As soon as any data has found its way from the mobile phone or modem into the fixed transmitter network, the same principles apply for mobile transmission as for making a phone call. In addition, Mallory has two extra methods of attack: one is the path between the end device and the Base Transceiver Station (a sender mast, of which there are several in each city), which is traversed by radio waves. The other is the path between the Base Transceiver Station and the Base Station Controller which controls how the call is transmitted onwards.

The stretch traversed by radio waves deserves special protection

The latter can be dangerous if the network operator cooperates with Mallory – a possibility also exists here for secret service agencies. More significant, however, is the stretch traversed by radio waves. As is normal with radio, it is not difficult to intercept the transmission signal with a suitable aerial.

Whether Mallory can actually do anything with the intercepted signals is another question, however. It depends on the network. Some older networks are analog and makes the task relatively simple: according to [BaHaJK] all that is required is a scanner and a decoder to reassemble the transmitted data. Expense: approx. 526 Euros. The majority of networks is digital, however, which makes matters rather

GSM allowed for encryption from the beginning

more difficult. These follow the GSM standard (Global System for Mobile Communication) which provides a constant change of frequency, making eavesdropping possible only with elaborate equipment. And GSM has one big difference: in contrast to the Internet, this standard allowed for encryption from the beginning (although only for the area bridged by radio transmission). This encryption ensures that it is difficult to make use of intercepted messages. Unfortunately, the process is not sufficiently secure to foil or deter financially powerful secret service agencies such as the NSA.

A certain amount of commotion has been caused by several reports about so-called IMSI-catchers (International Mobile Subscriber Identity). These deceive mobile phones into thinking they are the Base Transceiver Station, thereby making elementary eavesdropping possible.

3.2.6 Satellites

The use of satellites for Internet transmissions is coming

Satellites have long been used to transmit television signals. On the Internet they are becoming more and more popular. Satellites have the advantage of large bandwidth, and are independent of location. Satellite dishes can be set up regardless of cable connections. There is one clear disadvantage from our viewpoint: if Alice puts a satellite dish on her roof, then Mallory can do the same. Even if two-way satellite channels have become feasible in the meantime, it is still the case with most current systems that requests for data go via modem or ISDN while only delivery takes place by satellite. In this case, Mallory can only view the Web page that Alice has loaded, not the credit card number that Alice has sent for payment. Of course, satellites can be used to transfer more important data than Web pages, so it would not be out of place here to give a thought to uninvited eavesdroppers.

A satellite is a rewarding target for eavesdroppers

If one knows that the secret service agencies employ lots of Mallorys, it is not evidence of an excessive enthusiasm for James Bond films if one takes the following into consideration: a satellite is like the eye of a needle through which a large quantity of data flows. What then could be more effective than to tap into the system at exactly this point? Something of the kind might certainly be possible via a 'back door' built into the satellite by engineers.

3.2.7 Internet-specific attacks

The structure and the way that the Internet works offer Mallory several interesting means of attack that are independent of the medium of transmission, and therefore fall into the class of attacks on network nodes or attacks using diversion. The former are certainly the most dangerous.

Eavesdrop attacks on routers and gateways

A router is a node of special interest to eavesdroppers

A router offers a convenient point of attack for Mallory. Routers are normally found in companies, Internet service providers, and universities. Of course, a router is not normally accessible to just anyone, and is not accessible at all for complete outsiders. Which and how many people have access to a router varies greatly from case to case. Thus it is quite possible that an employee of an Internet service provider or a student involved in maintenance at a university might collaborate with Mallory to eavesdrop on the data flowing through a router. Secret service agencies also look favourably at such key locations. Once Mallory has gained access to a router, he will have no difficulty in reading or altering the data flowing through it.

If so configured, a router can divert data to an eavesdropper

In addition, a router can be so configured that it copies or diverts packets with specific attributes (possibly to a router under Mallory's control). Unfortunately for Mallory (and happily for Alice and Bob), no one knows in advance via which router a message on the Internet will find its way to its destination. It is not unusual for different parts of the message to follow different paths. If Mallory has the router of a service provider in his pocket, he can at least read all the messages going to or from its clients.

The sender can influence the path of a packet by source routing

A function of the IP protocol also offers Mallory an interesting possibility for eavesdropping. This stems from so-called source routing, by which the sender can determine via which router an IP packet should travel. If Mallory has an accomplice in the firm Crypt and Co., then the latter can arrange for all IP packets sent from this firm over the Internet to be sent via a router to which Mallory has access.

Even more interesting than a router for Mallory is a mail server. If Mallory has administrative rights over a mail server, it is possible for him to read or tamper with the mail of a whole company or of all the customers of an Internet service provider. Since an e-mail is always stored as a whole on a mail server and is even archived there, there is scarcely a more interesting location for Mallory to attack.

A real danger also emerges as the result of error-prone or wrongly configured mail servers. It can very possibly happen that Alice receives an e-mail that was addressed to someone else (say Zacharias). Of course, this might also be because the sender inadvertently typed in the wrong e-mail address.

Spoofing attacks

Falsification of information on the Internet is known as spoofing

It is not only the danger of eavesdropping that is a constant threat on the Internet. Mallory might also decide to falsify information being sent over the Internet. The process, in this case, is usually known as **spoofing**. The really annoying thing is that spoofing attacks can be carried out with very few means. Often Mallory only needs an Internet connection, sometimes his own domain (e.g. cryptoland.co.uk) and suitable software.

The most common form of spoofing is **IP spoofing**. Here Mallory generates an IP packet in which a false IP address has been given for the sender. Since the IP protocol does not contain any kind of measures against IP spoofing, IP spoofing is laughably easy with suitable software.

There are IP spoofing, Web spoofing and mail spoofing, among others
The most well-known form of spoofing is **mail spoofing**. Here Mallory creates a mail message with a false sender address. Anyone who can set up his or her own mail server will have no trouble with this.

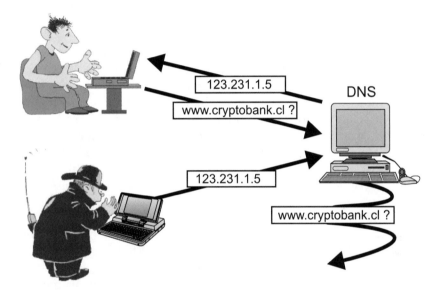

Figure 3.4 In DNS spoofing Mallory ensures that Bob receives a false IP address from the DNS.

In 1996 a report from Princeton University caused uproar by addressing the subject of **Web spoofing** for the first time [BaDeFW]. For Web spoofing Mallory uses a utility called URL-Rewriting that can be created using the current Web server products. URL-Rewriting makes possible the following scenario: if Bob calls up the 'http://www.mallory.cl/http://www.cryptostockexchange.cl' with his browser, then the request arrives first at Mallory's Web server (this has the address www.mallory.cl). Using URL-Rewriting, Mallory's Web server now calls the Web page www.cryptostockexchange.cl and sends this on to Bob. If Bob does not look carefully at the called address, he will not notice that Mallory has intervened. Of course, it becomes very dangerous if Mallory changes the contents of the original page. If Web spoofing is to work, Mallory must first palm off the false address to Bob. He can do this by referring to a Web page he set up at the false address.

DNS spoofing attacks are dangerous

Another dirty trick Mallory has up his sleeve is called **DNS spoofing** (see [MraWei] or [TegWün], for example). The DNS (Domain Name System) is an Internet service that provides the actual IP address (say 153.125.34.43) that belongs to a given text address, say (www.cryptostockexchange.cl). So when Bob types 'www.cryptostockexchange.cl' into his Web browser to call up share prices, his browser first sends a request to a DNS to obtain the relevant IP address (assuming that the browser doesn't already know it). With this IP address the browser then fetches the desired page and shows it to Bob.

DNS spoofing means that Mallory has palmed off a false IP address on a DNS user (in our case this is Bob's browser). This false IP address can then lead to a page forged by Mallory showing spurious share prices. If the forged page is well made (i.e. if it looks genuine), Bob has no chance of spotting the swindle. The modest sum he has invested in shares could quickly dwindle.

There are different varieties of DNS spoofing

There are different varieties of DNS spoofing. A general method runs something like: Mallory sends a DNS request to a DNS (let's call it DNS1), in which he requests the IP address for www.cryptostockexchange.cl. If Mallory is lucky, DNS1 does not know the requested address and now sends a request via the Internet to DNS2. Mallory, however, sends back a false answer to this request that arrives before the answer from DNS2. DNS1 now has the false address from Mallory instead of the genuine one. It therefore sends the false address as a reply back to Mallory (which is no longer of interest to him) and takes a note of it (technically speaking: it is saved in a cache). If subsequently someone requests the numerical address for www.cryptostockexchange.cl, he or she will then receive the address given by Mallory.

A Query-ID makes DNS spoofing difficult

The DNS protocol has at least one built-in hurdle: every request receives a 16-bit number (Query-ID) that must be detailed in the answer so that it is accepted. In order to be able to falsify a easy reply given by DNS2 to DNS1, Mallory must guess this Query-ID. This is not very difficult, however: many implementations of DNS simply increase the Query-ID number by 1 for each new request. Mallory only has to send a plausible request to his own address at DNS1 to find out the current Query-ID. He can then estimate the next Query-ID. To be certain, Mallory can also forge several replies with different Query-IDs and send them off in the hope that one is correct (most Name Servers are indifferent to repeated unacceptable answers). It is even conceivable that Mallory might send off 65,535 answers, all with questionable Query-IDs.

3.2.8 Compromising electromagnetic radiation

Tell-tale radiation is a means of attack on end devices

One of the most spectacular tools that Mallory can use is so-called **compromising electromagnetic radiation**. This is mainly useful for attacks on end devices and is based on the fact that data processing equipment such as computers, printers, modems and fax machines emit electromagnetic radiation [Luck96]. That this radiation as a kind of electro-smog might be damaging to humans is one thing. That it allows conclusions about the data being processed by the respective device is another. It has long been an open secret that it is possible to filter specific waves out of the chaos of electromagnetic waves that surround us constantly and tune in to a specific piece of apparatus. From Mallory's viewpoint, the results are astonishingly informative. This is especially the case when he can read what is currently being displayed on a monitor from intercepted electromagnetic radiation.

There are three ways to trap tell-tale radiation

Basically, there are three ways in which Mallory can trap electromagnetic waves: he can use an aerial to collect them, he can tap an electric cable in the appropriate room, or he can hope to extract them from some other metallic connection (e.g. mains cable). You should be very clear about the consequences: if Mallory has access to Alice's telephone cable, from this he can determine what Alice is typing into her computer. The same is possible if Mallory has access to the mains switchboard in Alice's cellar, or he can simply set up an antenna in the house next door.

Using tell-tale radiation, a monitor screen can be reproduced

We can only speculate how realistic such attacks are. The fact that such ideas are not pure science fiction was shown by experiments carried out at the technical college in Aachen, Germany: using primitive equipment it was possible to reproduce a monitor screen from a distance of several metres. This was done by capturing electromagnetic radiation from a monitor using an aerial and processing it to reproduce a readable copy of the original screen on another monitor. Frank Jones, a security specialist in New York, even went one step further: from across the caverns between the buildings of his home city he could gather valuable information from banks and Wall Street brokers, who were apparently unaware of the danger. The large areas of glazing in the office buildings made the task easier.

Specialists like the former East Germany security expert Hans Georg Wolf believe it possible that attacks of this kind can succeed from a distance of up to one kilometre, given a financial outlay of around 79,706.78 Euros. The thought of what secret service agencies, with their almost unlimited financial means, can achieve in this field can make one feel ill. A small taste of the capability of the secret service agencies was provided by the so-called PROMIS scandal [Schu96]. The American NSA (National Security Agency) is supposed to have doctored the PROMIS database program software so that it causes the hardware on which it runs to emit measurable radiation. It was mooted that the radiation could be sensed and interpreted via spy satellites.

Encryption is no defence against tell-tale radiation

The vital point about tell-tale radiation is that attacks on end devices using it cannot be countered by encryption. What Bob sees on his monitor or what is being processed in his computer is logically unencrypted. If Bob encrypts his data prior to transmission, it is already too late. Nevertheless, there are countermeasures to be taken: sealing a room with isolating material is one. Such an undertaking could turn into an expensive game, but inexpensive wallpaper with radiation-blocking qualities has now come on the market. Easier still is the installation of an interference transmitter to make the filtering of useful information more difficult. Apart from this, there are several things that should be considered when buying equipment: monitors with cheap housings should be avoided since these absorb only part of the emitted radiation. A high screen refresh rate also helps to reduce emitted radiation. It is a good sign if the monitor meets the TCO standard. This standard actually deals with the reduction of radiation to prevent damage to health, but the side-effect of protection from snoopers is certainly welcome.

There is equipment that is protected against tell-tale radiation

The ideal solution, of course, is to use only equipment that is specially shielded against tell-tale pulse radiation. Computers having this attribute are called TEMPEST (Transient Electromagnetic Pulse Surveillance Technology) computers. Since a TEMPEST computer can cost hundreds of thousands, only the military and national security authorities have warmed towards them up to now. TEMPEST computers also have the disadvantage of being technically less advanced by at least a year than normal computers on the market, which hardly adds to their popularity.

Tell-tale radiation attacks are onerous procedures

But even if Alice does not take any countermeasures, tell-tale radiation is only of limited use to Mallory. Even disregarding the cost of the necessary equipment, such attacks are troublesome and expensive. To trap the tell-tale radiation from a single piece of equipment, Mallory must pack his equipment into a van, set himself up in the right location and then find the correct signal from among the flood of ambient electromagnetic waves. Then he must wait until the data in which he is interested is being processed. How much easier it would be to record the messages from thousands of Internet users at a suitable network node and have them analysed by a computer program. Tell-tale radiation is therefore, in the main, suitable for a precision attack on an individual person or company. There are more effective tools for large-scale surveillance.

3.3   Some practical examples

In the previous section you have seen how dangerous Mallory can be for our heroes Alice and Bob. That such things don't only happen in theory I will now demonstrate to you through a few examples taken from actual practice.

3.3.1 Password snooping

Passwords are favourite targets for eavesdroppers

Among Mallory's favourite targets for his cracking activities are passwords of all kinds that are transmitted over the net. Widespread pilfering of passwords is not uncommon. [Anonym] reports the following cases in which Mallory's partners-in-crime were active:

- In February 1994, an unknown person installed a sniffer program (see Section 3.2.2) on various computer systems. By so doing, the unknown cracker recorded over 100,000 passwords transmitted over the Internet and the Milnet (a computer network operated by the US military).

- Another case happened just a few months later as an attacker once more installed a sniffer program on an American host. In only 18 hours, 268 passwords for computer systems accessible via the Internet were collected.

These are not the only cases demonstrating that unencrypted passwords are not a very secure method of authentication (see Section 13.2).

3.3.2 Echelon

Echelon is a worldwide surveillance system

I have mentioned several times that Mallory's partners are to be found mainly in secret service circles. Unfortunately, very little is known about the activities of the secret services around the world. Over the past few years, however, numerous details about the largest surveillance system in the world have trickled down. The name of this surveillance system is **Echelon**.

Echelon is a joint undertaking of the USA, the UK, Canada, New Zealand and Australia who came together in 1948 within the framework of an Anglo-American agreement. The driving force behind Echelon is the NSA (who else?). Echelon is a surveillance system that uses the best available technology to monitor satellite communications. Its activities are also aimed directly at civilian targets. Echelon spy stations include Menwith Hill (UK) and Sugar Grove (USA), not to mention stations on German soil such as at Bad Aibling (Bavaria). When one recalls what goes via satellite these days (phone calls, Internet packets, faxes, ...), it is easy to imagine the possibilities Echelon offers to the member states. Of course, Echelon focuses on evaluation just as much as on eavesdropping. Using a system of analysis called MEMEX it is supposed to be possible to scan the communication channels using artificial intelligence methods to seek out suspicious words and expressions. In this way the most interesting items are filtered from the overwhelming mass of data, and only the really interesting cases finally land on the desks of the executive officers.

The existence of Echelon was confirmed in an EU report

Only a few years ago, many people held Echelon to be a pipe-dream of cloak-and-dagger scientists. In January 1998, however, an EU report appeared in which the existence of Echelon was confirmed officially for the first time (the so-called STOA report [STOA]). According to the STOA report, Echelon had been in existence since the 1970s. The report also contained some interesting figures: 15 to 20 billion euros is the estimated yearly expenditure worldwide on communications spying. At least 30 countries are believed to have surveillance organisations similar to the NSA.

3.3.3 Siemens and the ICE

Siemens was the victim of an eavesdropping attack

The most spectacular case of spying known to date occurred in 1993 and concerned the firm Siemens [Ulfkot]. At that time, the internationally known Munich company was hoping to gain a contract from the government of South Korea to build an high-speed train. The French secret service succeeded in intercepting a fax stating the offer from Siemens, which they passed on to the French competitors. This allowed the French to make a lower offer and Siemens lost business worth billions.

3.3.4 Enercon

Another spectacular surveillance attack was carried out by the German firm Enercon, a manufacturer of wind turbines [Ulfkot]. In 1999 it was reported in the media that the NSA had monitored Enercon's communications. As a result, the NSA was in possession of secret design plans which it passed on to Enercon's US competitors. Estimated damage: 51 million euros and 300 new jobs.

3.3.5 The Serbs and NATO

The Serbs monitored NATO communications

In 1999, NATO bombed Serbia. Later, the US Department of Defense conceded that the Serbian military had gained detailed information about bombing targets through gaps in security. What these gaps comprised was explained by a spokesman of the US Department of Defense in reaction to a report in the *Washington Post*: various operational orders were sent by fax, without being encrypted, from NATO headquarters to the capitals of the NATO member states. The Serbs got hold of these orders by bugging the communication.

3.3.6 Other cases

Very few monitoring attacks are actually discovered

The cases described here, of course, form only the tip of a giant iceberg. It is safe to assume that only a fraction of the activities of Mallory and Co. ever come to light (many estimates claim that this is less than 5% per cent). Understandably, companies and organisations that suffer from eavesdropping attacks are not very forthcoming on the subject, so only a few of all cases discovered receive any publicity.

3.4 Summary

Nobody knows how big the danger of being monitored really is

It is not easy to approach the subject of the danger of eavesdropping on the Internet from the side of the eavesdroppers. Nobody knows just how great the danger of a message flowing through the Internet being intercepted by an eavesdropper like Mallory really is. The choice of useful literature on the subject is rather limited. Reports of eavesdropping attacks in connection with the Internet are astonishingly rare, most probably because the victims have no wish to parade their problems in public. What goes on in the secret service field is, in any case, beyond the ken of the private citizen. It would therefore, if only on the basis of speculation, seem wise to apply Murphy's first law of cryptography: Mallory is always more dangerous than one might think (see Section 32.5.1). Therefore we will continue to use the Alice–Bob–Mallory scenario, in which Mallory can intercept all communication between Alice and Bob, as a working hypothesis in this book.

Part 2

The principles of cryptography

Code Machine BC-243, 1943 Model
(from the IT-Security Teaching & Study Collection of the BSI)

Symmetric encryption

I do not trust any encryption process that I haven't been able to crack.
UNKNOWN

Key experience no. 4
In a hotel in Lynchburg (USA), in the year 1822, a certain Thomas J. Beale left a chest that he never called back for. In the chest were three coded texts that allegedly described the hiding place of hidden treasure. One of the three texts has since been decoded but contains insufficient information. The treasure, if it ever existed, remains undiscovered.

Bob sends the following e-mail to Alice:

```
Dear Alice,

As you know, tomorrow I am going away for a few days.
Could you please read my mail every day. My password
for Freecryptomail is 'crptlnd'. Could you also water
my flowers tomorrow? The key to my flat is under the
mat. If you need my bankcard, which you will find in
the living room, the PIN is 7650. While I'm away, if
you should see a nice birthday present for my
grandma while on a virtual window-shopping trip then
please buy it immediately. You can pay with my
credit card, the number is 6542 0957 7630 0064, and
it is valid until July 01.

Bob
```

Confidential information should not be sent by e-mail

Did anything strike you about this e-mail? Correct, it contains information that should not fall into the wrong hands. Since we assume, however, that Mallory can read all messages that Alice and Bob exchange over the Internet, Bob could be in deep trouble: Mallory can hit Bob's e-mail account on the basis of the intercepted information, and break into his flat to use his bank card and credit card number. Bob really ought to have encrypted his mail.

Bob should have encrypted his mail

High time then that we concerned ourselves with cryptography. Alice and Bob can use it to put a stop to Mallory's games. In this chapter we will first examine the principles of the simplest form of encryption: symmetrical or secret key encryption, as it is called.

4.1   What is symmetric encryption?

Now that Mallory has used Bob's e-mail to plunder his flat and bank account, Bob would like to encrypt all his correspondence. But this is easier said than done. True, it is not too difficult for Bob to think of an encryption algorithm. He is, however, in a bit of a quandary because he sends e-mails to various people, including Alice, his wealthy aunt, and the Inland Revenue. If Bob uses the same

Bob should not use the same code for all his mail

key for all his e-mail then the Inland Revenue can read his e-mails to his aunt, his aunt his e-mails to Alice, and Alice his e-mails to the Inland Revenue (if the e-mails should fall into their respective hands, of course). If Mallory – who can intercept all the messages – has an accomplice in the Inland Revenue, he can also read the e-mails Bob sends to his aunt and to Alice. So Bob must invent a unique encryption process for each communications partner, which can be a big undertaking in view of his wide circle of acquaintants. This can be expressed in general terms: in practice, it is not possible to set up an encryption process with each potential communications partner that the others do not know about.

4.1.1   Keys

Good encryption methods use keys

To get round the problem just described in practice, only encryption methods are used in which a secret element (the so-called **key**) is entailed. Depending on the method, a key is a password, a secret number, or simply just a sequence of bits. In good encryption methods it is easy for Alice and Bob, knowing the key, to decrypt the encrypted message. For Mallory, on the other hand, without knowledge of the key it is almost impossible, even if he knows the exact method being used. For Bob and his communication partners, the use of a key is a great help. Bob can use the same encryption algorithm for his e-mails to Alice, his rich aunt, and the Inland Revenue – he just needs to use different keys. Eavesdropper Mallory, on the other hand, has his nose put out of joint because he doesn't know the keys. And Bob doesn't even need to get his hands dirty – he can leave his computer to execute the encryption algorithm.

Encryption methods should not be kept secret

Since with suitable methods one can start from the assumption that security depends on the key alone, as a general rule the encryption algorithm need not be kept secret – at least not in commercial and academic fields. In fact, it would make sense to do just the opposite, and publicise the methods used as widely as possible. Only when enough experts have employed a method, when all imaginable weaknesses have been eliminated, and when no weaknesses have come to light, only then can we presume that Mallory (whom we know to be very astute, and consequently an outstanding code breaker) also has no chance. Apart from this, in practice it is often a thankless task trying to keep an encryption algorithm secret. Above all then, when an method is implemented in distributed software, sooner or later someone will take the trouble to analyse the source code and to make the method public knowledge. Making the method public takes the wind out of Mallory's sails since serious cryptographers can now begin cryptanalysis and discover any innate weak spots before he does. New encryption methods should not be trusted until their security has been thoroughly tested in like manner.

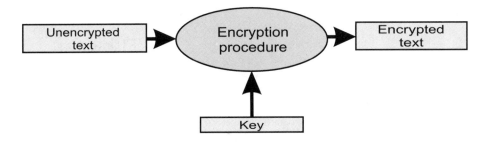

Figure 4.1 Good encryption methods entail the use of a key (a kind of password).

Security by obscurity is bad strategy Incidentally, what goes for encryption methods is also valid for other areas of computer security: the security of a system should never just depend on the mode of operation being kept secret. This kind of approach is called **security by obscurity** and is a very bad strategy.

4.1.2 Cryptographic terminology

At this point a few more technical terms are in order: encryption methods that by design work with keys are called **symmetric algorithms** or **secret key algorithms**. Later we shall see that there are also methods of encryption in which the key is not always kept secret and which are therefore described as asymmetrical encryption, or public key encryption. In this connection one speaks also of public key cryptography and of secret key cryptography. Such expressions as symmetric encryption, asymmetrical encryption, secret key encryption or public key encryption are in widespread use.

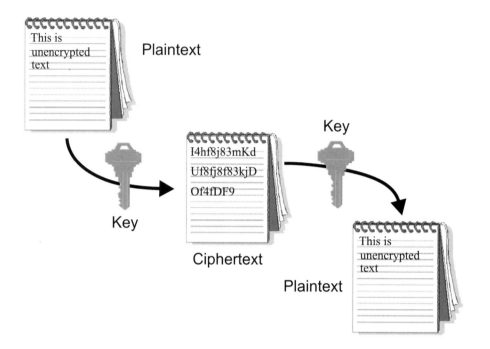

Figure 4.2 Some important terms in cryptography: the original message before encryption is known as plaintext. The encrypted message is known as ciphertext. The encryption algorithm is also known as cipher.

And here are a few more words that cryptographers use regularly: Before it has been encrypted, a message is known as **plaintext;** the encrypted message is known as **ciphertext** (even though it doesn't look like text in the accepted sense of the word). Encryption methods are also called **ciphers**. Expressed in mathematical terms, encryption and decryption are functions that can be represented by the letters e and d respectively. If k is the key, m the plaintext and c the ciphertext, then the following two formulae are valid:

$e(m,k)=c$

$d(c,k)=m.$

4.1.3 Attacks on ciphers

Ciphers can be attacked As you may recall, in this book we are assuming (not without cause) that Mallory can, at will, intercept any message exchanged between Bob and Alice. If Alice and Bob encrypt their messages, Mallory can still intercept the messages and, since it is no great secret, he also knows which encryption algorithm they used. However, he does not know the key that was used for encryption.

The word 'attack is used in cryptography
If Mallory now attempts to decrypt the ciphertext without the key, or to discover the key, this would be described as an **attack** on the encryption algorithm. Cryptanalysis is the science of attacks on encryption methods. Mallory is said to be trying to **break** the method or (less scientifically perhaps) to **crack** it. If he succeeds in obtaining the key by non-cryptanalytical methods (through stealing, bribery or whatever means), then he has **compromised** the key.

Attacks on encryption methods can be divided into different groups:

- If Mallory does not have the plaintext, it is a **ciphertext-only attack**.

- If Mallory has the plaintext and tries to discover the key for future use, this is called a **known-plaintext attack**.

- If Mallory wants to discover the key and has the chance of choosing the plaintext himself, this is called a **chosen-plaintext attack**.

The ciphertext-only attack is the most difficult

Without question, the most difficult method by far is the ciphertext-only attack. At the same time, it is the one that occurs most frequently in practice because, in most cases, Mallory does not know what the message says. If he does, then maybe he has no further interest in the key. Nevertheless, the two other attack methods are still important.

A known-plaintext attack can often be used if messages or parts of messages are repeated. If Alice always uses the same letterhead or begins all her e-mails with the words 'Hello Bob', then Mallory, if he is aware of this, knows at least part of the plaintext. He can now try to discover the key with a known-plaintext attack, and then go on to decrypt the rest of the e-mail. It is often a similar case with many messages that flow through the Internet: they often have a so-called header (a type of letterhead in which information about the message is stored), whose contents can be guessed.

Understandably, the chosen-plaintext attack is the dream of any cryptanalyst because it is the simplest. In the case of many former ciphers this attack is trivially easy, for modern methods happily not. A chosen-plaintext attack can be used, for example, in the Unix operating system to guess passwords. Passwords are usually stored there where anybody can get at them, even if encrypted. Since one can choose or alter one's own password to one's liking, one has all the prerequisites for a chosen-plaintext attack: a free choice of plaintext and access to the ciphertext.

Chosen-plaintext attacks are often realistic as well

But don't start celebrating too soon: the encryption algorithm used by Unix has shown itself to be very secure against chosen-plaintext attacks up to now. Things might be more promising, however, in the case of the encryption chip of a pay-TV decoder, for example. In this case, the key is stored in the hardware (smart card) and is not normally in readable form. However, since a decoder is easy to come by, there is a possibility of feeding one with a chosen plaintext, which is substantially more effective than constantly changing the password under Unix. Even with this chosen-plaintext attack, however, it is fair to say that the methods employed are only susceptible to such attacks under certain conditions.

A good method must also withstand even a chosen-plaintext attack

The moral of this story: a good encryption algorithm must also withstand a chosen-plaintext attack, otherwise it is not really secure. There again, if a known-plaintext or even a ciphertext-only attack might succeed, then the encryption algorithm belongs in the wastepaper basket.

4.2 Elementary encryption methods

After all these theoretical reflections, let us get down to business and take a look at some encryption methods. We shall start small, however, which means that I will first describe some elementary methods that are not used in the Internet because they are much too insecure.

4.2.1 Caesar cipher

The Caesar cipher is a simple encryption algorithm

Since Alice's and Bob's e-mails usually consist of text, one encryption algorithm option might be to replace each letter by another letter. For example, each letter might be shifted alphabetically by a number n:

If $n=1$, then A becomes B, B becomes C, C becomes D, ...

If $n=2$, then A becomes C, B becomes D, C becomes E, ...

The plaintext:

> PEOPLE MAKE MISTAKES, COMPUTERS ARE RESPONSIBLE FOR CATASTROPHES

for $n=5$, becomes the following ciphertext:

UJTUQJ RFPJ RNXYFPJX, HTRUZYJWX FWJ WJXUTSXNGQJ KTW HFYFXYWTUMJX

You have realised that n is the key in this algorithm, which is called the **Caesar cipher** (because Julius Caesar was said to have used it). The Caesar cipher (or Caesar shift cipher) has 26 different keys (the key 0 should be avoided for rather obvious reasons), for which reason even a ciphertext-only attack is possible here. To find the key Mallory must, by hand or with computer support, try all the numbers for n from 1 to 25. Such an attack, in which all possible keys are tested, is called a **exhaustive key search**, or a **brute force attack**. It goes without saying that a good cipher should withstand even a computer-aided brute force attack.

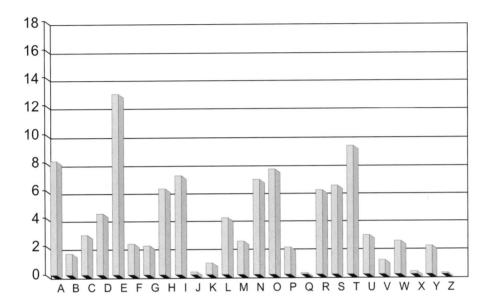

Figure 4.3 In English the letters of the alphabet are not used with the same frequency. 'E' is by far the most frequently used. Mallory can use this to crack a cipher.

Another way to attack the Caesar cipher is by so-called frequency analysis, which works outstandingly for longer texts. Frequency analysis is based on the simple fact that not all letters occur with the same frequency (this is valid for all languages). As the diagram shows, at 12.7% E is the most frequent letter in English, followed by T (9.1%) and A (8.2%). Mallory can use this by counting the number of occurrences of each letter. In the above ciphertext, for example, the following occurrences are found:

A	B	C	D	E	F	G	H	I	J	K	L	M	N	O	P	Q	R	S	T	U	V	W	X	Y	Z
0	0	0	0	0	5	1	2	0	9	1	0	1	2	0	2	2	3	1	5	5	0	5	7	4	1

You see that J with 9 occurrences is the most frequent letter in the ciphertext. Actually J is the substitution used for the letter E, and on this basis alone this Caesar cipher is already broken. That the second most frequent letter is X, and that here this substitutes for the letter S rather than T, is just one of those small trials sent to plague the cryptanalyst. In a longer text such deviation would not occur as a rule.

4.2.2 Substitution ciphers

A frequency analysis doesn't only work with Caesar ciphers, by the way, but whenever a cipher can be detailed with the aid of a table in which the corresponding cipher letter can be listed for each letter. In this case, one calls such a cipher a **substitution cipher**. The Caesar cipher is an example of a substitution cipher; the following table shows a further example (each letter in the top row is substituted by the cipher letter immediately below it):

A	B	C	D	E	F	G	H	I	J	K	L	M	N	O	P	Q	R	S	T	U	V	W	X	Y	Z
N	E	U	Z	Y	O	V	D	K	T	M	F	J	R	L	B	G	H	A	C	P	W	S	Q	I	X

Of course, in this more general case, it will not be enough just to determine the most frequent letters. Instead, Mallory must calculate the relative frequency for several (at best for all) letters. Once he has done this, and if the ciphertext is long enough, then Mallory will have no problem in extracting the plaintext with the help of the statistics displayed in Figure 4.3.

Using ASCII characters does not result in any significant benefits

Of course, Alice and Bob could make Mallory's task even more difficult. Instead of using just 26 letters they could instead use the 256 ASCII characters, for example. In this case Mallory would no longer be able to recognise words, blank spaces and punctuation marks as such. On top of this, it is much more onerous to set up a bar chart such as in Figure 4.3 for 256 characters. However, because we have to assume that Mallory knows very well the type of method being used (and thus also how the individual characters are coded), this would be only slightly more secure.

4.2.3 Permutation ciphers

We now take a look at another elementary class of ciphers that (taken alone) are equally insecure, the so-called **permutation ciphers**. In a permutation cipher the letters of the plaintext are not substituted, but only rearranged. If, for example, one looks at plaintext five letters at a time, then a permutation cipher is given by the following rule:

Permutation ciphers interchange the position of letters

Letter 4 goes to position 1, 1 to 2, 2 to 3, 5 to 4 and 3 to 5. This defines the key (in short form) as: (4,1,2,5,3).

The plaintext,

    THERE ARE TWO KINDS OF PEOPLE: THOSE WHO FINISH WHAT THEY
    START.

using this 4,1,2,5,3 cipher key, gives the ciphertext:

    RTHEE TAR WEN OKDIP SO EFEOPT: LEHOW SIH ONFWIS HHHA TETA
    YSRTT.

Permutation ciphers can be cracked

Mallory can usually break this kind of cipher by trial and error. Longer keys make it more difficult, of course, but a known-plaintext attack is no great problem for Mallory in any case. A further disadvantage of permutation ciphers lies in the fact that, even without decryption, the ciphertext offers various clues. Mallory can guess the language used from the frequency of individual letters. In addition, it can be seen from the ciphertext whether numbers or certain letters occurred frequently in the original plaintext. Permutation ciphers are therefore not especially secure. I have introduced them here only because, as will be seen later, Alice and Bob can put together outstanding encryption methods from a mix of permutation ciphers, substitution ciphers and one-time-pad (see Section 4.3.3). There is more on this subject in Chapter 5 on modern symmetric encryption algorithms.

4.3 Polyalphabetic ciphers

Neither permutation nor substitution ciphers are especially secure

As you may have noticed, all the methods described so far are anything but secure. Even ciphertext-only attacks scarcely bring a tired smile to Mallory's lips, not to mention the simpler known-plaintext and chosen-plaintext attacks. These weaknesses were known centuries ago and better methods were found. I would like to introduce you to three of these.

4.3.1 Vigenère cipher

The Vigenère cipher uses a word as the key

The reason why a frequency analysis is successful in the case of a substitution cipher is clear: each letter is always represented by the same substitution letter. Ciphers of this type are called **monoalphabetic**. Let's try our luck with a cipher that isn't monoalphabetic. The best known of these is the so-called **Vigenère cipher**. This was invented in the 16th century by a certain Blaise de Vigenère.

How the Vigenère cipher works

To understand the way in which a Vigenère cipher works, let's assume that Alice wants to encrypt the following plaintext:

```
IT IS ALL A SEQUENCE OF BITS.
```

In this case the key is a word, ALICE for example. To perform the encryption, Alice writes the plaintext with the key written repeatedly underneath as follows:

The Vigenère cipher anticipates column wise addition

```
IT IS ALL A SEQUENCE OF BITS

AL IC EAL I CEALICEA LI CEAL
```

Finally, Alice adds the letters column by column (A=0, B=1, C=2, ...; after Z she begins again at A):

```
IT IS ALL A SEQUENCE OF BITS

AL IC EAL I CEALICEA LI CEAL
```

```
- - - - - - - - - - - - - - - - - - - - - - - - - - - - -

IE QU ELW I UIQFMPGE ZN DMTD
```

The ciphertext then runs IE QU ELW … . Did you notice this? The Vigenère cipher is made up of several Caesar ciphers, i.e., exactly as many ciphers as the key has letters. As you see, the same letter can be represented here by various others; for example, the first L in ALL stays as L, but the second becomes W. A cipher with this attribute is said to be **polyalphabetic**.

Security of the Vigenère cipher

The Vigenère cipher is clearly more secure than the Caesar cipher

Naturally the Vigenère cipher is much more secure than the Caesar cipher, particularly as a brute force attack here is very onerous.

Even the Vigenère cipher can be cracked

Although it cannot be broken using frequency analysis, the Vigenère cipher can be broken easily with a ciphertext-only attack. The deciding factor for this attack is the length of the key. If Mallory knows this, then his only problem is that he has to break several Caesar ciphers, and as already discussed, this is not particularly difficult. To ascertain the length of the key it is often enough to search the ciphertext for sequences of letters that repeat themselves. If the sequence BJHG, for example, occurs twice at an interval of 56, this is an indication that 56 is divisible by the key length. If Mallory finds a further example that occurs twice, at an interval of 105 say, then the matter becomes clear: the divisors of 56 are 2, 4, 7, 8, 14 and 28, while the divisors of 105 are 3, 5 and 7. Since 7 is the only common divisor of 56 and 105, this is in all probability the key length.

There are other methods for determining the length of the key, but we will not pursue them because the Vigenère cipher is only of academic interest. In any case, it is clear that a computer-aided ciphertext-only attack presents no problems and that Mallory really will have no trouble with known or even random plaintext.

4.3.2 Vernam cipher

Although the Vigenère cipher is as old as it is insecure, it is by no means useless. It can be built up into a very secure cipher if Alice and Bob use the right keys.

The Vernam cipher is a special case of the Vigenère cipher

To make things as difficult as possible for Mallory, Alice and Bob should choose the longest key possible. The longer the key, the more Caesar ciphers for Mallory to break and the less text available to him for each Caesar cipher. Ideally Alice and Bob will choose a key for a Vigenère cipher that is as long as the plaintext itself. This special case is referred to as the **Vernam cipher** (named after its inventor, Gilbert Vernam). The Vernam cipher cannot be broken with the methods described in the previous section, such as a simple frequency analysis or a brute force attack. It is not absolutely secure, however. Where the ciphertext – and by definition the key – is long enough and both derive from a normal language (such as English), Mallory can make use of the fact that letters do not occur with the same frequency in the plaintext and the key, and that an erratic distribution must therefore occur in the ciphertext also. Once again, Mallory can apply frequency analysis. Of course, this is much more complicated than in the case of a simple substitution cipher; however, for a practised cryptanalyst of Mallory's calibre with computer support, this kind of thing is no more than an exercise.

4.3.3 One-time-pad

One-time-pad uses long keys

If Mallory wants to break the Vernam cipher in the manner described, then both key and plaintext must exhibit unsymmetrical letter distribution. If, however, Alice and Bob choose a key with a genuinely random letter sequence, then once again a frequency analysis cannot succeed. A Vernam cipher in which the key is a genuinely random sequence is called a **one-time-pad**. As the name says, with one-time-pad ciphers the key (which again has the same length as the plaintext) is used only once, otherwise that sequence of letters would no longer be random and an attacker would again be able to break a Vigenère cipher.

Security of the one-time-pad

One-time-pad is demonstrably secure

Is there any cryptanalytic method at all that can promise success against one-time-pad? Interestingly not, at least not if the key is genuinely random (what we mean by random is discussed in Chapter 9). In which case it can even be proven that the ciphertext is likewise completely random and so cannot be broken. Or in other words: any given plaintext can be encrypted into any given ciphertext with equal probability in each case – Mallory has met his match. Incidentally, one-time-pad in its various forms is the only encryption algorithm for which the following can be said: it is absolutely secure.

The binary XOR (exclusive OR) function

One-time-pad can even be used with only two characters

Of course, one-time-pad doesn't only function with the 26-letter alphabet. The 256 ASCII characters or another set of other characters could be used equally well. In modern cryptography, only the two characters 0 and 1 are used. In this case, the plaintext is a sequence of bits, the key likewise. Adding a plaintext bit to a key bit corresponds to the binary arithmetic **XOR (exclusive OR) function**. The XOR function gives the value 1 if the one input value is 0 and the other is 1. If the input values are both 0 or both 1, then the result is 0. The XOR function plays an important part in cryptography and will crop up again in this book.

Disadvantages of one-time-pad

Now, since we have already discovered an absolutely secure and, above all, simple encryption algorithm at the start of this book, why should we concern ourselves further with this subject? Quite simple: because one-time-pad also has its disadvantages. Basically, there are three of these.

One-time-pad is impractical

• Working with a key that is exactly the same length as the message is a bit unwieldy. If Alice and Bob want to use this method on the Internet, then for each bit transmitted there must also be a key bit, which is known only to Alice and

Bob. If all Internet users were to use one-time-pad, the Internet data traffic would be doubled.

- If a key is transmitted over the Internet, it can be intercepted. More on this subject in the chapter on the problem of exchanging keys (Section 6.1).

- It is substantially more difficult than one might think to create volumes of genuinely random numbers. More information can be found in Chapter 9.

These shortcomings are so serious that one-time-pad is not used on the Internet and other computer networks. There are, however, many methods that use the basic idea (DES for example, see Section 5.1).

One-time-pad is seldom used

One-time-pad has a certain importance in the secret service and military fields. For example, whenever Bob is travelling as a spy on behalf of the Cryptoland secret service, he always carries a sealed envelope containing a long sequence of random letters. In an emergency, Bob can use this sequence of letters as a one-time-pad key to send a message to the control centre in Cryptoland. The advantage of this practice is obvious: the encryption algorithm is simple to use and very secure. Even an amateur can encrypt a message reliably in just a few minutes using only pencil and paper.

4.4   The Enigma and other rotor cipher machines

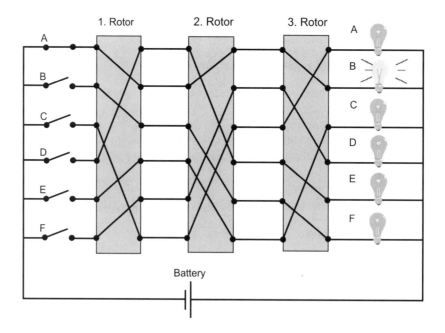

Figure 4.4   A rotor cipher machine with 3 rotors (instead of 26 letters only 6 are shown). If the A-key is pressed the rotor wiring leads to the B-lamp being lit up. The rotors then turn, causing the current path to be changed with each key press.

In the Second World War, rotor ciphers were employed

As recently as the First World War, descendants of the Vigenère cipher were used to encrypt radio messages. After that, the era of the so-called rotor cipher machines began and with them the most interesting chapter to date in the story of cryptography and cryptanalysis (see [Schu00] for an interesting article with many photos). The best-known example of a rotor cipher machine is the legendary Enigma encryption machine which played a decisive role in the Second World War.

4.4.1 How a rotor cipher machine works

Rotor cipher machines were invented in 1918

Rotor cipher machines were invented in 1918. At least four people independently and almost simultaneously came up with the idea of encrypting messages on this basis [Beth]. For example, in the USA, the inventor Edward Hebern had the idea of building an electromechanical encryption machine in 1918 (see Fig. 4.4). The design of this machine provides for one or more circular discs (rotors), each having 26 metal contacts on each side (presumably there were three rotors). Each contact on one side of the rotor is wired to a contact on the other side. The three rotors are linked mechanically, as in a tachometer. If a contact on the left side of the left-hand rotor is connected to the battery by pressing one of the 26 keys, current flows through all three rotors and causes one of the 26 connected lamps to light up. Each key is labelled with a letter, as is each lamp. With this arrangement, each letter is substituted for another as determined by the rotor wiring – which constitutes an encryption algorithm. This then becomes more complicated in that after each key press the left-hand rotor rotates one unit. After a full revolution the middle rotor turns one unit, followed after one complete revolution by the third rotor (just like a speedometer).

Inventing a rotor cipher machine did not bring Hebern good fortune

Incidentally, inventing a rotor encryption machine did not bring Hebern good fortune. True, he was granted a patent for his encryption machine in 1924, but after manufacturing just a few trial machines the company he had established had to file for bankruptcy in 1926. Some years later, in 1947, after the US military decided to adopt rotor cipher machines, Hebern sued for damages of 50 million US dollars. With only modest success, however: in 1958, four years after his death, his heirs were awarded 30,000 US dollars.

A rotor cipher is a polyalphabetic substitution cipher

From a cryptographic viewpoint, the Hebern machine produced polyalphabetic substitution ciphers. The process whereby ciphertext was derived from plaintext was changed after each letter because at least one rotor turned after each entry. The substitution process only repeated itself after the right-hand rotor had completed a full revolution. This did not happen until 26^3 (i.e., 17,576) letters had been pressed. Just like any good encryption algorithm, rotor ciphers also work with a key. Given that the wiring of the rotors is unchanged over a period and is known to Mallory, the key is constituted by the starting positions of the rotors. The size of the key is then the same as the number of rotor settings and amounts to $26^3 = 17,576$ letters. This number can be increased yet again by interchanging the rotors. For example, if five differently wired rotors are available and three of these can be used in any order, the size of the key is increased some sixty-fold to approximately one million. Most users of rotor cipher machines presume that attackers are not familiar with rotor wiring connections.

4.4.2 The Enigma

Scherbius invented the Enigma

Also in 1918, independently of Hebern, the German engineer Arthur Scherbius built an encryption machine using rotors. To his machine, which he patented in 1926, he gave the name **Enigma** (Greek for 'puzzle') – later to become a name known all over the world. In its most popular form the Enigma had three rotors. However, there was one extra component: behind the third rotor an additional, static rotor (the so-called reflector) was installed, having contacts on one side only. These were wired in pairs (see Figure 4.6). If one of the 26 keys was now pressed, the current flowed through the three rotors to the reflector and from there back again through the rotors, causing a lamp to light up. At the time, it was thought that the reflector would make the machine even more secure – a fatal error, as we now know.

Figure 4.5   The Enigma was used in the Second World War. It produced rotor ciphers and was the most famous encryption machine in the world. The photo comes from the IT-Security **Teaching & Study Collection** of the BSI (Bundesamt für Sicherheit in der Informationstechnik).

Scherbius like Hebern, could not take pleasure in his invention for very long. He died in 1926 following an accident. In 1934, his company went bankrupt. By the end of the 1920s, however, the German Army adopted the Enigma for military purposes, and by the end of the 1930s was providing the successor to Scherbius' company with viable orders.

4.4.3 Cryptanalysis of rotor ciphers

The Enigma was cracked How the Enigma, despite constant improvements, was cracked repeatedly by Polish and British cryptographers between 1928 and 1945 is probably the most exciting story in the whole history of cryptography.

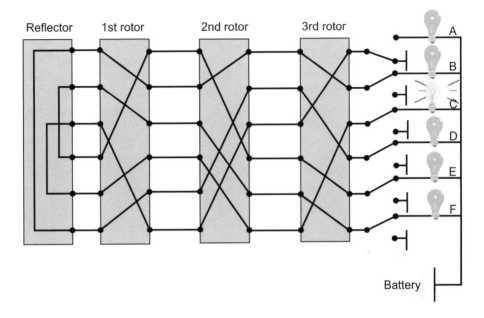

Figure 4.6 The Enigma creates a rotor cipher in which each rotor runs through twice. This is the effect of the reflector which has contacts on one side only.

History of Enigma cryptanalysis

The story begins in 1927, the year in which the Polish secret service obtained one of the commercially available Enigma machines and so learnt how the machine worked (which confirms that one should always presume that eavesdroppers know the method). The three Polish mathematicians, Marian Rejewski, Henryk Zygalski and Jerzy Rozycki, immediately applied themselves to the problem and soon registered their first success. With no small thanks to the help of a spy, in 1932 they succeeded in reconstructing the wiring of German Army Enigmas. Just one year later they were in a position to determine the rotor starting positions (i.e. the key), which meant they had cracked the Enigma. In 1938, Rejewski and his colleagues succeeded in constructing a machine that made the decryption of Enigma-coded messages much easier and which could be regarded as the forerunner of the modern computer. The inventor named the machine 'bomba' after the Polish word for an ice-cream bombe.

At least 50 versions of the Enigma were in use

A considerable problem for the Poles arose from the fact that the Germans used different versions of the Enigma (50 in total by the end of the war) and, where security was critical, added a fourth rotor and other improvements. This overwhelmed the Polish mathematicians, and in 1938 they let the British secret service into the secret. The British made full use of the information. They developed the Polish 'bomba' into a practical machine, which they called a 'bombe', not because it looked a little like an ice-cream bombe, but because the ticking noise made by the machine was reminiscent of the ticking of a time bomb. In their Government Code and Cypher School (GC&CS) at Bletchley Park, Buckinghamshire, the British pursued Enigma cryptanalysis with the aid of bombes on an industry basis until the end of the Second World War. Up to 7000 workers – including many women – were employed in decryption, under conditions of the utmost secrecy. Most of the workers only knew about their own working team and had no idea of the significance of their work in the enterprise as a whole.

The British could decode many German radio messages

With the help of the decoding factory at Bletchley Park, the British succeeded in decoding a large proportion of intercepted German radio messages. However, the numerous versions of the Enigma and diverse improvements proved a problem, and so there were some messages that the British could not read. One thing is now certain, however: the successful cryptanalysis of the Enigma had an enormous influence on the outcome of the Second World War. Certainly the U-boat war in the North Atlantic might have gone differently had the Enigma not been cracked – the Allies often had detailed information about U-boat locations which they gathered from intercepted and decoded radio messages. This let them steer their convoys wide of the danger zone and their warships attacked the U-boats instead. It is even possible that Germany might have suffered an atomic bomb in the Second World War if the Enigma machine had not been broken, and the war was undoubtedly shortened because of it. It was, after all, only three months after German capitulation that America dropped the first atomic bomb on Hiroshima.

The Enigma story was kept secret for a long time

After the end of the Second World War, the British public was told nothing of the dramatic story of the Enigma. The British prime minister, Winston Churchill, ordered the machines at Bletchley Park to be destroyed, and the success of the code breakers remained a state secret. The story only became public in 1974. The whole truth about the Enigma has probably not yet been told. One can speculate, for example, about the extent of the Soviet Union's knowledge. It is difficult to believe that the many outstanding Soviet mathematicians did not concern themselves with Enigma.

How Enigma cryptanalysis worked

Of course, Enigma cryptanalysis is more complicated than that for the Vigenère or Caesar ciphers. For this reason I cannot go into this subject in detail and must restrict myself to the most important facts. The first thing to realise is that a ciphertext-only attack on the Enigma is very difficult unless someone is familiar with the wiring. However, there are effective known-plaintext attacks. These enabled the Poles and British to discover the wiring of some machines.

The Enigma reflector caused a loophole in security

To find the key when the wiring was known (i.e. from the rotor starting positions) there is one means of attack where a feature of the Enigma itself is of use, the reflector no less – even though it was designed to make the machine more secure. As you can easily establish for yourself, the reflector ensures that during encryption no letter can be substituted by itself. If you knew a long word that might occur somewhere in the plaintext (wartime military vocabulary was rather limited), you passed this along the ciphertext until none of the letters in the word corresponded with a letter in the current ciphertext sequence. This meant that, with a fair degree of probability, you had found a plaintext–ciphertext match. The key could often be found on this basis.

Circumstances favoured the Poles and British

Despite all this rudimentary cryptanalysis, the Poles and the British would not have achieved much if circumstances had not come to their aid. These included the spy already mentioned and the fact that in 1941, a German U-boat fell into British hands, complete with a book of Enigma keys valid for the following months. Above all, however, this was due to the criminal carelessness of the Germans. They committed just about every mistake that one can make in the use of an encryption system. Again and again they used initial settings that were easy to guess (say AAA or ABC). A daily change of key offered no great problem for the code breakers because routine messages, often with the same sequence of words, were transmitted daily at the same time of day – which made possible a known-plaintext attack. These and similar mistakes naturally made the task of the Poles and British much easier.

Even without a reflector the rotor machine had weak spots

There is still the question of whether the Enigma without a reflector (i.e. with the same construction as the Hebern machine) would have been much more secure. Probably not, because the Hebern machine could also be cracked, even though using a guessed plaintext word would not work in this case. There are, however, other known-plaintext attacks and in the light of the countless errors the Germans made, these would undoubtedly have worked.

Modern symmetric encryption algorithms

It's better to be able to prove that an attack won't work than to have to guess that it won't because it's too much work.
COLIN PLUMB

Key experience no. 5
One of the first encryption machines was invented by the late president of the USA, Thomas Jefferson. The so-called Jefferson wheel produced a substitution cipher similar to a Vigenère cipher with a key length of 36.

Since Caesar, Vigenère and Vernam ciphers, as well as rotor ciphers, are so insecure and one-time-pad is impractical, Alice and Bob must look elsewhere if they want to protect their messages against Mallory. Their search need not take long, however, because in the past ten years a whole diary of encryption methods have been introduced against which Mallory has almost no chance. These methods are of course executed by computers, so from now onwards you should envisage plaintext, ciphertext and keys no longer as sequences of letters or numbers, but rather as sequences of *bits*.

5.1 The Data Encryption Standard (DES)

DES is the best-known encryption algorithm

The most well known of all modern encryption methods is the both famed and infamous **DES** (Data Encryption Standard). DES was developed in the USA by IBM during the 1970s. In 1977 it was acknowledged as the standard for data encryption by the US National Institute of Standards and Technology (NIST) and since then has become, as the name states, *the* standard for symmetric encryption.

DES meant a great leap forwards for cryptography because it provided the first modern, secure symmetric encryption algorithm that was known in great detail, was free from patent rights and enjoyed general acceptance.

The circumstances in which DES was developed were dubious

Unfortunately, the circumstances in which DES was developed were rather dubious, to say the least. The NSA was involved in the process and made certain that the design criteria for DES were kept secret, which did not exactly engender trust in the method. Nevertheless, over the years it became clear that the developers of DES had done a first-class job: cryptanalysts hit DES at all conceivable weak spots, only to be left gnashing their teeth in frustration. Therefore, despite its age, DES is still used today, both on the Internet and outside it. An end to the DES era is not yet in sight. Probably DES would enjoy eternal life if it were not for a huge weak point that, obviously under pressure from the NSA, the developers had built in deliberately. We are speaking about the short key length, to which we shall return later.

5.1.1   What was new in the DES?

DES can only sensibly be used in tandem with the computer

In contrast to the ciphers studied up to now, DES can only sensibly be used in tandem with the computer because it is rather more complicated than a Vigenère or rotor cipher. For all that it can outwit a supercomputer, DES is still remarkably simple. Therefore I shall go into DES, as the mother of all modern ciphers, in some detail. And here I would like to point out, once more, that I shall neither betray any secrets nor play into the hands of the hackers. The way DES functions is common knowledge, with full intent, because only a widely known algorithm can be exhaustively searched for weak spots. Also, in this book we are paying careful heed to Murphy's law of cryptography: Mallory is cleverer than you think. So he would know everything about any method used by Alice and Bob anyway (see Section 32.5).

DES encrypts 64-bit blocks

DES encrypts data in blocks 64 bits long (data can still be referred to as plaintext, even if it is not text in the actual sense of the word). For example, if Alice wants to encrypt a text that is stored in ASCII format (each character comprises 8 bits), she splits the text into blocks of 8 characters each. Should the final block comprise fewer than 8 characters, she fills the remainder with any other characters at random. Graphics, compressed files or audio files can be similarly encrypted. The only prerequisite is that the plaintext comprises a sequence of bits.

The DES working method is exquisitely clever

Each 64-bit block of plaintext is encrypted by DES into a 64-bit block of ciphertext. In other words, this means that the plaintext and ciphertext are of equal length, which is an important feature of DES. It would be admittedly much easier to develop a more secure encryption algorithm if the ciphertext could be longer than the plaintext. However, this advantage is forgone in DES and almost all other modern symmetrical algorithms because one wants to waste neither transmission capacity nor memory. As we shall see, DES is secure enough even without such an advantage.

The key in a DES algorithm is, like plaintext and ciphertext, a 64-bit block. Of these, 8 bits are used as a checksum so that the real key length in DES is only 56 bits. For this reason, and throughout the remainder of this book in connection with DES, I shall always speak of a 56-bit key.

DES is a combination of one-time-pad, permutation and substitution ciphers

DES is, if you like, a combination of one-time-pad, permutation and substitution ciphers that are applied to the two characters 0 and 1 instead of the letters A to Z. More precisely, in DES only the following downright simple functions are used:

- the XOR (exclusive OR) function (see Section 4.3.3)

- permutation (the order of a sequence of bits is changed)

- substitution (one bit sequence is replaced by a different one).

Experience from the past 20 years has clearly shown that these simple functions are all that is needed for effective secret key encryption. However, in themselves, none of these functions can effect secure encryption. Only through skilful combination and by frequent repetition can a secure algorithm be created. The fact that no complicated components are necessary for symmetric encryption algorithms has enormous advantages when it comes to building the hardware. In fact, the functions used in DES were chosen deliberately because they can be effectively performed by hardware. A DES encryption algorithm executed by hardware can achieve very high speeds.

5.1.2 How DES works

Finally we come to the modus operandi of DES, which is shown in Figure 5.1.

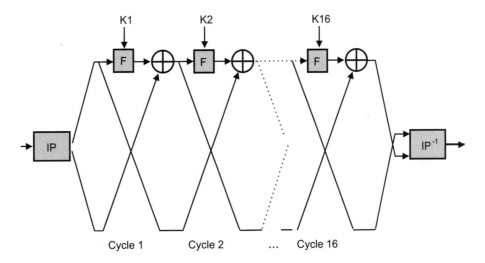

Figure 5.1 With a subkey as input, DES does 16 rounds. Function *F* is explained in the next diagram.

The 16 rounds of DES

The 64-bit block to be encrypted is first permutated (so-called **initial permutation**). The resulting 64-bit stream is then split into two parts, *L* (for left) and *R* (for right), of 32 bits each. The same process is then repeated 16 times (one talks about the 16 rounds of DES):

- Function *F* is applied to *L*. The result is XOR'd with *R*, the result then becoming the new *L*.

- *L* becomes the new *R*.

DES encrypts blocks that are 64 bits long   After the 16 rounds are complete, the resulting 64 bits are permutated again (**final permutation**), and in the exact inverse of the initial permutation. The resulting 64 bits are the product of the encryption, i.e. the resulting ciphertext block.

The decisive event in this process is the function *F*. This produces an output value that can be regarded as random. Using the XOR function, this output value is combined with an intermediate result of the encryption. We have met this process before in one-time-pad (Section 4.3.3). Part of the key is used as the input to function *F*, and of course another part is used in each round. I will explain how these subkeys come about (the so-called key transformation) shortly.

The function F

So that function *F* produces random bit sequences as its output, the input (32-bit block and subkey) must be cleverly combined. Surprisingly, function *F* does not involve lots of confusing operations, but is quite neatly structured (Figure 5.2).

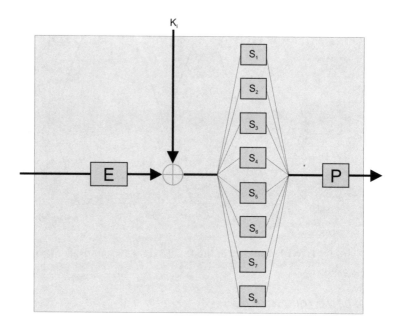

Figure 5.2   Function *F* is the most important part of DES. The input 32 bits are first expanded to 48 and then XOR'd with a subkey. Finally, every six bits are substituted by four new bits and are output, after permutation, as the resulting 32 bits.

Function *F* works as described on a block of 32 bits. This block is first permutated and, by doubling up some bits, expanded to 48 bits. This expansion is independent of the key and cryptographically meaningless in itself. The key now comes into play: the resulting 48-bit block is XOR'd with a 48-bit section of the key. This combination is coincidentally also the only point at which the key is input in DES. Since DES has 16 rounds, it is run through 16 times. The 48 bits that we have after combination with the part key are next split into 8 blocks of 6 bits each.

The S-boxes are an important component of DES

Each 6-bit block then becomes the input to one of the S_1 to S_8 functions (substitution boxes or S-boxes). Each S-box effects a different substitution: for each of the 64 possible input values, there is a specific 4-bit output value that is stored in a table. Eight output values to each 4 bits makes 32 bits in total, and it is precisely these 32 bits that constitute the output of function *F*.

5.1.3 Transformation of the DES key

To complete the description, we still have to discuss the process with which the 16 48-bit subkeys are generated from the 56-bit key of DES (i.e. key transformation). In comparison to some other processes, key transformation in DES is relatively simple, since only bit shifting and permutations are involved. There are no S-boxes in DES key transformation.

With the DES there are 16 sub-keys

As already described, a DES key comprises 64 bits, of which 8 are used as a checksum. The first step in key transformation consists of checking the correctness of the check bits and then erasing them or issuing an error message. The remaining 56 bits are the actual key from which, as you have seen, 16 48-bit subkeys have to be generated. The subkeys are therefore interdependent to a large degree, which does nothing to enhance security. Astonishingly, however, this apparent weakness of DES has not proved to be such.

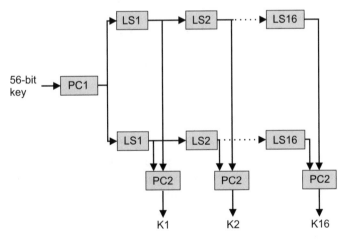

Figure 5.3 DES key transformation generates 16 48-bit subkeys from a 56-bit key. PC stands for a permutation (permuted choice), LS for left shift.

As illustrated in Figure 5.3, the 56 key bits of DES are split into two halves after permutation PC1. Both halves form the input to a further permutation (PC2), whose result is the subkey of the first round. In the following rounds, new halves are created by the two old halves each being bit-shifted, and subkeys again created in the PC2 permutations. Whether bits are single or double shifted is specified in a table that forms part of the DES specification.

5.1.4 Decryption with the DES

Decryption with DES works just like encryption

With a good encryption algorithm it is not only to be expected that Mallory has no chance of decrypting a text without the key. It is equally important, that decryption with knowledge of the key should be quick and easy to manage. This requirement is well fulfilled by DES because the way in which decryption works is remarkably simple: in exactly the same way as encryption. The only difference is the key transformation: the 16 subkeys are used in reverse order to how they are used in encryption. This feature of DES is no accident, of course; the DES developers intended it to be that way. If you look again at Figure 5.1 you will notice that this feature is independent of function *F*. It makes no difference which 16 functions are executed in the respective encryption rounds – if you subsequently run through the 16 rounds again and thereby apply the same 16 functions in inverse order, you get the plaintext back again.

5.1.5 DES security

DES has been well tested

DES is a prime example demonstrating that publication of the modus operandi of an encryption algorithm leads to increased security. In more than 20 years since its inception, cryptographers have tried every way imaginable to find any kind of weak spot in DES. The results have been such that today hardly any doubt exists about the security of DES. So it is little wonder that DES has been used in many areas for a long time: automatic teller machines and pay-TV boxes are only two of the more important examples. However, cryptanalysis has progressed in the meantime, with the result that DES is slowly being shelved. We will now look at this more closely.

Brute force attacks prior to 1997

The DES key length is too short

The relatively short 56-bit key length of DES was heavily criticised from the start. There would have been no great difficulty in prescribing a longer key. The developers at IBM probably wanted it (they were thinking of 128 bits), but they were prevented by the NSA: from a security viewpoint, the NSA saw their snooping activities being endangered and set the key length to 56 bits, a value that they could just about handle with the computing power they had available to them. One consequence in the face of the widespread adoption of DES was speculation about building a supercomputer that could crack DES by executing a brute force exhaustive key search in a reasonable time period (i.e. a known-plaintext attack).

DES-cracker machines are supposed to have been mass produced

At the end of the 1970s, such speculations were just mind games. It was not until the start of the 1990s that one could assume that, in the secret service field at least, such computers were in operation. For several years now it has been estimated that for several hundred million euros a new computer could be built that could crack

DES in seconds. It was rumoured that such machines were in mass production for the secret service. However, proof of their existence is still not to hand.

The above considerations and the financial assets of NSA and other secret service agencies led to the surmise that it was already possible during the early to mid-1990s to crack DES by performing a search for the key. Despite all these considerations and speculations about cracking DES, not a single successful known-plaintext attack against DES had been reported before 1997. That year saw a change in the situation, however.

The DES challenge

The DES can be cracked at great expense

The 18th of June, 1997 goes down in cryptohistory as the day when the first acknowledged known-plaintext attack on DES succeeded. The firm RSA Data Security had offered a reward of 10,000 US dollars for anyone who could crack DES by a brute force attack using a known-plaintext attack (the competition was named DES Challenge). Rocke Verser, a computer programmer from Colorado, wrote a program that executed DES encryptions and distributed it over the Internet. Over 14,000 Internet users made computer time available to help search for the key. On 18 June – some four months later – a Pentium user in Salt Lake City succeeded. He came up with the key and shared the reward with Verser. In four months, the shared search had checked only a quarter of all DES keys for correctness. With a little less luck, this cryptanalysis trial might have lasted a full 16 months.

The DES was broken several times

In the second round of the DES Challenge, an even greater success was achieved: the record for a known-plaintext attack on DES was beaten at the start of 1998 with 39 days. In the middle of the same year, American cryptographers under the banner of the civilian rights movement Electronic Frontier Foundation took just 56 hours [Koch99]. The computer they used had cost 250,000 dollars. In January 1999, in the third round of the DES Challenge, the 24-hour barrier was broken for the first time: under the direction of the Electronic Frontier Foundation, 100,000 Internet users conducted a successful known-plaintext attack in 22 hours. This record of 22 hours still stands today (summer 2002). The cryptology community has obviously lost interest in DES since nothing more has been heard about this topic lately.

Differential cryptanalysis

Differential cryptanalysis runs idle with DES

One of the methods that can be used to crack DES, other than a brute force attack, is the so-called **differential cryptanalysis**. This is a chosen-plaintext attack, and was developed in 1990 by the Israeli cryptographers Biham and Shamir. Differential cryptanalysis looks at the difference between two text blocks and makes use of the fact that, after a specific number of rounds, diverse differences bring out specific intermediate results with different probabilities. Based on this, and the known difference between input and output, a statistical forecast can be made about the key. If enough plaintext–ciphertext differences are used, the key can be determined. There are encryption methods with which this method can work with only a few hundred or even fewer correctly chosen differences. DES is not one of them. In this case the number of differences needed is so great that differential cryptanalysis brings no advantage over a brute force attack. This is no accident: the DES designers knew all about differential cryptanalysis and had chosen the S-boxes in such a way that the algorithm offered the smallest possible vulnerable surface to this attack. It was not until 1990 that such attacks were discovered – further proof that the DES developers had delivered first-class work.

Linear cryptanalysis

Linear cryptanalysis is only partly successful against DES

In 1992, Mitsuru Matsui in Japan invented **linear cryptanalysis**. With this method from the family of chosen-plaintext attacks, an algorithm (in this case DES) was approached using linear functions. With this method, in 1994 Matsui conducted a successful attack against DES, which occupied twelve workstations for 50 days. In addition he needed 2^{43} (i.e. 1,000,000,000,000) self-selected plaintext blocks – which roughly corresponds to the number of letters in 150 million copies of this book. That this is clearly better than a brute force attack is, however, scarcely relevant in practice.

Other attacks

There are other ways of attacking DES

In addition to the above attacks on the DES algorithm, there are still several real-world attacks, i.e. attacks that are aimed at special implementations (Section 15.6). Apart from these, many cryptographers have published attacks against DES with small changes in its working method. If only 8 rounds were used instead of 16, then Mallory's job would be much easier. This kind of result is not of much practical interest, however.

Summary

The short key length is the only genuine weak spot in DES

The short key length of DES and the constantly improving hardware have led to today's situation where you no longer have to be the NSA to crack DES. When it is a question of industrial secrets worth millions, or other extremely valuable data, DES should no longer be used. For applications such as online banking and online payments over the Internet, however, the algorithm is secure enough for the time being. New implementations of DES should be left well alone.

5.1.6 A stroke of genius comes of age

After my treatise on DES, perhaps you now understand why this algorithm (apart from the key length) was praised to the skies. The developers, with a touch of sheer genius, succeeded in creating a cipher that was as secure as necessary and as user-friendly as possible. Every function of DES was thought-through precisely and made secure against all known effective attacks. That DES has exactly 16 rounds is no more of an accident than is the arrangement of the individual rounds that makes it possible to encrypt and decrypt using the same algorithm. Even the S-box substitutions were carefully and cleverly calculated and are even secure against differential cryptanalysis, which didn't appear until ten years after the arrival of DES.

DES dispenses with many complicating functions

It is also astonishing how many complicated functions that might have made the algorithm more secure were omitted from DES. Instead, the algorithm was based on the following simple building blocks:

- The ciphertext is not longer than the plaintext.

- Only simple functions are used.

- The key affects DES at only one point per round.

- The key transformation could hardly be simpler.

- The subkeys are independent of each other to a high degree. From just 56 bits, 786 bits are produced.

DES has been discontinued

Obviously DES did not need any complications, it was secure enough already. On the other hand, DES is relatively easy to understand, simple to implement and, not least, very fast. The only cloud remaining on the DES horizon is the issue of the 56-bit key. This is the main reason for DES having now retired from service. Still, as described at the start, cryptography has much to do with relativity: if Alice wants to call up an encrypted bank statement from her online account, or doesn't want her boss to read her e-mails, then the DES algorithm is more than enough – at the end of the day, not many people have a DES-cracker in the cellar. However, if Alice is afraid of super-crook Mallory, or wants an encryption algorithm for the future, then she should seek an alternative to DES. In the following chapters some of them will be introduced.

Further information on DES is available in any good cryptography book, especially [Schn96], [Stinso], [MeOoVa] and [Beth]. A very detailed account is given in [Damm].

5.2 Other symmetrical ciphers

In addition to DES, there are many other algorithms

Of course, in addition to DES, there are dozens of other symmetric encryption algorithms. Some of them will be introduced in this section.

5.2.1 The transition from DES to other algorithms

The transition from DES to other algorithms will not happen overnight. First, let us take a look at why DES will take some time to fade from the scene.

Weaknesses of DES

The DES has further disadvantages

In addition to the key length, there are other drawbacks to DES, which, while they do not affect security, do still carry some weight:

- DES was designed for hardware implementation. It is therefore rather slow when executed in software. This is particularly valid for the permutations that DES uses: permutations can be effected without loss of time by purpose-designed hardware circuitry, but are very inefficient in software.

- DES was optimised for the hardware of the 1970s, not for the hardware of the 21st century. It could be faster, even in hardware implementation.

- The starting and ending permutations do not strengthen the algorithm but do slow things down, at least in software.

- DES has fixed block and key lengths (64 and 56 bits respectively). There are applications, however, that require a block length of 128 bits, for example.

- The DES design criteria are still only partly known.

There were enough reasons to look for an alternative to DES

Together with the key length, these points are reason enough for cryptographers to have tried to develop alternatives to DES.

The ideal key length for symmetrical algorithms

That the 56 bits of the DES key are not enough is probably clear by now. But how many would be enough? On the assumption that a brute force attack is the best method of attack, the effort Mallory will have to expend to break the algorithm doubles with each extra key bit. To gain an estimate of the time needed for a brute force attack, we also assume that Mallory can execute a brute force attack on a 56-bit key in just 1 second. This is a very pessimistic assumption because the world record for this is 22 hours. However, since we imagine Mallory to be in NSA circles and have a healthy respect for their capabilities, it might not be wholly unrealistic. On this basis the following table was drawn up:

Key length	Time needed
56 bit	1 second
64 bit	4 minutes
80 bit	194 days
112 bit	10^9 years

Key length	Time needed
128 bit	10^{14} years
192 bit	10^{33} years
256 bit	10^{52} years

The time needed for a brute force attack increases with key length

The magnitude of these figures should be seen against the age of the universe, which is estimated to be around 10^{10} years. It should be taken into consideration that only an attacker with a multi-million dollar budget would have a 50 per cent chance of achieving these figures.

If Alice and Bob want to outmanoeuvre Mallory, they should be dissatisfied with both 56 and 64 bits. On the other hand, with 80 bits it would have to be a very important and valuable message for Mallory to undertake a brute force attack.

128 bits cannot be cracked by a brute force attack

In the case of 128 bits, Mallory has no answer – even if he has access to all the computers in the NSA. Mallory will not even be able to use technical advances, because if he wanted to build a supercomputer that can execute a full-length 128-bit key search within a week, he would have to go against the laws of physics – he would require electrons to move faster than the speed of light. From this, the following can be concluded: a brute force attack on a key that is 128 bits long is ruled out from the start. For the outright paranoid user there are still 192 or even 256 bits available.

DES successors

There have been alternatives to DES since the start of the 1990s

Plans to develop an algorithm on a par with DES that would alleviate the weak spots proved to be more difficult than many thought. After the genesis of DES in the early 1970s, it took almost 15 years before any algorithms at all came on the market that could hold their own for quality. When serious alternatives finally became available during the 1990s, this by no means meant that they would push DES into retirement. After all, DES had resisted all attacks in superior style for years, while other ciphers were still tainted with not having been sufficiently tested. With time, however, it became apparent that several competitors could measure up to and even surpass DES when it came to security. In the following section the more important DES alternatives will be introduced.

5.2.2 Triple-DES

As described in the previous chapters, the Achilles' heel of the DES algorithm is still its relatively short key length. Might Bob and Alice still slip one past Mallory by applying DES more than once? They can, if they do it right.

Double DES provides for twofold application of the DES cipher

Double DES

True to the motto 'better safe than sorry', the closest alternative to DES calls for its twofold application. This means that Alice has to encrypt her message to Bob twice in succession (with two different keys, of course). So, if m is the plaintext, e the encryption function, c the ciphertext and k_1 and k_2 two keys, then:

$$c=e(k_1, e(k_2, m)).$$

Such twofold encryptions would be futile if, for any two keys k_1 und k_2, there was a key k_3, for which:

$$e(k_3,m)=e(k_1, e(k_2, m)).$$

Double DES is not as secure as one might think In this case, the double encryption could be replaced by a single encryption, and the security would be no higher. In mathematical terms this would mean that DES behaves as a group with regard to consecutive encryptions. That there is no such key k_3 as a general rule, and that hence DES is not a group, was surmised for a long time and has since been proved mathematically [CamWie]. Consequently one can now proceed on the assumption that with this simple ploy the security of DES can actually be increased. Contradictorily, this increase in security is not so great as it seems at first sight, however. Of course, a twofold encryption increases the key length to 112 bits, making a brute force attack by Mallory a thankless task from the outset. There is, however, another attack that makes it possible to shorten the search. This attack is called a **meet-in-the-middle attack** and belongs to the suite of known-plaintext attacks. Incidentally, it not only works with DES, but also with any secret key algorithm when twofold encryption is applied.

A meet-in-the-middle attack needs lots of storage capacity The way the meet-in-the-middle attack works is very simple. Mallory takes the (known) plaintext, encrypts it with all 2^{56} possible DES keys and stores all results. Then he takes the ciphertext, decrypts it with all 2^{56} possible DES keys and saves all the results. Now he compares the results of the encryption with those of the decryption. If everything is correct, there is a match (a 'meeting-in-the-middle') and the two DES keys which produced this match are the ones being sought.

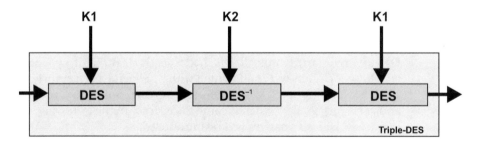

Figure 5.4 With Triple-DES, DES is applied three times consecutively. The second application is a decryption.

Naturally a meet-in-the-middle attack like this is very onerous, particulary because it needs a gigantic memory. If one assumes that there is enough memory and that it can be accessed with the speed required, then this attack on the twofold DES algorithm lasts only about twice as long as a brute force attack on the single DES, which is of course not quite realistic. This statement should not be treated with disdain; in the end a brute force attack on the twofold DES lasts 2^{56} (i.e. almost 10^{17}) times longer than with a single DES. Summary: If Mallory can crack DES with a brute force attack, then a meet-in-the-middle attack on the twofold DES is, because of the massive memory requirement, anything but child's play. Still, it is more realistic than a paranoid user regarding cryptanalysts with affection.

The way Triple-DES works

Now that a twofold DES encryption has been rendered insufficient help to Alice and Bob, they could try it threefold. And in fact this method proves to be a marked improvement: true, even the threefold DES (with three different keys) is not immune to a meet-in-the-middle attack, but on the other hand it is at least as secure as one would expect from a twofold DES – and that is more than enough. These threefold DES variations (the so-called **Triple-DES** or 3DES) are gaining more and more in popularity as the alternative DES algorithm. After all, this algorithm combines the security of the original DES with a greater key length.

The threefold DES is clearly more secure than the twofold

Since in DES there is no substantial difference between encryption and decryption methods, it is usual to replace the second of the three encryptions of Triple-DES with a decryption. This has no effect on security but does have one small advantage: if Alice only needs a simple encryption, she can use three identical keys. One encryption and one decryption then cancel each other out and leave a simple DES encryption. Here is the whole thing again in mathematical terms: if e is the encryption function, d the decryption function, m the message, c the ciphertext and k_1, k_2, k_3 three DES keys, then:

$$c = e(k_1, d(k_2, e(k_3, m))).$$

With Triple-DES only two keys are used for the most part

It is not absolutely necessary for three different keys to be used with Triple-DES. If k_1 and k_3 are identical, then the key length at 112 bits is of course somewhat shorter, but is more than long enough. Therefore, in practice, Triple-DES is usually used with just two keys.

With Triple-DES we now have our first algorithm that eliminates the most important weakness of DES – the short key length. In its place, the Triple-DES has one obvious drawback: it is three times slower than the single DES, which itself does not exactly qualify as the speedy Gonzales of symmetrical algorithms. This can be a great drawback on the Internet. It may be as well, then, to take a look at other methods.

5.2.3 IDEA

IDEA is the current most important DES alternative

The currently most important alternative to DES and Triple-DES is **IDEA** (International Data Encryption Algorithm). This algorithm was developed in Zurich at the start of the 1990s by cryptographers Xuejia Lai and James Massey. The experts praised it mainly for its theoretical foundations. More conducive to the popularity of IDEA, however, might have been that it had been in use for some time in the software PGP (see Section 26.3). Since, despite intensive testing, no weakness worth mentioning has been discovered in the eight years or so since its introduction, it is gradually approaching the stature of DES where quality of design is concerned.

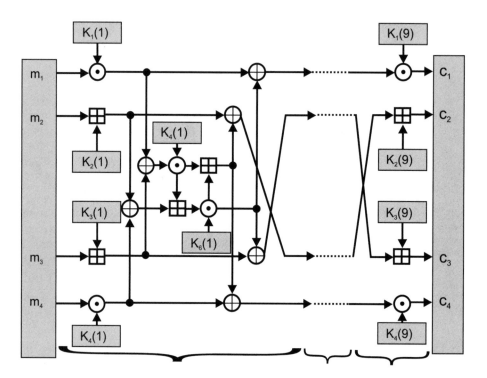

Figure 5.5 The International Data Encryption Algorithm (IDEA), like DES, uses only simple functions. In eight rounds plaintext (m_1 m_2 m_3 m_4) is changed to ciphertext (c_1 c_2 c_3 c_4). Six sub-keys are input with each round.

How IDEA works

The developers of IDEA did not reinvent the wheel. Instead, they used DES as a model in many instances. Many of the design criteria were obviously so well conceived that even after 15 years none better had been found. Like DES, IDEA uses only relatively simple functions, including addition modulo 2^{16} (if you don't know what that is, skip forward to Section 6.2), multiplication modulo $2^{16}+1$, and the indispensable XOR (exclusive OR) function. Another parallel to DES is the length of the encryption blocks at 64 bits. However, the key length is 128 bits and therefore more than double that of DES. In addition to a longer key, IDEA has yet another advantage: it is laid out for implementation in software and as such is *With Triple-DES* about twice as fast as DES.

only two keys were The way the IDEA algorithm works is set out in Figure 5.5. The 64 bits of the *used as a rule* plaintext block are first split into four blocks of 16 bits each (m_1, ..., m_4). The algorithm then runs through 8 rounds in each of which six 16-bit subkeys are input. In each round, four additions (modulo 2^{16}) and four multiplications (modulo $2^{16}+1$) are carried out. The eighth and last round is followed by two further modulo additions and multiplications, the four resulting 16-bit blocks finally coming together to form the ciphertext.

Following the DES model, decryption of an IDEA block uses the same algorithm as for encryption, expect that the subkeys are changed slightly (inverted) and applied in inverse order.

Assessment of IDEA

IDEA is rated as one of the best symmetric algorithms

Without a doubt, IDEA is one of the best symmetric encryption algorithms currently available. As with DES, the algorithm has passed all attack trials to date with flying colours. Differential and linear cryptanalysis do not work with IDEA. Since the key length is 128 bits, Mallory has no chance of success with a brute force attack.

Since IDEA is not only secure but also fast, it is the algorithm of first choice. It has one disadvantage, however: it is patented. Commercial users must pay licence fees.

5.2.4 Further symmetric encryption algorithms

As well as DES, Triple-DES and IDEA already considered, there are a number of other symmetrical algorithms that play a role in connection with the Internet. Some of these will be introduced below. Exact specifications for most of the algorithms mentioned can be found in [Schn96].

RC2

The RC2 symmetric encryption algorithm is one of many that have been developed by perhaps the greatest living cryptographer, Ron Rivest (see Section 30.1.7). RC2 stands for Rivest Cipher 2, and is a cipher with variable key length; until a short time ago, its working method was secret. The reason for opening up the algorithm was the desire to establish the e-mail encryption standard S/MIME (which includes RC2 as one of several algorithms). Up to now, RC2 has not been sufficiently tested in order for it to be classed as secure.

There are several RC algorithms

The RC family has several members: RC4 (Section 9.4.1), RC5 and RC6 (Section 5.3) are equally important symmetric encryption algorithms by Ron Rivest. RC1 and RC3 did not make it to the market.

CAST

CAST is a symmetric encryption algorithm from Carlisle Adams and Stafford Tavares. Since PGP software (see Section 26.3) uses CAST as well as Triple-DES and IDEA, the popularity of this algorithm has increased markedly. Today, CAST is classed as one of the more important DES alternatives.

The design of CAST is based on variability: both the S-boxes and key length are variable. In practice, the version described in [RFC2144], with fixed S-boxes and a 128-bit key, is used. CAST-256, a version with variable key length, is described in [RFC2612] and was one of the DES candidates (see Section 5.3). Both differential and linear cryptanalysis are ineffective against CAST; no other weaknesses are known.

Skipjack

Skipjack is one of the most talked about symmetrical algorithms of the past few years. Skipjack was developed by none other than the NSA. Work on this algorithm began as early as 1985 and was concluded in 1990. Skipjack formed part of the wrecked Clipper project (see Section 32.1.2).

The mechanics of Skipjack were originally kept secret by the NSA. All that was known was that it entailed a block cipher that encrypted 64-bit blocks in 32 rounds with an 80-bit key. It also worked about twice as fast as DES. All other details were just speculation. Since Skipjack only came on the market in hardware form, there was no way of analysing the working method of the algorithm.

In 1998, when there was no longer any mention of Clipper, the NSA published the working method of the algorithm. This confirmed what many cryptographers had expected: although the NSA had cryptological know-how far in advance of academic research, Skipjack used only well-known techniques (albeit excellent). The hope that the NSA might give away some of its secrets with Skipjack was not fulfilled.

Of course, cryptographers all over the world pounced on Skipjack. Some discovered that small modifications led to the algorithm becoming insecure, and that it could be cracked if the number of rounds was greatly reduced. But this could be said of virtually any encryption algorithm. The true sensation came with the discovery by cryptographers Eli Biham, Adi Shamir and Alix Biryukov: the three of them discovered a weak spot if, instead of 32 rounds, only 31 rounds were used. A similar (if only theoretical) weakness had not been found with, for instance, DES. This unexpected result allows only two conclusions: either the NSA was certain that this attack could not be extended to 32 rounds, or no one at the NSA had even noticed the weakness. Either conclusion would be highly interesting.

Although no actual weak spot has yet been discovered, Skipjack has hardly ever been used. Perhaps this is down to the general suspicion with which many people regard the NSA.

MISTY

MISTY is a symmetric encryption algorithm that was first published in 1996. It was developed by the company Mitsubishi [Matsui]. There are two versions, MISTY1 and MISTY2. Both use a key length of 128 bits, work with 64-bit blocks, and use a variable number of rounds.

At first sight, the structure of MISTY resembles that of DES without start and final permutations, and with a differently structured function *F*. The interesting thing is that this function itself looks like a three-round MISTY, and the function replacing *F* still has a similar structure. Only at this third level do S-boxes then come into play. This gives MISTY a recursive structure.

A big advantage of MISTY is its suitability for use in parallel, which is greater with MISTY2 than with MISTY1. The algorithm was also made secure against differential and linear cryptanalysis. MISTY is mainly of interest because a further development of it is intended for use in the new mobile phone standard UMTS (see Section 22.2).

Other algorithms

There are other secret key algorithms, which occasionally cross the paths of those interested in cryptography. These include the RC5, Safer, Blowfish, GOST, LOKI, Khufu and Khafre algorithms, to name just a few. Also, the predecessor of DES, Lucifer from IBM, should not be forgotten. Then there is that popular negative example, FEAL (see Section 32.1.5) – FEAL is so insecure that practically any cryptanalysis method can crack it.

In addition to the ciphers already introduced, Alice and Bob can also avail themselves of the AES and AES candidates (Section 5.3). There is also a whole class of other symmetric encryption algorithms termed stream ciphers (the algorithms described in this chapter are block ciphers). Stream ciphers are discussed in Section 9.4.

5.3 AES

It is rumoured that the way in which DES works was only made public by accident. The NSA allegedly wanted to restrict the use of DES to hardware implementations only. The way it works was supposed to remain secret. IBM took no notice of this imposition, however, and laid the algorithm bare to the world.

The NSA shot themselves in the foot with DES
Whether this story is true or not – the NSA really shot themselves in the foot with DES. This is because public knowledge of DES meant that cryptography was now common property, which is precisely what the NSA wanted to avoid. DES was the first instance of an algorithm that the NSA acknowledged as being secure. What was more obvious than to investigate this algorithm closely and to develop the techniques it used? Even though DES itself no longer represents an insurmountable hurdle for the NSA, with its successors such as Triple-DES or IDEA, even the all-powerful NSA will probably have its problems.

5.3.1 A new standard

After the lessons learned from the DES episode, the NSA obviously felt the urge for a new encryption standard. There was no serious movement until 1997, even in official circles, to find a successor for the ageing DES [LuWe99]. This was to be called **AES** (Advanced Encryption Standard).

Under the name of
AES, a DES
successor was then
standardised

In order to find a suitable algorithm for AES, the US standardisation body NIST appealed to all interested cryptographers all over the world to submit their suggestions by the middle of 1998. What they wanted was a well-documented block cipher with a reference implementation, which was equally suitable for hardware and software, and free from any patent rights. The algorithm was to allow three different key lengths (128 bits, 192 bits and 256 bits). The required length of a block was 128 bits (therefore twice the size of that used in DES).

Interestingly, the AES selection process was not intended to be secret. Instead, any cryptographer interested was given the opportunity to take part. All algorithms from which the selection was to be made were published. Cryptographers were able to present the outcomes of their research on the different algorithms at several AES conferences as well as on the Internet.

For the cryptographers of this world the publication of the 15 AES candidates opened an interesting field of action since most of the algorithms were largely unknown up to that time. All the same, CAST-256, LOKI97 and SAFER+ were three candidates known to the experts as variations of known algorithms. With Twofish (successor to Blowfish) and RC6 (another algorithm from Ron Rivest) at least the name sounded familiar. Algorithms like E2, MARS, DEAL, Crypton, DFC, FROG, Serpent, Hasty Pudding Cipher (HPC), Magenta and Rijndael, on the other hand were new even for expert cryptographers.

5.3.2 The first round

There were 15 AES
candidates

During the first selection round, it was merely the formal criteria that were of any concern. On 20 August 1998, NIST announced a list of 15 nominated algorithms (AES candidates) which fulfilled these criteria. The candidates examined were: CAST-256, Crypton, DEAL, DFC, E2, FROG, Hasty Pudding Cipher (HPC), LOKI97, Magenta, MARS, RC6, Rijndael, SAFER+, Serpent and Twofish.

5.3.3 The finalists

By the middle of 1999, of those AES candidates nominated, NIST had selected the following five algorithms as finalists on the basis of expert opinions [LW00/1]:

MARS comes from
IBM

- MARS: Not the chocolate bar, but IBM's official AES candidate. Among others, this was co-developed by Don Coppersmith, who also co-developed DES (DES also originates from IBM).

- RC6: This algorithm is another of Ron Rivest and his colleagues' developments. RC6 is impressive because of its speed and simplicity.

Rijndael comes from
Belgium

- Rijndael: This algorithm was developed by two Belgians, Joan Daemen and Vincent Rijmen. It is fast, simple and does not require much memory.

- Serpent: This AES candidate was developed by the three crypto luminaries Ross Anderson, Eli Biham and Lars Knudsen. To be on the safe side, the developers equipped the algorithm with 32 rounds, which made Serpent a comparatively slow algorithm.

• Twofish: This algorithm was developed under the management of Bruce Schneier (see Section 30.1.8). It is excellently documented, and there is even a book about it [SKWHFW]. Twofish is a very flexible algorithm which allows various parameters to be set. By doing so, the speed of encryption, memory requirement and other parameters can be changed and matched to user requirements.

5.3.4 The adjudication

The five AES finalists were, of course, put under severe scrutiny by the experts. Slight deficiencies in their performance under certain conditions ensured that MARS and RC6 lost their chances of victory. There were intense discussions about the three remaining algorithms before NIST finally announced the winner in October 2000: Rijndael had won [LW00/2].

Rijndael was the winner

Rijndael won through against Twofish because the latter algorithm was somewhat slower and more complex. Serpent had shown lower performance in software implementations. Looking at it this way, Rijndael is a worthy victor, even though some cryptographers had come out in favour of Twofish or Serpent on the basis of their higher number of rounds (it was also suggested – unsuccessfully, however – that the number of rounds in Rijndael ought to be increased).

The AES selection was carried out completely fairly and amicably

All the experts agreed that the work that NIST carried out during the whole AES selection process was first class. One particularly positive point is that the secrecy usually associated with DES failed to materialise. NIST's decisions were comprehensible and the whole selection method was conducted amicably.

5.3.5 Functionality of Rijndael

Rijndael supports a block length of 128, 192 or 256 bits. A variable also plays a part in the use of the algorithm. This is a so-called 'State'. The State is a four-row table of byte values. Depending on the block length, the number of columns in the table is 4, 6 or 8.

General functionality

Like almost all block ciphers, Rijndael also encrypts data in several identical concurrent rounds, whereby in each round another subkey is included. Before the algorithm is processed, the plaintext bytes are entered into the State a column at a time. For example, for a block length of 192 bits (24 bytes), this initially results in the following State:

Byte 1	Byte 5	Byte 9	Byte 13	Byte 17	Byte 21
Byte 2	Byte 6	Byte 10	Byte 14	Byte 18	Byte 22
Byte 3	Byte 7	Byte 11	Byte 15	Byte 19	Byte 23
Byte 4	Byte 8	Byte 12	Byte 16	Byte 20	Byte 24

In the case of a block length of 256 bits, another two columns are added. If there are only 128 bits, there are two columns less. Four functions, called ByteSub, ShiftRow, MixColumn and AddRoundKey, are involved in the encryption process. Each of the four functions processes the State. After the algorithm has been processed, the State contains the ciphertext. Rijndael has the following sequence of events:

- AddRoundKey

- n-1 rounds each with the following four components:

1. ByteSub
2. ShiftRow
3. MixColumn
4. AddRoundKey

- Last round with the following three components:

1. ByteSub
2. ShiftRow
3. AddRoundKey

The size of number n (and therefore the number of rounds) depends on the block length and the key length, which fluctuate between 10 and 14. The following table gives an overview of this:

	Block length		
Key length	128 bit	192 bit	256 bit
128 bit	10	12	14
192 bit	12	12	14
256 bit	14	14	14

At some points, Rijndael uses arithmetic operations in GF(2^8). You can read about the exact implications of this in Section 14.1.2.

ByteSub

The ByteSub function is at the start of each encryption round. For each byte b of the state, it carries out the following two operations one after the other:

1. First, b is regarded as an element of $GF(2^8)$. b is replaced by the inverse element of the multiplication in $GF(2^8)$, therefore $b = b^{-1}$.

2. b is then multiplied by an 8x8 matrix M and a value b^0 is added, therefore $b = Mb + b^0$.

b^0 has the value 11000110. The matrix M has the following content:

1	0	0	0	1	1	1	1
1	1	0	0	0	1	1	1
1	1	1	0	0	0	1	1
1	1	1	0	0	0	0	1
1	1	1	1	1	0	0	0
0	1	1	1	1	1	0	0
0	0	1	1	1	1	1	0
0	0	0	1	1	1	1	1

The two operators provide for a substitution and therefore together form an S-box. Similarly to DES, for Rijndael the S-boxes are also the most important components of the algorithm with regard to security. Interestingly, Rijndael gets by with one S-box, whilst DES uses eight. Another difference: in a Rijndael S-box (in the first step) a mathematical algorithm is used (the inversion in $GF(2^8)$), while the S-boxes of DES are merely used as substitution tables.

ShiftRow

The ShiftRow function takes second position in each round. In this function, the four lines of the State are each rotated to the right. The number of units by which they are rotated is variable: in the second row these are C1, in the second C2 and in the third C3 units. In the first row, nothing is rotated. The value of C1, C2 and C3 in turn depend on the block length, as the following table shows:

Block length	C1	C2	C3
128	1	2	3
192	1	2	3
256	1	3	4

ShiftRow consequently has the task of mixing up the contents of the State. Note that the mixing that ShiftRow carries out only takes place within the rows of the State. The MixColumn function is responsible for the mixing of content in the columns.

MixColumn

The MixColumn function (apart from in the final round) follows the ShiftRow function. In MixColumn the columns of the State are mixed up. However, the method is somewhat more complicated than that of ShiftRow. In turn, MixColumn interprets the bytes of the State as elements of $GF(2^8)$. The four bytes of a column are also treated as a vector and are multiplied by a matrix. The matrix has the following content (in hexadecimal notation):

02	03	01	01
01	02	03	01
01	01	02	03
03	01	01	03

Incidentally, this matrix multiplication is equivalent to a polynominal multiplication if you think of a vector of four elements from $GF(2^8)$ as polynominal.

AddRoundKey

The AddRoundKey function stands at the end of each round and is also processed before the first round. AddRoundKey adds (an addition is equivalent to a bitwise XOR) the State to a value derived from the key (to the so-called round key). Like the State, the round key is a table of bytes with four rows. There are the same number of columns as there are in the State and this number is thus dependent on the block length.

Key scheduling

In each round of Rijndael, a round key the same size as the State is added. A round key is also required before the first round. If there are n rounds, $n+1$ round keys are required. The purpose behind key scheduling is to map a key with a length of 128, 192 or 256 bits on $n+1$ round keys in the length of an encryption block.

In comparison to DES, in which key scheduling is almost trivial, the same operation performed for Rijndael is somewhat more time consuming. The algorithm used consists of two steps and uses the SubKey function:

In the first step (Key Expansion) a four-row table of bytes is generated from the key using the SubKey function. If the number of columns that the State has is labelled as s, then the number of columns in the table amounts to $s\,(n+1)$. The key is contained in the first s columns of the table.

In the second step (Key Selection) the round keys are taken from the table. The first s columns form the first round key, the second s columns form the second, and so on.

Since the AddRoundKey function is the first operation of the Rijndael algorithm and the first round key is equivalent to the key, the addition of the key to the plaintext is the first operation within Rijndael.

5.3.6 Decryption using Rijndael

One advantage of the way DES works is that decryption works in almost the same way as encryption, and completely independently of the structure of the function F. Neither of these facts applies to Rijndael. A Rijndael decryption therefore involves the individual steps of an encryption each being inverted and then being processed in the reverse order. However, this is not as difficult as it sounds, because the two inventors of Rijndael have designed the four subfunctions of the algorithm so that the inversion can be carried out without any problems. The mathematic operations in ByteSub and MixColumn are refined so that they can easily be inverted. The inversion of the shifts in ShiftRow is trivial, and AddRoundKey is even self-inverting (a second application of AddRoundKey therefore reverses the first). A Rijndael decryption consequently has the following sequence of events:

- Inversion of the last round with the following three components:

1. AddRoundKey

2. InvShiftRow

3. InvByteSub

- Inversion of the $n-1$ rounds each with the following components:

1. AddRoundKey

2. InvMixColumn

3. InvShiftRow

4. InvByteSub

- AddRoundKey

The key scheduling works in the same way as in the case of encryption, but with the round keys added in reverse order.

5.3.7   Evaluation of Rijndael

With a key length of at least 128 bits, a brute force key search is out of the question for Rijndael. As all attempts to discover other weak points have as yet proved unsuccessful, there is no doubt as to how secure Rijndael is. It is merely the fact that Rijndael only saw the light of day three years ago that gives any cause for concern. Normally you should wait a little longer before relying on the security of an algorithm. However, as Rijndael has been put under particularly intense scrutiny, an exception has been made in this case.

As Rijndael has also been given glowing reports with regard to its speed, flexibility and ease of implementation, it can confidently be seen as the algorithm of the coming decade.

Asymmetrical encryption

The multiple human needs and desires that demand privacy among two or more people in the midst of social life must inevitably lead to cryptology wherever men thrive and wherever they write.
DAVID KAHN

Key experience no. 6
Are you looking for a new career challenge? Then you should take a quick look at the home page of the British GCHQ (www.gchq.gov.uk). You will find a cryptographic puzzle waiting for you. If you can solve it, you can apply to become a code breaker. You must be a British citizen, naturally.

Let's look at another e-mail that Bob writes to Alice:

```
Dear Alice,
I propose that from now on we encrypt all our e-mails
using DES. As the key we can use the following seven
bytes: 234, 92, 13, 250, 32, 44, 199.
Bob
```

A secret key should never be sent over an insecure line Mallory loves this kind of e-mail. Since he knows DES and has learnt their key from the above e-mail, from now on he will have no problem in reading encrypted mail between Alice and Bob.

6.1 The key exchange problem

Alice's e-mail brings us to a fundamental problem in cryptography. It makes no sense if Alice and Bob agree on a common key over the same transmission channel that they use to send encrypted messages. If the transmission channel can be tapped into by Mallory, the key will fall into his hands. If the channel isn't tapped, Alice and Bob don't need to use encryption. To resolve this dilemma – known as the **key exchange problem** – there are the following options:

A key can be handed over personally • Alice hands the key over to Bob at a personal meeting or by telephone. This may not be very convenient for either of them. This option also has the disadvantage that it becomes very unmanageable if members of a large user group want to communicate using encryption. For example, if the 50 employees of the firm Crypt & Co. want their own keys on a person-to-person basis, then 1225 different keys will be required. In general terms, for n employees $n/2\ (n-1)$ keys are needed (see Figure 6.1).

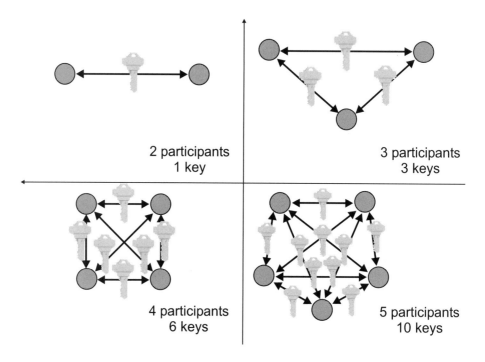

Figure 6.1 To use a symmetric encryption algorithm, each two participants must have their own secret key. This only makes sense for a small number of participants, otherwise the number of keys needed becomes too large.

- A key server is used. See Section 13.5.

- Alice and Bob use **public key cryptography** (the method described in this chapter).

How does this myth-surrounded public key cryptography work? The encryption algorithms we have described (e.g. DES and IDEA) are defined as secret key algorithms. There is only one key per encrypted message and it must be kept secret. Public key cryptography on the other hand always uses two keys per encrypted message (see Figure 6.2): one known only to the receiver (the **private key**), and another that is publicly known (the **public key**). They are of course interdependent and are usually assigned to one person, so that one can speak of Alice's public key and Alice's private key.

There are private and public keys

So, if Bob wants to send an encrypted message to Alice, he needs her public key. He can let Alice send this to him via the Internet with a clear conscience because eavesdropper Mallory has gained nothing if he intercepts it. After all, it is a public key and no secret. Bob now encrypts the message using Alice's public key and sends it to Alice. Alice then uses her private key to decrypt the message.

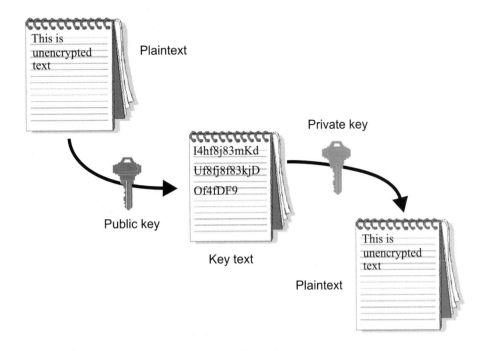

Figure 6.2 A public key encryption works as follows: different keys are used for encryption and decryption. The first is publicly known, the latter is kept secret (hence known as the private key).

Of course, the public and private keys are independent in so far as the private key cannot be derived from the public key. In mathematical terms, public key encryption can be described as follows: Alice has a public key a and a private key x. If m is the message, c the ciphertext, e the encryption function and d the decryption function, then:

$c=e(a,m)$ and $m=d(x,c)$.

If subsequently Alice wants to send something back to Bob, she needs Bob's public key with which to encrypt the message.

Public key encryption is a young science   If you are now a bit confused, no wonder. After all, humanity has needed thousands of years to discover public key cryptography. How are you supposed to grasp this leap forward in just a few minutes? The confusion that often arises at this point is understandable because it is not easy to find functions e and d that have the required features. However, they do exist and to study them we first need a little mathematical help.

6.2 A little maths

Public key cryptography can only be understood on a mathematical basis

I wish there were an easy example of a public key algorithm. Unfortunately, this is not the case. In general, there are only a few public key algorithms, and still fewer that are really secure. What they have in common is that some knowledge of mathematics is necessary to understand them. Some of this knowledge I shall pass on to you in this chapter. A mathematician might scoff at my efforts, but my main interest is to explain the more important mathematical relationships in the simplest possible terms without resort to theorems and proofs.

6.2.1 Modulo arithmetic

Let's begin our considerations with **modulo arithmetic**. Modulo arithmetic means calculating with natural numbers from 0 up to a given number n (we are counting 0 as a natural number, even if this is not general practice). There are no numbers greater than or equal to n. After $n-1$ we go back and start counting from 0 again. As an example, the hour hand on a clock can be regarded as a modulo-12 counter. It counts the hours from 0 to 11 and then starts again at 0. In the following, n is always a natural number. a and b are also natural numbers and always lie between 0 and $n-1$.

Modulo addition and subtraction

Modulo addition and **modulo subtraction** work in the same way as normal addition and subtraction, with just one change: if the result of an addition is greater than or equal to n, then n is subtracted from the result. Similarly with subtraction, if the result is smaller than zero, then n is added to the result. With modulo addition or subtraction the result is always a number between 0 and $n-1$. To distinguish a modulo arithmetical calculation from normal arithmetic, the expression '(mod n)' is added after the equation.

Examples:

        3+5=1   (mod 7)
        2+2=4   (mod 13)
        3-6=6   (mod 9)
        3+6=0   (mod 9)

Modulo multiplication

Modulo multiplication of two numbers can be derived from modulo addition. The multiplication is simply written out as repeated addition.

Example:

$$4 \cdot 5 = 4+4+4+4+4 \quad (\text{mod } 7)$$
$$= 1 \quad +4+4+4 \quad (\text{mod } 7)$$
$$= 5 \quad\quad +4+4 \quad (\text{mod } 7)$$
$$= 2 \quad\quad\quad +4 \quad (\text{mod } 7)$$
$$= 6 \quad\quad\quad\quad (\text{mod } 7)$$

There is a quicker way to perform modulo multiplication, however: simply multiply the two numbers in the normal way and then keep subtracting n until the result is a number between 0 and $n-1$.

Example:

$$4 \cdot 5 = 20 - 7 - 7 = 6 \quad (\text{mod } 7)$$

Modulo division

Division =
multiplication with
a reciprocal

First we must ask ourselves if for any number a there is a number b with the attribute $a \cdot b = 1 \ (\text{mod } n)$. If there is such a number, it is called the **reciprocal** of a and written a^{-1}. Since multiplication with the inverse of a number is the same as dividing by that number, this would give us **modulo division**. '$ba^{-1} \ (\text{mod } n)$' can therefore be written '$b/a \ (\text{mod } n)$'.

Is there always a inverse of a when calculating to modulo n? The answer is: if a and n have no common divisors.

Examples:

$5^{-1} \ (\text{mod } 7)$ exists, since 5 and 7 have no common divisor.
It is true for $5^{-1} = 3$.

$4^{-1} \ (\text{mod } 8)$ does not exist, since 4 and 8 have a common divisor.
(both are divisible by 4).

$7^{-1} \ (\text{mod } 10)$ exists, since 10 and 7 have no common divisor.
It is true for $7^{-1} = 3$.

The inverse can be
calculated with
Euclid's algorithm

So whether or not a number a has an inverse $(\text{mod } n)$ is simple to check. It is rather more difficult to calculate this inverse. This problem can be solved, however, using **Euclid's algorithm** (which I do not propose to go into here). This is normally used to find the greatest common divisor of a and n. It can be modified to calculate a^{-1} $(\text{mod } n)$ if that number exists. For the experts: the complexity of the algorithm amounts to $O(\log(n))$, and is hence about as quick as finding an element in a sorted field.

Modulo exponentiation

As you are no doubt aware, exponentiation (the exponential function) can be regarded as repeated multiplication. This applies equally in modulo arithmetic.

Example:

*There is also modulo
exponentiation*

$$3^4 = 3 \cdot 3 \cdot 3 \cdot 3 \quad (\text{mod } 7)$$
$$= 2 \cdot 3 \cdot 3 \quad (\text{mod } 7)$$
$$= 6 \cdot 3 \quad (\text{mod } 7)$$
$$= 4 \quad (\text{mod } 7)$$

This defines **modulo exponentiation**. In cryptography, mostly the inversions of modulo exponentiation are important.

Modulo logarithm (discrete logarithm)

One of the two inversions of modulo exponentiation is the **modulo logarithm**, usually called the **discrete logarithm**. For a, b and n the discrete logarithm is the number x such that $a^x = b \, (\text{mod } n)$. Proving the existence of a discrete logarithm for the given numbers a, b and n is no trivial matter. In cryptography, however, as you will see, we are only concerned with solving problems where the discrete logarithm actually exists.

The modulo root

The second inversion of modulo exponentiation is **modulo root extraction**. Its definition clearly might now be: for numbers a, b and n, a number x is sought for which $xa = b \, (\text{mod } n)$. x is then the ath root of $b \, (\text{mod } n)$. To answer the question of when a modulo root exists, we need the so-called φ-function, which shows how many natural numbers, which are larger than 0 and smaller than a number n, are not divisors of n.

Examples:

$\varphi(3)=2$, since 1 and 2 are not divisors of 3.

$\varphi(6)=2$, since 1 and 5 are not divisors of 6.

$\varphi(7)=6$, since 1, 2, 3, 4, 5 and 6 are not divisors of 7.

*Modulo root
extraction is also
important in
cryptography*

As you may have noted, $\varphi(n)=n-1$ if n is a prime number. On the other hand, if n is the product of two prime numbers p and q, then $\varphi(n)=(p-1) \cdot (q-1)$ is true. When calculating modulo roots, the following proposition is useful:

Proposition:

If a and n are natural numbers as before and $a<n$, then:

$$a^{1 \, (\text{mod } \varphi(n))} = a \, (\text{mod } n).$$

Which means in other words: $a^b = a \, (\text{mod } n)$ if $b-1$ is a multiple of $\varphi(n)$.
Example:

$$3^3 = 3 \, (\text{mod } 6), \text{ since } 3 = 1 \, (\text{mod } (\varphi(6))$$

With this proposition and algebraic transformation we can calculate the ath modulo root of a number. Given the numbers a, b and n we seek a number x for which:

$$x^a = b \pmod{n}.$$

If a and $\varphi(n)$ have no common divisors, then with Euclid's algorithm we can calculate the number c such that $c = a^{-1} \pmod{\varphi(n)}$. With this number we now exponentiate both sides of the equation:

$$(x^a)^{c(\bmod\ \varphi(n))} = b^{c(\bmod\ \varphi(n))} \pmod{n}.$$

A proposition gives the modulo root

.Applying the above proposition we can simplify the right side:

$$(x^a)^{c(\bmod\ \varphi(n))} = b^c \pmod{n}.$$

Since $a \cdot c = 1 \pmod{\varphi(n)}$, the left side becomes:

$$x^{1(\bmod\ \varphi(n))} = b^c \pmod{n}.$$

Again by the above proposition we get:

$$x = b^c \pmod{n}$$

The modulo root is not always easy to calculate

Now we also know the number x, which is the ath root of b, which we are seeking. Since x exists, a and $\varphi(n)$ must have no common divisors. If this is so and we know $\varphi(n)$, the root can be calculated without difficulty. However, we shall learn in the next chapter that $\varphi(n)$ is often anything but simple to calculate.

Groups and fields

Of special interest in mathematics and cryptography are values of n for which all numbers between 1 and $n-1$ have a reciprocal $(\bmod\ n)$. For this to be true, n must not be divisible by any number between 1 and $n-1$. This condition is met when n is a prime number (in which case p will be used instead of n). If p is a prime number, then any number between 0 and $p-1$ is divisible by any number between 1 and $p-1$ modulo p (division by 0 is not defined, as usual).

The modulo calculation of a prime number has some interesting features

With modulo multiplication the numbers between 1 and $p-1$ form a so-called **group**, which we write as $\mathbf{Z(p,\cdot)}$. In mathematics a group is a collection for which the following preconditions are given:

- A operation is defined (in this case this is modulo multiplication). That a connection is defined means that one can connect any two elements of the group with each other and thereby always obtain a further element of the group. The connection must be associative as well, which is true for modulo multiplication.

- There is a neutral element (in this case the number 1). A neutral element has the attribute that connecting it with another element gives the other element as the result.

- For each element there is a reciprocal element.

Note that p must definitely be a prime number, otherwise not all elements have a reciprocal element and then there is no group. In addition, null does not belong to group $Z(p,\cdot)$ because null has no reciprocal element.

Fields are formed using modulo computing

Incidentally, the numbers between 0 and $p-1$ also form a group with respect to modulo addition, a group named **Z(p,+)**. This time null is a member of the group (it is the neutral element).

The numbers between 0 and $p-1$ then form a group with regard to modulo addition as well as a group with regard to modulo multiplication (without the null). Such a double group is known as a **field**. A field that is derived as just described from the numbers 0 to $p-1$ is called a field of size p, or Galois field of size p. It is written **GF(p)**.

Subgroups

A group has subgroups

A **subgroup** is a selection of elements in a group that (with the same connection and the same neutral element) itself forms a group. Not every selection automatically forms a subgroup. A minimum requirement is, of course, that the neutral element is included. Also, many selections are not closed – this means that when two elements of a selection are connected the result does not belong to the selection.

Example: If we consider $Z(5,\cdot)$, then:

- {2, 3} is not a subgroup, because the neutral element is missing.

- {1, 3} is not a subgroup, because $3\cdot3=4$ (mod 5). However, 4 is not an element of the selection.

- {1, 4} is a subgroup, because $1\cdot1=1$ (mod 5), $1\cdot4=4$ (mod 5), $4\cdot1=4$ (mod 5) and $4\cdot4=1$ (mod 5). The subgroup is thus finite, because in all possible connections an element of the selection is formed.

It can be proved that the number of elements in a subgroup is a divisor of the number of elements of the original group. Since the group $Z(p,\cdot)$ has exactly $p-1$ elements, $p-1$ is always divisible by the number of elements in a subgroup.

The number of subgroup elements divides into the number of group elements

Example: the group $Z(13,\cdot)$ has 12 elements. The subgroups of $Z(13,\cdot)$ therefore have 1, 2, 3, 4, 6 or 12 elements.

It can also be shown that for the group $Z(p,\cdot)$, for every divisor of $p-1$ there is exactly one subgroup with this number of elements.

Example: for $Z(13,\cdot)$ there are subgroups with 1, 2, 3, 4, 6 and 12 elements respectively. The subgroup with 12 elements is the group itself. The subgroup with one element contains only the number 1.

Generators

One other thing that can be proved: if you take any element a from $Z(p,\cdot)$ then the amount $\{a, a^2, a^3, a^4, ..., a^{p-1}\}$ (mod p), forms a subgroup. a is called the **generator** of the subgroup. Each subgroup of $Z(p,\cdot)$ has at least one generator, including also $Z(p,\cdot)$ itself of course.

1											
2	4	8	3	6	12	11	9	5	10	7	1
3	9	1									
4	3	12	9	10	1						
5	12	8	1								
6	10	8	9	2	12	7	3	5	4	11	1
7	10	5	9	11	12	6	3	8	4	2	1
8	12	5	1								
9	3	1									
10	9	12	3	19	4	1					
11	4	5	3	7	12	2	9	8	10	6	1
12	1										

Figure 6.3 The subgroups of $Z(13,\cdot)$. The generators are listed at the left of each row.

In Figure 6.3, the subgroups of $Z(13,\cdot)$ are displayed. The number 1 is the only generator of the subgroup with one element. The subgroup with two elements has the generator 12. For the subgroup with three elements there are two generators: 3 and 9. The numbers 5 and 8 generate the subgroup with four elements. The subgroup with six elements was generated from 4 and 10. The numbers 2, 6, 7 and 11 are generators of the subgroup with 12 elements, i.e. $Z(13,\cdot)$ itself.

Generators play an important role in cryptography   The fact that there are also generators for $Z(p,\cdot)$ plays an important role in cryptography. As you can easily prove, the equation $a^x=b$ (mod p) is always solvable if a is a generator of $Z(p,\cdot)$ (where b is an element of $Z(p,\cdot)$) and cannot be null). In other words, the discrete logarithm in $Z(p, \cdot)$ always exists if the base is a generator of $Z(p, \cdot)$.

6.3   One-way functions and trapdoor functions

The inverse of some modulo functions can be calculated only with difficulty

The reason why the modulo calculations just described are so important in cryptography is as follows: some modulo functions are very simple to evaluate, but inverting the process to return the function from the result requires much effort. This is very useful in cryptography if one uses a simple calculation for encryption and the complicated inverse for decryption. There is a precondition, however: that there is a 'short cut' for the complicated inverse process, which is used as a key.

A function that is simple to evaluate, but is difficult to invert, is called a **one-way function**. If there is a 'hidden shortcut' (some extra information) that simplifies the otherwise difficult inverse process, then one speaks of a **trapdoor function**. With the mathematical tools from the last section, you are in a position to understand these cryptologically important backdoor and one-way functions.

6.3.1   The discrete logarithm

The discrete logarithm is difficult to calculate

With a suitable computer program, the result of a^b (mod n) is relatively easy to calculate, even for very large values of a, b and n. Even for numbers over 100 bits long it need not take a PC longer than a second. For the discrete logarithm, however, things look very different. Even with the biggest hardware set-ups and the best algorithms known, for several hundred bits one very quickly reaches calculation times longer than the life of our universe. This also gives us our first example of a one-way function: in the light of current knowledge, $f(x)=a^x$ (mod n) is just such a function. Admittedly, there is no mathematical proof for this. It is therefore theoretically possible that one day a fast algorithm for calculating the discrete logarithm will be discovered. But since this has been sought for a long time without success, we shall assume that it will not be found. It is not worth entertaining doubts about the security of cryptalgorithms based on the discrete logarithm. To search for a quick way of solving the discrete logarithm is also a fruitless exercise, for the same reason – at least for the novice cryptographer.

Modulo exponentiation is a one-way function

Unfortunately, the knowledge that modulo exponentiation is a one-way function is useless at first. Alice can encrypt a plaintext (in this chapter we take it that the plaintext is a number) using modulo exponentiation – but receiver Bob can no longer decrypt it because it is a question of a one-way function. Despite this, modulo exponentiation ranks as the most important one-way function in cryptography. What Alice and Bob can do with this will be shown in later chapters.

The factorisation problem

The multiplication of two prime numbers is a one-way function

A further important one-way function is the multiplication of two prime numbers (in this case modulo multiplication is not meant). The multiplication of prime numbers is easy to perform with a computer these days; even for larger numbers there is no problem. In contrast to this, no efficient algorithm is known that can determine two factors from the product of two primes. To help you to follow this, here is a small test: in your head, calculate the result of the multiplication of 13 by 17. Then, in comparison, try to find two prime numbers that give 217 when multiplied together (in your head, of course). From this you can imagine why the multiplication of prime numbers is regarded as a one-way function.

The factorisation problem is important in cryptography

There are more profound tests, of course, and these have produced similar results to modulo exponentiation: even if it cannot be proved that prime number multiplication is a one-way function, everything points that way. The splitting of the product of two prime numbers is called the **factorisation problem**, and plays an important role in cryptography (for interesting articles on this see [Buchma] and [GeLuWe]). The factorisation of a number like 217 might not embarrass a computer. However, factorising a several hundred-bit number would bring even the most powerful supercomputer to its knees.

Now that we have a second one-way function, we come to the trapdoor function. Interestingly enough, one can be fabricated from the prime number multiplication one-way function. To do this you must recall the modulo root extraction from the last section: the ath root of the number b modulo n can be calculated easily enough if $\varphi(n)$ is known. As I have already discussed, $\varphi(n)$ can be calculated for the product of two prime numbers p and q. In this case $\varphi(n)=(p-1)\cdot(q-1)$. The question now is: what if p and q are not known? In this case $\varphi(n)$ cannot be calculated in this manner, and consequently neither can the root. And as I have just said, it is exceptionally difficult to find two prime numbers p and q when only their product is known. Now comes the question, of course: is there another way to calculate the root?

Modulo exponentiation is a trapdoor function

The answer: not so far as is known today. The method using the φ- function is the only way. This makes modulo exponentiation into a trapdoor function where the back door is there to be used if the factorisation of the modulus is known. The most important algorithm that uses this trapdoor function is the RSA algorithm, which we will meet soon.

6.4 The Diffie–Hellman key exchange

After this mathematical excursion we go back to the starting point: Alice and Bob want to encrypt their Internet communications, but not to send the secret key over the Net (key exchange problem). One-way and trapdoor functions can help to solve this problem.

The Diffie– Hellman key exchange is a very elegant algorithm

An algorithm that uses the discrete logarithm to solve the key exchange problem was devised by cryptographers Whitfield Diffie and Martin Hellman, and is therefore known as the **Diffie–Hellman key exchange** (or simply the **Diffie–Hellman algorithm**). If there were a prize for the simplicity, power and genius of a cryptalgorithm, then surely it would go to the Diffie–Hellman algorithm. With their algorithm, Diffie and Hellman laid the foundations of public key cryptography and gave a giant boost to a science that had not long been taught in universities. No wonder that they published their research in 1976 under the title 'New Directions in Cryptography' [DifHel].

6.4.1 Diffie–Hellman working method

The Diffie–Hellman key exchange is based on discrete logarithms

To carry out a Diffie–Hellman key exchange, Alice and Bob agree on a prime number p and a natural number g. Ideally, g should be a generator of the group $Z(p;)$, but the algorithm also works when g takes on another value that is less than p. Alice and Bob can send the numbers p and g over the Internet openly because it doesn't matter if Mallory knows them. In practice, it is quite usual anyway for g and p to be predetermined and used by many users. In addition, Alice chooses a natural number x such that x is smaller than p, and Bob chooses a natural number y such that y is less than p. Alice and Bob keep these numbers to themselves. Now begins the following sequence:

1. Alice calculates the number $a = g^x \pmod p$

2. Alice sends a to Bob

3. Bob calculates the number $b = g^y \pmod p$

4. Bob sends b to Alice

5. Using b Alice calculates the number $k_1 := b^x \pmod p$

6. Using a Bob calculates the number $k_2 := a^y \pmod p$.

Mallory cannot calculate the key

Now that $k_1 = k_2$ (why, you can work out for yourself), we shall now write simply k. Mallory, who is eavesdropping as usual, does not know this k, nor can he calculate it. To do so he would need to solve the discrete logarithm and that, as already mentioned, is beyond current capabilities if the numbers are large enough.

And why is the whole thing now a public key algorithm? Because a is Alice's public key and x is her private key. Similarly, Bob's private key is y and his public key is b. One notes that, as expected, in both cases the public key depends on the private key. Also, if the Diffie–Hellman algorithm itself cannot be used for encryption, it nevertheless solves the key exchange problem. Therefore, it is rightly accepted as a public key algorithm and as the simplest representative of this guild to boot.

6.4.2 An example

3 is a generator of $Z(7,\cdot)$

Let us take a look at an example of the use of the Diffie–Hellman algorithm, using small numbers: Alice and Bob agree (and Mallory can overhear) that $g=3$ and $p=7$. As you can easily check, 3 is a generator of $Z(7,\cdot)$. Alice chooses 2 as her private key (x), and Bob chooses 5 as his private key (y). Now they can both calculate their respective public keys:

Alice's public key is $a = g^x \pmod p = 3^2 = 2 \pmod 7$

Bob's public key is $b = g^y \pmod p = 3^5 = 5 \pmod 7$

Alice now finds k_1 from $k_1 = b^x = 5^2 = 4 \pmod 7$

Bob can now calculate k_2 from $k_2 = a^y = 2^5 = 4$ (mod 7).

As planned, $k_1 = k_2 = k$. k has the value 4. Alice and Bob can now encrypt their messages using this key.

6.4.3 Security of Diffie–Hellman

With Diffie–Hellman any key length can be selected

With the Diffie–Hellman key exchange, any bit-length can be chosen for g, x and y, which means that there is no fixed key length (in contrast to DES, which provides for 56 bits). In this context it is basically true to say: the larger the numbers employed, the more secure the algorithm – but also the more burdensome. In contrast to DES and all other current symmetrical algorithms, a brute force attack on the key is not the most effective attack on Diffie–Hellman. This is because there are algorithms for calculating the discrete logarithm, which – despite the large effort involved – are still clearly faster than a simple frontal attack. Therefore, a longer key length ought to be used with Diffie–Hellman. If Bob and Alice were to choose 1024-bit numbers for all three values, for example, they would be on the safe side for the foreseeable future. Extra-paranoid users use 2048 bits and more. In practice, the use of 512 bits is still usual, and is enough for domestic purposes. A key of such a length could, however, be cracked by the NSA and similar powerful organisations.

The security of Diffie–Hellman depends on the length of the key

With keys of sufficient length, on the other hand, Alice and Bob have nothing to fear, even from the NSA. Despite intensive research, no one has yet succeeded in finding an algorithm that comes anywhere near calculating the discrete logarithm of a 1024-bit number within a human life span – not even with the most theoretically advanced computer conceivable.

6.5 RSA

The RSA algorithm is named after Rivest, Shamir and Adleman

I have already introduced Ron Rivest (see Section 30.1.7), probably the greatest living cryptographer, as the inventor of various symmetrical algorithms such as RC2, RC4, RC5 and RC6. And I have already mentioned his colleague Adi Shamir (Section 30.1.9) as co-founder of differential cryptanalysis. Together with Leonard Adleman, they developed a cryptological algorithm that is called the **RSA algorithm** in their honour. This is the oldest and, by some distance, the most important public key algorithm.

In comparison to a simple Diffie–Hellman key exchange, RSA is more versatile: it can be used not only for exchanging keys, but also for public key encryption. For this reason, RSA is rather more difficult to understand. Hopefully, however, the whole thing still falls within the scope of my earlier mathematical excursion. If you cannot follow the algorithm at first sight there are no grounds for panic. The important thing is that you know what it can do and that like all other public key algorithms it is based on a backdoor or one-way function. In this case it is not the discrete logarithm, but the factorisation problem already mentioned and the modulo root extraction connected to this.

6.5.1 How the RSA algorithm works

RSA is based on the factorisation problem

In contrast to secret key cryptography, in this context you should think of plaintext, ciphertext and key as natural numbers, rather than sequences of bits. This makes no difference to the computer anyway since all data is stored as a bit sequence. For numbers that are too big the plaintext is broken into blocks that are encrypted individually.

Encryption and decryption

If Bob wants to encrypt a message to Alice using the RSA algorithm, things proceed as follows:

1. First, Alice must choose two prime numbers p and q, and then multiply them together to give n.

A public RSA key contains the product of two primes

2. Next, Alice chooses a random natural number e, which is not a common divisor of $\varphi(n)$ (you may recall: $\varphi(n)=(p-1)\cdot(q-1)$). The numbers n and e are now together the public key that Alice makes public, and which Mallory can find out without Alice minding.

3. Alice solves the equation $d=e^{-1}(\mathrm{mod}\ \varphi(n))$. d is her private key, which she must keep to herself.

4. Bob knows Alice's public key e and uses it to encrypt his message m, which, as described above, he regards as being a number. To do this he solves the equation $c=m^e(\mathrm{mod}\ n)$. c is the ciphertext that he sends to Alice.

5. Alice can now decrypt the message c that she received from Bob by evaluating the expression $c^d(\mathrm{mod}\ n)$. The result is the exact plaintext m that Bob sent.

That Alice actually has the plaintext in her hands is shown by the following equation:

$$c^d = (m^e)^d = m^{1(\mathrm{mod}\ \varphi(n))} = m$$

Advantageous values for e

The number e can be chosen for ease of calculation

Since the encryption function m^e must be calculated for every message m sent to Alice, and the publicly known e always stays the same, it pays to choose an advantageous value for e. For this, the prime numbers 3, 17 and 65,537 have proved to be practical, since in binary form they contain few ones and so enable speedy exponentiation. If one of these numbers is used, then RSA encryption is logically several times faster than exponentiation with a 768-bit exponent, as is needed with Diffie–Hellman. Since consequently e is mostly small and constant, the size of the number n is almost always meant as the key length in connection with an RSA algorithm.

6.5.2 An example

Now we look at the RSA algorithm, using an example in which we use small numbers. Alice chooses *p*=5 and *q*=17, giving:

$$n = p \cdot q = 5 \cdot 17 = 85$$
$$\varphi(n) = (p-1) \cdot (q-1) = 4 \cdot 16 = 64$$

The example uses the prime numbers 5 and 17

If Alice also chooses *e*=3, then her public key comprises the numbers 85 and 3. She can easily work out her private key because she knows the factors of *n* and hence also knows $\varphi(n)$. This gives $d = e^{-1} = 43$ (mod 64), since $3 \cdot 43 = 1$ (mod 64). Therefore Alice's private key is 43.

Let us now assume that the message that Bob wants to send to Alice is the number *m*, which equals 2 in plaintext. Bob now calculates the ciphertext using Alice's public key and the equation:

$$c = m^e \text{ (mod } n) = 2^3 = 8 \text{ (mod 85)}$$

The ciphertext that Bob sends to Alice reads 8. Bob has calculated this without knowing Alice's private key. Using her private key *c* (i.e. 43) Alice can now decrypt the message *m* by solving the equation:

$$m = c^d \text{ (mod } n) = 8^{43} \text{ (mod 85)} = 2$$

6.5.3 RSA security

Also with RSA the key length is a matter of free choice

Since Alice can make *n* (and hence the key length) any size she likes, RSA is also a variable-length-key algorithm. As you might expect, the same principle applies here as for all good encryption algorithms: the longer the key, the more secure the algorithm. As with the Diffie–Hellman key exchange, with the RSA algorithm (in contrast to DES) there are also much faster attacks than a brute force key search, so that *n* must be considerably longer than the 56 bits of a DES key. Currently, the most popular size is 1,024.

When compared with DES, the RSA algorithm clearly offers more targets for cryptanalysis. One reason for this is that the values *p*, *q*, *e* and *n* can be chosen by Alice and Bob. The wrong choice can make Mallory's life much easier. Another reason is that it is an old cryptological maxim that complicated mathematical algorithms offer more openings for attack than the simple bit operations of current symmetrical algorithms.

RSA is secure when properly implemented

In the following sections I will introduce the most important results of the cryptanalysis of the RSA algorithm. I can, however, anticipate one of these results right now: in the light of current research, and when correctly implemented, RSA is a very secure algorithm.

General remarks on RSA cryptanalysis

Asymmetrical algorithms differ greatly from symmetrical algorithms. The aim of eavesdropper Mallory remains much the same, however. He wants to get at the plaintext or a private key. There are three ways of doing so: ciphertext-only, known-plaintext and chosen-plaintext attacks, as you already know from Section 4.1.3. For asymmetrical algorithms there are two additional types of attack:

- One of these is the **public-key-only attack**. Here Mallory tries to derive Alice's private key from her public key. He does not need an encrypted message for this.

Various attacks can be used against public key algorithms
- Another variation is the **chosen-ciphertext attack**. Here Mallory chooses a ciphertext and gets Alice to decrypt it. He then compares the resulting plaintext with the ciphertext and tries to deduce the private key. This type of attack could also be used against symmetric algorithms. They are not used due to the fact that all current symmetric algorithms are constructed in such a way that encryption and decryption are almost identical in operation. A chosen-ciphertext attack against a symmetric algorithm is therefore the same as a chosen-plaintext attack.

Let us therefore look at what RSA cryptanalysis offers.

Brute force key search

A brute force key search does not work for the RSA algorithm
In theory, Mallory can break the RSA algorithm using a brute force key search. In practice, this kind of attack is ruled out for keys more than 256 bits long (which are hardly ever met with today). For such an attack, Mallory must try on average 2^{255} keys (i.e. half the 2^{256} possible keys). This corresponds to 10^{76} keys – a number that is larger than the number of atoms in the universe. Since the universe is 'only' 10^{18} seconds old, Mallory must test at the rate of 10^{58} keys per second to have a hope of success within a measurable period of time. Summary: If Mallory can't come up with something better than a brute force key search, Alice and Bob are quite safe.

Factorisation attack

There are several factorisation algorithms
As already mentioned, a brute force key search is by no means the best way to attack the RSA algorithm. The closely following public-key-only attack is clearly better: Mallory takes the number n from Alice's public key and attempts to split this into two prime numbers p and q. With p and q he can then calculate Alice's private key without difficulty. This public-key-only attack is called a **factorisation attack**. The working method of the RSA algorithm relies on the derivation of p and q from n being particularly difficult – it is a one-way function after all. A factorisation attack therefore involves an attempt to invert a one-way function, and is very costly.

Just how lavish a factorisation attack is depends of course on the method used to find the factors of n. There are many ways of doing so – one could easily write a book on the subject. At this point, only one thing interests us, however: none of the previously known methods of factorisation are anywhere near powerful enough to *Factorisation is still being researched* factorise a 1,024-bit number at reasonable cost (if this was not the case, the RSA algorithm would never have succeeded). This will probably still be the case in future. Research may continue, and further progress can be expected – but a quantum leap in the process of factorisation is currently not yet in sight.

You are certainly now asking yourself what size of numbers can be factorised at present. The current world record stands at 512 bits (corresponding to 155 decimal places). This record was set up in 1999 by an international research group whose most prominent member was the Dutch cryptographer Arjen Lenstra. More than 250 computers were involved for a period of four months. In August 1999, the researchers were able to announce their success over the Internet.

The NSA can probably factorise numbers longer than 512 bits

This record only applies to known factorisations. It is doubtless the case that the NSA and other secret service agencies are in a position to factorise even longer numbers. From this we can conclude that an RSA key length of 512 bits is not sufficient for particularly security-sensitive data, but that 1,024 bits can be considered secure for the time being.

Low-exponent attack

As mentioned in Section 6.5.1, many RSA implementations use small values for e (mostly 3 or 17), since this enables particularly fast encryption. But care should be taken here: if the same message is sent to e recipients, and all are encrypted with the same number e, then there is an attack (**low-exponent attack**) with which the ciphertext can be regenerated. Even if only parts of the message are identical, this is still possible in part.

There are effective countermeasures to low-exponent attacks

Of course, there are effective countermeasures against low-exponent attacks. For example, a larger number can be chosen for e: 65,537 has about the same effect performance-wise as 3 or 17, but is clearly more secure. The PKCS#1 standard (Section 11.2.1) takes a different approach: it assumes that each message to be encrypted is prepared in a set manner whereby identical messages no longer occur.

TWINKLE

At the Eurocrypt Conference in Prague in 1999, Adi Shamir, co-founder of RSA, presented the idea of a machine to help with a specific factorisation algorithm [Luck99]. What was so special was that the machine was an optical-electronic apparatus rather than a computer. Shamir called his machine TWINKLE (The Weizmann Institute Key Locating Engine).

TWINKLE facilitates fast factorisation

Shamir estimated that a TWINKLE machine could be manufactured for around 5,000 US dollars each and, for factorisation process work, would replace between 100 and 1,000 PCs. As yet, no one has built a TWINKLE machine (at least as far as is known). It is clear, however, that in future RSA key lengths will have to be sized more generously than before.

Other attacks

In addition to those already mentioned, there are other effective attacks aimed at specific implementations of the RSA algorithm. These will be dealt with in Sections 11.2.2 and 15.6.

When is RSA secure then?

Numerous cryptanalysis results make two things clear: for one, the RSA algorithm is attackable when poorly implemented. Too short a key length, wrongly chosen parameters, and other mistakes can quickly lead to extensive holes in security. On the other hand, as already stated, the RSA is a very good algorithm if the mistakes just described are avoided.

As with Diffie–Hellman, a 1,024-bit key is also normal with RSA. A paranoid surcharge would take this up to 2,048 bits. 512 bits are already within the NSA's limits. In general, for the same key length, RSA can be cracked several percent faster than Diffie–Hellman.

6.5.4 Summary

The theoretical background that accompanies the RSA algorithm is not going to be explored further here

Since this book is supposed to be a practical introduction to cryptography, I will not go any deeper into the theoretical background of RSA and Diffie–Hellman. Instead, I would refer you to other books on cryptography that have already covered this subject in sufficient detail. Public key cryptography is treated, for example, in [Schn96], [Stinso] or [MeOoVa]. On the subject of RSA I can especially recommend [Frisch].

6.6   Other asymmetrical algorithms

The choice of algorithms in public key cryptography is only modest

In contrast to secret key cryptography, the choice of algorithms in public key cryptography is very modest. This is because the trapdoor functions that are based on public key algorithms cannot be redesigned at the drop of a hat. Instead, each public key algorithm must be accurately devised and, it seems, this has already been done for the most useful algorithms. If a public key algorithm is newly developed, there is no guarantee that it is also secure and practical. On top of this, it should be reasonably comprehensible if it is to be distributed to any degree worth mentioning. As far as this latter point is concerned, RSA is leading at the moment and seems likely to remain so.

Despite this, there are a few further public key algorithms, which I will now consider briefly.

6.6.1 Cailey-Purser

Cailey-Purser was invented by a 15-year-old Irish girl

Normally, the press takes virtually no notice of the invention of a new public key algorithm. Things were different for an algorithm created in 1998 called **Cailey-Purser** [Flanne]. However, the reason lay less in the algorithm itself than in its inventor, namely Sarah Flannery who, at the time, was a 15-year-old Dublin schoolgirl.

The algorithm discovered by Flannery was based, like RSA, on the factorisation problem, but is markedly faster. It will not continue to be distributed because it has been cracked by the inventor herself. Nevertheless, it was still an extraordinary feat for a 15-year-old to develop a new public key algorithm. We can hardly wait to see what else we can expect from this young Irish lady.

6.6.2 Algorithms based on elliptic curves

There are public key algorithms based on elliptic curves

The only algorithms that still play a role, after RSA and Diffie–Hellman, are those based on elliptic curves. These algorithms, however, involve rather more mathematics than we have met up to now. So as not to put off our less mathematically minded readers, I have left the chapter on this interesting class of cryptalgorithms until the third part of this book (Chapter 14).

6.6.3 Other algorithms

Of course, there are further public key encryption algorithms into which we neither can nor ought to go into in detail here. Most of them have been broken and are therefore of no practical interest. In any case, on the Internet the main roles in public key matters are played by RSA and Diffie–Hellman. The only others that might in time become alternative algorithms are those based on elliptic curves.

6.7 Hybrid algorithms

RSA and all other public key encryption algorithms have one big drawback: because of the large key sizes and the onerous mathematical operations (such as exponentiation) they are very slow. An RSA decryption is around 1000 times slower than the same process with DES. Encryption, even with a small prime number, is still more time-consuming than a DES encryption. Especially with long messages, which have to be split into individual blocks, such a delay is very burdensome. In practice, RSA and other public key encryption algorithms are therefore rarely used to encrypt whole messages. Instead, a key for a symmetric algorithm is transmitted, with which the remainder of the communication is encrypted. So rather than being used as an encryption algorithm, in practice RSA is used as a key exchange algorithm (like Diffie–Hellman). The combined use of secret key and public key in this way is called a hybrid algorithm. Practically all the cryptographic software used on the Internet works with hybrid algorithms. RSA is predominantly the public key distributor, while DES is having to surrender the secret key part more and more to competition such as IDEA.

If RSA is not used, then Diffie–Hellman is almost always used instead. In practice, hardly any other public key algorithms are used. Hybrid algorithms are also the reason why secret key and public key algorithms are currently not in competition. Instead, they enhance each other's standing in the field.

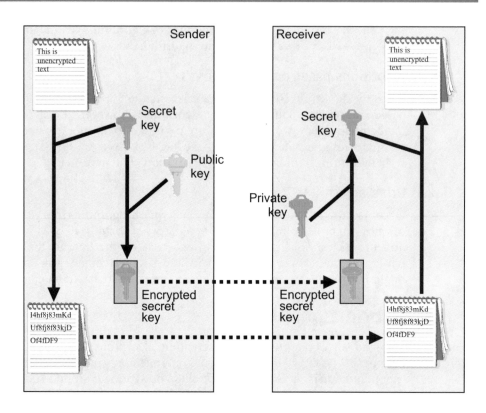

Figure 6.4 Symmetrical algorithms (such as DES) and asymmetrical algorithms (such as RSA) are usually used in combination. The asymmetrical algorithm is only used to send the key used to encrypt the remainder of a message.

6.8 Differences between public and secret key

There are numerous differences between secret key and public key algorithms

I hope that by now the important difference between public key and secret key algorithms has become clear: in the case of public key algorithms, there is no problem with key exchange as the encryption key is public knowledge anyway. Nevertheless, there are important differences in the use of the algorithms:

- Most current secret key algorithms use simple, mathematically undemanding functions. Public key algorithms, on the other hand, only work with mathematically demanding functions.

- The fact detailed in the first point means that it is very difficult to invent a new public key encryption algorithm. New secret key algorithms, on the other hand, can be developed in number.

Public key algorithms are slower than secret key algorithms

- The most important difference in practice is connected to the first point: a public key encryption requires substantially more computing power than a secret key encryption. Taking the RSA and DES as an example, RSA is around a 1000 times slower than DES.

- Public key algorithms are more prone to weakness than secret key algorithms in the face of mistakes in implementation. This difference can also be traced back to the first point.

- For secret key algorithms, one should picture the key, plaintext and ciphertext as bit sequences. Public key algorithms, on the other hand, should be pictured as large numbers or pairs of numbers. This difference relates to the majority of the respective algorithms.

- The previous point has the consequence that fixed-length keys are provided for most secret key algorithms (e.g. 64 bits for the DES, 128 for the IDEA). For public key algorithms, the key length is variable, which means that the number used has no fixed size.

As you can see, there are substantial differences between public key and secret key algorithms. You should note these differences if you wish to get a fair idea of what goes on in cryptography. I consider this to be a lot more important than knowing the algorithms in intricate detail.

The differences between public key and secret key are not proven

The differences that have been mentioned are all a matter of experience, and have not been proven mathematically. It remains one of the open questions of cryptography, whether there might not after all be public key algorithms that use only simple bit operations and require a key length of only 128 bits.

Digital signatures

Whoever wants to proceed safely must do so slowly.
JOHANN WOLFGANG VON GOETHE

Key experience no. 7
Despite increasingly widespread usage, digital signatures are still frequently confused with written signatures that are scanned in. In an article in an Internet magazine in 1997, a product for scanning signatures was even associated with the German signature law. That this concerns not handwriting traits but digital certificates plainly did not disturb the supplier's spokesperson: 'Then we will just get one of those certificates ourselves as well.'

Alice has had a washing machine delivered from online-dealer Oliver, which she didn't order. The reason: once again, she has been tricked by Mallory. Although Bob and Alice have been making things difficult for him by encrypting their messages, Mallory has once again found a way to outmanoeuvre them. He simply sent an e-mail to Oliver pretending to be Alice. Unfortunately, it is only too easy to falsify the sender of an e-mail, and it doesn't take much imagination to picture what devilment Mallory can get up to because of it. This is known, however, and therefore the trust with which e-mail is viewed is in general not very high, especially in business circles.

A digital signature is the counterpart to a handwritten signature

The spoof sender problem is not confined to computer networks. After all, the post also can be used by anyone with the inclination to send a letter sporting any sender details he or she wishes. In the real world, this problem is solved by a signature. On the Internet, one uses a **digital signature**.

7.1 What is a digital signature?

A digital signature is not a handwritten signature that has been scanned

By digital signature one should of course not picture a handwritten signature that has been scanned and digitally stored. This could easily be copied and misused. Instead, one understands it to be a (very large) number that, in connection with a digital document, has the same attributes as a handwritten signature on a written document. So that the designation signature is warrantable, this number must fulfil the following requirements:

- It must be proof against forgery.

- Its authenticity must be provable.

- It must not be transferable between documents without detection.

- The document to which it belongs must not be subject to alteration without detection.

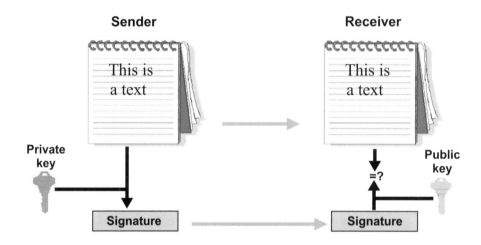

Figure 7.1 A digital signature is created with a private key. Proof of authenticity comes via the public key.

The first point is ingeniously resolved by including a password (here also called a private key) in the digital signature. By doing so, anyone can generate their own unique digital signature, provided nobody else knows the key. The problem with this, however, is that it must be possible to check the authenticity of the signature also without knowing the key. Luckily, this can be resolved by using a public key (here again a term already known to you from public key encryption).

The private key is used for signing
Here is the whole thing in mathematical terms: a message m is given, which Alice wants to sign. To do this she has a publicly known key a and a secret key x. The act of signing is emulated by evaluation of the function $u(m,x)$, the result being the signature s. Since only Alice knows x, only she can calculate s. If Bob now wants to authenticate (**verify**) the signature, he uses another function v. He evaluates the equation $m'=v(a,s)$. If $m=m'$ then the signature is genuine.

7.2 RSA as a signature algorithm

That there are usable digital signatures is not obvious
Obviously, a and x are interdependent. It is less obvious, on the other hand, how one selects functions so that the whole thing not only works, but is also secure. It is not even obvious that there is such a thing as a usable digital signature.

7.2.1 Working method

Fortunately, there are usable algorithms for digital signatures and amazingly, I don't even have to introduce you to a new algorithm. For digital signatures, Alice and Bob can use the RSA algorithm introduced in Section 6.5 – they need only exchange the use of the keys. If Alice wants to sign a message, she 'decrypts' it with her private RSA key d (although the message has not been encrypted). The resulting 'plaintext' is the digital signature. Bob can verify this by 'encrypting' it with the RSA algorithm using the values e and n. If he gets the original message back, the digital signature is genuine.

The RSA algorithm can also be used for digital signatures

It is not easy to see that the RSA algorithm used in this way functions as a signature algorithm. However, I would like to spare you the proof of this at this point, as it is enough for you to remember that RSA can be used both for encryption and for signing. Independently of RSA, signature algorithms also depend closely on public key encryption algorithms, which is why they are also counted as public key cryptography. Unfortunately, signature algorithms suffer the same drawbacks as public key encryption algorithms: they are few in number and they are really slow.

RSA is the number-one signature algorithm

Among signature algorithms, RSA enjoys a similar standing as it does in public key encryption algorithms. In the 20 years since its creation, the RSA algorithm has developed into the most important pillar of cryptography. No other public key algorithm is simultaneously so versatile in its application, so well researched, and so easy to implement. There is no alternative in sight, and it is expected that it will even outlive the monumental DES.

7.2.2 Security

Longer keys are often used for signatures than for encryption

What I said in Section 6.5.3 about the security of the RSA algorithm is also valid when applied to digital signatures. One should allow 1,024 bits for the modulus these days. Those who are paranoid think 2,048 bits are necessary. For digital signatures, longer keys are often used than for encryption. On the one hand, a digital signature must normally have a long lifespan (a contract can often run for years), while for public key encryption a key is normally agreed for one message exchange and holds no long-term interest. On the other hand, at least in the case of the RSA algorithm, verification of a message proceeds speedily since the value e need only be small.

7.3 Signatures based on the discrete logarithm

There are many signature algorithms based on the discrete logarithm

In the field of digital signatures, RSA is almost without competition. Nothing has come close for a long time. Of practical significance, however, is the very versatile family of signatures on the basis of the discrete logarithm (**DLSSs**, discrete logarithm signature systems). These are a further development of Diffie–Hellman key exchange and so are based on the problem of the discrete logarithm (Section 6.4). This means that Bob's private key is the natural number x and the public key is $g^x \bmod p$. In total there are over 13,000 variations of the signature algorithm based on the discrete logarithm – we are interested only in the two most important: ElGamal and the Data Signature Algorithm (DSA).

7.3.1 ElGamal

The simplest DLSS is the algorithm of ElGamal. Although this was almost never used in practice in its original form, it provides the basis of the DSA algorithm we shall discuss later.

Working method of ElGamal

The ElGamal algorithm is a DLSS

For an ElGamal signature, one first needs a large prime number p and a number g, which is a generator of $Z(p,\cdot)$ (hopefully you remember all this from Diffie–Hellman). Alice, who wants to sign her message, needs a secret key x such that $x<p$, from which she calculates the public key using the expression g^x (mod p). Alice sends this public key to Bob. He needs it to verify Alice's signature. Whenever Alice wants to sign a message m, she generates a random number y that is relatively prime to $p-1$ (i.e. has no common divisor except 1). Using y she calculates the number r from the expression $r=g^y$ (mod p) and then applies the following equation:

$$m = x\cdot r + y\cdot s \quad (\text{mod } p\text{-}1)$$

An ElGamal signature comprises two parts

In this equation, x, y, m and g are known. The newly introduced variable s is dependent on these values and can be evaluated by Alice using an algebraic transformation. The two numbers r and s together form the digital signature for the message m. How Bob can verify the signature is apparent if one takes the above equation as the exponent to base g. To do this one needs the proposition described in Section 6.2, which stated that $a^{1 \ (\text{mod } \varphi \ (n))} = a$ (mod n), if a and n are natural numbers such that $(a<n)$:

$$m = x\cdot r + y\cdot s \ (\text{mod } p\text{-}1)$$

$$=> g^m = g^{x\cdot r + y\cdot s \ (\text{mod } p\text{-}1)}$$

$$=> g^m = g^{x\cdot r + y\cdot s} \ (\text{mod } p) \quad \text{(from the described proposition)}$$

$$=> g^m = g^{x\cdot r} \cdot r^s \ (\text{mod } p)$$

If the equation balances, the signature is authentic

In the last equation you see that Bob can calculate both sides without knowing the secret numbers x and y. For this he only needs the numbers g and m, which he knows, the public key g^x and the variables r and s, which constitute the actual signature. So, using this equation, Bob verifies the digital signature: he calculates the left and right sides and compares the results. If they agree, then the signature is authentic.

Example

Let us look at an example using small numbers. Let's assume that Alice chooses $p=13$ and $g=7$. 7 is a generator of $Z(13,\cdot)$ and therefore a reliable value for g. $p=13$ and $g=7$ are publicly known values. Alice also chooses $x=3$ as her private key. From this she calculates her public key g^x (mod p) = 7^3 = 5 (mod 13).

If Alice now wants to sign the message $m=10$, she chooses a further random value. This might be $y=5$ (5 is a relative prime to $p-1=12$). From this Alice gets $r = g^y$ $(\bmod\ p) = 7^5 = 11\ (\bmod\ 13)$. She applies this to the following equation:

$m = x \cdot r + y \cdot s\ (\bmod\ p-1)$

$<=>10 = 3 \cdot 11 + 5 \cdot s\ (\bmod\ 12)$

$<=>10 = 9 + 5 \cdot s\ (\bmod\ 12)$

$<=>s = 5\ (\bmod\ 12)$

The signature hence comprises the numbers 11 and 5. Let us now look at how Bob can verify this signature. Bob uses the following equation:

$g^m = g^{x \cdot r} \cdot r^s\ (\bmod\ p)$

$7^{10} = 5^{11} \cdot 11^5\ (\bmod\ 13)$

$4 = 8 \cdot 7\ (\bmod\ 13)$

$4 = 4\ (\bmod\ 13)$

Since the equation balances, Bob knows that the signature is authentic.

7.3.2 DSA

The Digital Signature Algorithm (DSA) is also based on the discrete logarithm

The reason why so many signature algorithms are based on the discrete logarithm is that the equations used for verification can differ in so many ways. Out of the many possible variations, however, only one is of practical importance for the Internet, the **Digital Signature Algorithm (DSA)**. How this works is laid down in the Digital Signature Standard. The DSS is the work of the US National Institute of Standards and Technology (NIST), which published it in 1991 and standardised it in 1994. Many could not understand how an algorithm without a name could become a standard instead of the widespread RSA, and this led to lively discussions. So it is should be no cause for surprise that the DSA could not prevail against RSA. It is, however, still the undisputed number 2.

Mathematics of DSA

Subgroups play a part in the DSA

To understand the way that DSA works, we must once again have recourse to the mathematics detailed in Section 6.2. There you learnt that each group of type $Z(p, \cdot)$ has subgroups. For each divisor of $p-1$ there is just one subgroup. For each subgroup there is at least one generator.

Given that g is a generator of a subgroup of $Z(g, \cdot)$, b is an element of the subgroup generated from g, and the statement $a^x = b\ (\bmod\ p)$ is true, asking the following question now becomes important: with the given provisos, is it simpler to calculate x (the discrete logarithm) when – as required by Diffie–Hellman and ElGamal – g is itself a generator of $Z(g, \cdot)$? It can be shown that the answer is no. Awareness of the generated subgroup offers no advantage when calculating the discrete logarithm – only a brute force key search is simpler, but that is out of the question if the subgroup is big enough. DSA makes use of this fact.

How DSA works

With DSA, calculations take place in a subgroup with q elements
For a DSA signature, Alice and Bob once again need a large prime number p. In addition, Alice chooses a prime number q that is a divisor of $p-1$. In contrast to the ElGamal algorithm, the trick with DSA is that calculations take place in a subgroup with q elements.

As you know from our previous considerations, there is just one subgroup of $Z(p,\cdot)$ that has q elements. From this subgroup, Alice chooses a generator g. Alice now calculates her key pair. For this she chooses a private key x such that x is smaller than q and from this calculates the public key $g^x \pmod p$. This method corresponds to the ElGamal algorithm, except that x must be smaller than q. Alice sends the public key to Bob. He needs it to verify her signature.

Whenever Alice wants to sign a message m, she calculates a random number y, which is smaller than q. Using y she calculates the number $r=(g^y \pmod p) \pmod q$ and then applies the following equation.

$$m = y \cdot s - x \cdot r \pmod q$$

A DSA signature also comprises two parts
In this equation x, y, m, r and g are known. The newly introduced variable s can be calculated using algebraic transformation. The two numbers r and s together form the digital signature for the message m. Note that this equation resembles that of the ElGamal algorithm. It is, however, calculated to modulo q so as to remain within the subgroup of the quantity q. Also, DSA provides a minus sign instead of a plus sign – this difference has no deep importance, however, it is just one of many possible variations for calculating a signature.

Bob then applies the following equation:

$$g^m = r^s / g^{x \cdot r} \pmod p$$

If the equation balances, the signature is authentic. DSS, in which DSA is defined, makes conditions about parameter sizes: p must be a multiple of 64 and be between 512 and 1,024 bits long. The length of q must be 140 bits.

An example

In the example there are two possible generators
Here is an example of a DSA signature. We assume that Alice chooses $p=13$ and $q=3$. Since p and q are prime numbers and also q (=3) is a divisor of $p-1(=12)$, the preconditions are fulfilled. Now Alice still needs a generator g of the subgroup $Z(13,\cdot)$ with q (=3) elements. As you can see from Figure 6.3, there are two possible values for g, 3 and 9. Alice chooses 9.

Now Alice generates her pair of keys. For this she chooses $x=1$ as her private key. Her public key she calculates as $g^x \pmod p) = 9^1 = 9 \pmod{13}$. Now Alice signs the message $m=1$. For this she chooses 2 as the random value of y. Using this she evaluates $r = (g^y \pmod p) \pmod q = 9^2 = (3 \pmod{13}) \pmod 3 = 0$. She can now put numbers to the following equation:

$$m = y \cdot s - x \cdot r \pmod q$$

$$\Leftrightarrow 1 = 2 \cdot s - 1 \cdot 0 \ (\text{mod } 3)$$

$$\Leftrightarrow 1 = 2 \cdot s \ (\text{mod } 3)$$

The signature Solving s gives $s=2$. The signature is hence the pair of numbers comprising 0 and 2.
comprises the
numbers 2 and 0 If Bob wants to verify this signature, he applies it to the equation:

$$g^m = r^s / g^{x \cdot r} \ (\text{mod } p)$$

$$\Leftrightarrow 9^1 = 0^2 / 9^0 \ (\text{mod } 3)$$

$$\Leftrightarrow 0 = 0 \ (\text{mod } 3)$$

Since the left and right sides of the equation balance each other, the signature is authentic.

7.4   Security of signature algorithms

Mallory tries to If Mallory attacks a signature algorithm, he has two possible aims: either to forge
forge a signature Alice's signature or, better still, to learn Alice's key.
or to learn the key

Attacks that also work with encryption algorithms

Most of the attacks that can be used against RSA when used as an encryption algorithm (see Section 6.5.3) can also be used against RSA used as a signature algorithm. So Mallory can try a brute force key search or a factorisation attack. A low-exponent attack would only work if Bob signs the same message several times with different private keys. And the reaction attacks described in Section 15.6.1 can be used against RSA whether used for encryption or for signatures.

Signature algorithms based on the discrete logarithm behave similarly to RSA algorithms. Since they are based on the same principle as Diffie–Hellman, the same attacks can be effective. A particularly valid point is that Mallory can crack any DLSSs by calculating the discrete logarithm.

Attacks on signature algorithms

As well as the attacks already described, there are other attacks that only work with signature algorithms. With these attacks, Mallory tries to forge Alice's digital signature, or to learn Alice's key:

Some attacks • Mallory can create a message that matches an already existing signature used by
only work with Alice. How this works and what Alice can do about it is covered in Chapter 8.
signatures

• With the RSA algorithm Mallory can present a message he has created to Alice for decryption. Since RSA decryption is practically the same thing as an RSA signature algorithm, Mallory receives a valid signature (provided he gets at the result of the decryption). Alice can avoid this kind of attack by protecting her decrypted data. Also, in practice the RSA algorithm is used in a manner that obviates this attack (see Section 11.2.1 about PKCS#1).

The representation problem is only difficult to solve

- Mallory can alter Alice's signature software so that what Alice sees on the screen is not what she is actually signing (see [Fox] and [Pordes]). This attack exposes, without doubt, the biggest weakness of digital signatures (one talks about the **representation problem**). If Mallory succeeds in manipulating Alice's software via a virus or trojan, digital signatures quickly become a farce: if Alice orders 100 shares over the Web and signs the order, a manipulated Web browser can change "100" to "1000" before the order is signed. This alteration will not appear on the screen of course, so Alice is unaware of it. The fact that the signature itself might be produced on a smart card is of no consequence, since the data is only sent to the smart card after being manipulated. Unfortunately there is no really satisfactory solution to the representation problem – one can only take the usual security measures to protect against viruses and trojans. Also, Alice should only create important digital signatures on her own computer – after all, someone else's could be manipulated.

Despite everything, digital signatures rank as sufficiently secure

Despite these possibilities of attack, digital signatures are sufficiently secure to replace actual handwritten signatures.

7.5　Differences between DLSSs and RSA

Instead of knowing the fine details of individual signature algorithms, you should once again note the differences between RSA and signature algorithms based on the discrete logarithm. Here are the most important:

- RSA can both encrypt and sign. A DLSS, on the other hand, can only be used for signatures. However, there are also encryption algorithms based on the discrete logarithm.

- While generating a signature takes about the same time with both algorithms, the RSA algorithm is about ten times faster than a DLSS. This applies especially if a small value is used for e with RSA.

There are a few differences between RSA and DLSSs

- In practice, the public key is usually 768 or 1024 bits long for RSA. DLSS can provide the same level of security using rather shorter key lengths.

- DLSSs need to generate a random number for each signature. RSA algorithms, on the other hand, only need to generate a random key. This drawback of DLSSs should not be underestimated since the generation of random numbers is much more difficult than it may appear (see Chapter 9).

As you can see, apart from their shorter key lengths, everything speaks against DLSSs and for the RSA algorithm. That DLSSs nevertheless have their share of the market, and an increasing one at that, has several reasons:

- The fact that DLSSs can't be 'misused' for encryption appeals to many national agencies with an interest in the control of encryption.

DLSSs can be implemented with the aid of elliptic curves

- DLSSs can be implemented, with the aid of elliptic curves, so that they are decisively faster than RSA (of course, there is also an RSA variant based on elliptic curves, but this is hardly ever used). For more on this matter see Chapter 14.

- The RSA algorithm was protected by a patent in the USA until the year 2000. DSA and ElGamal, on the other hand, were not patented (although the legal situation is not quite certain). The patent protection was one reason why the US National Institute of Standards and Technology (NIST) opted for a DLSS instead of RSA.

7.6 Other signature algorithms

Of course, there are signature algorithms other than the RSA and DLSS family. Worthy of special mention are the algorithms based on elliptic curves (although strictly speaking, these are a DLSS variant). These algorithms with their related mathematics will be introduced in Chapter 14.

There are relatively few digital signature algorithms

Apart from this, the choice of signature algorithms is even more modest than it is for public key encryption algorithms. Except for RSA, DLSS and the elliptical curve algorithms, there is almost nothing that might be ready for practical use in the foreseeable future.

Cryptographic hash functions

Q: I understand how MD5 works, but I can't figure out how to 'decrypt' the resulting ciphertext. Can you please explain how to decrypt an MD5 output?
A: MD5 is not an encryption algorithm – it is a message digest algorithm. There should be no feasible way to determine the input, given the output. That is one of the required properties of a message digest algorithm.
RON RIVEST WEB PAGE

Key experience no. 8
Some well-known authors become fascinated by cryptography and describe cryptographic problems in their works. The best known are the two stories 'The adventure of the dancing men' by Arthur Conan Doyle (with Sherlock Holmes as the hero) and 'The Gold-Bug' by Edgar Allan Poe. In both cases there was a Caesar cipher, which was promptly cracked.

From the chapter on public key encryption you already know that asymmetric encryption algorithms like RSA are much more demanding than symmetric algorithms. In practice, Alice and Bob therefore use asymmetric encryption algorithms only to transmit a key, which is then used for a symmetric algorithm (hybrid algorithm). Whole messages (especially longer texts) are almost never asymmetrically encrypted.

Digital signatures are resource-hungry
A similar problem as with asymmetric encryption presents itself when a message is to be digitally signed. Since similar or even identical algorithms are used for signatures as for asymmetric encryption, a signature algorithm takes a similar amount of time. If Alice wants to sign a long message, this becomes a computing-power and time-consuming algorithm. It requires Alice to split the message into blocks of suitable length, and then sign each block individually. For receiver Bob, who has to check the signature, a similar game then begins: he has to check each block individually. It is also a drawback that the signatures created are very unwieldy, since in total they equal the length of the message itself.

A cryptographic hash function produces a value that is signed instead of the message
To get round the problem just described, as a rule whole messages are never signed. A checksum of manageable length is derived from the message and only this is signed instead.

This checksum is known as a **hash result**. An algorithm for calculating a hash result is called a **hash function**. In this chapter we shall concern ourselves with hash results, hash functions and their role in cryptography.

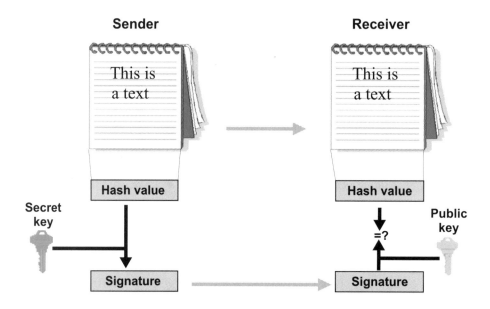

Figure 8.1   From a whole text a single hash result is formed in practice. A cryptographic hash function is used for this.

8.1   What is a cryptographic hash function?

The message can be much longer than the hash result

The calculation of a hash result using a hash function is an everyday event in information technology. Therefore, in the following section we shall address the subject without regard to any questions concerning cryptography.

8.1.1   Hash results and hash functions

Mathematically speaking, the matter can be expressed thus: if f is the hash function, h the hash result and m the input value (e.g. the message to be signed), then the expression $h=f(m)$ is valid. The range of values for h is limited, while m must be selectable from a much larger or even unlimited range of values.

A non-cryptographic case

Hash functions are not used only in cryptography

A typical application for a hash function, not from cryptography, might be the following: the Cryptobank (the leading banking house in Cryptoland) allots numbered accounts to its clients. Since the bank only has a few thousand clients, four-figure account numbers are big enough to give each account a unique number. From experience, however, the Cryptobank knows that its clients often forget one figure of their account number. Therefore the Cryptobank has decided that, instead of four-figure account numbers, five-figure account numbers will be used. The last figure in this case is a hash result, which is derived from the first four digits. If Alice now mistakes one figure in her account number, then normally the hash number will no longer check out, and it becomes immediately apparent that the account number is wrong.

Collisions

Collisions should be avoided with hash functions

In our case, there are 10,000 input values (all four-figure numbers), for which only 10 hash results (the numbers 0 to 9) are available. Of course, it can happen that a hash result is correct although the first four figures are not. This case, in which two different input values have the same hash result, is called a **collision**. With a good hash function of course, such collisions should occur only very rarely. If this is to be the case, the hash function, must fulfil the following requirements:

- If one tests all the input values, then each hash result should occur with virtually the same frequency.

- The hash result should be changed even by minor changes in the input value. In the present example, if Alice gives the first four figures of her account number inadvertently as 0816 instead of the correct 0815, this should be apparent from an altered hash result.

A simple hash function

The cross-sum is an example of a hash function

In our example, the Cryptobank has various options for defining the necessary hash function. The simplest is to add the first four figures together (cross-sum). If the cross-sum is greater than 9, the last figure is used – mathematically speaking, the hash result is the cross-sum modulo 10. For 0815 the cross-sum is 0+8+1+5=14, the hash result then being 4. Using this hash function then, Alice's full account number is 08154. If Alice inadvertently inputs her account number as 08164, the hash result 4 is no longer correct and it is instantly apparent that the number is wrong.

Each hash result should recur virtually the same number of times

Let us now check to see if the described hash function fulfils our stated requirements. Using the cross-sum method, each hash result recurs virtually the same number of times because each occurs exactly a thousand times. The fact that a small change in the input value effects a change in the hash result is also apparent – if one ignores the fact that figure inversion (e.g. 0851 instead of 0815), which occurs frequently in practice, does not change the hash result and so leads to collisions. Given this, both requirements for a good hash function appear to be met. I will leave the explanation of what a hash function can look like for a later exercise.

Of course, there are many other applications for hash functions, which also have nothing to do with cryptography. It is always a question of a large number of input values being represented by a significantly smaller, finite number of hash results. In any event, it is important that all hash results recur with roughly the same frequency, and that even a small change in an input value will change the hash result.

8.1.2 What is a cryptographic hash function?

The cross-sum method is not safe for digital signatures

Let us return to the original problem: Alice, instead of signing a whole message, would like just to sign a hash result so that the signing doesn't take up her whole evening. She could use the hash function described in the previous section – cross-sum modulo 10 (if the message consists of ASCII characters she might then use, say, the cross-sum of the related ASCII code numbers). This algorithm is extremely insecure, though. For Mallory, it would be no great problem to produce a second message with the same hash result, so that Alice's signature is transferred to a text that she hasn't signed. Let us assume that Mallory intercepts a message with a hash result 6 that has been signed by Alice. Mallory can now try to replace this intercepted message with 'I order 100 washing machines'. If the hash result is wrong, Mallory replaces the number 100 with 101, 102, 103 ... and so on, until the hash result 6 eventually appears. If he succeeds in this, Mallory has an order, signed by Alice, for 100 or more washing machines that Alice knows nothing about. Mallory's friend, a washing machine dealer, will be very happy.

Cryptography places high demands on hash functions

If Alice, instead of the cross-sum method, takes one of the numerous other hash functions that are suggested in the literature on non-cryptographic applications, the problem remains. In every case, Mallory will not find it particularly difficult, for a given message, to find a second with the same hash result (and with it a collision). This is quite simply because hash functions, which have not been developed specially for cryptographic purposes, are not suitable for these. We then are confronted with a problem that you will meet frequently in this book (for instance in Chapters 9 and 12): cryptography makes higher demands than other types of application.

Requirements for a cryptographic hash function

Let us look at the requirements for a hash function intended for signatures:

Each hash result should recur equally in cryptography, too

• That each hash result should recur equally often also applies to signatures. If a hash result recurs particularly frequently, then in many cases it is easier for Mallory to find a forged message with the same hash result as the genuine one.

• That a small change in the input value (in this case the message from Alice) should change the hash result, is equally an attribute that is required both within and outside cryptography. If Mallory, for instance, were easily able to alter the value in a digitally signed cheque without changing the hash result, then due to the ease with which a collision is caused, a digital signature would be worthless.

- Unknown outside cryptography is the requirement that it must be as difficult as possible for attacker Mallory to bring about collisions. For a given message it must not be possible with a realistic degree of effort to find another with the same hash result. This, of course, implies that it ought to be altogether impossible to find a matching message for a given hash result.

Cryptographical hash functions are used in cryptography

A hash function that fulfils the above three requirements is called a **cryptographic hash function**. Accordingly, a hash result that has been generated with a cryptographic hash function is called a **cryptographic hash value**. Cryptographic hash functions have long been an area of cryptography with which cryptographers have concerned themselves almost as intensely as with encryption and signature algorithms.

Terminology

Unfortunately, in the field of cryptographic hash functions, terminology is very untidy. One could fill half a page with terms used instead of 'cryptographic hash function' alone. Terms such as footprint function, Manipulation Detection Code (MDC), secure hash function or Message Integrity Code (MIC) are used equally along with cryptographic checksum algorithm or one-way hash function – all meaning generally the same thing. Correspondingly, there are innumerable alternative names for the cryptographic hash value, such as footprint, digital fingerprint, Message Digest (MD) or cryptographic checksum. This flood of names is a contrast to the astonishing fact that, for several things that are intrinsic to cryptographic hash functions, there are no special terms at all – as you will see, I have therefore allowed myself to introduce several new terms.

The most important design considerations

Cryptographic hash functions use symmetric cryptography techniques

Modern cryptographic hash functions do not work with cross-sum or similar methods, but with techniques that you already know from symmetric cryptography. All current algorithms divide a message into blocks and process each block through several rounds. Since a cryptographic hash function ought to be markedly faster to calculate than a digital signature, simple bit operations are always used. In this connection, therefore, you should imagine a message not as a number but as a sequence of bits or bytes. A typical hash result is 160 bits long; the input value is always of arbitrary length.

Important facts here are that with cryptographic hash functions nothing is encrypted and there is no key. So anyone (even Mallory) can calculate the cryptographic hash value of a message. There are several exceptions to this rule, though, which you will meet in Section 8.3.

8.1.3 Attacks on cryptographic hash functions

Mallory tries to find collisions

Before we take a closer look at the way in which some cryptographic hash functions work, we will first ask ourselves what an attack on a cryptographic hash function might look like. The aim of an attack on a cryptographic hash function is not, of course, to find a key. Instead, Mallory's aim is to find collisions.

What types of attack are there?

Free collisions are the easiest to find

Similarly to how one can divide attacks on encryption algorithms into ciphertext-only, known-plaintext and chosen-plaintext attacks, there are different grades of attacks on cryptographic hash functions:

- The easiest way is for Mallory to find a collision between two messages. Neither of the messages must have a purpose or fulfil any kind of task. In this book, such a collision will be termed a **free collision** (I cannot find another apposite term for this in current cryptological use). Cryptographic hash functions, which are not susceptible to free collisions, are known as **strongly collision-resistant** (this expression is not my invention).

Bound collisions are more difficult to find

- It becomes more difficult for Mallory if he has to find a collision for which one of the two messages is predetermined. Such a collision I call a **bound collision** (I cannot find a term in current literature for this). Correspondingly, a cryptographic hash function will be described as **weakly collision-resistant** if it does not admit bound collisions (again, this expression is not my invention).

You must realise that it is not enough for Mallory to find free collisions because, in practice, one message is always predetermined (for example, one that Mallory has captured from Alice). Normally, therefore, weakly collision-resistant cryptographic hash functions are adequate for creating hash results for signatures. Despite this, in practice no one is satisfied with a weakly collision-resistant cryptographic hash function. This is certainly down to Murphy's first law of cryptography ('Mallory is always cleverer than you think', see Section 32.5.1).

Strongly collision-resistant hash functions are available

However, it might also have something to do with the fact that strongly collision-resistant cryptographic hash functions are available – making the weaker option redundant. There is also another reason: there are applications for cryptographic hash functions in which free collisions must also be avoided (in this book, however, such applications are not considered).

If one wants to be precise, the division into bound and free collisions is not enough. In practice, it is not enough for Mallory to find just any bound collision. It must, more importantly, be a message that not only has the same hash result as a predetermined message, but also has a purpose that Mallory can use to advantage (say, to order a washing machine). On the other hand, Mallory often gains an advantage because Alice does not take care with the exact wording of messages she sends so long as the content is correct. So if Alice signs an order for an alarm clock,

Mallory can try to attribute a message ordering an alarm clock to her, which he can very simply change into a message ordering a washing machine with the same cryptographic hash result. However, I shall spare both of us a closer look at the prospects opened up by such attack possibilities.

Substitution attack

A substitution attack is very simple

Surprisingly, there is a very simple attack on cryptographic hash functions with which Mallory can find bound collisions from which he can largely determine the content of the second message. This attack basically works with any cryptographic hash function and can only be foiled by a measure that I shall introduce to you after the description of the attack. Unfortunately, I can find no current terminology for this attack, therefore I have decided on the name **substitution attack**.

In order to understand how a substitution attack works, let us assume that Mallory has intercepted a message from Alice, with a signed cryptographic hash result, which is an order for a washing machine. Mallory is now looking for a text with the same hash result in which one washing machine is ordered. To do this he first sets up the following text:

```
I hereby order a washing machine of type Cryptowash Plus.
Please deliver it before 1600 hrs Saturday.

Alice Onliner
```

Mallory searches for elements he can replace

In this text he now looks for words that he can replace without substantially changing the meaning. Here are a few examples:

- 'Saturday' can be replaced by 'Sat.'.

- '1600 hrs' can be replaced by '4 pm'.

- 'Alice Onliner' can be replaced by 'A. Onliner'.

- 'hereby' can be omitted.

There are many chances for a substitution attack

Suppose Mallory has found n possible replacements. Using different combinations of replacements he can generate 2^n washing machine orders with the same meaning but with varying hash results. Mallory now calculates these hash results, one after the other, until he finds a washing machine order with the same hash result as the intercepted message. He has then succeeded in finding a bound collision. If the length of the hash result of the cryptographic hash function is less than n (i.e. less than the number of possible replacements), then there is a high probability of Mallory finding a bound collision with this method.

Of course, there are better possibilities for a substitution attack than the replacement of words. For example, a space character can often be replaced by another, non-printing, character without a noticeable difference, or spaces can be added at the end of the text. In many formats (say HTML or programming languages) there is the possibility for comments that Mallory can change while leaving the content essentially unchanged.

The hash result should be of sufficient length

Therefore, in principle, substitution attacks work with any cryptographic hash function and any type of message. The only countermeasure Alice can take is to choose a hash result of sufficient length, because the longer the hash result, the greater the number of messages that Mallory must test. If the hash result is, for instance, 160 bits long, then Mallory must correspondingly seek 160 replacement possibilities (or more) and from these create 2^{160} hash results that he must then test. If we assume that on average he will succeed after only half the values have been tested, he still must have tested $2^{159}=7,3\cdot10^{47}$ values, which, even with the best supercomputers imaginable, will take longer than the remaining estimated life of the universe.

Birthday attack

The birthday problem has a surprising solution

Just try to answer the following question: How many people must be present in a room so that there is a 50 per cent probability of at least two of them having the same birthday?

What this question (known as the **birthday problem**) has to do with cryptographic hash functions, I shall explain later. First let us simply consider the answer: when only 22 people are gathered in a room, the probability is approximately. 50 per cent. This means: if we assemble a number of groups containing more than 22 people, then in more than half of them there will be two people who celebrate the same birthday.

The birthday problem can be described in general terms. Let us assume that a year has d days. Then the number of people who must be assembled in order that there is a 50 per cent probability of a birthday pairing is always more than the square root of d.

What does this have to do with cryptographic hash functions? Quite simple: if Mallory wants to know how many messages he must test on average before he has found a free collision at random, he need only remember the birthday problem. The number of possible hash results becomes the number of days in the year, and the number of tested messages becomes the number of people. If the hash result has a length n, there are 2^n possible hash results. The square root of 2^n is $2^{n/2}$, which means that Mallory will find a free collision on average after $2^{n/2}$ attempts.

A birthday attack finds collisions

An attack that makes use of the birthday phenomenon is called a **birthday attack**. You are already familiar with the birthday attack in its simplest form: the application of a cryptographic hash function to all possible messages, until a free collision is found. For a 128-bit hash result, using this method Mallory needs 2^{64} attempts, therefore, for instance, 10^{19}. To attempt this on a PC, Mallory will need tens of thousands of years. The NSA, with its supercomputers, could do it rather more quickly, which is why all new cryptographic hash functions use hash results of 160 bits or more.

The birthday attack can be combined with a substitution attack

Of course, there are other forms of the birthday attack. If Mallory can, in advance, formulate messages that Alice signs, then the following method would work (n is here the length of the hash result in bits): Mallory, who knows that Alice intends to order a box of paper clips, uses a substitution attack to formulate $2^{n/2}$ versions of an innocent-looking order message (for instance 'I order a pack of paper clips. Alice'). Then he formulates a message with his preferred content (for instance, 'I order a washing machine. Alice'). He then continually alters the latter message using the substitution attack method, and in each case calculates the hash result. He then compares each of these with the hash results of the $2^{n/2}$ innocent-looking messages. He repeats the whole process until he finally finds a collision between a paper clip order and a washing machine order. He then sends the innocent-looking paper clip order for Alice to sign (Alice is not suspicious, because she wanted to order some paper clips anyway). He then gives the washing machine order message with the same hash result to his friend, the washing machine dealer. For a birthday attack of this type to succeed, Mallory must test on average $2^{n/2}$ washing machine order messages. This was scarcely feasible for a 128-bit hash result and for a 160-bit value would be absolutely hopeless.

Summary

Both substitution and birthday attacks show that attacks on cryptographic hash functions are easier than attacks on symmetric encryption algorithms. Since both attacks work independently of the design of their respective cryptographic hash functions, one can only counter them with a hash result of ample length. This should be longer than the key length of a symmetric algorithm. The standard used today is 160 bits.

There are still other attacks on cryptographic hash functions

Of course, substitution and birthday attacks are only the tip of the cryptanalysis iceberg in the sea of cryptological hash functions. In addition to these, there are numerous other attacks on cryptographic hash functions. These are, however, dependent on the way that their respective algorithms work. So, for example, the principles of differential and linear cryptanalysis of symmetric cryptography are applicable to cryptographic hash functions.

8.2 The most important cryptographic hash functions

There is comprehensive literature on the theme of cryptographic hash functions

After considering various attacks on cryptographic hash functions, we now come to the algorithm itself. I shall introduce the most important of them, SHA-1, in detail. A few others I shall cover rather more superficially. If you want to delve deeply into this theme, you should get hold of the books from Schneier [Schn96] or Menezes, Oorschot and Vanstone [MeOoVa] (for further details of these books see Section 31.2). Schneier describes a whole array of cryptographic hash functions in great detail, including their strengths and weaknesses. With Menezes and his two colleagues you will find a systematic treatment of the theme, in which numerous classifications and terminology are explained.

8.2.1   Hash functions from encryption algorithms

Block ciphers can be used as hash functions

The simplest way to construct a cryptographic hash function consists in the application of a block cipher. There are several variants of this: the most frequently used is an algorithm in which the message to be processed is divided into blocks that match the key length (i.e. 56 bits for DES). The hash result is found by encrypting an arbitrary starting block (64 bits long for DES) using each of the 56-bit blocks as a key in turn. This method is only practical if the key transformation is easy enough (for several of the new block ciphers such as Blowfish this is not the case).

The algorithm just described can be varied, of course. For example, a fixed key could be used, with which the message could then be encrypted block by block. Each block would then be XOR'd (exclusive OR'd) with the previous block. Because an encryption using a known key is easily inverted, however, Mallory can find bound collisions in this variant (although none in which the found message has a purposeful content). Further possibilities for the use of encryption algorithms as hash functions can be studied in [Schn96]. Or you could figure some out for yourself, in which case please proceed carefully since so many designs have proven to be insecure.

Hash functions based on encryption algorithms are little used

Although there are quite usable cryptographic hash functions based on encryption algorithms, in practice those in use today have been specially developed for this purpose. We will meet the most important of these in the following sections.

8.2.2   SHA-1

SHA-1 is currently the most important cryptographic hash function

The currently most important cryptographic hash function is **SHA-1**. The acronym SHA stands for Secure Hash Algorithm. The 1 was added to the name after the function had been slightly altered (previously it was known simply as SHA). Both SHA and SHA-1 were developed by the NSA. The development ran parallel with that of the Digital Signature Algorithm (DSA), also from the NSA, which I have already described in Section 7.3.2. Both DSA and SHA were made public in 1991. Although NSA developments are always viewed with some suspicion by cryptographers, time has shown that both SHA and SHA-1 are very good cryptographic hash functions. The back doors always credited to the NSA have not been discovered so far. It cannot be claimed, however, that the NSA has used completely new cryptographic knowledge in SHA-1 – in fact it is a development of the cryptographic hash function MD4, which will be covered in Section 8.2.3. Incidentally, other developments of MD4 are all currently viable cryptographic hash functions.

SHA-1 working method

Chaining variables are used in SHA-1

SHA-1 processes blocks that are 512 bits long, and generates hash results 160 bits long. If Alice hashes a message m, she must divide it into 512-bit blocks. We can call these 512-bit blocks m_0, m_1, m_2, m_3, ... and so on. Since as a rule message lengths are not exact multiples of 512 bits, the SHA-1 algorithm describes a method for padding out the final block.

Five 32-bit chaining variables (**32-bit-word buffers**) play an important part in the functioning of SHA-1. These are set to predefined values at the start, and change their value with each block. The variables are labelled as a_j, b_j, c_j, d_j and e_j, where j takes the values 0, 1, 2, 3, 4 etc. and stands for the respective round. The predefined initial values are correspondingly a_0, b_0, c_0, d_0, and e_0. These values (in hexadecimal notation) are a_0=67452301, b_0=EFCDAB89, c_0=98BADCFE, d_0=10325476 and e_0=C3D2E1F0.

A further important part of the method is the so-called **compression function**, which we shall designate by the letter f. The compression function accepts five 32-bit values and one 512-bit value and converts them into five 32-bit values.

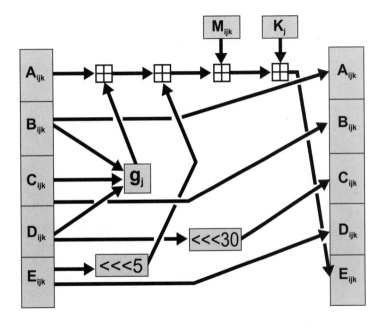

Figure 8.2 This operation is executed 20 times in each round of SHA-1. The function g_j changes with each round.

SHA-1 now proceeds with each 512-bit block in sequence as follows: the current value of the chaining variable and the current 512-bit block are processed with the compression function. The five output values from the compression function become the new values of the chaining variables. The five values finally saved in the chain variables together form the hash result. Mathematically expressed:

$$(a_j, b_j, c_j, d_j, e_j) = f(a_{j-1}, b_{j-1}, c_{j-1}, d_{j-1}, e_{j-1}, m_j)$$

The SHA-1 compression function has four rounds The compression function operates in four rounds. Each round consists of 20 identical operations. The execution of one operation is shown in Figure 8.2. The framed + symbol stands for an addition, <<<n for a circular left shift of n bits. The five input values for the operation are called A_{ijk}, B_{ijk}, C_{ijk}, D_{ijk} and E_{ijk}. i is the number of the block, j the number of the round and k the number of the operation (j=0,1,2,3,4; k=0,1,..., 20). Then:

$$(A_{i00}, B_{i00}, C_{i00}, D_{i00}, E_{i00}) = a_i, b_i, c_i, d_i, e_i$$

SHA-1 works with blocks of 512 bit length

As can be seen in the diagram, a part-block M_{ijk} of the current 512-bit block m_i is input to the calculation. This is the only point at which the text to be hashed affects the hash result. In addition, in each operation three values of the g_j function are brought in. The function g_j and the constant K_j change with the round number. g_j changes as follows:

- $g_1 = (B_{i-1} \wedge C_{i-1}) \vee ((\neg B_{i-1}) \wedge D_{i-1})$

- $g_2 = B_{i-1} \oplus C_{i-1} \oplus D_{i-1}$

- $g_3 = (B_{i-1} \wedge C_{i-1}) \vee (B_{i-1} \wedge D_{i-1})$

- $g_4 = g_2$

The final values of the 5 chaining variables is the hash result.

The constant K_j also takes another value in each round, which is fixed in the specification. As you may have noticed, the written algorithm calls for a total of 80 32-bit blocks from each 512-bit m_i block, although each m_i block only has 16 of them. For this purpose, the SHA-1 specification provides another expansion function, which I shall not look at in more detail.

After all the blocks of the text to be hashed have been processed, the contents of the five chaining variables are output as the hash result.

SHA-1 security

With its 160-bit hash result, SHA-1 is sufficiently secure against substitution and birthday attacks. Furthermore, despite intensive research, no other effective attack has been discovered to date. Alice and Bob can therefore assume that by using SHA-1 they have nothing to fear from Mallory. It is highly likely that SHA-1 will remain first choice amongst cryptographic hash functions for the foreseeable future.

8.2.3 MD4

MD4 is the basis for many other cryptographic hash functions

A further cryptographic hash function that you might meet on your expeditions through the Internet is **MD4** (Message Digest 4). MD4 is one of the numerous developments from Ron Rivest (see Section 30.1.7).

It is no accident that MD4 bears a striking resemblance to SHA-1. The reason for this is that SHA-1 is a development of MD4.

Working method

MD4 is also the basis of SHA-1

Since MD4 and SHA-1 are so similar, I shall just give a description of the differences between them:

- MD4 produces a hash result of length 128 bits (for SHA-1 it is 160 bits). For this reason there are only four chaining variables.

- MD4 uses only three rounds (SHA-1 uses four).

- MD4 uses only 16 operations per round (SHA-1 uses 20).

- The MD4 operations are rather differently structured than in SHA-1.

MD4 security

There is no doubt that MD4 is an influential algorithm. From a security viewpoint, however, it falls a long way short of today's standards. Using attacks discovered in the past few years, it is possible to find collisions even with modest means. MD4 should not be used further.

8.2.4 MD5

MD5 is based on MD4

The failings of MD4 caused Rivest to make small changes to the algorithm. The result, called **MD5**, became probably the most-used cryptographic hash function in the Internet. Since then, MD5 has been standardised by the IETF and is described in [RFC 1321].

Method of operation

MD5 is also very similar to SHA-1. Both algorithms use 512-bit blocks, 32-bit chaining variables, a compression function, and four rounds per block. The way that MD5 works is therefore easier to describe by observing the differences from SHA-1:

- MD5 produces a hash result 128 bits long (with SHA-1 is 160 bits). Therefore, it uses only four chaining variables.

- MD5 uses 16 operations per round (SHA-1 uses 20).

- MD5 operations differ structurally from SHA-1 operations.

MD5 security

Although MD5 is still widely used, it is rarely used in newer implementations. One reason for this is the length of the hash result: 128 bits are on the low side these days, 160 bits are more in demand.

MD5 has a weakness in theory

A further weak spot was discovered by the German cryptographer Hans Dobbertin, of the Bundesamt für Sicherheit in der Informationstechnik (BSI). In 1996 he succeeded in finding collisions in the MD5 compression function (thereby gaining international recognition as a leading German cryptographer). Although not yet extended to collisions for MD5 itself, this attack casts serious doubts on the strength of MD5 as a collision-resistant hash function.

8.2.5 RIPEMD-160

RIPEMD-160 is fast becoming popular

In addition to SHA-1, a hash function developed in Europe called **RIPEMD-160** is becoming very popular. Like SHA-1, RIPEMD-160 is an extension of MD4 with a hash result of 160 bits (hence the name). One of the developers of RIPEMD-160 and its predecessor RIPEMD (which still produced 128-bit hash results) is Hans Dobbertin, who also discovered the best-known attack on MD5.

8.2.6 Summary

That all currently popular secure hash functions stem from MD4 does not mean that extending MD4 is the only way. So it is no wonder that dozens of other algorithms have been published. That these did not break through is partly due to their security failings, and partly due to the mistrust with which any new algorithm is regarded. With the successors to MD4, one at least knows what to expect. In my opinion, SHA-1 and RIPEMD-160 are therefore the shape of the future.

8.3 Key-dependent hash functions

There are also key-dependent hash functions

As you have seen in this chapter, cryptographic hash functions normally do not include a key. This is of no importance because it doesn't matter if Mallory can calculate a hash result. There are exceptions, however.

What is the purpose of key-dependent hash functions?

Alice sends Bob a message that need not be kept secret (Mallory may also read it). However, Alice does not want the message to be changed by Mallory without it being apparent. Now to achieve this, Alice could of course sign her message (or a cryptographic hash result of it) digitally. There is another possibility, however: Alice could use a cryptographic hash result that can only be calculated using a key. Since she has already been exchanging secret keys with Bob for a long time, Bob can likewise also calculate a received hash result and then check that the message has not been changed. However, Mallory cannot do this as he does not know the key.

The term Message Authentication Code is also used

A cryptographic hash function that needs a secret key for the calculation of a hash result is known as a **key-dependent cryptographic hash function**, or simply as a **key-dependent hash function**. Another name that is often used is **Message Authenticity Check (MAC)**.

Perhaps you are now asking yourself, why are key-dependent hash functions necessary when there are digital signatures (or vice versa)? The answer is: a key-dependent hash function needs much less computational power than a digital

Digital signatures have advantages over cryptographic hash functions

signature, and can use a shorter key. From the efficiency viewpoint, a key-dependent hash function is more attractive.

On the other hand, a digital signature has one advantage over a key-dependent hash function: it is incontestable. Only Bob can create a digital signature with Bob's private key. If Bob wants to order a book from online-dealer Otto, then Otto can have recourse to the law if Bob denies his signed order. On the other hand, if Bob agrees a secret key with Otto and uses a key-dependent hash function for the order, then Otto has no claim. Bob can always maintain that Otto might have generated the key-dependent hash function himself. Since Otto knows the key, this could be the truth.

The most important key-dependent hash functions

When designing key-dependent hash functions there is no need to reinvent the wheel. All current key-dependent hash functions are extensions of already known cryptographic hash functions. Here are the most important examples:

- A simple method for converting a normal cryptographic hash function into a key-dependent function consists in Alice encrypting the hash result with a symmetric algorithm (e.g. DES).

- Alice can also attach the secret key to the message to be hashed and then use a cryptographic hash function.

Key-dependent hash functions an be generated from encryption algorithms

- There are several ways to generate a key-dependent hash function from a symmetric encryption algorithm alone.

Further details are available in [Schn96] or [MeOoVa]. Alice and Bob can at any rate choose from a satisfactory number of algorithms.

8.4 Further applications

Up to now we have only considered cryptographic hash functions with respect to digital signatures and as key-dependent hash functions. However, there are other applications, which I will examine in more detail in the course of this book. Here is a brief summary:

There are different uses for cryptographic hash functions

- Cryptographic hash functions can be used as pseudo-random generators (more on this in Chapter 9).

- Cryptographic hash functions provide algorithms that can be used to determine whether someone is who he or she claims to be (authentication, see Chapter 13).

As you can see, cryptographic hash functions are important tools in the hands of a cryptographer. They will reappear often enough in the course of this book.

9

Cryptographic random generators

The moral of the story is that random numbers should not be generated with a method chosen at random. Some theory should be used.
DONALD KNUTH [KNUTH]

Key experience no. 9
During 2000, the film '*U-571*' was released. The cracking of the Enigma played an important role in this film. '*The Mercury Rising*' with Bruce Willis is another film in which cryptography is important. The classic film '*War Games*' is more concerned with IT security than with cryptography per se.

The generation of random numbers is often underestimated

From previous chapters you will have realised that random numbers play an important role in cryptography. Alice and Bob need them mainly for generating keys. This might be a DES key or even a one-time-pad key, which is as long as the message to be encrypted. Not just any random number can be used for an RSA key, because such keys are generated from two prime numbers. On closer examination, however, all practical prime number generators comprise normal random generators that simply discard all non-prime numbers. Public key algorithms on the other hand, which, like Diffie–Hellman, ElGamal or DSA, are based on the discrete logarithm, need random numbers that exhibit no special properties. On top of this, each ElGamal or DSA signature requires, as well as a key, a unique random number to be generated. In all cases, Mallory can crack even the most secure algorithms if he learns the key generated by the random generator. This should serve to make you aware of the importance of random numbers in cryptography.

There are many random number generators

However, it is not that obvious why a whole chapter of this book is dedicated to random numbers. After all, any of the better compilers offers a random number generator that can be used for cryptographic purposes. Why can't Alice and Bob use one of these? The answer is simple: nearly all current random number generators offered by compilers or operating systems are not good enough for cryptography. In fact, there is no area of cryptography that is so often and so thoroughly underrated as the generation of random numbers. So we will now consider the matter more closely.

9.1   Random numbers in general

Keys are generated with random numbers

By a **random string** we understand, in this context, a long, random sequence of zeros and ones (a definition of the term 'random' comes later). How these zeros and ones are interpreted – in groups of eight as ASCII codes, for example, or simply as binary numbers – is immaterial. A **random number** is a section of a random string with a fixed length (e.g. 56 bits, if the random number is to be used as a DES key). A **random generator** (also called random number generator) is a procedure that delivers a random string as its result.

You are already aware that random numbers are important in cryptography. Certainly you also know that there are many uses for random numbers outside cryptography: computer games decide at random on the direction from which an alien comes who must be shot down; simulation programs determine at random which countries sink into the sea and how many people die from an illness; probability algorithms use random numbers to calculate an approximate value if an exact calculation is too complex. These and other uses have led to a growing mountain of literature on the subject of random numbers.

9.2   Random numbers in cryptography

Cryptography makes high demands on random generators

Anyone who thinks that current procedures for generating random numbers can also be used in cryptography without any problem is mistaken. The crux of the matter is that the above-mentioned uses such as simulations or computer games have much smaller expectations of random numbers than does cryptography – similar problems arise with cryptographic hash functions (Chapter 8) and with cryptographic protocols (Chapter 12).

Probabilistic algorithms and most simulations only need random strings that have specific statistical attributes. In these cases it is enough to define 'random' as 'statistically well distributed'.

Computer games have a further requirement: that it must not be possible for a player to forecast easily the direction from which the alien will come. Here 'random' thus means 'statistically well distributed and not easily predictable'.

9.2.1   Requirements of cryptography

Cryptography has stringent requirements for random numbers

By contrast, cryptography makes markedly more stringent demands than computer games or simulations: it must not be possible for Mallory, even at great cost and after many attempts, to predict a random number. Mallory does not have to succeed in guessing an RSA, DES or one-time-pad key at the first attempt. It is often good enough for him if he succeeds only with the help of a supercomputer and after billions of attempts – even if it takes weeks. If he should succeed in guessing a key in this manner, then the most secure encryption algorithms become ineffective. In cryptography 'random' thus always means 'not predictable at realistic cost'.

Cryptographic random numbers must not be predictable

Most random generators mentioned in the literature or implemented in compilers do not meet these special requirements of cryptography. They do provide statistically usable results (if not always), and are as a rule unpredictable. For an eavesdropper of Mallory's class, who shrinks from neither effort nor expense, numbers generated in that way are mostly easy to guess – especially if we can assume that Mallory knows the algorithm being used. For this reason cryptographers must develop new random generators that take account of the special requirements of cryptography.

You may now be thinking that despite everything it must be possible to find a simple method of constructing random generators suitable for cryptographic use. This is not so, however, as Netscape, for example, discovered. Originally, Navigator used a very simple procedure for generating random numbers. Since students Ian Goldberg and David Wagner could extract the procedure from an analysis of the machine code, it was child's play for them to crack an encrypted message [GolWag]. Netscape had to admit to a gap in security, which they were quick to close.

9.2.2 Real random generators

Real random generators are based on a physical process

Let us assume that Alice wants to generate random numbers to acquire a key for her communications with Bob. Her aim is to generate random numbers that Mallory, even at great cost, cannot guess. The best way to do this is to use a physical process that cannot be reproduced. Such a random generator is called a **real random generator**. Good examples of real random generators are the toss of a coin or the roll of a die. Both actions generate indisputably unpredictable results. To obtain a truly random 56-bit key, Alice has to toss a coin 56 times or throw a die 22 times (why 22 exactly I leave for you to figure out).

Standard hardware can also be used for random generation

For obvious reasons, coins and dice are not used on the Internet in practice. It would be better to use a special hardware module that can generate random numbers from specific measured values. In practice, these are usually voltage variations measured across a resistance or diode. The advantage of such hardware modules is that they produce a large volume of random numbers per unit of time. But solutions of this kind have been rather expensive up to now: you must be prepared to shell out hundreds of pounds. But this could change if demand was great enough. Maybe we might even find PCs equipped with hardware random number generators as standard.

Instead of using an expensive random module, Alice can of course fall back on existing hardware. The times between successive disk accesses, key inputs, mouse movements etc. are sufficiently random for occasional key generation. Certainly Alice won't achieve a large throughput and still keep things safe. But if, at the start of communications, a key is needed for that session only, this kind of action might be usable.

The great advantage of real random generators lies in the fact that they are difficult to guess, and hence secure. As a result, they are often expensive and can sometimes be manipulated.

9.2.3 Pseudo-random generators

Computers are not designed to act randomly

The generation of random numbers would be much easier, of course, if Alice did not need hardware to do it. A random generator which works without physical measurement and instead uses an algorithm implemented in software is called a **pseudo-random generator**.

Unfortunately, it is very difficult to generate unpredictable random numbers using software. This is because a computer is designed to act in a predictable manner. Its job is to produce a specific output for a specific input using a specific algorithm. This determines everything, so if Alice develops a random generator using only a software program, then the output random string is predictable for Mallory (who probably knows the program) and is in the first instance simply not suitable for cryptography.

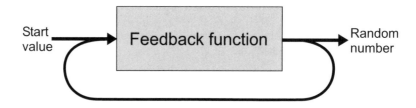

Figure 9.1 A pseudo-random generator repeatedly processes a start value.

Feedback functions

Since, strictly speaking, there are no pseudo-random generators that are suitable for cryptography, in cryptology it is always assumed that a real random number (unknown to Mallory) can be used as the input. In cryptography, a pseudo-random generator is therefore always a procedure that changes a random initial value (**seed**) into a random string of any length. This is done by applying a function f (**feedback function**) to the seed x a number of times. In mathematical language this means that the seed x is the first random number, $f(x)$ the second, $f(f(x))$ the third, $f(f(f(x)))$ the fourth, and so on.

But be careful: if Mallory finds out a random number and knows the function f, he can calculate all subsequent random numbers. To avoid this, there are two methods:

A pseudo-random generator should not output the whole of the current value

- The pseudo-random generator can just output part of the current value, or a cryptographic hash result of this.

- A key-dependent feedback function can be used.

For Alice to be able to use a random string produced by a pseudo-random generator cryptographically, two conditions must first be met: Mallory must not be able to guess the seed, and the function f must be chosen such that no inferences can be drawn about the generated random numbers without knowledge of the seed. Of course, we assume here also that sly fox Mallory knows the function being used (but not the seed). This means: a cryptographic pseudo-random generator does always produce predictable results. However, if the seed is not known, the results are not predictable. As you have surely noticed, the seed fulfils the function of a secret key.

What does a feedback function look like?

A pseudo-random generator reprocesses a seed repeatedly

If you are thinking that Alice could program a usable feedback function by combining, as obscurely as possible, as many computations as possible, then you are wrong again. If one examines the output of such pseudo-random generators statistically, then as a rule you will see that some random numbers appear very frequently, others seldom or even not at all. The repeated application of such functions also reveals that number sequences repeat themselves quite soon.

Therefore, you should remember the following: pseudo-random generators should never be generated pseudo-randomly (an old cryptographers' rule). In the light of this, it is no wonder that there are now stacks of literature on the subject of cryptographic pseudo-random generators. There have been some successes: good algorithms are available in ample quantity today.

Pros and cons of pseudo-random generators

Pseudo-random generators are good to analyse

Pseudo-random generators have a decided advantage over real random generators: they are very rewarding to analyse because they are independent of outside influences and also produce the same random string from the same seed. Not least therefore, a large part of the literature concentrates on pseudo-random generators.

However, there are still two drawbacks: One of these is that pseudo-random generators normally produce repeatable random series. The other is that a pseudo-random generator is worth very little without a truly random seed (initial value).

9.2.4 The grey area between true and pseudo

There is a grey area between true and pseudo

Alice enters the grey area between truly random and pseudo-random if she draws on, say, the contents of a specific area of memory for random generation. It is ideal if she generates a hash result like this from any areas of memory that change and are difficult to predict. If the area of memory is directly influenced by hardware, this method has the character of a real random generator. However, if areas which are changed by software, are used, it is more of a pseudo-random generator. When executed correctly, the use of areas of memory is very secure. Unfortunately, these methods are difficult to analyse – and cryptographers don't like that.

9.2.5 Mixing random sources

If Alice wants to be extra secure, she has the option of mixing different random sequences (see also [RFC1750]). To do this, she must use a function (**mixing**

function) that converts any number of input bits into a short bit sequence, which is then used as a random number. The output of the mixing function must be statistically well distributed and may only be guessable when all input bits are known (we assume that Mallory knows the mixing function itself).

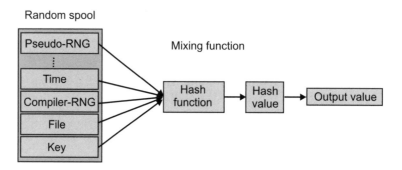

Figure 9.2   The mixing of random numbers from different sources, using a hash function, is a good way to generate random sequences.

The generation of secure random numbers is comparable to squaring the circle

The stated requirements for a mixing function are fulfilled almost perfectly by a (true) cryptographic hash function (see Chapter 8). The generation of secure random numbers requires that an area of memory (**random pool**) be filled with random numbers from differing sources. These random numbers can be derived, for example, partly from a pseudo-random generator and partly from some hardware parameter values. Another source might be data from an area of memory that the operating system accesses frequently, and which therefore changes often and unpredictably. The time, a keyboard input, or a secret key can then possibly be used to fill the random pool. The random pool is then converted into a short bit sequence using a cryptographic hash function as a mixing function. If Mallory now wants to guess the output, he must know every input value.

9.3   The most important pseudo-random generators

There are pseudo-random generators of varying effectiveness

After the long preamble let us now take a look at which pseudo-random generators Alice and Bob can actually use. All the pseudo-random generators described in the following have been developed specially for cryptographic purposes and are deemed (unless otherwise stated) to be secure.

9.3.1   Cryptographic hash functions as feedback functions

An obvious idea for a pseudo-random generator is for Alice to use a cryptographic hash function as a feedback function (see Chapter 8). She can reiterate a seed of, for instance, a length of 160 bits using the cryptographic hash function SHA-1. Since SHA-1 outputs a 160-bit hash result, in this way she obtains a series of random 160-bit values. For key generation she should not use more than 80 bits each, so that Mallory cannot continue the random series if a key should fall into his hands. If Alice wants to use the full 160 bits, she should use a key-dependent hash function (and keep the key secret, of course).

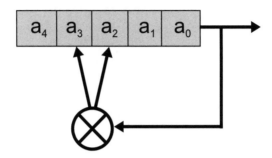

Figure 9.3 Example of a linear feedback shift register (LFSR). a_2 and a_3 are the tap variables.

9.3.2 Linear feedback shift register

A classic, decades-old method for building a cryptographic random-generator is the use of linear feedback shift registers (**LFSR**).

How a linear feedback shift register works

An LFSR consists of a sequence of n variables that can be written as $a_0, a_1, ..., a_{n-1}$. Each variable can only accept the values 0 or 1. If Alice needs a random bit, she reads the value of a_0. The value of a_1 is then shifted into a_0, a_1 receives the value from a_2, a_2 the value from a_3 and so on. The new value of a_{n-1} is calculated in each case from the recent value of a_n.

LFSRs use tap variables

For an LFSR, the **feedback function** is the application of the XOR function to some of the a_n variables. For example, if $n=5$, then say a_2 and a_3 can be designated as the variables used for input to the feedback function. These variables are called **tap variables**. An alternative description of the feedback function runs as follows: if, prior to shifting, the tap variables contain an uneven number of ones, a one is inserted in a_{n-1}. If not, a zero is inserted in a_{n-1}.

The values output from an LFSR build a random sequence that Alice can use for key generation. Which variables are used for input to the feedback function and how many variables there are, Alice should keep secret, and consider this to be a part of the key (and the initial values also).

An example

In this example there are five register variables

An LFSR holds five variables a_0, a_1, a_2, a_3 and a_4. The tap variables are a_2 and a_3. As the initial value Alice chooses 01100, giving the following variable values:

Random bit	a_0	a_1	a_2	a_3	a_4
1	0	1	1	0	0
2	1	1	0	0	1
3	1	0	0	1	0
4	0	0	1	0	1
5	0	1	0	1	1
6	1	0	1	1	1
7	0	1	1	1	0
8	1	1	1	0	0
9	1	1	0	0	1
10	1	0	0	1	0
11	0	0	1	0	1
12	0	1	0	1	1

The resulting random sequence is derived from the value of a_0. This reads 011001011100. The first five bits of the random sequence are identical to the initial value.

The application of LFSRs

LFSRs offer a simple method for generating random sequences

A random sequence can be generated easily using an LFSR. Just how difficult it will be for Mallory to predict a value of this random sequence depends on how many variables are used (the more, the better) and which of them are used as tap variables. Much has been written about LFSRs. The development of an LFSR structure that is unfavourable to Mallory has been thoroughly researched.

After several sections on LFSRs, it will perhaps come as a surprise for you to learn that the security of an LFSR pseudo-random generator is only rather modest. There are two reasons why LFSRs are covered in all good books on cryptography (including this one): first, LFSRs are easily realisable in hardware, where they allow very high-speed generation. Secondly, LFSRs can be combined with other techniques to form secure cryptological procedures. An example of this is to be found in Section 9.4.2.

9.3.3 Other pseudo-random generators

Blum Blum Shub is a pseudo-random generator

Of course, there are numerous other pseudo-random generators. Hence a block cipher (e.g. DES) can be used as the feedback function instead of a cryptographic hash function. Worthy of mention is the pseudo-random generator with the beautiful name **Blum Blum Shub**, whose security, like the RSA algorithm, is based on the factorisation problem.

9.4 Stream ciphers

A stream cipher is a pseudo-random generator used specially for a one-time-pad

As you discovered in the previous section, a pseudo-random generator can produce a long random sequence from a short seed (which has the function of a key). Alice and Bob can exploit this not only to generate keys for the already described symmetrical algorithms such as DES and IDEA, but can also use the resulting random sequence for one-time-pad (Section 4.3.3). This means that they both use a random sequence that is exactly the same length as the plaintext that is to be encrypted. For encryption, Alice XOR's the plaintext with the random sequence. For decryption, Bob uses the Exclusive OR function on the ciphertext and the random sequence. To ensure that Alice and Bob use the same random sequence, they must both use the same seed.

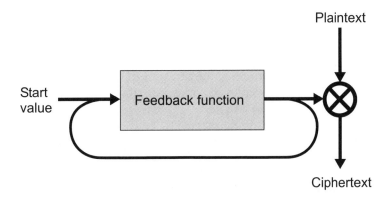

Figure 9.4 In a stream cipher the plaintext is processed with the result of a pseudo-random generator.

How a stream cipher works

A pseudo-random generator which is conceived for use as a one-time-pad, as just described, is called a **stream cipher**. A stream cipher is therefore a symmetric encryption algorithm, which can be used in the same way as DES or IDEA. The seed of the pseudo-random generator is here the secret key of the symmetric algorithm. As you may recall, DES, IDEA and other algorithms already mentioned are block ciphers. All current symmetric encryption algorithms are either block or stream ciphers.

Stream ciphers are much less widely distributed than block ciphers

Stream ciphers are much less widely distributed than block ciphers. This is mainly for historical reasons: DES is a block cipher, and is the most tried and tested of all algorithms. Therefore, the first alternatives to DES were also block ciphers, and stream ciphers could never challenge their dominance, although in many respects they are their equal or even superior to them. On the other hand, there are no cogent grounds for preferring stream ciphers. Therefore, block ciphers will no doubt continue to be more widely distributed in future. Only block ciphers could be put forward as candidates for the AES (Section 5.3).

9.4.1 RC4

The best-known and most important stream cipher is **RC4**. This algorithm is one of the numerous developments from Ron Rivest (currently perhaps the greatest cryptographer in the world (see Section 30.1.7)) who also co-developed the RSA algorithm. RC4 stands for Rivest Cipher No.4. Rivest developed this cipher as far back as 1987, but to the chagrin of many cryptographers, he kept the working method secret. So the *schadenfreude* was correspondingly great when, in 1994, the source code of the algorithm turned up on the Internet (from an unknown source, of course).

How RC4 works

RC4 is very simple After the modus operandi of RC4 leaked out, everyone involved in cryptography, i.e. the whole 'crypto world', was surprised at how simple it was. In fact, RC4 is the simplest modern cryptological algorithm I know. There are programmers who can implement RC4 from memory (just try doing that with DES!). With a little practice, RC4 can even be deployed manually without any support from the computer (also difficult to do with DES).

At the core of RC4 is a sequence of 256 variables, in which every number between 0 and 255 occurs precisely once. We want to name the 256 sequence members as $s_0, s_1, ..., s_{255}$. We also need two variables i and j, which have the value 0 at the start, as well as another variable k. The sequence $s_0, s_1, ..., s_{255}$ is now processed using the following feedback function:

```
i = i+1 (mod 256)
j = j+s_i (mod 256)
Exchange s_i and s_j
k = s_i + s_j (mod 256)
```

RC4 has a variable key-length The random number that is now output is s_k. After each feedback a byte is output, which Alice can use for XOR'ing with the plaintext (and Bob for XOR'ing with the key text).

The key length of RC4 is variable, and can vary between one and 2,048 bits (a multiple of 8 works best). It is most sensible to have a key length of 128 or 256 bits. In practice, 40 bits are frequently used (this is of course not secure, but did meet the US export regulations, valid until just recently). The seed for the number sequence is calculated from the key: for this, the number sequence is initialised with $s_0=0$, $s_1=1, s_2=2, ..., s_{255}=255$. In addition, the key is written byte-wise in another number sequence $k_0, k_1, k_2, ..., k_{255}$ (for a key length of 2,048 bits this fits exactly). If the key length is shorter than 2,048 bits, then it is written several times, one after the other. Before the encryption can begin, the following algorithm is worked out:

```
for i:=0 to 255
    j:=j+s_i+k_i (mod 256)
    exchange s_i und s_j
```

Even the key transformation is simple with RC4

This completes the key transformation for RC4 – it could hardly be any simpler.

Properties of RC4

The RC4 algorithm is, without doubt, the work of a genius. It is not only remarkably simple, but also extremely fast. The encryption speed is about ten times faster than DES.

The security of RC4 is also exceptionally high. Weaknesses worth mentioning have not come to light as yet, despite the simple way in which it works (with the proviso that a key of sufficient length is used).

9.4.2 A5

A5 is used in GSM mobile phones

Another important stream cipher bears the name **A5**. This is an encryption algorithm that is used all over the world to encrypt transmissions from mobile phones to the nearest Base Transceiver Station (i.e. the stretch covered by radio-waves). That it makes good sense to apply encryption in mobile phone communication you have already discovered in Section 3.2.5. The GSM Standard – and hence A5 – applies to all major British mobile telephone networks.

How A5 works

The A5 algorithm appeared in the mid-1980s, along with the GSM standard at the European Telecommunications Standards Institute (ETSI). Current literature contains no clues as to who the developers are. As with RC4, the working method of A5 was initially kept secret. Over time, several details about the modus operandi were made public, and the whole algorithm has been known for some years now.

A5 is based on LFSRs

A5 is a stream cipher that is based on LFSRs (see Section 9.3.2). Three LFSRs are used, and these are 19, 22 and 23 bits long. The variables that are adopted in the feedback function are illustrated in Figure 9.5. The random sequence with which Alice can encrypt her message comes from the output bits of the three LFSRs being XOR'd with each other. When a random bit is generated, all three LFSRs are not necessarily shifted. Instead, each LFSR is shifted only when its related variable (**clocking tap**) has a certain value. Clocking taps are located around the centre of the respective LFSRs (the positions are fixed precisely, see Figure 9.5). If there are more ones than zeros in the three clocking taps, the LFSRs whose clocking taps have the value 1 are shifted. If there are more zeros in the clocking taps, then similarly the LFSRs with the respective clocking tap value of zero are shifted. In this way, at least two LFSRs are always shifted per random bit.

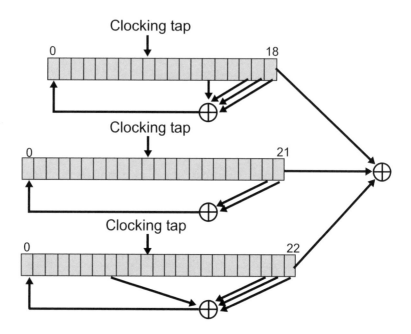

Figure 9.5 Working method of the A5 encryption procedure. There are three LFSRs whose output is combined with the plaintext. It is now known that this is a very weak procedure.

The key length of A5 is 64 bits. Following a particular process, these 64 bits generate the start values of the three LFSRs. Before the cipher outputs any random bits, several 'warm-up rounds' are carried out, so that the key cannot be derived from the random sequence.

There are two variants of A5   The method described here is known as A5/1. It is used mainly in Europe. In addition there is the weaker Version A5/2, which is used in Australia, for example. A5/2 has a fourth LFSR that controls the shifting of the other three LFSRs.

A5 security

A5 is not particularly secure   A5 is fast (especially in hardware) and the way in which it works is very simple. Is A5 therefore a serious alternative to DES, IDEA and RC4? No, because A5 is downright insecure. As more knowledge was acquired over the years about how A5 worked, the clearer it became that A5 is not the answer. In principle, the idea of three LFSRs did not turn out to be wrong. However, the developers of A5 have obviously not chosen the optimal lengths and tap variables. The very style and manner of these faults lead one to suspect that the developers knew what they were doing and that the intention with A5 was to establish a crackable algorithm for use with millions of mobile phones.

There are several disturbing cryptanalysis results that have been published over the past few years concerning A5 [LuWeZe]. The most spectacular result comes from Biryukov, Shamir and Wagner [BiShWa]. They describe a method with which it is possible to derive the key inside one second using a known-plaintext attack on a PC. Apart from extremely comprehensive preliminary calculations, the plaintext and key text are also required, which are produced in the first two minutes of a phone conversation. The level of A5 security is worlds apart from that of other modern crypto procedures described in this book.

The security of A5/2 looks even worse. This method is obviously more of a joke than an encryption algorithm. According to cryptanalysis outcomes of recent years, the effective key length of A5/2 is about 17 bits. A brute force key search would be child's play.

9.4.3 Other stream ciphers

There are yet more stream ciphers

Of course, there are still more stream ciphers than I can deal with at this point. The stream cipher SEAL, for example, is a procedure that is approximately as fast and secure as RC4. A stream cipher was also the method that is used by the compression software Winzip (and compatible programs). Winzip, while being widely used for data compression, does, however, offer a password option. If this is activated, the aforementioned stream cipher (which does not have a special name) is used for encryption. Unfortunately, the procedure has proved to be very insecure.

9.5 Prime number generators

The generation of prime numbers is very important in cryptology

If Alice generates an RSA key pair, she needs two prime numbers (for algorithms based on the discrete logarithm, prime numbers are also needed, but need not be kept secret, nor be able to be used simultaneously by a group of users). Alice must also be in a position to generate two large prime numbers, which are so random that Mallory cannot guess them.

At this point, two questions become pertinent: first, whether a 'prime number generator' exists at all, with which Alice can generate her prime numbers, and second, whether there are enough prime numbers to make it sufficiently difficult for Mallory to guess them.

Are there enough prime numbers?

There are enough prime numbers

As you may be aware, there is an endless supply of prime numbers. This doesn't help to answer the second question, however, because Alice actually needs a prime number of fixed length (say 512 bits). The number of 512-bit primes is limited, of course. This is no cause for worry, however: there are 10^{50} prime numbers 512 bits long, and the number increases in proportion to the bit length. At 1,024 bits there are around 10^{100} primes. It must be very clear from this that Mallory hasn't the slightest chance of guessing a randomly selected prime number.

How a random prime number is generated

Prime number generators use random generators

Since there is no lack of prime numbers, the question now arises – how can Alice generate a random prime number? Here again there are enough publications on this subject to fill a whole book. We must make do here with a bare minimum. This embraces the fact that all current prime number generators work on the same principle: first a random number is generated, then it is tested with a probabilistic algorithm to see if it is prime. If not, a new random number is generated and also tested. This procedure is repeated until a prime number is eventually found. 'Probabilistic' means here that the algorithm gives an incorrect result in exceptional cases, and judges a number to be prime when it is in fact not. The probability of such exceptions occurring can be made optionally small through the choice of suitable parameters (the cost climbs, however, with falling probability). A good algorithm, which can be used to determine whether a number is prime or not, will reduce the probability of exceptions while holding down the effort to an acceptable level.

Of course, it would be better to use a non-probabilistic algorithm for testing primes. However, all known methods for this are so onerous that a probabilistic method is inevitably the best choice.

The Rabin–Miller procedure

The Rabin–Miller procedure is the most important in the generation of prime numbers

The most important procedure by far for generating prime numbers is the Rabin–Miller procedure. This works on the principle described above. It uses a very effective probabilistic prime number test and is easy to implement. How the procedure works is described in standard works such as [Schn96] and [MeOoVa].

Part 3

Advanced cryptography

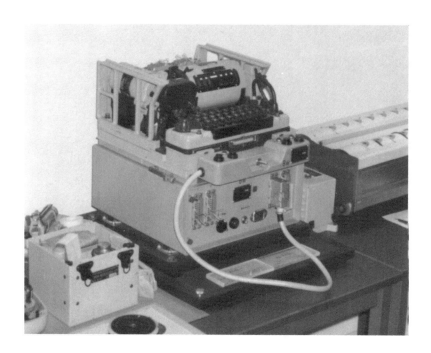

Coding Machine KL-7, Madel ca. 1950
(from the IT-Security Teaching & Study Collection of the BSI)

Standardisation in cryptography

The nice thing about standards is that you have so many to choose from. Furthermore, if you do not like any of them, you can just wait for next year's model.
ANDREW S. TANENBAUM [TANENB]

Key experience no. 10
Out of the more than 3000 RFCs that exist today, there are some that were published on 1 April. RFC 1149, for example, which is concerned with the transfer of IP-packets in transport aircraft. Equally useful is RFC 2324 in which the Hypertext Coffee Pot Control Protocol (HTCPCP) is described. RFC 2325 covers the management of coffee machines.

The use of cryptography must be standardised

Alice would like to invite Bob to the cinema by e-mail. She encrypts this invitation with a secure encryption algorithm (let's assume she uses a hybrid procedure using RSA and Triple-DES). Mallory, who as always tries to spy on the message, is out of luck – he can't decrypt the message. Is Bob and Alice's visit to the cinema secure? No, because although Alice and Bob have agreed on which crypto procedure to use, they have not agreed on details such as the message format. Bob is now scratching his head over what the encrypted Triple-DES key and the encrypted message in the e-mail are. He is equally unaware that Alice converted the Triple-DES key into a number before applying an RSA encryption. While Alice waits outside the cinema, Bob is still tearing his hair out, trying to read her e-mail.

10.1 Standards

Standards are indispensable

Bob's failure to decrypt Alice's e-mail would have been avoided if they had agreed beforehand not only on the encryption algorithm, but also on details such as the message and number formats. This axiom applies even more if, instead of just Bob and Alice, millions of Internet users are involved. If cryptography is to be adopted for general use, uniform **standards** (norms) will have to be agreed, and adhered to universally. Who develops such standards, and everything else worth knowing about standards in cryptology, you will learn in this chapter.

10.1.1 Standardisation bodies

The importance of standards extends far beyond cryptography and the Internet. Standards are always demanded whenever uniformity will bring advantages. By virtue of this, there are innumerable groups (standardisation bodies) developing standards for every conceivable thing. Many of these are national authorities or represent industrial groups. In the following we take a look at the most important of the standards bodies.

International Organisation for Standardisation (ISO)

The ISO is an important standards organisation

Indisputably, the most important standardisation organisation in the world is the International Organisation for Standardisation (ISO). This issues standards for just about everything that can be standardised. Covering such diverse things as the tear-resistance of condoms, the dimensions of freight containers or quality control in management (ISO 9000), the ISO bodies have compiled some 11,000 standards. The standardisation authorities of all the main countries belong to the ISO, including the Deutsche Institut für Normung (DIN) and the American National Standards Institute (ANSI). Many standards created by industrial organisations have been adopted in part by the ISO. For us, the most important ISO standard is the ISO OSI Layer model, which will be discussed in Chapter 21.

Standardisation of computer networks

The following organisations are involved with standards for computer networks.

- The ITU (International Telecommunication Union) is the international organisation of the telephone companies. The ITU-T (formerly the CCITT) department is responsible for telecommunications standards. The X.509 Standard, which will be described later in detail, stems from this body.

Standards are developed by various organisations

- ETSI (European Telecommunications Standards Institute) is a European standards organisation that develops standards for telecommunications. The GSM Standard stems from the ETSI.

- The IEEE (Institute of Electrical and Electronics Engineers (say 'I-triple-E') is a worldwide engineering confederation that also issues standards. To us, the IEEE 802.3 (Ethernet, Section 3.2.2) and IEEE P1363 (Public key algorithm, Section 10.5) standards are the most important.

- The National Institute of Standards and Technology (NIST) belongs to the US Department of Commerce. The Data Encryption Standard (DES), the Digital Signature Standard (DSS) and the Secure Hash Standard (SHS) stem from this authority.

- The IETF and the World Wide Web Consortium also develop standards. This will be discussed in the next section.

10.1.2 Standardisation on the Internet

The standardisation body for the Internet is the IETF

The above-named organisations all play a role in the Internet. However, the Internet has its own ways and means of standardisation, which have been reformed and now operate on a more formal basis than they did previously.

IETF

The IETF publishes RFCs

The main focus of attention is the Internet Engineering Task Force (IETF), which is divided up into eight work areas: Applications, Internet, Operations and Management, Routing, Security, Sub-IP, Transport, and User Services. The IETF is a large open international community of network designers, operators, vendors, and researchers. It meets at regular intervals and the members otherwise communicate by e-mail and mailing lists. When the need for a standard to be developed arises, a working group is set up in the relevant work area to draw up an **Internet Draft**, a sort of standard proposal. The Internet Engineering Steering Group (IESG) must now concur with the Internet Draft, following which, the Internet Draft becomes a Request for Comment (**RFC**). The first stage of an RFC is the Proposed Standard. If, after six months, two independent implementations of the RFC are in existence, the Internet Engineering Steering Group then elevates the RFC from a Proposed Standard to a Draft Standard. After further tests through the IESG, the RFC finally becomes an official standard. Note that the term RFC is also used to label closed standards.

Not every RFC is a standard

Not all RFCs are standards or potential standards. Some RFCs define specific procedures or provide information on a given subject. RFCs are numbered sequentially; currently they number around 3,000. Many of these are made redundant by later RFCs and are no longer of interest. The RFCs and Internet Drafts of interest for us are, of course, those concerned with cryptography.

World Wide Web Consortium

The W3C develops W3C standards

As well as the IETF, the **World Wide Web Consortium (W3C)** also develops standards for the World Wide Web. In contrast to the IETF, the W3C is an industrial association and its meetings are not open to anyone who might be interested, but only to representatives of the member companies. The W3C therefore works rather more effectively and can develop standards more quickly. W3C standards often undergo the procedure described above, and so can become official Internet Standards.

10.2 Standards in the real world

A standard is only a piece of paper

When it comes right down to it, a standard is only a piece of paper. Whether a standard prevails or not depends on many things, but only rarely on the standards body. As a result, many standards turn out to be prone to error or are too complicated. Many standards appear too early, some too late, and many fail simply because another standard has already established itself. Business practical politics can also come into it: when a company rules the market, it can often succeed in imposing its own standards, to which others must adhere (while grinding their teeth perhaps). In short: there are standards that prevail, and others that do not. A successful standard becomes a bible: anyone who wants to sell his or her product must observe it to the letter. A standard that does not prevail is just a paper tiger, not worth the paper on which it is printed. Standardisation bodies, organisations, and working practices are not therefore so important for us. What is important is what is successful. Almost all successful cryptographic standards relevant to the Internet are covered in this book.

10.3 What you ought to know about standards

Before we look at some examples of standards, at this point I would like to consider some important aspects of standards themselves.

Standard versions

There are often
standards in several
versions

As with software, many standards are never completed. Instead, every now and again a new version appears, which corrects some deficit or other in the old version. One problem here, of course, is that the new standard must be compatible with the old. Not least for this reason, as time passes many standards grow into monster works of several hundred pages.

OIDs

It often happens that different standards use the same procedures or objects. Because of this, the ISO has brought in the so-called **OID** (Object Identifier). An OID is a unique identifier (actually a string of numbers) denoting a procedure or object, which ideally denotes the same thing in all standards worldwide. OIDs have a hierarchical structure. All Internet IDs, for example, begin with the numbers 1.3.6.1 because the ISO has assigned this sequence to the Internet controlling organisation IANA. In the field of Internet security, all OIDs start with 1.3.6.1.5.

OIDs denote
standardised objects

Of course, OIDS are also important in cryptography. There are numerous OIDs that denote crypto algorithms. If an algorithm can be used with different key lengths, or in different modes, then there are normally several OIDs. Incidentally, most crypto OIDS do not begin with the Internet security sequence 1.3.5.1.5 since they are also used in other areas. For example, the OID for RC4 is 1.2.840.113549.3.4. The sequence 1.2.840.113549 is the start of all OIDs applied for by the company RSA Security.

10.4 PKCS standards

There are currently
13 PKCS standards

You are going to meet cryptography standards aplenty in this book. As a starter I would like to introduce you now to a family of standards which will be frequently mentioned: the **Public Key Cryptography Standards (PKCS)**. When considering crypto standards it makes sense to begin with these because the formats described in them are used by numerous other standards, which I have not yet discussed in this book. The PKCS standards are one of a series that were developed by RSA Security. The standards mainly specify the data formats for various areas of public key cryptography. The series came into being in 1991, and has been continually expanded ever since. You can read about the current standards on the RSA Web site (http://www.rsa.com).

PKCS is a series of crypto standards

At the moment, the series consists of standards PKCS#1 to PKCS#15. PKCS#2 and PKCS#4 have been incorporated in PKCS#1. There are currently 13 PKCS standards. Despite the name, PKCS standards do not only cover asymmetrical algorithms. Some of them also give specifications for symmetrical algorithms. The various PKCS standards are independent of each other. The PKCS series can therefore be regarded as a cryptographic toolbox, offering formats and algorithms for many basic problems.

PKCS standards are so important that I shall treat them all individually. In the next section I shall begin with some of the less relevant and then investigate the important PKCS#7 standard. The remaining PKCS standards will be met in later chapters in the appropriate settings.

10.4.1 PKCS#3, PKCS#9 and PKCS#14

To begin, I shall introduce some of the simpler or less important standards:

PKCS#3, PKCS#9 and PKCS#14 are less important

- **PKCS#3** describes a method for the implementation of the Diffie–Hellman Key Agreement [PKCS#3]. This is one of the simpler PKCS standards. It mainly describes the data formats and methods for representing keys. It also specifies an OID for the Diffie–Hellman key exchange to PKCS#3. The OID is 1.2.840.113549.3.

- **PKCS#9** describes extensions to PKCS#6, PKCS#7 and PKCS#8 [PKCS#9].

- **PKCS#14** is currently in development and concerns pseudo-random generation [PKCS#14].

10.4.2 PKCS#7 Cryptographic Message Syntax Standard

Now we want to examine one of the most important PKCS standards in detail: PKCS#7. This standard defines a general syntax for messages that include cryptographic enhancements such as digital signatures and encryption, as used in Alice's messages to Bob [PKCS#7]. A PKCS#7 message can hold six types of content. The content type is dependent on whether the message is encrypted, signed or hashed.

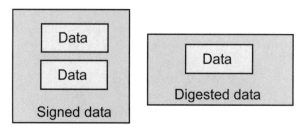

Enveloped data

Figure 10.1 PCKS#7 describes a recursive format for encrypted, signed and hashed data. In this diagram a signed data unit and a digested data unit are contained within an encrypted unit.

PKCS#7 is set up recursively. This means that some of the data types anticipate a format which itself contains a PKCS#7 message. The six types of content are set out in the following:

Content type: Data

This content type describes a simple format for data that is neither encrypted, nor signed, nor hashed. Through this content type, PKCS#7 can admit messages that have not been subjected to cryptography.

Content type: Signed data

PKCS#7 standardises the format of messages to which cryptography has been applied

This content type standardises the format for a signed message. Only the hash result is signed (as usual) and not the whole message. RSA is used as the signature algorithm. The signature format corresponds to the PKCS#1 standard (see Section 11.2.1). The message to be signed is itself a PKCS#7 message. Apart from this message, the PKCS#7 format provides other information that is also to be signed. This includes the OID of the applied cryptographic hash function and of the signature algorithm, as well as a version number (the current PKCS#7 version is 1.5) and information about the digital certificate of whoever is signing it (see Chapter 16). This additional information makes it much easier for Bob to verify Alice's signature – how was he supposed to verify a signature without knowing the applied algorithm?!

Content type: Enveloped data

PKCS#7 includes a digital envelope

This content type standardises a format for data to which a hybrid procedure has been applied (see Section 6.7). The format anticipates a message that has been encrypted with a symmetric algorithm. The secret key used is encrypted with the receiver's public key, and the resulting encrypted key becomes a component of the format. The encrypted message itself is again a PKCS#7 message. A message in this format is also called a **digital envelope**.

Content type: Signed and enveloped data

This content type provides a format for a signed message which is also encrypted with a hybrid method. The message itself is once again a PKCS#7 message.

Content type: Digested data

This content type specifies a format for a message to which a cryptographic hash function has been applied. The message itself is once again a PKCS#7 message.

Content type: Encrypted data

PKCS#7 also allows for encrypted data

This content type describes a format for a message that has been encrypted with a symmetric algorithm. The message itself is once again a PKCS#7 message.

Application of PKCS#7

As you can see, apart from the first, all content types anticipate a format which itself contains a PKCS#7 message. If Alice wants to apply PKCS#7, she needs first of all a message to which she can give the data content type. She can then use this message for any other content type and thus obtain a new PKCS#7 message. Through the recursive structure of PKCS#7 she can now use this again for another content type.

10.5 IEEE P1363

P1363 offers a cryptographic tool chest

Along with the PKCS standards, another set of standards is being established that also specifies formats and basic procedures for public key cryptography: IEEE P1363, or **P1363** for short. Like PKCS, P1363 is also a cryptographic toolbox, from which a user can help himself when implementing crypto procedures. In contrast to PKCS, P1363 is clearly less RSA-heavy (which is hardly surprising, since PKCS standards are from the company RSA Security after all). There is therefore more room in P1363 for algorithms like DSA and Diffie–Hellman. The development of P1363 began in 1994. In 1997, P1363a was brought into being. The aim here was to deal with areas of public key cryptography that were already established in P1363, so as to be able to finalise a first version within a few years. This plan seems to have been successful: following a first draft at the start of 1999, further drafts have been published which allow hope of an early finalisation of the standard. P1363a, on the other hand, is concerned with areas in which a speedy standardisation does not seem possible. A schedule for the coming years is in course of development.

Up to now, P1363 has been far less important than PKCS. However, it is a very interesting standard that could gain a lot more importance as the years go by. In this book, P1363 will be investigated in Sections 11.2 and 14.3.2.

Block cipher modes of operation and data transformation for asymmetrical algorithms

It does no harm if the strong grow stronger.
JOHANN WOLFGANG VON GOETHE

Key experience no. 11
In the 16th century, Mary Queen of Scots was imprisoned by Queen Elizabeth. Despite her guards, she succeeded in exchanging several encoded messages with her supporters. The letters fell into the hands of Sir Francis Walsingham, Private Secretary to the queen, whose code breakers were able to decipher them. One encoded message, in which Mary Stuart gave her assent to a plot against Elizabeth, finally sealed her fate: Elizabeth had her beheaded. Even today, it has not been established that the fateful message was actually genuine.

Supplements are intended to improve crypto procedures The crypto methods that I have introduced in this book so far are counted as secure and suitable for very different purposes. As you will see in this chapter, however, in practice there are many situations in which crypto procedures show weaknesses. These can be gaps in security, but can also be drawbacks of a different kind. To alleviate this problem, cryptographers have given consideration to various supplements, which are intended to make existing crypto procedures more secure, and to resolve other practical problems. These supplements, which play an important part in the Internet, are dealt with in this chapter.

11.1 Block cipher modes of operation

For Alice and Bob, the encryption of a message with a symmetric algorithm (DES, for example, or IDEA) is one of the easiest exercises. But even for this simple process there are several variants, all of which have their pros and cons. Such a variant is called a **mode of operation**. The four most important modes of operation for symmetrical algorithms are examined in this section. These observations of course apply mostly only for block ciphers. For stream ciphers there are significantly fewer possible modes, which will be briefly examined at the end of the section.

In the following, we always start out from a block cipher that processes blocks of 64 bits (such as IDEA or DES). However, similar forms of the mode of operation also apply to all other block lengths.

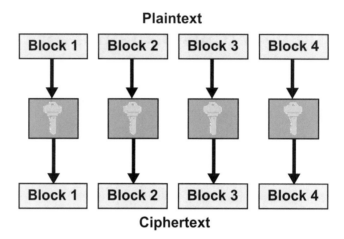

Figure 11.1 In ECB mode every plaintext block is encrypted independently of the others. This makes ECB the simplest mode of operation.

11.1.1 Electronic Codebook Mode

ECB is the simplest mode of operation

When using symmetric encryption algorithms such as DES or IDEA, we have previously assumed the following process: when Alice encrypts a message to Bob, she divides it into blocks 64 bits long and applies the algorithm to each block individually. This simplest of all modes of operation is called **Electronic Codebook Mode** (ECB or ECB mode).

The name therefore suggests that in order for Alice to encrypt a message, she could, in theory, prepare a codebook in which all possible plaintext blocks (i.e. 2^{64} for DES or IDEA) are listed with their corresponding ciphertext blocks. This kind of codebook would certainly be rather costly, since every key must have its own book. However, in theory it is possible.

Drawbacks to the ECB mode

ECB mode has several drawbacks

Of course, the cryptographers of this world discovered disadvantages in ECB mode a long time ago. The fact that this mode of operation theoretically allows frequency analysis is certainly not one of them – unless Alice and Bob encrypt hundreds of millions of gigabytes without ever changing the key. Of much greater practical relevance is the fact that Mallory can remove blocks from a message encrypted in this way, or change their sequence. He can also mix up blocks from different messages, provided the same key was used in each case.

Another drawback is that identical blocks are always encrypted identically. This is a drawback when, for example, lists of passwords are encrypted (as in Unix and Windows NT). If Alice's encrypted password looks the same to another user as it does to herself, she knows that this is the same password.

Another problem with ECB mode occurs when the data that Alice wants to encrypt is supplied in small units (say byte by byte). Alice then always has to wait for a 64-bit buffer to be filled before she can encrypt it. In some cases, this can be a drawback.

Plaintext

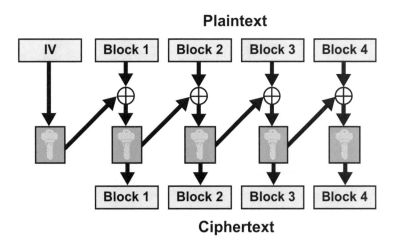

Ciphertext

Figure 11.2 In CBC mode each plaintext block is combined with the preceding ciphertext block.

11.1.2 Cipher Block Chaining Mode

One problem with Electronic Codebook Mode is that the same plaintext blocks are always encrypted into the same ciphertext blocks using the same key. This can easily be prevented by Alice adding the existing ciphertext block to the next plaintext block after encrypting a plaintext block (i.e. a bit-by-bit XOR-ing). This mode of operation is called **Cipher Block Chaining Mode** (CBC).

An initialisation vector is needed for CBC mode

When decrypting, after decrypting a block Bob must correspondingly subtract the previous ciphertext block bit by bit. If Alice encrypts her data in CBC mode, then her message can contain any number of identical blocks without Mallory noticing this in the ciphertext. So that the first plaintext block of a message can be combined with a ciphertext block prior to encryption, CBC mode uses a dummy block for the first encryption. This dummy block is called the **initialisation vector** (IV), which does not need to be kept secret.

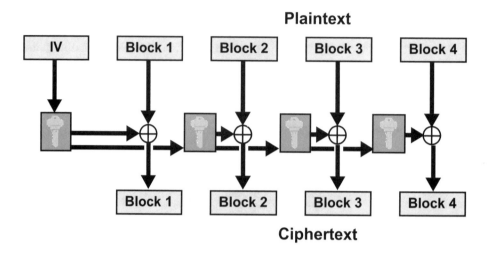

Figure 11.3 In CBC mode each plaintext block is linked to the previous ciphertext block.

11.1.3 Output Feedback Mode

OFB mode works like a stream cipher

Neither ECB nor CBC solves the problem that Alice always needs a whole 64-bit block before encryption can begin. Sometimes, however, it is necessary to encrypt data in smaller bundles. Encryption in small morsels is a strength of stream ciphers (see Section 9.4). Some stream ciphers can even encrypt bit by bit.

One obvious idea would be for Alice to use a block cipher such as DES in the same way as a stream cipher. This mode of operation of a block cipher is known as the **Output Feedback Mode** (OFB). For an OFB encryption, Alice needs an initial value (also known as the initialisation vector) in the form of a 64-bit block, which is stored in a 64-bit register. The value stored in the register is now encrypted any desired number of times using the block cipher as an iteration function, in which the result of each encryption replaces the contents of the register. After each encryption of the register, Alice uses a certain number of bits (we shall call this number b, which is usually smaller than the block length) in order to perform an exclusive OR addition with this and the plaintext. Those same b bits are then pushed into the register, causing b bits to be pushed out of the end of the register. The next encryption can now begin.

OFB mode wastes resources

One drawback of OFB mode is, or course, that as a rule a large part of the effort that goes into encryption is wasted. For each encryption process, 64 bits of register content but only b bits of plaintext are encrypted. In return, however, OFB mode is very fast if the register is encrypted in advance. If this is done, the encryption of the plaintext only comprises an Exclusive-Or connection.

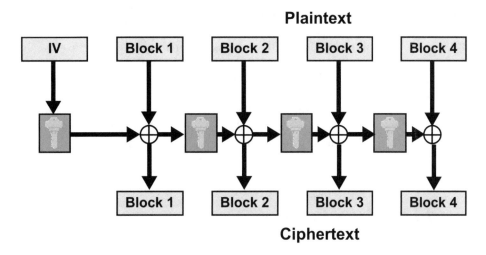

Figure 11.4 In CFB mode the combination of a plaintext block and an intermediate result produces a ciphertext block and an intermediate result for a new block.

11.1.4 Cipher Feedback Mode

The last mode of operation we will now look at is **Cipher Feedback Mode** (CFB). This mode of operation works in the same way as the OFB mode, except that after encryption of the register, the result of the Exclusive-Or connection (i.e. the ciphertext block of length b) is pushed into the register. In OFB mode, on the other hand, the register content of length b, which was used for the Exclusive-Or connection, is used. Of course, the CFB also needs an initialisation vector.

An advantage of CFB mode is that errors, which Mallory causes by altering the ciphertext, are more easily discovered.

11.1.5 The importance of modes of operation

Modes of operation play an important role

Although there are other modes of operation for block ciphers, in practice only the four modes described above are relevant. These four modes are important. As regards the Internet, the simplest mode of operation – ECB mode – is only rarely used. In contrast, CFB mode is very popular. As for Alice and Bob, the different modes of operation mean that they have to agree on which mode as well as on which algorithm they will use. For this reason, for each of the current block ciphers there are several OIDs – one for each specific mode of operation. Along with the OID, for CBC, CFB and OFB the generation of the initialisation vector is also specified.

Incidentally, modes of operation are not so important for stream ciphers. As a rule, because of their design, stream ciphers work in OFB mode. Many could also be used in CFB mode. However, ECB and CBC modes make no sense for stream ciphers.

11.2 Data transformation for the RSA algorithm

Preparing the data for the RSA algorithm is wise

The following also holds true for asymmetrical algorithms: each algorithm can be used in different variant forms. These variants are even more important than the operating modes of block ciphers because, if wrongly implemented, asymmetrical algorithms very quickly demonstrate gaps in security. Since with asymmetrical algorithms the differences lie mostly in the transformation of the data rather than in the application of the algorithm, we shall address **data transformation** – especially data transformation for the RSA algorithm, as described in the **PKCS#1 standard**. Both [PKCS#1] and [JohMat] contain interesting information on this topic. The P1363 standard also deals with the subject of data transformation for asymmetrical algorithms, covering RSA and others.

11.2.1 The PKCS#1 standard

PKCS#1 standardises methods for data transformation

The PKCS#1 standard is one of the 15 PKCS standards discussed in Section 10.4. This standard covers how the RSA algorithm is used in practice. Firstly, it defines how a sequence of bytes is interpreted as a natural number. This definition is necessary because plaintext and ciphertext must always be presented as natural numbers for the RSA algorithm. Lastly, PKCS#1 describes the well-known operation of the RSA algorithm, including possible error messages (e.g. 'message representative out of range', if the plaintext is too long.) On top of this, PKCS#1 contains formats for public and private RSA keys, as well as various OIDs.

There are two versions of PKCS#1

The most interesting parts of PKCS#1 are the descriptions of the procedures for data transformation. We shall examine these procedures in detail in the following. In total, there are four data transformation procedures in PKCS#1: in version 1 of the standard one procedure is described for digital signatures, and one for encryption. Version 2 describes new procedures intended to replace those of version 1. For compatibility, however, version 2 also retains the version 1 procedures.

11.2.2 Data transformation for encryption

An RSA encryption without data transformation has drawbacks

If Alice wants to encrypt a plaintext using RSA (e.g. the key for a symmetric algorithm), she can make matters easy for herself and encrypt the unaltered plaintext. However, this entails several problems:

- If we assume that the plaintext is a random number (as is the case with a secret key), then after encryption it cannot be determined whether the result of the encryption truly represents the plaintext. If Bob, the receiver of the message, accidentally uses the wrong key, he obtains a false result without knowing it. The same happens if the ciphertext is changed during transfer.

PKCS#1 prevents a low-exponent attack

- As we know from Section 6.5.1, RSA encryption proceeds very speedily if Alice uses a small exponent (the numbers 3 and 17 are most suitable for this). However, if Alice encrypts the same text with a small exponent on several occasions (with several public keys), Mallory can begin a low-exponent attack. If Alice encrypts all her plaintexts without changing them, the danger is of course increased.

- From Section 7.2 you should be aware that Mallory can present a message for RSA encryption to Bob and thereby obtain an RSA signature (mathematically, an RSA encryption and RSA signature are seen as the same thing).

As you see, it is worth while for Alice to prepare the data that she encrypts with the RSA algorithm in advance.

Transformation for encryption according to PKCS#1 version 1

PKCS#1 extends the RSA plaintext What Alice can do about the first two of the above problems is not difficult to guess. To resolve the first problem, before encryption she must give the plaintext an identifier, which enables Bob to recognise that it is actually a permitted plaintext. For the second problem, it helps if, prior to encryption, she also gives the plaintext a random number. The first version of the PKCS#1 standard allows for the latter form of transformation.

The prepared plaintext has the following components, according to PKCS#1:

1. The first byte of the prepared plaintext always has the value 00000010. This is the identifier by means of which, after encryption, Bob can establish that it is the correct plaintext.

2. The first byte is followed by any number of random bytes, other than null. Alice should choose different random bytes for each encryption process. This ensures that the prepared plaintexts differ from each other, even when the original plaintexts are identical.

3. The random bytes are followed by a byte with the value 00000000. This byte separates the random bytes from the following part.

4. The last part is the original plaintext.

The plaintext can be recognised as such After Bob has decrypted the message from Alice, he first checks whether the first byte has the value 00000010. If so, he knows that it is a prepared plaintext. Then he looks for the first byte with the value 00000000. Everything that follows this is the original plaintext.

In 1998, cryptographer Daniel Bleichenbacher discovered a weak spot in data transformation according to PKCS#1 version 1. Mallory can use this weak spot for an attack of the **side-channel attack** family (see Section 15.6.1). Under certain circumstances, Mallory can use it to decrypt a message that Bob has encrypted with Alice's public key. The aforementioned side-channel attack anticipates that Mallory changes the message encrypted by Bob using a certain method and thereby produces in total around a million altered messages. He sends these messages to Alice. If Alice decrypts each of the messages and in each case Mallory learns whether the format of the decrypted message is correct, he can then, using the procedure described by Bleichenbacher, reconstruct the genuine plaintext. Of course this attack is not always realistic. In addition, Mallory only receives the plaintext (not the key, however). Nevertheless, this weakness was sufficient grounds for improving the data transformation process of the PKCS#1 standard.

Data transformation for encryption to PKCS#1 version 2

The procedure described for data transformation for RSA encryption prevents the most important attack possibilities. However, there are two problems:

- Since each prepared message begins with a byte containing 00000010, Mallory can mount a known-plaintext attack (but only to a certain extent, since he still doesn't know the whole message).

- If Mallory can influence the random bytes, he can use a chosen-plaintext attack (again only to a certain extent, because he can influence only a part of the prepared message).

To eliminate these weaknesses, version 2 of PKCS#1 requires a more comprehensive transformation for RSA encryption. This is known as **OAEP encoding** (the acronym stands for Optimal Asymmetric Encryption Padding), and also plays a part in the P1363 standard. In PKCS#1v2 it is recommended, in the future, to implement the OAEP encoding, whereby an implementation conforming to PKCS#1 must still also support the original method according to PKCS#1v1. The OAEP encoding requires that Alice does not simply write her random bytes between the identifier and the plaintext. Instead, she must take the random bytes (normally 32 bits) as the initialisation vector for a pseudo-random generator (see Section 9.2). In this way she generates a random sequence with which the plaintext is XOR'd.

Through masking bits can no longer be predicted
The result is called masked plaintext, the process being known as **masking**. Masking is similar to one-time-pad and results in the masked plaintext being unpredictable for Mallory. The initialisation vector for the random generator is placed before the masked plaintext. This is itself also masked, however, whereby the masked plaintext forms the initialisation vector.

The masking can easily be reversed
Since Bob knows the length of the masked initialisation vector, he can easily re-create the initialisation vector and then the plaintext. From the identifier he knows that it is a valid plaintext.

The advantage of OAEP encoding lies in the fact that Mallory cannot know or influence a single bit of the prepared plaintext, even if he can trick Alice into taking a plaintext. The initialisation vector chosen by Alice, and the transformation, ensure that Alice ultimately encrypts a random value.

11.2.3 Data transformation for signatures

Data transformation is also worthwhile for signatures

For RSA signatures, Alice can also simplify things if she takes the text to be signed, applies a cryptographic hash function, and finally signs the hash result. Of course, it makes sense here if Alice appends some additional data to the message (such as the OID of the algorithm being used), to be included in the hash result. Additions of this type are standardised, for example, in PKCS#7 (see Section 10.4.2) and need not be examined here. Of much more interest is what Alice does with the hash result. If she signs this without alteration, then again two problems arise:

- If the message hash result does not agree with the result of the decryption with Alice's public RSA key, Bob knows that the digital signature is wrong. However, he does not know whether the hash result has a false signature or a genuine one. For signatures, it is also better if the hash result to be signed is a random one.

- For this reason, PKCS#1 also specifies data transformation methods for digital signatures. Here it should be noted that the typical length of a hash result is 160 bits, but RSA usually encrypts data blocks of length 768, 1,024 or 2,048 bits (the length of a data block corresponds to the key length). For this reason a PKCS#1 transformation consists mainly of an extension of the hash result.

Transformation for signing according to PKCS#1 version 1

The transformation of a hash result according to version 1 of PKCS#1 is very simple. The format consists of four parts:

Data transformation to PKCS#1 version 1 is very simple

- The first byte of the prepared hash result always has the value 1. This ensures that the prepared hash result is smaller than the modulus.

- This is followed by as many bytes with the value 255 as are necessary to make the total length of the prepared hash result correspond to that of the modulus.

- There is then a byte with null content.

- The fourth part consists of the hash result and an OID of the hash algorithm.

    If, after using Alice's public key on a signature, Bob gets a value that does not correspond to the described syntax, he knows immediately that it cannot be a correct signature. This solves the first of the two problems mentioned at the start of this sub-section.

Transformation for signing in accordance with PKCS#1 version 2

Version 2 of PKCS#1 allows for masking of digital signatures

The drawback to the described procedure is of course that the data structure is immediately evident. To avoid reaction attacks, version 2 of PKCS#1 uses a masking function, as in the transformation for encryption.

By this means a random value (salt) is included in the hash result in addition to the message. The salt is also part of a data block that also contains a block of null bytes, which extends the prepared message to the length of the key. The hash result is used as the initialisation vector for the masking function. As a consequence of the masking, Mallory does not know a single bit of the prepared plaintext beforehand.

11.2.4 Transformation for other asymmetrical algorithms

Data transformation is less important for DLSSs

Data transformation is less important for algorithms based on the discrete logarithm than it is for RSA algorithms. Diffie–Hellman needs no data transformation at all because encryption is not involved and only generates a shared key.

With signature algorithms based on the discrete logarithm (DLSSs) – such as ElGamal and DSA – the transformation of the hash result is appropriate, but not so important as it is for the RSA algorithm. The reason for this is that each signature contains a random value (see Section 7.3). This means that any two signatures are necessarily different, even when they have the same hash results. Another reason is that with current DLSSs there is no verification result that Bob can examine for a specific structure. So it avails nothing to extend the hash result by some kind of identifier. Should transformation still be desirable, however, the two algorithms described in the P1363 standard can be used [P1363].

Cryptographic protocols

Security is mortal's chiefest enemy (Macbeth, Act III, Scene 5)
WILLIAM SHAKESPEARE

Key experience no. 12
Signing a contract digitally over the Internet has its pitfalls. If one party has signed, it cannot be sure that the other party has also signed the contract. Fortunately, cryptographers already have a solution to this basic problem: contract signing. This calls for an alternating signing in stages. If one party has signed the entire contract, then the other must have at least 90% completed signing it. What a 90% signature is worth is still arguable, though.

In the previous chapters you read something about the procedures that Alice and Bob can use to encrypt their messages or to process them cryptographically in some way. You will then certainly have noticed that there are procedures designed to be applied by two or more people acting together. One example of this is the Diffie–Hellman key exchange, in which Alice and Bob send each other messages from which they then generate a secret key that Mallory cannot read.

A protocol is a series of steps that two or more parties agree upon to complete a task

So that a procedure in which several people are involved can work, a plan of ordered execution is needed, to which all parties must adhere. Such a plan is known as a **communication protocol** (or simply just **protocol**).

12.1 Protocols

Protocols have nothing to do with cryptography. A protocol is needed to let Alice and Bob communicate over a computer network. This will control who sends a specific message and when, and what meaning this has in the particular context. Alice and Bob are of course substitutes for any two people or computers; there cannot be more than two partners involved in the communication. The protocol regulates who should or must say or do something, and when.

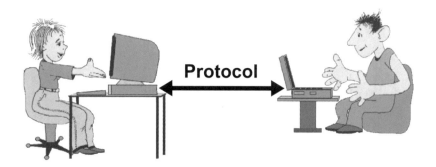

Figure 12.1 Using a suitable protocol, Alice's computer can communicate with Bob's.

12.1.1 An example

Let us now consider the example of a protocol that enables Alice to question Bob on certain matters over the telephone. It might read something like the following:

1. After Alice has dialled Bob's number, Bob lifts the receiver and answers 'Bob Offliner'.

2. Alice replies with 'Alice Onliner'.

3. Bob says 'Hello Alice!!'.

4. Alice asks one of the following questions:
   - Would you like to play tennis with me today at <Time> ?
   - Shall we go to the cinema at <Time>?
   - Shall we meet in the pizzeria at <Time>?

5. Bob replies with 'yes' or 'no'.

6. If Alice has another question, she returns to item 4, otherwise she takes her leave with 'Bye Bob'.

7. Bob takes his leave with 'Bye Alice', and both hang up.

Each step in a protocol must be defined precisely   If we imagine Alice and Bob to be computers, it is important that both use the same protocol and that both adhere to it. Because computers are infamously stupid, it would cause problems if, for example, Alice asks 'Shall we play squash at <Time>?'. This question is not anticipated in the protocol and hence Bob cannot answer.

12.1.2 Roughly specified protocols

A roughly specified protocol is inadequate for implementation   In many cases, a protocol at the level described above will be adequate. The description took just over 10 lines. Obviously such a protocol could not be implemented without being amended, as the individual steps are not specified with sufficient precision. If a protocol is only vaguely described in this way, we speak of a **roughly specified protocol**.

Roughly specified protocols are very useful for demonstrating a plan of execution or to discover holes in one. As the basis for implementation as software they are not suitable.

12.1.3 Finely detailed protocols

Finely detailed protocols can be implemented

If a protocol is to be implemented, a much more detailed protocol specification is needed than in our example. The specification must set out, bit for bit, which pieces of data are to be transmitted under which circumstances, and what importance these have. Omissions and errors must be catered for, of course, so that Alice does not, for example, wait for Bob's answer hours after he has already hung up. A good protocol must also provide for such things as compatibility with older versions, support for standard formats, and much more.

A protocol that is so finely detailed that it can be implemented is called a **finely detailed protocol**. To meet the said requirements, a finely detailed protocol can soon fill several hundred pages. Incidentally, the terms **finely detailed protocol** and **roughly specified protocol** are terms of my own invention. I have not found any corresponding terms previously defined, although in my opinion this distinction would have been very apt.

protocol messages

In a protocol, protocol messages must be defined

The development of a finely detailed protocol requires the prior definition of a number of permitted message types (so-called **protocol messages**). A protocol message bears a resemblance to a command in a programming language and can likewise be provided with an argument. In the above protocol one could define, for instance, the protocol message 'Name(<Forename>, <Surname>', 'Greeting (<Forename>)', 'Question(<Question Number>,<Time>)', 'Answer(<yes/no>)' and 'Farewell (<Forename>)'. Our protocol would then have the following sequence of execution:

1. Bob->Alice: Name('Bob','Offliner')

2. Alice->Bob: Name('Alice','Onliner')

3. Bob->Alice: Greeting('Alice')

4. Alice->Bob: Question(1/2/3)

5. Bob->Alice: Answer('yes'/'no')

6. Alice->Bob: continue with 4 or Farewell('Bob')

7. Bob->Alice: Farewell('Alice')

Protocol messages have headers

In practice, most protocol messages still have a part in which additional information (addresses of the sender and receiver, the length of the message, and so on) is stored. This part is known as the **header**. The content relevant to the execution of the protocol (say, 'Name('Bob','Offliner')') is known as the **payload**.

Examples of finely detailed protocols

HTTP, IP and TCP are finely detailed

You will meet finely detailed protocols again in this book, especially in Chapters 21 to 28. Pertinent examples of these are the Internet protocols HTTP, IP, TCP and FTP.

12.2 Protocol properties

Since protocols cover a wide field, we must first ask ourselves what properties protocols can or must have. We are not thinking only of crypto protocols, but of protocols in general.

Perhaps the most important method of classifying protocols is the so-called OSI reference model, which will be explained in Chapter 21. In this chapter, however, I first want to introduce some attributes that are independent of this model.

12.2.1 Error tolerance

A protocol can be tolerant of errors

Unfortunately, there is something that, in practice, makes the development of protocols much more difficult: errors occur during the transmission of protocol messages. So it happens fairly frequently that a message from Alice never reaches Bob, or that a part is missing. One attribute that a finely detailed protocol therefore must have is **error tolerance**.

To guarantee error tolerance, a protocol description must ensure suitable actions in response to any eventuality, and provide error messages where appropriate. In an emergency, both Alice and Bob must be able to break off communications.

Finely detailed protocols must be error tolerant

With roughly specified protocols, which are only supposed to describe the communication sequence in principle, the necessary provisions for error handling are usually dispensed with. However, error tolerance is indispensable for finely detailed protocols.

12.2.2 Negotiation ability

Some protocols use contexts

There are many details in a protocol that can be covered in various ways. Among these are the questions of what format the payload is transmitted in, which protocol version is to be used, whether a compression function is to be applied, and so on. Naturally, such demands must be accurately clarified if communication is to succeed. However, in order to permit a certain degree of flexibility, many finely detailed protocols make it possible for Alice and Bob to agree on certain parameters. For example, in a suitable protocol message, Alice might announce a choice of parameters (say 'I support versions 1.0, 1.1, 1.2 and 2.0 of the protocol'), and Bob would then select the most suitable parameter from that selection.

If a protocol supports this kind of trading in parameters, one speaks of **negotiation ability**. Most finely detailed protocols have negotiation ability. On the other hand, in roughly specified protocols, as a rule negotiation ability is dispensed with because such abilities depend largely on implementation details that are outside the scope of a rough outline document.

12.2.3 Statelessness

Many protocols use contexts If, in our protocol described earlier, Alice wants to ask Bob one of the three questions, she must of course remember which question she has asked. If she does not, Bob's answer ('yes' or 'no') is meaningless to her. For a computer, this means that it must use an area of memory to record certain information about the previous execution of the protocol. This area of memory is termed a **context**. The entire entity of Alice's and Bob's contexts and the intermediate communication link is termed an **association**. Naturally it would be ideal if Alice and Bob would each note in their respective context which stage of the communication they have reached, because it would then be easier to react suitably to missing or erroneous protocol messages.

A context can, of course, store different values. For our protocol, Alice's context might, for instance, hold the following values (we will leave the time on one side for now):

- Initial value

- Bob's name input and own name sent

- Bob's greeting input, question 1 asked

- Bob's greeting input, question 2 asked

- Bob's greeting input, question 3 asked

- Question answered by Bob with 'yes'

- Question answered by Bob with 'no'

- Ending 1: Alice and Bob play tennis

- Ending 2: Alice and Bob go to the cinema

- Ending 3: Alice and Bob eat pizza

- Ending 4: Alice and Bob do not meet at all

Each of these values, which the context can hold, is called a **state**. Of course the context cannot lead from any one state to just any other (ending 1 only takes place if Bob has answered question 1 with 'yes'). Which other states can follow from a given state must be defined precisely. In an error-tolerant protocol, Alice and Bob must also be able to return to an earlier state in order to repeat a part of the communication. Additional states may be necessary to achieve this. If various dimensions such as the time of day are added, many more states will result.

The number of states that are possible is of no interest to us here, however. What is important is to know that many protocols get by without a context at all. In this case, Alice and Bob arrive at their decisions purely on the basis of general rules and with the help of the message received last. Such a protocol is called **stateless**. In the other case, a protocol is called **stateful**. Stateless protocols are naturally simpler and easier to implement than stateful. The latter are more competent, however.

Whether a protocol is designed to be stateless or not is mainly a question of the implementation. Statelessness is therefore an attribute that is relevant to finely detailed protocols.

12.3 Protocols in cryptography

Protocols are important in cryptography. Usually it is not enough just to encrypt some data or sign it. In practice, a procedure must be laid down with which two or more people can achieve a specific aim.

Protocols are important in cryptography

We talk about a **cryptographic protocol** (or **crypto protocol**) if Alice and Bob use cryptographic techniques (in particular, encryption, digital signatures, and cryptographic hash functions) in a protocol in order to guard against attack from Mallory.

Of course, a cryptographic protocol can also be a roughly specified or finely detailed protocol. You are already familiar with examples of roughly specified cryptographic protocols. The Diffie–Hellman key exchange is one of these. If Alice and Bob apply a hybrid procedure for key exchange and encrypted communication, this is also a roughly specified cryptographic protocol.

Crypto procedures must be finely detailed

In the case of a finely detailed cryptographic protocol, the crypto method used must be precisely determined with all formats. The PKCS standards (Section 10.4), for example, are frequently used as the basis for finely detailed cryptographic protocols.

Of course, more than two people communicating with one another can be involved in a cryptographic protocol. As a rule, however, only two collaborators are involved – Alice and Bob in our case.

12.4 Attributes of cryptographic protocols

Cryptography makes serious demands on protocols

Cryptographic protocols also have attributes, which we shall now examine more closely. Naturally, the attributes described in Section 12.2, which are of general interest when dealing with protocols, play an important part. As you will see, the demands on cryptographic protocols go beyond those already described.

12.4.1 General attributes

Let us first examine those attributes that are also relevant for non-cryptographic protocols.

Error tolerance in cryptographic protocols

As with any protocol, error tolerance is also an important attribute with regard to cryptographic protocols. As with cryptographic hash functions (Chapter 8) and random generators (Chapter 9), the following also holds good: the demands that cryptography makes are much higher than in other framework conditions. With a cryptographic protocol, we not only have to reckon with a message going astray during transmission or a bit flipping over accidentally. We also have to take into serious consideration the fact that eavesdropper Mallory tries by deliberate changes or fraudulent conversion to get one over on us. For cryptographic protocols, error tolerance therefore means the same as manipulation tolerance.

Protocols can be attacked   The details of what Mallory can do to attack a protocol are covered in Section 12.5, which also covers the defensive measures to which Alice and Bob can have recourse.

Cryptographic protocols with negotiation ability

As you might think, the ability to negotiate is an important aspect of cryptographic protocols. We are not so much interested here in protocol details such as the protocol version or the data representation (although such things cannot be ignored in cryptographic protocols of course). Here we are much more interested in that fact that Alice and Bob can negotiate the application of crypto procedures and relevant parameters

The ability to negotiate is advantageous in cryptographic protocols   There are many opportunities for negotiation in cryptographic protocols: at the start of a communication Alice can inform Bob in a protocol message about which algorithm she supports for key exchange, along with the length of the public key, which symmetric encryption algorithm she is using, the length of the symmetrical key and which modes of operation she is using. From this information, Bob can then choose the combination that suits him most. To this end, the individual algorithms and parameters are identified with the help of OIDs.

Many protocols do not fix on a specific algorithm   If a cryptographic protocol has the ability to negotiate, then it not only has the advantage that Alice and Bob can use their favourite algorithms. It is also an advantage that it is simple to introduce new algorithms into an existing (finely detailed) crypto protocol. For this reason, nearly all finely detailed protocols do not specify a particular algorithm for each purpose. More often, a list of supported algorithms is given, from which the implementer and later the user also can make his or her choice. As a rule, this list can be expanded without the need to change the protocol specification.

Statelessness in cryptographic protocols

States are also important for cryptographic protocols. Just imagine, Alice and Bob exchange a key using the RSA algorithm and then encrypt their communication with a symmetric algorithm. In this case, Alice and Bob need at least a context in which they can save their secret key. Even such a simple protocol cannot be designed without states. Incidentally, an association is called a **security association** in the case of cryptographic protocols.

12.4.2 Special attributes

Cryptographic protocols often have special attributes

Cryptographic protocols may or ought to have attributes for which there is nothing comparable in non-cryptographic protocols. We shall examine these attributes now.

Level of confidence

For cryptographic protocols, the level of confidence is important. There are three levels:

- If the two friends, Alice and Bob, are communicating over a secure connection, they have mutual confidence.

- If Alice is communicating with online shop owner Oliver, they do not trust each other. Alice is afraid that she will not receive the goods she orders. Oliver is afraid that Alice will not pay for them.

The level of confidence is critical

- If Alice is communicating with the Cryptobank, and we assume that Alice trusts her bank, then this an example of a situation where one communications partner trusts the other, but the reverse is not true.

Many protocols run through several stages: at the start, neither communications partner trusts the other. However, as soon as Alice knows that Bob is on her side, a one-sided trust is established. If Bob also knows that he is really communicating with Alice, a reciprocal trust is created. However, there are also protocols in which reciprocal mistrust is maintained during the whole process.

Minimum disclosure

Minimum disclosure is a desirable attribute

Normally, a protocol message is not completely encrypted. Especially on the Internet, for example, the addresses must remain unencrypted. Nevertheless, it must be the aim to transmit as little unencrypted data as possible. This aim is called **minimum disclosure**. What it entails depends, of course, on the individual protocol. The protocol payload should always be encrypted. For genuine minimum disclosure, the header fields should also be included in the encryption. As you will learn, a complete protocol message can be transported in the payload part of another protocol message.

Perfect Forward Secrecy (PFS)

PFS should prevent any subsequent encryption

Let us assume that Alice and Bob encrypt their communication with a symmetrical and a key-exchange algorithm (for instance, RSA or Diffie–Hellman). Mallory records all encrypted communications between Bob and Alice. Some time later – the magnetic tapes have been stacking up in his cellar – Mallory succeeds in getting hold of a key. Can Mallory use this to decrypt all the recorded communications retrospectively?

The answer depends on which key Mallory has got hold of and on which algorithms Alice and Bob used. If they both used RSA for the key exchange, and they have never changed the RSA key which Mallory has gained by sharp practice, they are out of luck: Mallory can now read the whole of the recorded messages. On the other hand, if, against the same background, Mallory gains a symmetrical key, it will avail him little: Alice and Bob use a new symmetrical key for each communication, and so Mallory can decrypt just one specific communication with his symmetrical key.

PFS is a possible attribute of cryptographic protocols

Of course, it is better if a protocol gives Mallory no chance from the outset to decrypt recorded protocol messages with a known key. This attribute is called **Perfect Forward Secrecy (PFS)**. PFS is created, for example, if Alice and Bob use the Diffie–Hellman key exchange and use a new Diffie–Hellman key pair every time. Even if Alice and Bob use the RSA algorithm for the key exchange, PFS can be achieved: if Alice transmits the RSA encrypted key in each case, then Bob must generate a new RSA key pair each time and send the public key to Alice. Of course, Alice must generate a new secret key for each communication.

PFS is expensive

PFS is a property that can only be realised at great overhead expense. As a rule, Alice and Bob will also take into consideration that fact that a compromised key can result in many decrypted messages.

12.5 Attacks on cryptographic protocols

There are attacks on protocols

Let us now take a look at the attacks Mallory can initiate on a cryptographic protocol. This is of course quite clear: if Mallory succeeds in cracking one of the applied cryptographic algorithms, then even the best protocol is of no further use to Alice and Bob. The reverse is not true, however: if Alice and Bob use secure crypto procedures, this does not by a long way mean that they have triumphed over Mallory. There are actually attacks on protocols that work even with secure crypto procedures. These are the subjects of the next section. We assume, of course, that Mallory knows the protocol being used by Alice and Bob. When protocols are being attacked, Mallory may not just be considered as an eavesdropper listening-in to communications between Alice and Bob. It is also very possible that Mallory might be an apparently harmless acquaintance who is taking his communication partners for a ride. Mallory might even try to start up communication with Bob while pretending to be Alice.

12.5.1 Replay attacks

Protocol messages can be reused by Mallory

Alice is conversant with share dealing and would like Bob to join in. For this reason they have agreed on a simple protocol, which just consists of a single protocol message. The protocol message is 'Buy shares in company <companyname>', into which the name of a company will be inserted. Whenever Alice gets a hot tip, she sends one of these messages to Bob. So that Mallory cannot eavesdrop, Alice encrypts the payload of the message with the IDEA algorithm, which is well known for its security. Since Alice and Bob have a common key, they need not worry about exchanging keys.

Does Mallory have to throw in the towel? No, because he can attack the protocol without needing to crack the IDEA algorithm. This attack is so simple: Alice sends a message to Bob, in which she advises him to buy shares in Crypt & Co; Mallory is eavesdropping and, a few days later, sends it again. Bob thinks Alice wants him to buy shares in Crypt & Co. a second time and buys them. Days later the share price falls and Bob loses his savings.

A replay attack works despite encryption

An attack on a protocol in which Mallory resends an old message is called a **replay attack**. The special thing about a replay attack is that usually Mallory cannot read the message because it is encrypted. He can, however, choose a moment to repeat a message. Replay attacks are especially dangerous in connection with authentication (Chapter 13).

Timestamps help against replay attacks

The best way to guard against a replay attack is obvious: Alice and Bob have to include a **timestamp** in the protocol message. If the timestamp is too old, Bob does not accept the message. But there is another way to defeat a replay attack: Alice and Bob can agree that each message will be accompanied by a number that is incremented each time. The aim in each case is to spot a repeat because no two messages are identical.

12.5.2 Spoofing attacks

Authentication guards against spoofing

Since Mallory knows the protocol that Alice and Bob use for communication, he can try to communicate with Bob while pretending to be Alice. Such an attack is called a **spoofing attack**. Spoofing is very simple with non-cryptographic protocols. For this reason, it is a fairly simple exercise for Mallory to give the wrong IP address in his messages (IP spoofing). Spoofing attacks can be prevented by authentication.

12.5.3 Man-in-the-middle attacks

Alice and Bob use the Diffie–Hellman algorithm to exchange keys (as you know, the Diffie–Hellman algorithm is a protocol). Although the algorithm itself is very secure, Mallory can attack the protocol if he can change the protocol message without it being noticed.

The attack is easy to describe: if Alice sends her public key g^x to Bob, Mallory intercepts it, replaces it with his own public key and sends it on to Bob. If Bob then sends his public key g^y to Alice, Mallory also replaces this with his own public key. Then Alice and Bob each generate a secret key from the public key they received. They both now think they have a mutually secret key $k=g^{xy}$ – in reality, however, Alice now has a secret key k_1 in common with Mallory and Bob equally has a key k_2 in common with Mallory. If Alice now sends a message encrypted with k_1 to Bob,

Mallory intercepts it, decrypts it, encrypts it again with k_2 and sends it to Bob. If Bob sends a message to Alice, the process runs in reverse. Alice and Bob think they are communicating with each other, but in reality they are both communicating with Mallory.

Using a man-in-the-middle attack, Mallory joins in the communication

Such an attack, in which Mallory actively joins in the communication between Alice and Bob, is called a **man-in-the-middle attack** (not to be confused with the meet-in-the-middle attack). With a man-in-the-middle attack, Mallory changes protocol messageprotocol messages in a way that brings him an advantage. This is a danger with cryptographic protocols with negotiation ability. For example, Mallory can use it to change the crypto algorithm that Alice tenders to Bob. He can thus ensure that they both utilise an insecure algorithm – or even none at all.

Figure 12.2   In a man-in-the-middle attack, Mallory actively joins in the communication between Alice and Bob.

A man-in-the-middle attack normally only works in the starting phase of a protocol. As long as Alice and Bob have a mutual secret key and use it correctly (for encryption or for a key-dependent hash function), Mallory is helpless. How to avoid a man-in-the-middle attack is revealed in Chapter 13 and Section 16.1.4.

12.5.4   Hijacking attacks

In a man-in-the-middle attack Mallory limits himself to the targeted alteration of protocol messages. Mallory can do more, however: he can block the protocol messages from Alice at a given point in time and continue the communication with Bob himself. This is called a hijacking attack. If you like, a **hijacking** attack is a combination of a man-in-the-middle attack and a spoofing attack. You are therefore familiar with the countermeasures: Alice and Bob can forestall Mallory using authentication with encryption or a cryptographic hash function.

12.5.5   Illegal state change

In stateful crypto protocols, the current protocol state is often important. If a protocol contains, say, a request for a password, then it is, of course, not exactly beside the point to ask whether the state 'password not yet entered' or 'password already entered' is the current state. Mallory can therefore try to attack a protocol by causing an **illegal change in state**. How and if Mallory can achieve such an illegal change in state depends of the protocol, of course. The best defence against such an attack is a clean implementation.

12.5.6 Traffic analysis

Encryption cannot prevent traffic analysis

Even after Alice and Bob securely encrypt everything that they send to each other, and also apply a secure protocol, Mallory still has one last possibility of finding out something about a communication: he can compile statistics about when and how Alice and Bob communicate. This attack is called **traffic analysis**.

In practice, traffic analysis can be more dangerous than you might think. If, say, after receiving each e-mail from Alice, Bob sends an e-mail to his online broker, Mallory deduces that Bob is receiving share-market tips from Alice. If the boss of Crypt & Co. suddenly starts a brisk correspondence with the boss of a competitor, this could indicate a merger. If Alice sends most of her mail unencrypted over the Net, but occasionally encrypts messages to Bob, this could point to very important data exchanges.

Traffic analysis can hardly be prevented

In practice, of course, traffic analysis can never be completely prevented. However, there are two effective countermeasures that can make things difficult for Mallory: on the one hand, Alice and Bob should encrypt everything they send over the Net (not only important items). By doing so, Mallory will find it difficult to sift the important things from the unimportant. On the other, the protocol that is used should work on the principle of minimum disclosure. This means that not only should the payload of a protocol message be encrypted, but practically everything apart from the recipient's address.

12.5.7 Denial-of-service attack

Denial-of-service attacks are usually the easiest

When Mallory has exhausted his bag of protocol attacks, he can still attempt a **denial-of-service attack**. Such an attack has the exclusive aim of preventing communication between Alice and Bob. There are two ways of doing this, which are widely used:

- Mallory can block a protocol message from Alice, or change it so that Bob can do nothing with it.

- Mallory can flood Bob with fake protocol messages, so that these prevent the timely assessment of Alice's news.

There are many openings for a denial-of-service attack

There are often other means Mallory can use to prevent communication by fake protocol messages. Such might be the case with an erroneous implementation that permits a fake protocol message to cause a breakdown.

Incidentally, denial-of-service attacks are also often more effective than they might appear. For example, if Mallory changes every encrypted protocol message from Alice to Bob so that Bob cannot decrypt them, then the pair will, sooner or later, come to doubt the quality of their encryption software and, for simplicity's sake, exchange unencrypted messages. Mallory will profit from this immensely.

12.5.8 Other attacks

There are still other attacks on protocols

Of course, there are also attacks on protocols other than those described above. In each case, the important thing to remember is that secure crypto algorithms by no means ensure a secure protocol. Protocol development has become a separate discipline of cryptography, a fact that should be acknowledged when developing crypto products.

12.6 An example of a protocol: blind signatures

Blind signatures are an example of another attack

To round off our consideration of cryptographic protocols, let us look at one more example of a roughly specified cryptographic protocol. This is a protocol that can be used to create so-called blind signatures. There are two reasons for choosing this protocol: firstly, it shows that the performance of current cryptographic procedures can only be enhanced by the application of suitable protocols. Secondly, the described protocol is one that is actually used in practice (see Section 27.4.1).

12.6.1 What is a blind signature?

When Alice signs a message digitally, she usually sees what she is signing. However, there are cases where the signer neither needs nor ought to see the exact contents of a message to be signed. When a message is signed without the signer having full knowledge of its contents, this is called a **blind signature**.

A typical application for a blind signature arises when cash is to be simulated by means of software alone. To do this, a digital note must be digitally signed by a bank (or similar institution), otherwise anyone could make his or her own digital notes. Because of data protection, however, the bank may not know the serial number of a digital note. A protocol must therefore be found with which the bank can sign digital notes without knowing the serial number.

12.6.2 A protocol for blind signatures

Blind signatures can be easily demonstrated

In the following, I shall describe how such a protocol can look. Let us assume that Alice wants to draw a 100-Cryptodollar digital note from her bank (the Cryptobank). The Cryptobank signs notes only shortly before issuing them to customers. The Cryptobank should have no way of noting the serial numbers of the notes. The protocol outline is as follows:

1. Alice produces ten notes with a value of 100 Cryptodollars each (although she can't sign them as only the Cryptobank has the private key necessary for this). She uses a different serial number for each note. She encrypts these ten notes (with a symmetric algorithm) using ten different keys and sends them to the Cryptobank.

2. The Cryptobank chooses one of the ten unsigned, encrypted notes at random, and signs it. The bank then tells Alice which note it has signed.

3. Alice now sends the nine keys with which the nine unsigned notes were encrypted to the Cryptobank .

4. The Cryptobank decrypts the nine unsigned notes and checks to see if these were properly produced by Alice (and in particular whether the value is really 100 Cryptodollars). If everything is in order, Alice receives the ten signed notes.

After the devolution of this protocol, Alice has a signed note whose serial number is unknown to the bank. Of course, Alice can abuse the protocol by giving one of the ten notes a value of 100,000 Cryptodollars (instead of 100) and hoping that the Cryptobank does not choose this particular note to decrypt. The odds of this attack working are ten to one in favour (it belongs to the 'illegal change in state' type). If this is too dangerous for the Cryptobank, it can demand 100 or even 1000 notes from Alice instead of ten.

Blind signatures can be created with the RSA algorithm

In practice, blind signatures are created with the RSA algorithm. This has an appreciable advantage: a simple modulo multiplication can be used as the symmetric encryption procedure. Alice can regenerate these from the bank's signature. This provides Alice not only with a signed, encrypted note, but also with a signed, unencrypted note.

12.7 Other protocols

There are numerous other cryptographic protocols

In his work [Schn96], Bruce Schneier describes a collection of several dozen (roughly specified) protocols. He starts with simple protocols, such as key exchange, or public key encryption with multiple keys. He also lists numerous signature protocols, such as proxy signatures, group signatures, blind signatures, or simultaneous contract signing. The high points are, without a doubt, such protocols as mental poker, online voting, or virtual coin tossing. Interesting as these protocols may be, they are of little practical interest for the Internet, which is why I shall not investigate them here.

Authentication

Love all, trust a few.
WILLIAM SHAKESPEARE

Key experience no. 13
The importance of proper authentication was demonstrated in the fairy tales of the brothers Grimm. There, as everyone knows, the seven little goats opened the door to the wolf, which had previously eaten chalk and smeared his paws with dough. It was their own fault: a smooth voice and white paws do not amount to reliable and sufficient authentication – perhaps the seven kids should have read this book.

Authentication is the proof of genuineness

In our daily life, we often check if a particular person genuinely is who he or she purports to be. For example, Alice checks the authenticity of Bob when she meets him on the street or speaks to him on the phone. Alice proves her own genuineness with her personal identity number at a cash machine or with her passport at international checkpoints. When Alice receives a letter, she checks the genuineness of the sender by looking at the signature. This process of checking genuineness (authenticity) is known as **authentication**.

13.1 Authentication and identification

In this book, **authentication** – as already stated – means the act of proving whether someone really is the person he or she purports to be. So, when Alice gets cash from the automatic cash machine at a bank, she authenticates herself with her personal identity number (PIN). Simultaneously the cash machine authenticates Alice. Just to confuse things, there is the term **identification**. In this book, this means a process with which Alice gives her name (or some other means of identifying herself, such as her bus pass, for example). Normally, identification (Alice states her name) comes before authentication (checking shows that it really is Alice). The term identification is also used in connection with biometrics (see Section 13.3).

Generally speaking, authentication has nothing to do with the Internet, nor with computers, and with cryptography, even less. Authentication is more of an everyday process that we meet constantly outside the world of computers.

Nonetheless, there are points of contact between authentication and cryptography. On the one hand, cryptography needs authentication, and on the other, provides work tools for it that are indispensable on the Internet.

Figure 13.1 When Bob enters his PIN at the cash machine, this is an example of authentication.

13.2 Authentication procedures

Authentication can be established in different ways Let's take a look at procedures that can be used for authentication outside the Internet. To do so, we assume that Bob wants to check Alice's authenticity. He has three basic ways of doing this:

- Bob checks whether Alice knows a certain fact (*something you know*). Examples are passwords, secret numbers, secret keys or personal information. This is called **authentication by knowledge**.

- Bob checks whether Alice is in possession of any object that is difficult to forge (*something you have*). The most important example here is a passport. In this case one talks of **authentication by possession**.

- Bob checks an unmistakable, difficult to fake, personal characteristic of Alice (*something you are*). Examples here are her facial image, her fingerprints and her signature. In technical terms, this is **authentication by personal characteristics**.

In short: one authenticates oneself through something one knows, something one has, or what one is. These three authentication variants will be examined more closely in the following chapters.

A decisive question when considering an authentication procedure is whether Alice can only use it to authenticate herself to someone she knows (such as Bob), or also to a complete stranger (such as Zak). In the latter case, a **trusted third party** **(TTP)** is required. A TTP might be a passport authority, for example.

13.2.1 What one knows

Let us begin our examination with authentication by knowledge (what one knows). This has the advantage that it is quite simple, because Alice and Bob need no material object or measuring apparatus.

Passwords

Passwords have been used for ages   The fact that a person can authenticate himself by knowing some piece of information has been known, at the latest, since the time of Ali Baba and the 40 Thieves. The cry 'Open Sesame' was nothing more than a password that allowed access to a cave. Although passwords are no longer used to gain access to caves, their use is still widespread: as bank cards, or in computerised accounts or online banking, passwords are omnipresent (passwords and secret numbers are the same thing in this context).

Alice and Bob can agree on a password   Of course, Bob and Alice can also use a password if they have agreed one beforehand. It would be difficult for Alice to check the authenticity of Zak in this way, however, because they do not know each other and have had no opportunity to agree on a password. Passwords are therefore a typical means of authentication without a trusted third party. Ali Baba learnt about one drawback of passwords: if someone learns your password, your doors are open to him. Against this, passwords, like authentication by knowledge in general, have the advantage that Alice and Bob can use them for mutual authentication on the phone or the Internet.

Passwords are frequently forgotten   Another drawback of passwords comes to mind: they are frequently forgotten. The current flood of passwords contributes to the fact that hardly anyone can remember all of them. Passwords are used today to secure EC identity cards, Internet access, Internet bank accounts, answering machines, car radios, mobile phones, office doors, PC access, intranets, databases, and placing on order in the online bookshop, to name just a few of the more important examples. Having to remember 20 passwords is no longer a rarity.

Ergonomic substitute for passwords

Faces are easier to remember than passwords   Because passwords are frequently forgotten, it seemed a good idea, instead of passwords, to use some piece of information that the human brain can remember more easily. The one I like best is the method that the English firm ID Arts has patented. This method does not require Alice and Bob to use a password, but to select one from several available portrait photos. Which photos are to be used, and which of them is the correct one, has to be agreed between them beforehand. It is conceivable that they could use a set of nine photos. If the procedure has to be made even more secure, Alice and Bob must utilise several sets, in each of which Alice must remember one photo.

The advantage of this method – it could be used in bank ATMs or for computer access – rests on the fact that people remember faces better than words or numbers. Photo recognition is consequently more ergonomic than a password. And a face cannot be recorded, especially if Bob presents the photos in a set in a different order each time of asking. So one needn't be afraid that someone might write the information needed for access on a ticket stuck on the monitor.

Figure 13.2 Firm ID Arts offers an authentication system in which Alice must select one specific face from several. The advantage of this is that a face is easier to remember than a password.

Personal information

Personal information can be used for authentication

To avoid forgotten passwords, another variant of authentication by knowledge can be used. This consists in Bob asking Alice about some item of personal information that Mallory cannot know. This information might be the name of Alice's favourite film, the colour of the wallpaper in her living room, or her grandmother's birthday. It is to be supposed that – in contrast to a password – Alice won't forget such details. Since Mallory cannot answer such questions automatically, this form of authentication is very secure when properly applied. A precondition is, however, that Alice and Bob have agreed on the relevant information beforehand. This means that authentication by personal information is only possible between people who know each other personally.

13.2.2 What one has

Passports are a popular means of authentication

The possession of an object as evidence of authenticity is a widespread method of proving identity. Using a passport, Alice can check the genuine identity of an unknown person such as Zacharias, which provides us with a classic example of authentication by the mediation of a trusted third party. This function is fulfilled by the authority that issued the passport. However, documentary evidence can also be used without third party involvement: a library ticket, for example, is issued by a library and as a rule is recognised by that institution alone.

13.2.3 What one is

What one is used most often for authentication

Personal characteristics are used very often in everyday life for authentication, mainly without people even realising it. Normally it is simply Alice's facial image, voice and behaviour that Bob uses to determine that it is, in fact, Alice whom he has met on the street. This authentication by sight happens without any third party, of course, and presupposes that Bob knows Alice.

The matter becomes more interesting if a computer is to carry out authentication by personal characteristics. This is possible if the computer, for example, records fingerprints by means of suitable sensors, or the execution of a signature. This subject (biometric authentication) is so interesting that I will examine it in detail in Section 13.3. Biometric authentication is also executed without a trusted third party as a rule, such as when, for example, the authenticating computer has stored relevant biometric data of someone.

13.3 Biometric authentication

Biometrics is the measurement of biological systems

The term **biometrics** applies to a broad range of measuring techniques that employ physical characteristics of living objects as a means of authentication. They include, for example, the measurement of blood pressure in humans or the estimation of the yield in a field of wheat. Of course, we are not interested here in the application of biometric techniques in medicine or agriculture, although they may well be highly interesting subjects. Our interest lies in the application of biometric techniques for authentication purposes. In fact, some measurable characteristics of the human body are so unique and constant that they can be used for authentication. This is the basis of **biometric authentication**. A device used for biometric authentication is called a **biometric system**.

Biometrics can be used for authentication

Biometric authentication belongs to the field of authentication by attributes. Examples of measurable characteristics of the human body that can be used for authentication include fingerprints, retinal patterns and hand geometry. Other examples will be mentioned below.

13.3.1 The basics of biometric authentication

In the following, we assume that the Cryptobank (the leading financial institution in Cryptoland) wants to install biometric authentication in their automatic teller machines. If Alice, who is a customer of Cryptobank, wants to withdraw cash from the ATM, but in future no longer have to input her personal identity number, she will instead have to subject herself to biometric authentication.

Reference values

Reference values are needed for biometric authentication

In order to use biometrics, the Cryptobank must equip their automatic cash machines with the corresponding biometric system (e.g. a fingerprint reader and related software). In addition, for each customer the Cryptobank must store the appropriate measurement value for comparison purposes – such as the relevant parameters of Alice's fingerprints. This measurement value (so-called **reference value**) could be stored in a database. It would be better, however, if each customer could carry his or her own reference value on a smart card. The reference value is compared with a newly measured value when Alice wants to withdraw cash. Before Alice can use the newly equipped automatic cash machine, she will have to have the relevant physical characteristic (say her fingerprints) measured and recorded to provide the data to be stored in the smart card (**reference value construction**).

For the authentication itself, there are two possibilities: firstly, the Cryptobank can provide for Alice to give her name before the measurement process. After the measurement, the software must determine whether the measured value actually belongs to Alice. This variant is called **verification** (not to be confused with the verification of a digital signature). Secondly, the Cryptobank can equip their teller machines in such a way that Alice need not make any additional input. The software finds the correct person in the database on the basis of the measured characteristic alone. This possibility is termed **identification** (not to be confused with the identification defined in Section 13.1). Of course, identification is more user-friendly than verification, but less effective.

False acceptance rates and false rejection rates

The false acceptance rate should be low

Of course, it is in Cryptobank's own interest that Mallory cannot withdraw cash from Alice's account. To guarantee this, the biometric system on the teller machine must not mistakenly reconcile Mallory's actual measurement with Alice's reference value. Should this happen, however, one speaks of a **false acceptance**. If many people attempt to access Alice's account illegally, the proportion of false positive matches is called the **false acceptance rate** or **FAR**.

The false rejection rate should also be low

On the other hand, it can be Alice's misfortune that the teller machine does not recognise her measurement value even though her reference value is in the database (perhaps because of an error in the measuring device). Such an event is called a **false rejection**. The proportion of false negative rejections of valid users in a given number of authentications is called the **false rejection rate** or **FRR**.

For a given biometric system, both the false rejection rate and the false acceptance rate should be as low as possible. For either rate to be zero is impossible in practice, but rates below 1 per cent can be achieved. As shown in Figure 13.3, the false acceptance rate falls and the false rejection rate rises if a greater margin for error (tolerance) is allowed when comparing measurements (an exact match is almost never found). The degree of tolerance for comparisons is configurable in most biometric systems. The Cryptobank must find a compromise: Alice should have to return home without cash as rarely as possible, while Mallory should also succeed in withdrawing cash from Alice's account as rarely as possible.

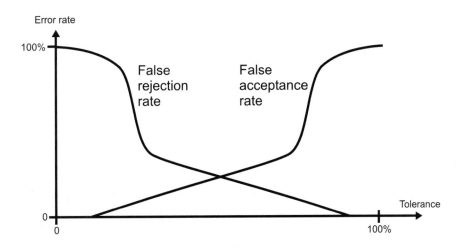

Figure 13.3 False acceptance and false rejection rates for a biometric system.

13.3.2 Biometric characteristics

After the theoretical preamble, I would now like to examine different measurable dimensions of the human body (so-called biometric characteristics) that can be used for biometric authentication. The appropriate attributes for biometric characteristics must be easy to measure, uniquely different, unchangeable and constant over the long term. They should also be difficult to replicate artificially (replica recognition).

Fingerprint recognition

A fingerprint is a biometric characteristic In the world of police detection it has long been known that a human fingerprint is unique and almost unchangeable. If one uses a fingerprint scanner (usually optical or capacitative) as the measuring device, a fingerprint can serve very well as a biometric characteristic. This fact seems to have done the rounds, because the number of fingerprint recognition systems on the market is hard to overlook (there must be more than 100). Correspondingly, there are also numerous mechanical procedures that can be used to compare a fingerprint with a reference value.

In favour of fingerprint identification systems is the long experience accumulated in this field. The technology is simple to use and the cost is reasonable (a fingerprint scanner can be bought at around 100 euros).

Fingerprint recognition is often viewed with suspicion from a hygiene point of view. For this reason, fingerprint readers are often used for protecting access to PCs or mobile phones, but are not often to be found in much-frequented locations such as automatic teller machines or busy entrances.

Many fingerprint readers can be outsmarted

In tests, many fingerprint readers have shown themselves to be easy to outsmart (i.e. there is no effective live recognition). However, capacitative readers in particular seem able to offer a measure of security in order for fingerprint recognition to find a suitable practical use. Obviously, capacitative readers cannot even be outsmarted by the amputated finger of an authentic user (it is hoped that this only takes place in criminal circles).

Facial image recognition

For facial image recognition, a camera is used as the measuring device. With the help of image processing techniques, the biometric system determines whether a photographed face is consistent with one stored in a database.

Figure 13.4 Facial image recognition is a biometric variant that causes relatively few acceptance problems.

Facial image recognition can be used for authentication

Without a doubt, facial image recognition has a certain appeal. After all, we humans recognise each other by our faces, so why shouldn't a computer do likewise? Also, suitable cameras are one of the cheaper measuring devices, a good model being available for around 100 euros. From experience, users are quite accepting of this technique, since people are quite used to being photographed with cameras nowadays. The false acceptance rate for well-implemented facial image recognition is average when compared with other biometric systems. A negative factor is that people's faces change with time; beards and spectacles often cause problems. So a high false rejection rate can be expected if the facial image recognition system is not capable of learning (adaptive).

No facial image recognition system is perfect authentication

In 1999, *c't* magazine published a test of the leading facial recognition systems performed by biometrics expert Marco Breitenstein (I was involved as co-author of the article, see [BreSch]). None of the systems tested produced perfect results, but two of the systems could be classed as good, or at least usable. These were the German systems ZN Face from ZN (test winner) and BioID from DCS. These results showed that Germany is a world leader in the facial recognition market. The other systems included in the test (predominantly cheaper products from the USA) would qualify for prosecution under customer protection laws. False acceptance rates of 20 to 50 per cent make these systems a poor buy, not to mention replica recognition failings (often a photograph would be enough to trick the system). It can be said that these products should not be on the market – unless they are to be used as entertaining party games (whoever is not recognised loses).

Hand recognition

Hand geometry is a biometric characteristic

Hand geometry can also be used as a biometric characteristic. The length, width and thickness of the fingers are sufficiently unique to recognise a human being by them. The advantage here is that it is a simple biometric variant whose biometric characteristic remains unchanged over a long period. However, the question of hygiene also comes to the fore again, just as with fingerprints. Again, the false acceptance rate for such systems is quite high.

Recognition of typing behaviour

Typing behaviour is a biometric characteristic

The cheapest, and for the user, simplest, variant of biometrics is the recognition of typing behaviour when using a computer keyboard. This variant makes do with a keyboard (which is usually available anyway) as the measuring device. The biometric system continually measures the time lapse between successive keystrokes by the user. If the measurements are repeated while Alice types in a text, then a pattern is created that is sufficiently characteristic to recognise her by. Recognition of typing behaviour belongs to the more exotic biometric variants up to now, so there is little record of it. However, it can be assumed that the false rejection rate is quite high.

Signature recognition

A signature can be used as a biometric characteristic

Signature recognition measures the movement of a pen during the execution of a signature. The measuring device can comprise a pad equipped with sensors, or a special sensor-pen (or even both together). A signature is difficult to forge, especially if the speed of writing and the downward pressure are included in the measurement. Since Alice's signature can vary so much, however, the margin for error must be set relatively high. High user acceptance and low-cost equipment mean that signature recognition is an interesting biometric variant.

Figure 13.5 Signature recognition requires a high degree of cooperation from the client.

Voice recognition

In the case of voice recognition, a human voice is recorded using a microphone as the measuring device. Using suitable algorithms, sufficient characteristics can be extracted from the recording to define a human voice. To ensure that a voice recognition system cannot be tricked by a recorded tape, a key word that Alice must pronounce is usually included in her recording.

Voice recognition is cheap and simple

Voice recognition is also cheap and simple to use. This method is predestined for telephone use. The greatest drawback is the high false rejection rate, which can be increased by hoarseness, for example. There are also often acceptance problems in practice: who enjoys talking to a machine? If Alice has to call her laptop to life several times during an important meeting, this tends to breed mockery rather than confidence.

Iris recognition

Iris scanning is one of the best biometric variants

Iris recognition works because the coloured ring surrounding the pupil of the eye (the iris) is uniquely patterned. A high-resolution digital camera is used as the measuring device for iris recognition, which produces a recording of the eyes.

Iris recognition is without doubt one of the most interesting biometric variants. When well implemented, the false acceptance rate is very low and is only bettered by retinal pattern recognition. On top of this, it is uncomplicated to use. However, experience has shown acceptance problems, mostly due to it being continually confused with retinal recognition. The manufacturer of the sole iris recognition system maintains that it cannot be tricked by a photograph because the measurement process registers movements in the iris that are not present in a photo. Since such dimensional changes can be caused by a pulse of light, a video film will not work either.

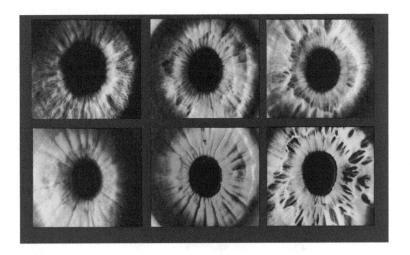

Figure 13.6 A human iris is uniquely different. It can therefore be used as a biometric characteristic.

Retina recognition

When using the method of retina recognition, the rear wall of the eye is used as a biometric characteristic. Strictly speaking, the expression retina recognition is incorrect, since it is not the retina (membrane lining of the eye) itself that is used, but the arteries lying behind it. These arteries create a pattern that is so unique that retina recognition shows the lowest false acceptance rate of all the procedures described here. Since it is difficult to simulate the rear wall of the eye with a photo, retina recognition is acceptable even to paranoid users.

Retina recognition is very secure   In practice, retina recognition is only recommended for those who are paranoid, as it is useless for normal use. This is because the photo of the rear wall of the eye cannot be obtained in a manner acceptable to the user. A special camera is needed, which illuminates the retina with an infrared light beam. To authenticate herself, Alice must look into a tube that looks like a gun barrel and bring a row of dots into focus. I feel that it is inconceivable that a bank might ask its clients to do such a thing. Retina recognition is therefore only of use in high-security zones (secret or military installations). Its high price will also ensure that it does not find general application.

Other methods

There are still other biometric variants, including odour recognition, ear recognition and the bodily motion analysis of a walking man. Combinations of several characteristics are also possible. DNA analysis is still in the realms of fantasy, however. Although the false acceptance rate would be virtually zero, the measuring device – a spit-absorbent towel fitted with sensors – would be rather unappetising.

Figure 13.7   Retina recognition system: retina recognition is a very secure biometric variant; however, there are problems with user acceptance.

13.3.3 Summary

Without doubt, biometrics is a fascinating subject. In my field of work I have always found exceptionally high interest in it. In comparison to cryptography, where procedure improvements are effected in nuances, biometrics is still in its infancy. However, it is becoming more apparent that despite strong interest, the readiness to part with money for biometrics is not yet very appreciable.

There are also drawbacks to biometrics   There are other drawbacks. These include the fact that in the end, biometrics is based on measurements that, in principle, can be replicated illegally. Whether face, fingerprint or voice – with appropriate outlay (photo, monitor, wax model, tape recording) Mallory can always forge the biometric characteristic. The system manufacturers can only try to make the practical application of such forgeries more difficult – they cannot stop them completely. Fingerprints do have one feature that can be significant – they cannot be changed like a password, even if they can be copied.

Biometrics is a theme for the future

Biometrics is an interesting theme for the future, which in the next few years will surely produce some novel items. If you want to delve into this further, I can recommend the article [Wirtz]. The only book covering the basics of the subject I know of is [Ashbou] – for which the contents hardly justify the high price. There is also a book of collected articles on the subject [JaBoPa]. A good overview of the subject is contained in the diploma thesis of Marco Breitenstein [Breite].

13.4 Authentication on the Internet

After our general excursion into authentication, we shall now look at how authentication can be achieved on the Internet (or any computer network). As you might imagine, authentication is important on the Internet because in this anonymous, world-embracing network, almost anyone can pretend to be anyone, without arousing suspicion.

Authentication on the Internet also results from what one has, is or knows

As always, we assume that Alice sends a message to Bob. This time, however, Mallory is not so intent on interception. He is much more interested in forging messages that Bob will think come from Alice. Bob's task is to find out whether a message he has received is in fact from Alice, or whether it is a forgery.

13.4.1 Characteristics of authentication on the Internet

Authentication on the Internet is always linked to a protocol

Although very different rules apply to the Internet compared to real life, authentication cannot be redefined for it. This means that the following also holds for the Internet: the decisive thing is what one is, what one knows, or what one has. On the Internet, authentication is always linked to a protocol and consequently to a protocol message. Strictly speaking, on the Internet it is always a question of the receiver (Bob) checking whether a protocol message really stems from the alleged sender (Alice). Again, this means that Alice and Bob try to prevent spoofing, man-in-the-middle and hijacking attacks. Even the blockage caused by replay attacks can be prevented with a suitable authentication (and in some cases an additional measure).

Authenticity is closely bound to integrity

So that these kinds of attacks can be reliably deflected, it is not enough for Bob just to ensure that a protocol message actually stems from Alice. It must further be guaranteed that the protocol message arrives unaltered. The authenticity of data is therefore closely bound to its unchanged state (**integrity**). An integrity check is therefore a part of an optimal authentication.

13.4.2 Simple password requests on the Internet

Passwords are simple but not secure

The simplest means of authentication on the Internet is the password (in cryptography this is often the same thing as a secret key). Telnet, FTP, SNMP and other Internet protocols use passwords for authentication when establishing a connection. For this, Alice sends the password to Bob in her first protocol message. Thereafter, the communication between them runs without further security measures. This very simple method of using passwords is, of course, very insecure. It has at least four drawbacks:

- Mallory can eavesdrop on the password sent from Alice to Bob and reuse it (this is a very simple form of the replay attack).

- Only the first protocol message contains the password, while all following messages are not involved in the authentication.

- There is no form of integrity protection. Therefore, man-in-the-middle and hijacking attacks are possible.

- Alice and Bob have to agree on a password beforehand (this is the well-known key exchange problem).

Passwords are often used on the Internet

Although the simple sending of a password in the first protocol message is not exactly the most secure thing to do, this method is often used. This is because of the simplicity of this way of working. Of course, there are numerous alternative ways to model a more secure authentication. When one looks at these alternatives however, one notices that many of them succeed in resolving only the first of the four problems listed above (it is possible to eavesdrop on the password). There are two reasons for this: for one, the danger of a password being eavesdropped on is markedly greater than that of an attack in which Mallory actively interferes with the communication (problems two and three in the list). In order to get at a password, it might be enough for Mallory simply to look over Alice's shoulder while she is typing. To change protocol control messages or even to falsify them completely, on the other hand, requires much more overhead expense. The second reason is that the three other problems can only be solved if Alice herself can apply cryptography. Points two and three could be resolved by suitable encryption or cryptographic hash functions. It is known that the key exchange problem can be solved by an asymmetrical algorithm. Nevertheless, Alice herself is often unable to apply cryptography. Thus many protocols are not supported by encryption. It should also be clear that Alice doesn't want to perform any cryptographic operations when buying something over the phone.

Passwords can also be used without cryptography

For the reasons mentioned, attempts to replace the simple password request by something more intelligent are often undertaken just to make eavesdropping and reuse more difficult for Mallory. We will now look at what other methods are available.

One-time passwords

An obvious way to counter the eavesdropping of passwords is the so-called **one-time password**. As the name suggests, Alice and Bob have to agree on several passwords, of which each will be used only once. Mallory's hope of using an acquired password a second time is thereby foiled from the start.

One-time passwords are used in online banking, for example. If Alice wants to use this service at her bank (the Cryptobank), she obtains a list of passwords from them (usually called transaction numbers (**TANs**)). Each time she connects to the bank and starts a transaction, she must use a TAN from her list, following which this TAN becomes invalid. Once all TANs have been used, Alice must get another list from the bank.

One-time passwords offer more security than passwords

A one-time password procedure can be realised very effectively using a cryptographic hash function. To do this, the Cryptobank generates a random number p_0. It then runs this through a cryptographic hash function (see Chapter 8) and gets the TAN p_1, from which it produces p_2 using a second run. This procedure is reiterated several times until, say, p_{10} is produced. The Cryptobank gives p_0 to p_9 to Alice as the TAN list and takes a note only of p_{10}. Alice's first TAN is p_9. The bank can check its correctness by running p_9 through the cryptographic hash function once and comparing the results. The next TAN is p_8, which in turn must produce p_9 if it is sent through the secure hash function.

One-time passwords are standardised as an OTP system

The procedure just described for generating one-time passwords is standardised in RFC1938 as a **One-Time Password (OTP)** system. The US firm Bellcore has implemented the procedure for all current operating systems under the name **S/Key**. The name is often used for the procedure itself. The Bellcore implementation selectively uses one of the cryptographic hash functions, MD4 or MD5.

The OTP system has two main advantages: the Cryptobank need not store any large TAN lists, and Mallory will find no usable passwords if he gains access to the bank's computer. One drawback of one-time passwords is obvious, however: Alice must carry a password list around with her. If Mallory steals this, or Alice loses it, her modest savings can quickly dwindle.

Passwords and cryptographic hash functions

Even one-time passwords do not offer optimal protection

An alternative to one-time passwords consists of Alice using only one password, but, instead of sending it over the Net, she submits only a cryptographic hash value of the password to the Cryptobank each time. So that the cryptographic hash value is not the same each time (and thus reusable by Mallory), some additional data must be processed in the hash value. This extra data might be the current time, for instance, or simply a random number. The additional data need not remain secret; Alice can send it over the Net.

The described way of proceeding is most secure when the additional data comes directly from the bank. For this, the Cryptobank sends a random value (challenge) in a protocol message to Alice. From this value and the password she then builds the answer (response), which she sends back to the Cryptobank. A procedure that follows this principle is called a **challenge–response procedure**. There are innumerable variations of the challenge–response procedure.

There are many versions of the challenge–response procedure

The use of a cryptographic hash function is clearly more effective than a one-time password list. One drawback is that Alice must have the possibility of calculating the cryptographic hash value. A smart token can be used for this (see Section 15.3.2).

13.4.3 More complex password methods

More secure methods can be devised using passwords
The methods described so far for authentication with passwords are quite widely used, but they are not particularly secure. Therefore, we now turn to procedures whereby an authentication through knowledge can be formed more effectively on the Internet. There is one proviso, however – not only the Cryptobank but also Alice must be able to apply cryptographic methods in comprehensive form. And in the methods described in the following, the whole protocol (not just the first or the first two protocol control messages) must be involved in the authentication.

Digital signatures and authentication

One simple possibility for authentication would be to employ digital signatures. If Alice signs her digital message, the Cryptobank can verify that the message actually comes from Alice. Because Alice uses a private key (i.e. a quasi password) for it, we have here a further case of authentication through knowledge. If Alice saves her private key on a smart card, we have authentication through possession.

At first sight, authentication on the Internet using digital signatures is a good thing, as the following arguments confirm:

Digital signatures can be employed for authentication
• If Alice uses a digital signature, a replay attack through reuse of a password is not possible.

• If each protocol message from Alice is digitally signed, the danger of a man-in-the-middle or hijacking attack is avoided.

• A digital signature offers integrity protection.

• Alice and the bank do not need to agree on a password, thus avoiding the key exchange problem.

Does this mean that digital signatures provide the ideal method for authentication on the Internet? No, because they are too onerous. As you know from Chapter 7, digital signatures need plenty of computing power, which would work against communication between Alice and her bank. Therefore, digital signatures are not usually used when authentication is demanded. Digital signatures are needed more when connectivity is requested, thus when Alice has no opportunity to contest the authenticity of a protocol message. However, most protocols do not demand connectivity and so digital signatures are avoided.

Use of symmetrical algorithms

Since digital signatures are often too onerous, we come back to passwords. In the process, we want to introduce passwords in the form of a secret key with fixed bit length. If Alice and the Cryptobank have a shared secret key and Alice is in a position to employ cryptographic methods, the obvious form of authentication is

Symmetrical encryption algorithms can be employed for authentication

to use symmetric encryption (DES, for instance). For this, sender Alice encrypts each protocol message with the secret key, and the Cryptobank decrypts it. If Mallory changes something in the message or sends one of his own, after decryption, the Cryptobank sees only garbage and knows that something is wrong. Of course, this form of authentication only works if the plaintext can be distinguished from data garbage (if it contains sufficient redundancy). However, this is the case for written words and most other data and in other cases it can be guaranteed using suitable checksums. The advantage of symmetric encryption algorithms in authentication is: Mallory is not only unable to alter the text, he can't even read it.

Key-dependent hash functions can be used for authentication

If secrecy is not required, Alice and the Cryptobank can also employ a key-dependent hash function. In this case, each protocol message must include a key-dependent hash value. By checking the hash value, the Cryptobank can check whether each protocol message is genuine.

Authentication and key exchange

By using a secret key, Alice and the Cryptobank can work out a protocol by which a replay attack will not succeed, each protocol message is protected, and integrity protection is also provided. This leaves only the key exchange problem to be solved. This can of course be achieved by a key exchange being carried out at the start of the protocol using an asymmetrical algorithm (RSA or Diffie-Hellman). Unfortunately, however, these algorithms are sensitive to a man-in-the-middle attack. You can find out what you can do about this in Section 16.1.4.

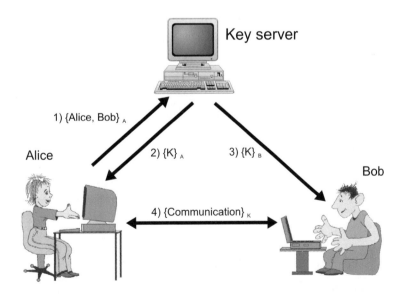

Figure 13.8 A key server and a suitable protocol enable a key exchange without the use of public key cryptography.

An alternative to using an asymmetrical algorithm to solve the key exchange problem is to employ a trusted third party, which will supply both communication partners with a shared secret key. Such a trusted third party is called a **key server**. If Alice wants to make use of a key server, then to get things started, she must agree on a common secret key A with this key server by secure means. Her communication partner (Bob, for example) must proceed in like fashion to set up secret key B. If Alice and Bob now need a shared secret key, they work through the following protocol:

A key server enables
a key exchange

1. Alice sends a message to the key server, which contains her and Bob's names. She encrypts this message with key A.

2. The key server decrypts the message and checks whether its content is consistent (thereby authenticating Alice). In the positive case it generates a secret key K, encrypts it with key A and sends it to Alice.

3. The key server encrypts key K with key B and sends it to Bob.

4. Alice and Bob now have a common secret key K, and the key exchange problem is solved.

Of course, Alice can also work through the same protocol with Carol or the Cryptobank, provided these have also established a shared secret key with the key server. In practice though, an expanded variant of this protocol is more often used. This is the subject of Section 13.5.

13.4.4 Further authentication methods on the Internet

Authentication on
the Internet not only
relies on knowledge

Up to now, in the context of the Internet we have spoken almost exclusively of authentication by knowledge. Let us now take a look at what else there is.

Biometrics on the Internet

The use of biometrics on the Internet brings problems. If Alice sends a biometric characteristic value over the Net to the Cryptobank, Mallory can intercept and change it. The Cryptobank has no way of finding out whether the value actually comes from a biometric measuring device or from some other source.

Biometrics plays an
increasingly
important role on
the Internet

Despite this, biometrics plays an increasingly important role on the Internet. It is actually possible, with the help of biometrics, to control access to a secret key that Alice has stored on her hard disk in encrypted form (it might also be saved on a smart card).

Authentication by possession

Authentication by
possession is also
possible on the
Internet

The possession of a passport or some other difficult-to-forge item cannot be proven directly over the Net. But this form of authentication still plays a part on the Internet. It is actually possible to store a secret key on a piece of hardware (usually a smart card) in unreadable form. Possession of the key is thereby the same as possession of the hardware. Examples of this are given in Chapter 15.

Summary

Since only data can be sent over the Net, authentication on the Internet is ultimately always connected with authentication by knowledge. There are, however, ways to tie in authentication by possession or characteristic.

13.5 Kerberos

After our reflections on the topic of authentication on the Internet in general, let us now look at one the most important authentication protocols for the Internet. This bears the name **Kerberos**.

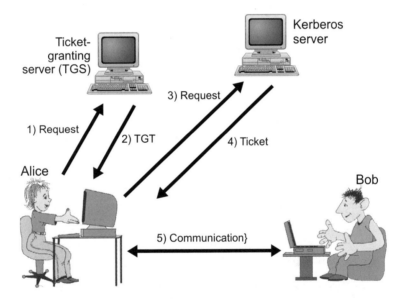

Figure 13.9 Kerberos provides two trusted third parties for the execution of a key exchange. Public key cryptography is not required for this.

In Greek legend, Kerberos is a three-headed dog that guards the entrance to the underworld. The name of this mythological being was adopted and adapted by the American elite university MIT (Massachusetts Institute of Technology) for an authentication with a trusted third party protocol – namely Kerberos. Using the Kerberos protocol, two users (Alice and Bob) are supplied with a shared secret key for encrypting their communications. This dispenses with asymmetric algorithms. Following the Kerberos implementation, MIT has developed a software packetage and a standard [RFC1510], both of which are available on the Internet.

13.5.1 How Kerberos works

Kerberos uses two trusted third parties

The most important feature of Kerberos is that it uses two trusted third parties at the same time: the **Kerberos server** and the **ticket-granting server (TGS)** (see Figure 13.9). There can be several ticket-granting servers on a network, but in our case we will be satisfied with just one. Before Alice and Bob can use the Kerberos protocol, they must first establish a secret key each with the Kerberos server (e.g. by personal contact with the administrator). Communication between Bob and Alice now proceeds as follows:

1. Alice sends an initialisation message to the Kerberos server, in which she specifies a TGS.

2. The Kerberos server now generates a DES key K_1, which it encrypts using Alice's secret key. It also creates a so-called **ticket-granting ticket (TGT)**, which consists of Alice's name, the newly generated DES key K_1 and several other items. It encrypts the TGT using the secret key of the TGS. The Kerberos server sends the encrypted DES key K_1 and the encrypted TGT to Alice.

3. Alice sends the unaltered encrypted TGT on to the TGS. With it she sends a message that basically consists of her own name and is encrypted using the DES key K_1 that she has received from the Kerberos server.

Kerberos only uses symmetrical cryptography for exchanging key

4. The TGS now generates a DES key K_2, which it encrypts with K_1. It also creates a so-called ticket that consists of Alice's name, the newly generated DES key K_2 and some other items. It encrypts this ticket with the secret key from Bob. The TGS then sends the encrypted DES key K_2 and the encrypted ticket to Alice. As you may have noticed, step 4 works like step 2, except that the TGS replaces the Kerberos server and Bob replaces the TGS.

5. Alice sends the unaltered encrypted ticket on to Bob. She also sends a message consisting mainly of her own name, and which is encrypted with the DES key K_2 she has received from the TGS. This step corresponds to step 3, again with different parties involved.

6. Alice and Bob now have the shared DES key K_2. With this they can communicate with each other without being challenged by Mallory.

Kerberos allows for a two-stage authentication

As you can see, Kerberos is not simply a server that supplies Alice and Bob with a shared key. Instead, the Kerberos server gives Alice a key that she has in common with the TGS. The TGS then supplies Alice with a key that she has in common with Bob. This two-stage method makes a lot of sense: the exchange of messages with the Kerberos server usually takes place when Alice logs in. She only communicates with a TGS when she wants to exchange encrypted messages with Bob. If she later wants to communicate with Carol, she only needs to contact the TGS, provided Carol has established a password with this TGS.

13.5.2 Pros and cons of Kerberos

Servers make an ideal target for Mallory

The great advantage of the Kerberos protocol is that asymmetrical algorithms – which are known to be very onerous – can be dispensed with. This plus point must, however, be set against the fact that the Kerberos server and the ticket-granting server must be constantly reachable online. On top of this, central servers are an ideal target for an attack by Mallory – if he succeeds in gaining control of the Kerberos server, he has practically the whole system at his mercy.

The consequence of the two drawbacks is that Kerberos is employed almost exclusively in university and company networks in which a certain amount of trust can be placed in the operator. On the world wide Internet, on the other hand, the use of public key infrastructures is preferred (see Chapter 16).

13.6 RADIUS and TACACS

AAA servers facilitate authentication

Alice's employer, Crypt and Co., would like to offer tele-working to several employees. This means they will have the opportunity to work from home, logging-in to their computers in the office. Field service worker Alice also needs remote access (e.g. over the Internet) to various computers of Crypt & Co. And finally, there are clients of Crypt & Co. who by agreement can call up certain information over the Net. It is clear that all these actions must be protected by a reliable authentication process. You already know the appropriate procedure.

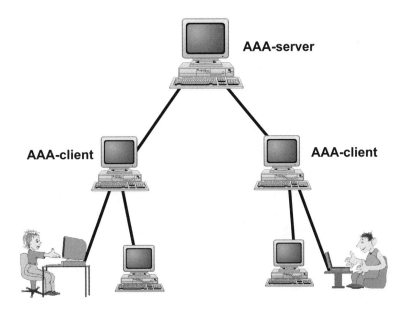

Figure 13.10 A policy for the authentication of AAA-clients can be fixed with the help of an AAA-server.

A unified authentication policy is important

It is also clear, however, that this can cause problems: if Alice has access to various computers of the company, the authentication must apply to all of them, otherwise it becomes unmanageable. For example, if Alice needs a separate password for each computer, and must update them at regular intervals, there is a great danger that careless errors will creep in. If Alice eventually leaves Crypt & Co. and consequently each access point must be individually blocked, it can easily happen that the system administrator forgets one of them, and Alice still has access to one of the company computers as a result. The decision about on which computers Alice has which rights should also be carefully considered and centrally recorded. The same goes, of course, for the tele-workers and clients of Crypt & Co. when they access their facilities. If clients pay for the use of a service, how long and to what extent that happens must be centrally recorded anyway (accounting). In short: if various people have access to various computers on a local network, a unified authentication policy must be decided upon and carried through. Otherwise, especially on a heterogeneous network with hundreds of users (as frequently occurs in practice), it will quickly come about that nobody any longer knows who has access through which door to which part of the network.

13.6.1 AAA-server

An AAA-server enables the pursuit of an authentication policy

This problem can be solved in the following way: all authentication data (such as passwords, one-time passwords, public keys) and all information about access rights are recorded on a central server and dial-in points are made available online. The server is usually called an **AAA-server** (AAA stands for Authentication, Authorisation, Accounting) and correspondingly a dial-in point is called an **AAA-client**. The third entity involved is the user, for instance the field service worker Alice, who wants to log-in. The typical process now looks as follows:

1. Alice connects to the AAA-client.

2. The AAA-client challenges Alice to authenticate herself (through the input of userID and password, for example).

3. The AAA-client decides whether it will engage the AAA-server for authentication, or whether it will perform this itself (we assume the former case, of course).

An AAA-server and AAA-client are involved as well as the user

4. The AAA-client sends a message to the AAA-server (Access Request), which tells it that Alice would like authentication. Alice's userID and password (or its hash value), as well as an identifier of the AAA-client and its password are included in this message.

5. The AAA-client waits for an answer. If this takes too long, it can send further access requests (to other AAA-servers as well).

6. The AAA-server authenticates the AAA-client with its password.

7. The AAA-server checks Alice's password and determines which access rights she has. It uses a database for this. If this does not have the necessary information

stored, the AAA-server can itself send an access request to another AAA-server. The result of the password check and the access rights are finally sent back to the AAA-client.

8. The AAA-client grants Alice access or rejects her.

Double authentication is provided

Whether one-time passwords or normal passwords are used has no effect on this process. Both are protected against Mallory by a hash (which includes the message ID). For a challenge–response procedure, an exchange of messages between the AAA-server and AAA-client is also necessary.

A characteristic of the described process is the double authentication: Alice authenticates herself to the AAA-client, which in turn authenticates itself to the AAA-server. Passwords, other authentication data, information about access rights, and accounting data are all saved exclusively on the AAA-server. The access point for Alice to use can therefore be configured centrally. Also, Alice only needs to change her password on the AAA-server rather than on each individual computer. If Mallory succeeds in gaining access to a company computer, he will not find any authentication stored there data that he could use for pretending to be Alice. The only drawback: the AAA-server needs special protection. If Mallory actually gains access to it, he has the whole system at his mercy.

13.6.2 RADIUS

RADIUS is an AAA standard

The best-known standard that implements an AAA-server is the **Remote Authentication Dial-In User Service (RADIUS)**. RADIUS was developed by the company Livingstone and was also specified in an RFC [RFC2058]. Since then, there have been a further 14 RFCs covering RADIUS extensions or other RADIUS themes. Although none of these RFCs is an Internet standard yet, RADIUS has long been a de facto standard that has been put into practice in numerous products. The operation of the RADIUS protocol is very similar to the process described above, if some labels are changed (AAA-server and AAA-client to RADIUS-server and RADIUS-client). RADIUS is one of the Internet services that UDP (and not TCP) uses as a transport protocol (see Section 21.2.2).

13.6.3 TACACS

TACACS is similar to RADIUS

The TACACS protocol, which provides for two-stage authentication similar to RADIUS [RFC1492], was written with the participation of the firm Cisco and is described in RFC1492. With the inclusion of access rights and accounting, this was developed into **TACACS+**, which is still in the Internet Draft stage. TACACS+ is not that different from RADIUS, but is not compatible with it. The only substantial difference: TACACS+ uses TCP and not as it does RADIUS UDP.

13.6.4 A replacement AAA standard

Another AAA standard is planned

In the IETF there is a working group that deals with the subject of AAA-servers. This group does not come under the Security Working Area, but under the Operations and Management Area instead. The aim of this working group is to develop a unified, effective AAA standard. It might take some time before this is ready, however, because the working group is relatively new. So far, it has only produced some preliminary documents in which the requirements for a standard are described.

13.7 Packaging of authentication mechanisms

The packaging of authentication mechanisms is logical

The authentication methods described in this chapter offer a sufficient choice of procedures to cover any practical application. This abundance has its drawbacks, however: users and administrators are confronted with a confusing choice of different authentication procedures for any given purpose. This means, for example, that Alice must remember ten or more different passwords, each having different default values with regard to the number of letters, number of special characters and maximum validity period. Fortunately, more and more passwords are being replaced by smart cards and smart tokens. However, this has the unfortunate side-effect that Alice's purse is becoming stuffed full of cards and tokens. Seen from an administrator's point of view, the matter is scarcely any better – when all is said and done, the access rights for various systems still have to be monitored, along with their respective authentication devices.

There have been several packaging attempts

For these reasons, in the past few years, various attempts have been made to bring authentication proceedings in tune with each other. These attempts mainly concerned company-internal networks, since their administrators would benefit from a unification of passwords, cards and account handling procedures (although most package suppliers on the open market prefer to exploit their own people). The three most important attempts to package authentication devices are introduced briefly in the following. It should be made clear, however, that each of these attempts represents a subject in itself, which in this context I can only cover superficially.

13.7.1 Single Sign-on (SSO)

One way to package authentication mechanisms is **Single Sign-on (SSO)**. This term – sometimes called Secure Single Sign-on (SSSO) – is currently one of the buzzwords in IT security. It incorporates two ideas: first, Alice should be able to authenticate herself to different computer systems using the same method (i.e. with the same password). Second, only one authentication procedure should be necessary for Alice to use all systems (which means, for example, that she will only need to enter it once).

Currently, SSO systems are mainly of interest to the operators of company networks. In this way, one-time authentication could be integrated into the operating system log-in. Once Alice logs-in to the operating system, she then, according to the SSO principle, will also have access to the SAP-R/3 system, to various database servers, and to the intranet and other applications, without having to enter her password or PIN, or insert her smart card, again.

The SSO server switches between client and server

Technically, SSO systems are usually implemented with the help of a server (SSO server), which switches between the company workplace computer and the respective application server. The operating system log-in is thus linked with authentication to the server. For example, if Alice starts her R/3 client, the SSO server performs the authentication to the R/3 server, without Alice knowing anything about it. The final communication then takes place directly between Alice and the application server, without the SSO server switching in.

From a security point of view, SSO is an advantage because it reduces the burden on the user. This boosts its acceptance and ensures that passwords that are written down or easy to guess, or a stack of cards in the wallet, are avoided. The drawback to this is clear: the SSO server is a particularly worthwhile target for Mallory. If he controls the SSO server, he can create havoc on a network.

13.7.2 Management of cross-platform warrants

Packaging also has benefits for management

Alice's problems with multiple authentications are only one side of the coin. Administrators have similar problems. For example, if the firm Crypt & Co. operates an R/3 server, a database server, and a Web server for the intranet, then administrative assistants must enter Alice into each of these systems individually before Alice can use the respective system. Any changes to Alice's rights, or even a denial perhaps, must also be undertaken individually in each system.

The said proceedings can be simplified if **cross-platform warrant management** is implemented. To do this, a central computer is set up, which has interfaces to all the server systems in question. Software on this central computer gives the administrator the ability to register new users and warrants. These details are then transmitted to the respective systems via the interfaces.

Cross-platform warrant management is complex

It goes without saying that cross-platform warrant management is a complex matter. For it to succeed, all the different server systems must be brought under one roof. In many cases this will be uneconomic, because the administration overhead can be considerable.

13.7.3 Company cards

A further interesting approach to packaging authentication mechanisms consists in using the same smart card for different applications. Since the greatest interest is currently to be found in large companies, people normally talk about company cards (or in other fields, student cards or employee cards).

Ideally, Alice can use her company card to log-in to the operating system, which simultaneously takes care of her authentication to the SSO server. She will also be able to use the same card to open doors, to clock in, or to pay for her lunch in the canteen. Since the card also carries her portrait, it can also serve general identification needs.

14

Cryptosystems based on elliptic curves

Crypto is not mathematics, but crypto can be highly mathematical, crypto can use mathematics, but good crypto can be done without a great reliance on complex mathematics.
W. T. Shaw

Key experience no. 14
One of the numerous earth-shaking problems that can be solved by cryptography is the coin flipping problem. The problem here is for Alice and Bob to toss a coin without either of them looking or cheating. The problem can be solved with the help of a special cryptographic protocol that you can study in [Schn96] – by the way, a coin is not actually needed.

Public key algorithms are overhead intensive The big drawback of public key algorithms is that they are heavy on overheads when compared to secret key algorithms. Although this situation is unlikely to change soon, there are ways of reducing the advance of symmetrical algorithms. The most promising possibility to date is offered by the so-called cryptosystems based on elliptic curves. This does not call for completely new cryptographic algorithms, but looks to an appreciable speeding up of algorithms based on the discrete logarithm, such as Diffie–Hellman, DSA or ElGamal. To understand the present chapter, you should be conversant with these algorithms.

14.1 Mathematical principles

Cryptosystems based on elliptic curves are mathematically the most demanding procedures to be addressed in this book. In the following, we will therefore be talking once again about mathematical principles. This said, I do not intend to delve too deeply into mathematics, but instead I will try to explain it all as simply as possible. You will find a more scientific explanation in [Rosing]. Other sources from the literature are [Certic] and [Johnso].

14.1.1 Yet another field

Crypto methods based on elliptic curves are mathematically complex

From Section 6.2.1 you already know that a group is a set by which a connection is defined. This connection is often called addition or multiplication, but is not necessarily the addition or multiplication you remember from elementary arithmetic. By definition, a group has a neutral element with respect to its connection and each element of the group has a reciprocal element. If the connection is described as an addition, the term 0 is normal for the neutral element. If the term multiplication is used, the neutral element becomes 1. The reciprocal element of element a is written as a^{-1} or $-a$, depending on the nature of the connection.

A group has two connections

As you already know, a field is a set for which two connections are defined, which are mostly either addition or multiplication. A field, with respect to addition, is a group. Without the 0, it also forms a group with respect to multiplication. The best-known field is the group of real numbers R, for which addition and multiplication are defined in the known manner. In Section 6.2.1 you learnt that for every prime number p there is a field with p elements, called GF(p). In the process, modulo-addition functions as addition, and modulo-multiplication functions as multiplication. There is one more demonstrable fact that I have not yet mentioned, however: for each prime number p and each natural number n there is exactly one field with p^n elements. If $n=1$, we have the special case in which modulo arithmetic can be used.

In the following, we shall only consider the special cases $n=1$ and $p=2$, i.e. GF(p) and GF(2^n), as cryptosystems based on elliptic curves can best be implemented with these Galois fields. In the following, GF(m) means any field with the form GF(p) or GF(2^n).

14.1.2 Calculations in GF (2^n)

The elements of GF(2^n) are written in binomial form

You already know how to calculate in GF(p). Calculating in GF(2^n) is somewhat more complicated. The elements are not written as natural numbers, but as binary numbers or as a polynomial with the coefficients 0 and 1. Here are some examples from GF(2^4):

$0101 = x^2+1$

$1111 = x^3+x^2+x+1$

$1010 = x^3+x$

Addition in GF(2^n) is defined as the bitwise Exclusive-Or connection of two binary numbers. In polynomial form, this corresponds to a polynomial addition with coefficients from GF(2). Here are some examples from GF(2^4):

A sequence of bits can also be written as a polynomial

$1001+1111 = 0110 = (x^3+1) + (x^3+x^2+x+1) = x^2+x$

$1000+0001 = 1001 = (x^3) + (1) = x^3 + 1$

In the following, polynomial always means a polynomial with coefficients from GF(2). Multiplication in GF(2^n) is defined as the polynomial multiplication modulo of an irreducible polynomial to the power of n. A polynomial is irreducible when it cannot be represented as a product of polynomials of lower degree. There are different algorithms that can be used to determine whether a polynomial is irreducible. For our purpose, however, it will suffice to take a polynomial of the desired degree from a table. For each degree $n>1$ there is an irreducible polynomial. In the following examples, the irreducible polynomial x^4+x+1 is used to define multiplication in $GF(2^4)$:

$$(x^3+1)\cdot(x^3+x^2+1) = x^6+x^5+x^2+1 = x^3+x^2+x+1 \ (\text{mod } x^4+x+1), \text{therefore } 1001\cdot1101 = 1111$$

14.1.3 Elliptic curves

An elliptical curve is defined as a curve of a group that fulfils the following equation:

The elements of GF(2^n) are written as a polynomial

$$y^2+a_1xy+a_2y = x^3+a_3x^2+a_4x+a_5$$

This definition embraces a point that lies at infinity and is termed as 0 (not to be confused with the point of origin of the coordinate system). It can be shown that elliptic curves (and only these) have the following interesting attribute: if a straight line cuts such a curve, then there are exactly three points of intersection. This includes the following cases (see Figure 14.1):

1. For a straight line that runs parallel to the y-axis, there is an intersection at point 0.

2. For a straight line tangential to the curve, the point of contact counts as a double point of intersection.

3. For all other straight lines, the three points of intersection are obvious.

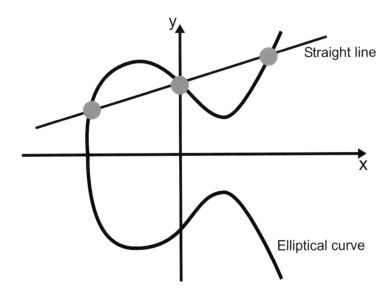

Figure 14.1   If tangential points count as double, and the intersection at infinity is included, then a straight line always cuts an elliptical curve at exactly three points.

From elliptic curves Based on this attribute, and using elliptic curves, a group can be defined which we
a group can be shall call E(K). Its elements are all the points on an elliptical curve, including *0*.
defined Addition is defined as follows: two points are added by drawing a straight line
through them (if the two points are identical, the line is a tangent to the curve). In
accordance with the above attribute, there must be a third point of intersection
between the straight line and the curve. The reflection of this point on the *x*-axis is
the result of the addition, where the reflection of *0* is still *0*. *0* is the neutral element
of the group, for which *P+0* = *0+P* = *P* for all points *P* of the elliptical curve. To
obtain the reciprocal of a point, a line is drawn through it, parallel to the *y*-axis. If
this line is a tangent, the point is its own reciprocal element. If the line is not a
tangent, in accordance with the above attribute, there is exactly one other intersect.
This is the reciprocal element.

In cryptography, only elliptic curves of the form $E(GF(m))$ (i.e. $E(GF(p))$ and
$E(GF(2^n)))$ are utilised, even if all the procedures named in the following would
also function using $GF(p^n)$.

14.2 Cryptosystems based on elliptic curves

For historical reasons, the connection for the group $E(GF(m))$ is called addition. As
mentioned, multiplication would also be possible, whence the expression
exponential function is justified for the multiple addition of points on $E(GF(m))$.
Similarly, the inverse of this computation can be expressed as the logarithm.

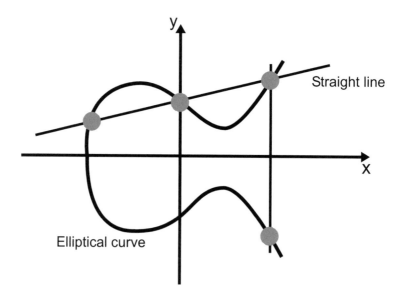

Figure 14.2 Two points on an elliptical curve are added by drawing a straight line through
them. The sum of the two points is given by the reflection on the *x*-axis of the third intersect
between the line and the curve.

The following attribute of $E(GF(m))$ is of central importance for cryptography: there are effective algorithms for the calculation of an exponential function, but not for the calculation of the logarithm. The result of this is that all cryptographic algorithms described that are based on the discrete logarithm can be implemented *ECCs are based* with the help of $E(GF(m))$. An **elliptical curve cryptosystem** (ECC) is thus an *on the discrete* asymmetrical algorithm based on the discrete logarithm, in which calculations in *logarithm* $E(GF(m))$ are used instead of calculations in $GF(p)$. Instead of a modulus, a group $GF(m)$ and the group $E(GF(m))$ built up from this are specified. All parameters that form the exponent are (as before) natural numbers; the base of the exponential function is an element of $E(GF(m))$.

14.2.1 Why ECCs?

ECCs need The addition of two points from $E(GF(m))$ consists of several calculations in *shorter keys* $GF(m)$. Exponentiation using $GF(m)$ is less onerous than exponentiation using $E(GF(m))$. The known algorithms for calculation of the discrete logarithm using $GF(p)$ are, however, much less efficient than those that calculate the logarithm using elliptic curves. The main advantage from using $E(GF(m))$, therefore, is that a set with smaller cardinality can be used with the same degree of security. This results in shorter key lengths, shorter signatures and shorter computation times.

According to [FoxRöh], the complexity of the discrete logarithm in $E(GF(m))$ increases linearly with m, while the complexity in $GF(m)$ only increases logarithmically. For a cryptosystem based on the discrete logarithm, a key length of 1024 bits can be reduced to 200 bits through the use of elliptic curves, without sacrificing security. This is said to reduce the computing time by a factor of 10.

ECCs offer a high Compared to the RSA algorithm, cryptosystems based on elliptic curves have still *degree of security* greater advantages as regards key length than algorithms based on the discrete *even with shorter* logarithm without elliptic curves. An RSA key length of 1024 corresponds to a key *keys* length of 160 for ECCs and has the same degree of security. Even here, an ECC is faster by a factor of 10. On top of this, the resulting signature (or ciphertext) is shorter. Because of these savings in computation time and bandwidth, ECCs are of special interest for use in smart cards (see Chapter 15 and [Hühnle]). If algorithms such as RSA or algorithms based on the discrete logarithm (without elliptic curves) are to be implemented on a smart card, this will only be possible through the use of a coprocessor. This would mean increased cost, however, which, for the high numbers in which smart cards are usually issued, gives cause for concern. However, ECCs can also be used without coprocessors, without performance suffering too much.

14.3 Examples and standards for ECCs

There are ECC To finalise our considerations, let us now look at some examples for ECCs and cast *standards* a glance over the standards that are intended to ensure their uniform use.

14.3.1 The most important ECCs

Since all ECCs are algorithms with which you are familiar from previous chapters (except that calculations were made in $GF(p)$), we will only take a brief look at the two most important here.

ECDH

ECDH is an ECC The acronym **ECDH** stands for **Elliptic Curve Diffie–Hellman** and designates the Diffie–Hellman algorithm based on elliptic curves. Instead of agreeing on p, Alice and Bob agree here on a group $E(GF(m))$. The public keys x and y are natural numbers, while g is an element of $E(GF(m))$, upon which Alice and Bob agree.

ECDSA

ECDSA is another The acronym **ECDSA** stands for **Elliptic Curve DSA** and designates the ECC variant *example* of the DSA algorithm, which, as is well known, is used for digital signatures. Once again, Alice and Bob agree on a group $E(GF(m))$. The public key x and the number y are natural numbers, while g is an element of $E(GF(m))$, upon which Alice and Bob agree. The only problem with porting the DSA algorithm into the ECC world lies in the fact that the number g^y is actually a point on an elliptical curve but is nevertheless also used in the exponent (the exponent must only contain natural numbers, however). Alice can solve this problem by using a natural number in the exponent derived from g^y. The x-coordinate of the point g^y is normally used for this. As long as Mallory cannot guess the derived number, this does no harm to the security of the procedure (after all, there are thousands of possibilities for varying the equation used for verification with DSA).

14.3.2 ECC standards

There are several In years gone by, various standardisation bodies have ensured that there is no lack *ECC standards to* of ECC standards to choose from. We shall restrict ourselves to the most important *choose from* exemplars.

P1363

The P1363 standard, already mentioned in Section 10.5, specified five ECCs in total (these are in P1363, not in P1363a). These include three key exchange algorithms: two ECDH variants and an algorithm called MQV, which works in a similar way to ECDH. P1363 also standardises ECDSA variants and an ECC version of the Nyberg–Rueppel algorithm, which is similar to DSA.

PKCS#13

You have already met PKCS standards in Section 10.4. **PKCS#13** is concerned with the topic of elliptic curves [PKCS#13], is currently being developed. It is already clear, however, that this standard will follow on from P1363. It is highly likely that PKCS#13 will be more restrictive, which is why this standard can also be described as a P1363 profile.

Other ECC standards

There are still other ECC standards There are still more standards in which ECCs are specified. These include ANSI X.9 and ISO/IEC 14888. However, I presume that P1363 and the largely compatible PKCS#13 standard will become established as the more important standards.

Implementing cryptography

Within a few years even backward Americans will have smart cards in their wallets.
BRUCE SCHNEIER [SCHN96]

Key experience no. 15
A special form of encryption (steganography to be more precise) was devised at the end of the 1990s by a research group in New York. They expanded the DNA from a human cell using synthetic sections in which a message was encoded. In this way it is possible to transfer a message in a dehydrated drop of liquid DNA.

Up to now, we have been concerned with algorithms, protocols and standards that Alice and Bob can use for communication. However, algorithms, protocols and standards by themselves cannot send a single bit down a line – instead, Alice and Bob need an implementation to put all their theoretical knowledge into practice.

The type of implementation is important
This chapter discusses how a cryptographic method is used in practice. This will teach you two things: first, that there are many ways in which cryptography can be implemented, and second, that a bad implementation can render even the most secure procedure useless.

15.1 Crypto hardware and software

To start with, we ask one of the most crucial questions in cryptography: should cryptographic procedures be implemented in hardware or software? There are arguments for both methods.

15.1.1 Pro software

Cryptography can be implemented in software
If cryptography is to be implemented in software, then a piece of software must be produced that, along with encryption and signatures, takes care of other tasks. An example of this is the PGP software (see Section 26.3), which can run on most of the current operating systems. PGP encrypts and signs e-mails and files using cryptographic algorithms integrated in the software. When cryptography is implemented in software, this has the following advantages:

- Writing computer programs is easier and cheaper than designing hardware.

- When the source code for a piece of software is known, then back doors and unintentional flaws are more easily spotted than in hardware.

- DEA, RC4 and other symmetrical procedures were developed mainly for software implementation.

- Hardware is affected by the cost of materials. Software, on the other hand, is not.

- Software has a high degree of portability. Once implemented, an algorithm can usually be ported onto other systems.

15.1.2 Pro hardware

Cryptography can be implemented in hardware

Cryptography can also be implemented in hardware. This means that a hardware module is developed that is used exclusively for the execution of cryptographic procedures. The message to be processed, together with a key in some instances, is fed to the hardware module, which returns the result (the ciphertext, for example). Basically, hardware can fulfil the same functions as software. In hardware, however, the crypto algorithms are transferred to an external module, while with crypto software, everything takes place on the same computer. Crypto hardware also has its advantages:

- In many implementations, hardware is faster than software. For encryption on a high-throughput transmission cable, there is no alternative to purpose-designed hardware. DES – still the most popular symmetric encryption procedure – is optimised for hardware.

Crypto hardware rates as secure

- If the source code for a software implementation is available, Mallory can try to manipulate it. For example, he can try to push software onto Alice and Bob that always uses keys that Mallory can guess. A similar effect can be achieved with special computer viruses or trojans. Hardware, on the other hand, is much more difficult to manipulate.

- Software is easier to analyse than hardware. So if you want to keep a procedure secret, you should only build it into hardware products. Of course, this is security by obscurity and, in view of Murphy's second law of cryptography ('It is impossible to keep a crypto procedure secret'), not to be recommended. Despite this, however, it still happens.

The key must not leave the hardware

- With hardware implementations, secret keys can be stored in such a way that they never leave the module. If the module is also protected with a password, Mallory can never learn the key, even if he steals the module.

- Another advantage of hardware is that Alice can always carry her own module with her. No matter where she goes, she can encrypt, decrypt and sign with her own key.

15.1.3 Summary

For high security requirements, hardware is mandatory

Hardware is the more expensive solution, but is more secure and usually faster. For the highest security needs, hardware is indispensable. On the other hand, software is less expensive, less secure, and usually slower. The main advantage of hardware has proven to be that Alice can carry her own module around with her, on which her secret key is stored. Since the secret key never leaves the module and is also unreadable, a hardware module offers special protection against Mallory. A hardware module of this type is usually a smart card, which is what we shall look at next.

15.2 Smart cards

There are different forms of plastic cards

You almost certainly carry a plastic card around in your wallet. Perhaps you travel with a railway card, make calls with a telephone card, pay with a credit card, or obtain cash from an automatic teller machine using a Eurocheque card. All these plastic cards may be the same size, but sometimes have completely different functions.

15.2.1 Plastic cards

Let us look at the different types of plastic card, and how they can be used for cryptography.

Magnetic strip cards

Magnetic strip cards can store data

If a plastic card has a dark strip, approx. 1 cm wide, on the back, it is a **magnetic strip card** (Figure 15.1). The magnetic strip has three invisible channels, in which data can be stored. According to the relevant ISO 7811 standard, 226 bytes fit on a strip and hence on a card. The stored data can be read or changed with suitable devices. A magnetic strip card is thus a storage medium like a diskette or fixed disk, even if a storage capacity of 226 bytes is hardly conducive to creativity. Nevertheless, this version of the plastic card is in use in great profusion, mainly because it is so cheap. Cheque or credit cards, for example, are mostly (still) implemented as magnetic strip cards. Seen from a security point of view, however, magnetic strip cards give rise to indigestion rather than feelings of well-being.

Magnetic strip cards are not specially secure

If a card falls into Mallory's hands, he can change the data stored on it as though it were a diskette. He can even copy data from one card to another or fill a blank card with his own data. Credit card companies and banks protect themselves against this by using various devices: holograms, which are difficult to forge, are supposed to guard against duplication. Key-dependent hash values stored on the card are there to ensure that no one changes or forges the content. A user can normally have a stolen card blocked at any time. Automatic teller machines can also make online checks to make certain that a card is valid and not blocked.

Chip cards

Substantially more powerful than a simple magnetic strip card is the second important model of plastic card, the **chip card** (Figure 15.1). You can usually recognise these by a gold-coloured metal contact surface about the size of a fingernail on the front (there are also non-contact chip cards, but these are not of interest here). Telephone cards are the most well-known example of this species of plastic card. Behind the contact surface on a chip card there is a hardware chip, which is markedly more powerful than a magnetic strip.

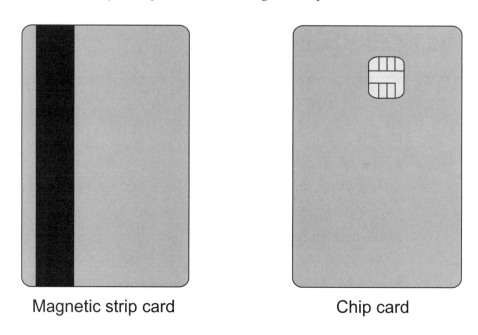

Magnetic strip card   Chip card

Figure 15.1 Magnetic strip cards can be recognised by a dark strip on the reverse side. Chip cards can be recognised by a metal contact surface.

There are two kinds of chip card: **memory card** and **smart card** (externally these are the same). On a memory card, the chip is only used to store data and is not able to compute or control access to the stored data. A smart card, on the other hand, is a miniature computer: it has a processor, a genuine read-only memory (ROM), a working memory (RAM) and an electronically erasable programmable memory (EEPROM). These components are coordinated by a special smart card operating system. Input and output is via the contact surface on the front.

A chip card is a computer in miniaturised form Smart cards nowadays typically have 16 Kbyte ROM, 2Kbyte EEPROM and several hundred bytes of RAM available.

Further information on the technology of smart cards is available in [EffRan]. There is also a technical magazine (*Card Forum*) that deals with this subject.

Further plastic cards

There are cards with both a strip and a chip

For the sake of completeness it should be mentioned that there are also plastic cards with neither a chip nor a magnetic strip, and which serve only to replace a piece of paper. You may also have a so-called hybrid card in your wallet that has both a magnetic strip and a chip. The Eurocheque card is the best-known example of this. The magnetic strip is present only for compatibility with existing reading devices and offers no other advantage.

15.2.2 Successful model smart cards

Smart cards are a successful product

The smart card is not a new invention. The first patents date back to the late 1960s and early 1970s. At that time, hardware was still bulky and expensive, making the smart card inconceivable as a mass product. Only in the mid 1980s did the smart card develop into a success story of computer technology. According to [Lemme], the number of smart cards produced worldwide to date runs into ten figures, which must be a record for technical devices. Up to now, smart cards have been used mainly in banking and as a means of payment. Pay-TV, telephone cards and mobile phones are further areas of application that are becoming increasingly important. The age of the smart card has only just begun, however: in the offing is their use in the field of medical and social care, as personal IDs and as a means of payment on public transport. They are becoming increasingly accepted as a substitute for cash. Lending weight to the argument, more and more PCs are being equipped with card-reading devices, and in a few years, time these may well be standard equipment. A considerable increase in the use of smart cards seems certain in the years to come.

Smart cards are more popular in Europe than in the USA

That the smart card boom is only just beginning is shown by the fact that the USA is still a chip-card-development country: nearly all patents stem from Europe, and most manufacturers are located here. In the form of credit cards, smart cards are almost unknown in the USA and the average American carries almost no other kind of smart card. This may well soon change, however, as is confirmed by Bruce Schneier's quotation at the start of this chapter. It is to be hoped that European manufacturers will be ready and waiting.

15.2.3 Smart cards and cryptography

Smart cards are ideal for cryptography

It is as though smart cards were invented just for cryptography. Above all, they are suited to the execution of cryptographic algorithms that need secret keys. They take in data to the chip via the contact surface, encrypt it with the secret key, then sign or process it in some way. The data is then output via the same contact surface. The secret key used is stored in the chip on the card and never leaves it. In this way, smart-card-owner Alice can carry her own little crypto service module around with her. She can slide her card into a reading device controlled by Mallory, since the reading device has no chance of accessing the secret key. Alice also has nothing to fear if she loses her card or has it stolen, because the key to the card cannot be decrypted (at least in theory). On top of this, the smart card only works if a password (PIN) has been entered beforehand. In contrast to a magnetic strip card, the smart card is almost uncopiable. However, there is one drawback: in contrast to most other variants of cryptological hardware, they are very slow.

Symmetric encryption and decryption using smart cards

There are many applications for smart cards in cryptography

Smart cards are ideally suited for symmetric encryption (and decryption) if speed is not essential. Alice feeds the data to be encrypted to her smart card, where it is encrypted with DES or some other symmetric algorithm. Data can similarly be decrypted. At first sight, such a use would be ideal for pay-TV: the pay-TV sender could encrypt their programs with DES and distribute smart cards to all clients. These cards would have the DES key stored on them and would be connected between the antenna and the television with a special device, in order to decrypt incoming signals. So far, this method has two catches: first, TV pictures are mostly analog at present and are therefore difficult or even impossible to encrypt with any algorithm looked at in this book. Secondly, smart cards are too slow to decrypt a TV picture as they can't manage more than a few Kbytes per second. The solution: in practice, (enforcedly weak) analog encryption procedures are used. However, the key is changed every few seconds, which is enough to spoil non-paying TV viewer Mallory's fun. Each new key is encrypted with a symmetric key and sent with the TV pictures to the receiver, where a smart card decrypts the key and can then decrypt the picture. The fact that it is possible to crack pay-TV encryption with a standard PC is due to the fact that, despite frequent key changes, the weak analog encryption is open to attack if the attacker has sufficient computational power – in contrast, the strong encryption of the smart card is secure.

Asymmetric decryption with smart cards

The private key can be stored on the smart card

Asymmetric algorithms like RSA are mainly used for the exchange of keys. Small quantities of data such as this can easily be processed with a smart card. First, however, Bob encrypts the session key with Alice's public key without using a smart card (this is not necessary because no private key is involved). When Alice receives the encrypted key, she feeds it to her smart card, which decrypts it with her private key and delivers it back to her decrypted. Alice can now use the session key. If Alice uses a terminal that has been manipulated by Mallory, he can acquire the session key, of course, but not Alice's private RSA key.

Digital signatures with smart cards

As far as cryptography is concerned, the most valuable service rendered by smart cards is connected with digital signatures. For example, if Bob has written a text with his word processor and would like to sign it, he inserts his card in the reading device on the computer and clicks on the menu option 'Sign'. The software now asks Bob for his PIN and then fabricates a hash value with a cryptographic hash function, which it sends to the smart card together with the PIN. If the PIN is genuine, the smart card then signs the hash value and returns the signature.

Authentication with smart cards

Authentication can be performed with smart cards

Authentication based on a challenge–response procedure can be implemented using a smart card. Crypt & Co. can use this, for example, to secure access to its PCs (usually it only uses passwords for this, despite the known drawbacks). So that Crypt & Co. employee Alice can use authentication by smart card, she needs a smart card reader, some dedicated access software and, of course, a smart card. Stored on this smart card is a secret key, which must also be known to the PC. When Alice wants to log-in, she inserts her smart card into the reader. The computer now asks for her PIN and sends this and a random number (challenge) to the card. The card checks the PIN and if it is OK applies a key-dependent hash function to the random number using the secret key stored on the card. The result is sent back to the PC and checked (the PC also has the secret key and can therefore undertake the verification). If everything is OK, Alice is logged-in.

Smart cards can be used for logging in

Summary

Without a doubt, smart cards and cryptography are excellently suited to each other. For Alice and Bob, there is scarcely any more effective way of guarding their private keys than on a smart card, because on such cards the key is not readable. Not in theory at least, because of course hackers have already tried to get round the protection mechanisms of smart cards and to read the secret contents – you will find a couple of cryptanalytical methods for this in Section 15.6. Less cryptanalytical, but nevertheless effective, Mallory can proceed by freezing the chip in liquid helium and viewing it with an electron microscope. It is possible that he can discover and extract the secret key in this way. To prevent this and similar attacks, smart card manufacturers had a few ideas: the memory cells of smart cards that are dedicated to cryptography are normally and deliberately concealed. There are dummies that cannot be distinguished from genuine cells. The connecting circuits take diversions that make them difficult to follow. Further security precautions mean that the memory content will be erased if the memory is bombarded with electrons, thus preventing it from being read. Operation at a lower resonant frequency (which could allow changes in the memory to be observed) is not allowed by many chips.

Procedures based on elliptic curves are very suited to smart cards

Quite another problem with the use of smart cards lies in the fact that public key procedures are computationally very demanding, and smart cards are very slow. If procedures such as RSA, Diffie–Hellman, or DSA (without elliptic curves) are implemented on smart cards, this almost certainly means excruciatingly long waiting times if adequate key lengths are used. To get round this problem, many implementations (like Eurocheque cards) do away completely with public key procedures. An alternative is to use cryptographic coprocessors, which increases the price of the chip, of course. The ideal solution, however, is undoubtably the use of cryptosystems based on elliptic curves (see Chapter 14). For the same level of security, these need only a tenth of the computing power needed by RSA or DSA. True, this is still notably more than is needed by DES or IDEA. However, the saving

Eurocheque cards are well suited to smart cards

is big enough to do without a coprocessor, provided the chip EEPROM is enlarged a little. For this reason, cryptosystems based on elliptic curves are enjoying increasing popularity in smart card circles.

15.2.4 Smart cards on the Internet

Up to now, smart cards have enjoyed only rarity value on the Internet, but this need not continue. There is an array of promising applications that could become household names in years to come. Before these can break through, however, smart card reading devices must first become established as normal computer components. Here are the more important possible applications:

On the Internet there are many applications for smart cards

- Authentication: Telnet, access to databases over the Net, special Web pages and similar services are still usually protected with passwords. This task could be undertaken by smart cards for very security-critical applications.

- Payments: whether as a chip-bedecked credit card or as a substitute for cash – in the future, smart cards will perhaps play an important part in effecting payments on the Internet. After Alice has filled her virtual shopping trolley in the cyber mall, she will pay by inserting her card in the reading device and perhaps entering her PIN.

- Signatures: some software programs for the Internet (e-mail programs, Web browsers) support smart cards for signing messages.

- Encryption: asymmetric encryption with smart cards is rather slow but is conceivable for high-security applications. In any case, it is wise to place only the private RSA key on the smart card.

On the Internet the advantages of smart cards become apparent

When used on the Internet, the advantages of smart cards become more apparent. No matter whether Alice logs-on to the Internet from home, from her place of work, or from an Internet café – she always has her secret key with her on the smart card. Even a contaminated computer can do Alice no harm, since her key is stored on the card in unreadable form.

15.3 Other crypto hardware

There are further examples of hardware cryptography

Smart cards are by far the most popular means of executing cryptographic operations with a special hardware module, but there are many other ways of demonstrating how cryptography can be implemented in hardware.

15.3.1 Hardware security module

The biggest drawback to the smart card is a chronic lack of speed. However, there are applications in which a higher performance is required. This is the case, for example, for the certification of a public key infrastructure (see Section 17.1). If the

Cryptobank issues digitally signed account statements for their clients, they cannot do so without the use of a smart card.

An HSM functions like a smart card

For those cases where a smart card is too slow, the market offers the **hardware security module (HSM)**. The function of an HSM is similar to that of a smart card: a secret key is stored on the HSM in unreadable form. The HSM can execute signature and encryption operations on data fed to it via an interface provided on the HSM.

Compared to a smart card, an HSM is significantly larger (about the size of a PC). It is also expensive, being priced around 10,000 euros. There is one other difference: unlike smart cards, most HSMs make it possible to prepare a backup copy of the secret key. This is achieved with a special accessory that can make the copy and store it. The HSM accessory can be stored in the office safe as a backup of the secret key, which, incidentally, is not in readable form and is only of use when restored to the HSM.

15.3.2 Smart tokens

smart cards need a reading device

Smart cards have the drawback that they are useless without a reading device. As yet, however, only a few PCs and other machines have been equipped with them, which is why many users are looking for an alternative. For authentication purposes there is an alternative in the form of the so-called **smart token**. A smart token is a small object with an inbuilt computer chip and a display. Most smart tokens look like a small pocket calculator, although some are in the form of wrist watches or key fobs. Many smart tokens have a keyboard, making them more likely to be mistaken for a pocket calculator.

Smart tokens facilitate the challenge-response procedure

With a smart token, Alice can authenticate herself through a challenge–response procedure (see Section 13.4.3), without owning a smart card reader and without the software she uses having to support cryptographic functions. Smart tokens are thus a secure alternative to passwords.

To explain how a smart token works, we assume that Alice wants to access her online account at Cryptobank and uses a smart token to achieve this. Typically this works as follows:

1. Alice sends her name and account number to the Cryptobank.

2. The Cryptobank sends a number (challenge) back to her.

3. Alice inputs the challenge to the smart token (via its keyboard, for example).

4. The smart token now calculates the response to the challenge with a key-dependent hash function and shows this on the display screen.

The password is shown on the display

5. Alice reads the response from the display and sends it as a password to the Cryptobank.

6. The Cryptobank checks the response and grants Alice access to her account, or not, as the case may be.

There are as many variations of this scenario as there are smart token manufacturers.

The SecurID card

The SecurID card is the best-known smart token

The best-known and most successful smart token product is the **SecurID card** produced by RSA Security. The most important feature of the SecurID card is that the current time (correct to the minute) is used as the challenge. In this case, the server does not need to send a challenge and Alice does not have to type it in. Instead, the challenge is delivered automatically from a clock contained on the chip. Since the server also knows the current time, a transmission of the challenge is not necessary. The actual response is displayed continuously on the SecurID display and changes once every minute.

Internally, the SecurID card is not designed to calculate the response directly from the current time. The chip contains a pseudo-generator which, starting from an initial setting, changes every minute. The response displayed is produced from the current value. Obviously, the initial setting must be different for every SecurID card. How the pseudo-generator works is, unfortunately, an RSA Security secret.

In this case, the challenge is the time

Since a SecurID card does not accept an external challenge, it does not need a keyboard. However, there is a SecurID variant with a keyboard that enables the additional input of a PIN.

Figure 15.2   The SecurID card (shown left in key fob, right in cheque card format) is a smart token.

The SecurID card is a very simple, but also very successful product. RSA Security has made a fortune out of it. It was probably its very simplicity that led to its success: a simple, easily integrated, repeatable smart token solution is preferred by many companies to a smart card solution, which, although more secure, is more burdensome.

Vasco

The smart token from the company Vasco contains a small scanner that can read the challenge from the screen for itself. This method is – like any challenge–response procedure – more secure than a simple password request. Authentication by knowledge and authentication by possession are thus combined.

15.3.3 Crypto boxes

Crypto boxes facilitate the application of cryptology

In this book, a **crypto box** is a piece of hardware that is an imperceptible part of a communication connection and encrypts or decrypts data. The key is stored in the crypto box. The purpose of a crypto box is not just to store the key in a secure external hardware module. Its purpose is much more to facilitate very fast encryption.

Crypto boxes are a widespread form of hardware cryptography. They are many applicable communications protocols (IP, X.25, IDSN, ...) for them. In client–server architectures they are often used only on the server side, while the clients make do with less productive software. Crypto boxes are very important in connection with VPNs (see Sections 22.4 and 23.6).

15.3.4 Further opportunities for hardware cryptography

There are further opportunities for hardware cryptography

Obviously there are still more opportunities for using cryptography in hardware form. There are small hardware modules that function like smart cards, but use the USB port instead of a smart card reader as the interface. Modules with similar functions are also available for the PCMCIA slot. There are also several random generator hardware modules for the serial port on the market. And last but not least, dongles (hardware modules that prevent software pirate copying) often use cryptographic techniques.

15.4 Crypto software

Even if hardware modules are admirable and secure, most crypto implementations are still software programs that execute the cryptographic functions themselves (and do not export the task to an external module). The drawbacks with crypto software were covered in Section 15.1. Here we want to consider the three most important drawbacks from the security point of view:

- Crypto software is not as secure against manipulation as crypto hardware.

- Crypto software offers less secure key storage than crypto hardware.

- With crypto software it cannot easily be arranged for Alice always to have her secret key with her.

Let's assume Alice's employer Crypt & Co. wants to develop some crypto software. How can Crypt & Co. best allow for the known drawbacks of crypto software?

15.4.1 Security against manipulation

Crypto software is easier to manipulate than crypto hardware

Controlled manipulation of hardware is no easy matter, even for Mallory. The manipulation of software is much easier, especially if Mallory has the source code.

If Mallory can manipulate crypto software to suit his purpose, security flies out the window. For example, by suitable tampering, Mallory can arrange things so that when keys are generated they will be easy to guess. There are many other ways in which Mallory can build back doors into software.

Crypto software must be protected against tampering

If Crypt & Co. wants to produce its product without any special hardware, it should take care that the product reaches customer Bob without Mallory having any opportunity to tamper with it. For his part, Bob should make certain that no one has access to his computer and that viruses and trojans are avoided. If Mallory is denied access to the software in this way, neither Bob nor Crypt & Co. need fear his attempts at manipulation.

15.4.2 Key storage with software

A very critical matter that Crypt & Co. must take care of in its software is the storage of secret keys. A secret key must be accessible for the software when needed, but must be stored in unreadable format in case Mallory gets his hands on the computer on which the software is installed.

Keys must be stored securely

If secret keys are stored externally on a smart card, the problem is solved. But since we assume that Crypt & Co. wants to sell its software without hardware support, we must look for other methods. One solution would be for customer Bob to remember his key and type it in when needed. For a 128-bit IDEA key or a 1024-bit RSA key, poor Bob would be hopelessly overtaxed.

Derivation of a key, PKCS#5

Another possibility is to derive the key from a password of moderate length that Bob can remember. This method is described in the **PKCS#5** standard, see [PKCS#5] and Section 10.4. The key can be generated from a password using a cryptographic hash function (MD2 or MD5). The standard uses DES as the encryption algorithm. A similar method can be used with other symmetrical algorithms.

A password can be changed into a key

For asymmetrical algorithms, on the other hand, it is very complicated and possibly insecure to generate an RSA or Diffie–Hellman private key (even if it is possible). For this reason, in practice, the transformation of passwords into keys is only used for symmetrical algorithms.

Since we assume that Mallory knows the method with which Bob transforms his password into a key, Bob must definitely select a secure password. His surname, date of birth and similar entities are not suitable, and where possible he should also avoid other words fraught with meaning. If he doesn't, Mallory can try to guess the password as a simple way to get at the key.

PKCS#8 standardises the encrypted storage of keys

Encryption of keys, PKCS#8

Mainly because of the fear that passwords that are simple to guess will be used, the method of deriving keys from passwords is not used in a direct form. Instead, software implementations usually store secret keys in a file, which is itself encrypted. To encrypt this file (and the key with it) Bob cannot use a key derived from a password. The advantage of this method is that a more secure (i.e. more random) key, which cannot be derived from a password, can be used for the encryption of the communication. In addition to this, Bob can change the password without having to change the secret key.

PKCS#8 can use PKCS#5

A format for the encrypted private keys of asymmetrical algorithms is described in the **PKCS#8** standard [PKCS#8].This format provides a data structure that holds other details as well as the key itself. These other details include, for example, a version number and the OID of the algorithm with which the key can be used. PKCS#5 can be used for the encryption.

Biometrics can also be used for securing an encrypted key (see Section 13.3). For example, Bob might be made to have his fingerprint checked before he can encrypt his secret key.

Secret keys as memory remnants

A secret key can remain in storage

Even if Bob stores his secret key in an encrypted file, he is still not safe. This is because whether encrypted, decrypted or signed, the key must at some time be decrypted by the software. Since areas of working memory are often swapped out to the hard disk by the operating system, there is always the danger that a key will be left on the hard disk. Even an explicit erasure often avails nothing, because operating systems usually 'erase' areas of memory simply by releasing them for overwriting – leaving the data untouched for the nonce. If at some stage Bob's PC falls into Mallory's hands, Mallory can search specifically for such memory remnants and perhaps even find a secret key. With modern technology (such as an electron microscope) it is even possible to resurrect explicitly erased areas of memory. It is feasible that Mallory might rummage around in Bob's waste bin and come across an old hard disk on which he will find several keys that Alice and Bob have used at some time or other. If Mallory was in the secret service, such a scenario might well be a reality.

Erased data can be restored with an electron microscope

For the above reasons, Crypt & Co. should make sure that its software protects the secret key, even against erroneous temporary storage and pseudo-erasure processes. However, even the best crypto software can do much to outwit the electron microscope. If Bob wants maximum security, he will do well to go over old hard disks with a hammer before throwing them away.

Summary

Hardware is an advantage for key storage

If we fear that Bob's PC might fall into Mallory's hands, then key storage is a major problem for crypto software implementations. Although there are ways to ameliorate this problem, it cannot be completely solved. A good hardware implementation is always more secure than a software implementation, because a key can never be completely hidden with software. There is always a moment when a secret key must be available in decrypted form. If a trojan or other with evil intent software chooses this moment to strike, it will capture the key.

15.4.3 Portable keys in software

A private key can also be stored on a server

Crypt & Co. still have the third software problem to deal with: an encrypted, stored key is more difficult for Bob to carry around in his trouser pocket than a smart card. But even for this there are solutions: for example, Bob can carry his secret key stored on a diskette in encrypted form. Another possibility: the encrypted keys are stored on a server and can be downloaded over the Internet with a Java applet. Although these possibilities are not quite so secure and effective as a smart card, in many cases they are adequate.

15.5 Universal crypto interfaces

Standardised crypto interfaces are practical

The purpose of crypto hardware is to store cryptographic software functions in a secure, portable and often faster module. Obviously, a standard interface for such hardware modules would be an advantage – this might actually enable any given software to work together with any given crypto service module.

Even with crypto software, cryptographic functions are often stored in a library that can be used by other implementations. The interface to such libraries should also be standardised.

A universal crypto interface has three components

For the above reasons, several interfaces have been standardised over the past few years, which facilitate uniform access to cryptographic hardware and software modules. In this book, such interfaces are known as **universal crypto interfaces**. When one considers the diverse standards in this field, one is reminded of the old adage: the great thing about standards is that there are so many of them to choose from. There are, of course, many standardised universal crypto interfaces designed to achieve similar goals with similar means, but these are incompatible.

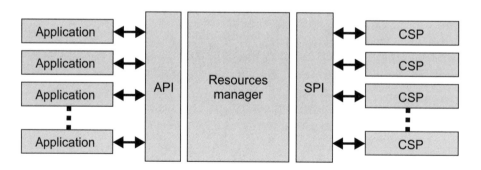

Figure 15.3 A universal crypto interface makes different crypto modules (CSPs) available to applications over a resource manager.

15.5.1 Structure of a universal crypto interface

A universal crypto interface is best imagined as a three-part object, which stands between any number of software programs and any number of crypto modules (see Figure 15.3). These crypto modules, depending on their standards, are implemented in hardware or software, normally both. A software program that accesses a crypto module over the universal crypto interface is often termed the **application** in this connection, and the crypto module is termed the **cryptographic service provider (CSP)**.

How a universal crypto interface works

In the centre stands the resources manager

At the centre of the three-part interface is the **resources manager**. This component controls communication between applications and CSPs. The application accesses the resources manager over an interface, which is called the **application program interface (API)**. The interface between the resources manager and CSPs is called the **service provider interface (SPI)**.

The crypto interface is addressed over an API

The normal operating sequence of a universal crypto interface requires an application to call up the execution of a cryptographic function over the API (say the encryption of a message). The resources manager takes this function call and forwards it via the SPI to a CSP, which executes the function. Via the SPI, the CSP now gives the result back to the resources manager, which sends it back to the application via the API. This sequence can be regarded as a protocol between the application and CSP. In the terminology of Chapter 12, it is a finely specified, usually state-regimented protocol. It is not a crypto protocol in the usual sense, however, because communications between application and CSP are not authenticated and also not further encrypted.

Contribution of the resources manager

An important point of difference between the diverse universal crypto interfaces is the form of the resources manager. At one extreme, it is an intelligent component that manages the control of communications between applications and CSP. At the other, the resources manager (and the SPI along with it) is not even present and the function calls go directly via the API to the CSP.

A resources manager can be set out differently

An intelligent resources manager is primarily suitable for 'dumb' hardware modules, which can do little more than encrypt, decrypt and sign. The resources manager notes which hardware modules are currently available and, where needed, can also generate error messages. In the case of a simple or absent resources manager, the CSPs must supply the necessary intelligence themselves.

15.5.2 PKCS#11

PKCS#11 standardises a crypto interface

PKCS#11 is another standard from the PKCS suite ([PKCS#11], see Section 10.4). It specifies a universal crypto interface called **Cryptoki (Cryptographical Token Interface)**, pronounced crypto-key. Cryptoki is quite clearly set out for hardware modules (which does not mean that it only supports these). CSPs are called tokens in PKCS#11. A token is usually a smart card or an HSM, but can also be a software module. PKCS#11 provides an intelligent resources manager that controls the tokens.

PKCS#11 follows a simple object-based approach. The resources manager, the tokens and the so-called slots (a slot corresponds approximately to a smart card reader) are each modelled by their own object. A token can itself store objects, keys for example.

PKCS#11 is without doubt a very important interface, used by many software products (Netscape Navigator®, for example). Since most smart card operating systems do not themselves support PKCS#11, many manufacturers offer drivers that connect between control object and slot and thus emulate PKCS#11-compatible smart cards.

PKCS#11 allows many profiles

The big problem with PKCS#11 is that even this standard cannot overcome the heterogeneous nature of the smart card world. Of necessity, PKCS#11 is generic in some places and thus allows different profiles. For this reason, it cannot be guaranteed that a PKCS#11-controllable smart card will work with all software that supports PKCS#11.

15.5.3 PC/SC

PC/SC is a smart-card interface

As the name indicates, **PC/SC** is an interface specification that is intended especially for connecting smart cards to PCs. In contrast to PKCS#11, PC/SC is more closely tailored for smart cards. PC/SC is not a genuine crypto interface, because the card also provides cryptography-independent functions such as the reading of files. PC/SC provides an intelligent resources manager, which controls negotiations with smart cards and card readers. PC/SC is supported by numerous products, including Windows 2000®.

15.5.4 Microsoft CryptoAPI

CryptoAPI stems from Microsoft

CryptoAPI is a universal crypto interface developed by Microsoft, which is used mainly in the 32-bit environment of Microsoft operating systems (Windows 95, 98, 2000 and NT). As the name suggests, CryptoAPI doesn't provide a resources manager – the applications communicate directly with the CSPs. The CSPs must therefore be rather more intelligently constructed than in the case of a universal crypto interface with a resources manager.

CryptoAPI makes a whole series of function calls available, with which all conceivable cryptographic processes can be set in motion. These processes range from the encryption and hashing of messages with popular algorithms to the verification of digital signatures and the duplication of an encrypted message.

Several Microsoft products support CryptoAPI

Since CryptoAPI comes from Microsoft and is supported by several Microsoft products (such as Windows 2000 and Internet Explorer), this interface is widely used. Outside the world of Microsoft, however, other universal crypto interfaces are used.

15.5.5 CDSA

CDSA stems from Intel **Common Data Security Architecture (CDSA)** is a universal crypto interface developed by Intel. CDSA provides a resources manager called the **Common Security Services Manager (CSSM)**. CDSA offers numerous cryptographic functions. Thanks to the wide choice of functions and the well-thought-out design, CDSA is one of the best universal crypto interfaces. Unfortunately, CDSA is not nearly so widespread as most other universal crypto interfaces described here. However, it is supported by Apple and Hewlett-Packard.

15.5.6 GSS-API

The GSS-API is standardised in several RFCs The **Generic Security Service Application Program Interface (GSS-API)** is a universal crypto interface, which, in contrast to most others, does not stem from just one firm, but from the IETF. It is described in [RFC1508], and extensions are described in other RFCs, including [RFC1509], [RFC1964], [RFC2025], [RFC2078] and [RFC2479].

The GSS-API specifies a universal crypto interface specifically for crypto protocols. The specification anticipates that in the working out of a crypto protocol, both communication partners (Alice and Bob in our case) have recourse to a GSS-API implementation. That being so, with the help of the GSS-API, different protocols can access the same crypto library.

The GSS-API does not provide a resources manager The GSS-API does not provide a resources manager and therefore needs intelligent CSPs. Among the function calls supported by the GSS-API there are also commands for the creation and control of contexts, with which a state-regimented protocol can be implemented. The GSS-API supports Kerberos and PKI functions amongst others (see Chapter 16). The use of SSL (see Chapter 24) is also possible, if not yet standardised.

15.5.7 Further universal crypto interfaces

There are still other universal crypto interfaces The range of universal crypto interfaces continues to grow. For example, there are **Java Cryptography Architecture (JVA)** and a **Java Smart Card API**. There are also several interfaces from the field of biometrics (such as the **BioAPI**), although these can no longer be called crypto interfaces. In future we shall therefore have to live with a multiplicity of standards in this field.

15.6 Real-world attacks

Real-world attacks If Mallory wants to eavesdrop on the encrypted communication between Alice and Bob, he can try to attack procedures and protocols. It is often simpler, however, if his attack is directed at the respective implementation. Such an attack is known as a **real-world attack**. The most important real-world attacks will be introduced in this section. We start with the very real assumption that Mallory can not only eavesdrop on communication between Alice and Bob, but also has access to their end devices. If Mallory should steal Alice's smart card, this would be such a case.

15.6.1 Side-channel attacks

Normally we assume that, when attacking an encryption algorithm, Mallory only uses the ciphertext and sometimes the plaintext for unauthorised decryption. In practice, however, there are often other things that can give Mallory an indication of the key. This is the case when Mallory has direct access to the implementation (which is exactly what we are assuming).

Mallory can also use indirect results

An attack which includes and evaluates such indirect results is known as a **side-channel attack**. Side-channel attacks on PKCS#1 implementations of the RSA algorithms were introduced in Section 10.4. This attack enables Mallory to determine the key of an RSA implementation when he feeds this with specially selected (nonsensical) ciphertext. The indirect result of the encryption here is the reply of the implementation, whether or not the respective input ciphertext was decrypted into a valid plaintext. Some further side-channel attacks will now be introduced.

Differential time analysis

Differential time analysis was discovered by Kocher in 1995

The oldest of the real-world attacks described here is the **timing attack**, which, on the grounds of uniformity, I call **differential time analysis** [Koch95]. This attack was discovered in 1995 by the American cryptographer Paul Kocher. With a differential time analysis, Mallory can extract the secret key from an implementation (say an RSA-compatible smart card) by feeding it with specific values and in each case measuring the time that the implementation needs for the encryption. Just a few thousand encryptions with the RSA algorithm should return enough information to determine the key. With a smart card this takes only a few hours. For this reason, differential time analysis counts as a major threat for smart cards.

Differential time analysis works very well with public key procedures

In principle, differential time analysis works very well with public key procedures, which of course need more time for calculation and also exhibit greater differences in the computing time that they require. Symmetrical procedures make things are more difficult for Mallory: DES, for example, uses only Exclusive-OR combinations, substitutions and permutations – these operations are largely independent of the processed values. IDEA, on the other hand, uses a greater number of multiplications, causing a difference in computing time. Up to now, however, this has not led to a successful differential time analysis of the IDEA procedure. In any case, it is not all that difficult to prevent differential time analysis attacks: it only needs artificial delays to be built in.

Differential error analysis

Differential error analysis was invented in 1996

In September 1996, three colleagues of the US company Bellcore, Dan Boneh, Richard Lipton and Richard DeMillo, laid the foundations for a further side-channel attack, called **differential error analysis**. In the case of differential error analysis, an implementation is falsely activated or damaged in order to infer the key from the errors that ensue.

The three Bellcore researchers damaged smart cards either through heat or mechanically. By comparing the correct and the false results they could partially reconstruct the key. Adi Shamir and Eli Biham – the founders of differential cryptanalysis – transported the idea of the Bellcore attack to symmetrical procedures and established the term 'differential error analysis'. Ross Anderson and Markus Kuhn suggested that, as a further variant, an abrupt change in the resonant frequency could lead to revealing errors.

Differential error analysis has not been evaluated in practice to date

Differential error analysis is also suitable for smart cards, which offer the easiest access to Mallory. In fact, this attack has caused a great stir in smart card circles. But up to now there has been no confirmation that in practice a differential error analysis can be evaluated. Obviously it is very difficult to damage a hardware module in such a way as to facilitate this specific attack.

Differential power analysis

Another form of reaction attack is **differential power analysis** [JuJaKo]. This attack only works on hardware implementations (such as smart cards) and assumes that Mallory can attach a suitable measuring device to the hardware module. The aim, once again, is to reconstruct the apparently unreadable stored key.

Differential power analysis was also invented by Kocher

The principle of differential power analysis is very simple: Mallory feeds the module with different messages, which it then encrypts. During the encryption process, Mallory measures and draws conclusions about the key from the fluctuations in power consumption.

Differential power analysis was invented in 1997 by Paul Kocher and two other cryptographers (Kocher is also the inventor of differential time analysis). It is supposed to be possible to reconstruct a DES key after around 100,000 encryption operations. However, the success of this attack depends strongly on the respective implementation – some modules are not susceptible to it. There are also effective countermeasures against differential power analysis: such attacks can be obviated by the careful selection of electronic components in the hardware module, and by measures that vary the power consumption.

Summary

There are other possibilities for side-channel attacks

There are still other means of side-channel attacks. For example, the electro-magnetic radiation from a crypto implementation could be measured. Other variables are conceivable which, in coming years, might be used for other attacks.

The numerous attacks that have just been described could easily give the impression that crypto hardware offers no real improvement in security compared to software. This is not so, as is shown by the following:

- We have assumed the extreme case that Mallory has direct access to the hardware module and can operate it (he must therefore know the PIN). In this case, the hardware module makes it a lot more difficult to access the key than does software.

In the main, side-channel attacks can be easily prevented

- The attacks described can be largely prevented by suitable manufacturing measures. These attacks must therefore be seen as part of the battle between hackers and manufacturers.

- Many of the attacks described have a rather theoretical character. How well they work in practice remains to be seen.

In each case, side-channel attacks clearly demonstrate that security in cryptography means much more than secure crypto procedures.

15.6.2 Further real-world attacks

There are further real-world attacks

For the transposition of procedures into practice, there are still numerous real-world attacks, as well as side-channel attacks, which must be prevented. To go into these individually would be an arduous undertaking. At this point I shall only name the weaknesses that favour real-world attacks.

Implementation errors

Every long program contains errors and the number of errors climbs in increasing proportion to the length [BelChe]. In cryptography, this truism from software development has fatal implications. A small error, which would hardly be noticed in another program, can make a whole crypto implementation insecure. Even worse: in cryptography, things are rated as implementation errors that would not be considered so elsewhere – who would regard small differences in runtime or fluctuating power consumption as errors in normal software? If crypto software stores secret keys on the hard disk in plaintext, this is also classed as an implementation error – this kind of thing would soon be revealed by PGP software.

Implementation errors can be dangerous

Since implementation errors occur frequently, and cryptography makes high demands on correctness, this must be given special consideration when constructing a cryptographic system.

Sabotage by programmers

Many gaps in security were intentionally built in

Mistakes can, of course, be intentional. Again and again, programmers sabotage software in order to spite their employer. Concealed back doors are much favoured; these, with or without the client's knowledge, are built into encryption programs just in case someone might want to eavesdrop. As always in cryptography, in this instance one should never make a calculation without considering the secret services, who may be to blame for so many manipulations (such as the Promis case, see [Schu96]).

Carelessness by users

The user is often the biggest weak spot

A sloppy approach to encryption was not just the cause of the accelerated defeat of Germany in the Second World War. The same phenomenon is still responsible today for many accidents with encryption: passwords that are easy to guess are chosen again and again, or written down and stuck up somewhere in full view. Often, encryption is dispensed with completely, simply because of laziness and convenience. Even top quality encryption is useless if it is not given a chance.

Weakness in the face of social engineering

The term **social engineering** describes an attack in which Mallory tries, under false pretences, to evade security measures (for instance to obtain Alice's key). A simple form of social engineering consists in Mallory calling an administrator of Crypt & Co. and, under some pretext, asking for a valid password. Mallory might also get himself hired as a cleaner at Crypt & Co., or simply walk in and stroll around, picking up the odd diskette here and there. A good source of information is often the wastepaper bin in the company yard. Social engineering can only work if the victim is foolish enough, which amazingly they are.

False integration

Integration is important

Any computer owner wanting to print something out simply buys a printer and connects it to the port provided. However, security is not a printer. Security cannot be bought as an off-the-shelf product under special offer. Instead, all components of a computer system must follow a specific security policy. Cryptography should also be planned into systems beforehand rather than added as an afterthought. What is the point of a super file encryption program if unencrypted data is stored temporarily and is not deleted? And what is the use of the best cryptographic protection for database access if it is possible to read the data directly from the hard disk?

Summary

Real-world attacks are a big problem

In my opinion, real-world attacks are currently the biggest problem in cryptography. It is simply not enough to use algorithms that deliver security until the end of the universe, if Mallory can get at the key because of programming errors, or carelessness on the part of user Bob. I would even describe this as a fundamental crisis in cryptography: ever more and improved algorithms are being developed, but it seldom happens that they find adequate and reliable application.

15.7 Evaluation and certification

Security cannot be measured

Alice's employer, Crypt & Co., has developed some brand new encryption software and wants to put it on the market. However, customers are cautious of new developments because of the countless pitfalls that can appear during the development and operation of such crypto solutions. After all, who knows whether the software has a hidden back door, and even if Crypt & Co. lays all its cards on the table (say, the source code), purchaser Bob never knows if he is dealing with an error-prone implementation or whether perhaps some important component has been forgotten. In this context it would be ideal if security could be measured – like the computing speed of a processor or the capacity of a hard disk. However, security is not a hard disk or processor, but an abstract concept and thus not subject to measurement.

15.7.1 ITSEC and Common Criteria

Evaluation is the assessment of a product against specific criteria

Of course, methods have been sought that can provide a certain measure of the security of hardware or software. As a rule, such methods consist in an attempt to classify implementations into levels of security using fixed criteria. Of course, manufacturers may not undertake the classification themselves because they would be accused of dishonesty. Instead, this is the task of a national authority or a recognised independent body. The assessment by such a body to determine whether a product fulfils set criteria is known as **evaluation**. If a product evaluation is favourable, this can be documented in a document (a certificate) that the manufacturer can hang on the wall. This is called **certification**. To avoid misunderstandings: this certification has nothing to do with digital certificates (Chapter 16).

ITSEC

ITSEC and the Orange Book specify evaluation criteria

The idea of certification and evaluation according to security criteria was first put into practice in 1983 in the USA, when the Department of Defense-associated National Computer Security Center (NCSC) published the Trusted Computer Security Evaluation Criteria (TCSEC). Since the criteria were contained in a thick volume with orange-coloured binding, they are also known as the **Orange Book**. The Orange Book permits the grading of complete computer systems (especially of operating systems) into classes A1, B1, B2, B3, C1, C2 and D, where D is the lowest.

While the Orange Book has prevailed in the USA, in Europe the **Information Technology Security Evaluation Criteria (ITSEC)** are recognised, having been introduced in 1991 in Germany, France, the UK and the Netherlands (see [Verste] for example). In ITSEC, numerous ideas from the Orange Book have been adopted and developed further, so that the ITSEC is the more flexible. If Crypt & Co. wants to have its software evaluated according to ITSEC, it must first state which attacks against it are possible. This can entail a detailed threat and risk analysis. The measures offered by the software against the specified risks are those to be assessed with the ITSEC criteria. The criteria lay down a number of degrees of rigour known as Assurance Levels.

ITSEC evaluation proceeds in two stages

This assessment is carried out in two stages: in the first stage, the software is checked for correctness (implementation errors are potential security failings, of course). Here it is true to say that the more complicated the successfully assessed procedure, the higher the classification. In the second stage it is assumed that the software is error-free, and based on this premise the efficiency of the security measures is tested.

ITSEC assurance levels

ITSEC issues certificates at the following levels:

ITSEC has levels ranging from E0 to E6

- E0: Every product automatically has this level.

- E1: An E1 certificate is granted if security aims are defined and there is an informal description of the system architecture.

- E2: For this level, an informal but detailed specification of the system architecture is necessary. It must be established that the system is generally available, and it must be proved whether or not security measures are applied during production and configuration.

- E3: A test of the source code is necessary for an E3 certificate. In addition, appropriate distribution, maintenance and configuration procedures must be defined.

- E4: For this level, a formal model of the security policy and a structured description of the architecture must be presented. In addition, detailed tests of the logical vulnerability of the certified product must be performed and documented.

- E5: At this level a detailed outline must be reconciled with the source code. The logical vulnerability of the product must be tested at source code level.

- E6: For this highest level a formal description of the system architecture must be presented.

There are three levels of efficacy

Three levels of effectiveness are distinguished: low, medium and high. For example, if Crypt & Co. is given an 'E2 high' certificate, the product has high-level security measures but was tested for implementation errors at a comparatively superficial level. 'E5 low', on the other hand, means that the implementation is very probably free from error but offers only moderate means of defence against attack.

Common Criteria

Common Criteria have replaced ITSEC

The USA, Canada, Germany, the Netherlands, the UK and France have agreed a new set of criteria to replace the Orange Book and ITSEC, and to provide a new uniform standard. The new criteria are known as the **Common Criteria** [Brauer].

What are the benefits of evaluation?

Evaluation is expensive

It is unnecessary to mention that the ITSEC evaluation of their software cost Crypt & Co. a lot of money. An E4 evaluation will cost at least 30,000 euros for a simple product. Beyond this, there is no set limit to cost. This makes evaluation a rewarding business for the several bodies and organisations that have been authorised to issue certificates. Evaluation documentation (meeting all the necessary requirements for certification) has been an important business for some time now.

Evaluation is a very tedious process, of course. After E4, the evaluation of an already available product is almost impossible. This means that various measures should be undertaken during product development towards an evaluation that can take several years. For complicated products such as word processors, operating systems or development environments, anything above E2 is utopian.

In the face of all these organisational and financial overheads, it must be asked whether an evaluation is really worth it. In many cases the answer is obviously yes, because a relevant brochure of the BSI (in Berlin) names almost 100 products – from operating systems to smart card readers and databases – that have been accredited. Incidentally, there are also products that do not appear in any statistics and whose evaluation is secret. The most frequent level listed in the brochure is E2 and there are not many higher than that. The highest level achieved in Germany by a non-secret product is E4.

Not many products have been evaluated   Even if there are quite a few evaluated products, their proportion of all available products is still quite small [Rannen]. Up to now, certificates have been demanded mainly in the fields of military or aviation security. In the meantime, the German signature law (Section 29.2) also requires evaluation. For some components this level is E4, for others E2, both at a high level.

Part 4

Public key infrastructures

Coding Machine Siemens Geheimschreiber T52, 1938 Model
(from the IT-Security Teaching & Study Collection of the BSI)

Public key infrastructures

Security, like correctness, is not an add-on feature.
ANDREW S. TANENBAUM

Key experience no. 16
Quantum cryptography is one of the branches of cryptography that are not dealt with in this book. Quantum cryptography makes it possible to transmit a key using quanta of polarised light. Because, according to the laws of physics, the polarisation of light quanta cannot be measured without it being changed, Mallory cannot intercept the key without being detected. Quantum cryptography therefore provides a demonstrably secure exchange of keys – it's just a pity that it is not yet used in practice.

PKIs are currently an important topic in cryptography

Asymmetrical algorithms such as RSA, Diffie–Hellman and DSA have revolutionised cryptography, but in themselves they are no guarantee of a carefree crypto life. This is due to the fact that the practical application of asymmetrical algorithms is full of pitfalls that can only be avoided by constructing a suitable infrastructure. Such a structure is termed a **public key infrastructure (PKI)**. The building of public key infrastructures is currently the most important subject in cryptography, especially in connection with the Internet and mobile phones. For this reason, I have dedicated a whole chapter of this book to the topic of PKI.

16.1 Trust models in public key cryptography

The application of asymmetrical algorithms creates problems

In order to understand how a PKI works, and why one is needed, a little preparatory work is in order. To begin, we shall deal with the most important problems arising from the use of asymmetrical algorithms without an additional infrastructure. Then we shall look at three ways in which these problems can be solved.

16.1.1 Problems with asymmetrical algorithms

Problems with the use of asymmetrical algorithms without an additional infrastructure can be divided into four areas. These are described in the following.

Authenticity of the key

Key ownership is not apparent

Alice would like to send an encrypted e-mail to Bob. To do so she uses Bob's public key (see Sections 6.4 and 6.7). If the villain, Mallory, palms off Alice's own key as Bob's without her noticing, then he can decrypt the mail himself.

Mallory has several ways of carrying out this kind of attack. If Bob sends Alice his public key over the Net, Mallory can intercept it and replace it with his own (man-in-the-middle attack). He can also do this if Alice downloads Bob's key from a server. In addition, Mallory can try to distribute his own key on the Net under the pretence that it is Bob's.

The problems arise because there is nothing about a public key that indicates to whom it belongs.

Revoking keys

Keys must often be revoked

Mallory has stolen Alice's private key from her hard disk. This means that he can use it to read all messages that were encrypted with the associated public key. In addition, using Alice's private key he can forge her digital signature. Fortunately Alice has noticed the theft. She immediately generates a new key pair and does not continue using the old private key (this is called **revocation** of the old key). But how can these with whom she is communicating know that Alice's old key has been revoked?

The problem is that one cannot tell from a public key whether it has been revoked or not.

Non-repudiation

Ownership of a key cannot be proved

The purpose of a digital signature is to ensure non-repudiation. This means that Alice cannot contest her completed signature in retrospect. When all is said and done, a digital signature is an excellent way of meeting this requirement. If Alice keeps her private key secret (which is in her own interests), then no one else can imitate it. However, Alice does have one way to contest a signature: she simply claims that the key used in the transformation of the signature was not hers.

The problem here is that there is no way of proving that a particular key belongs to Alice.

Enforcement of a policy

A policy must be carried through

Crypt & Co. is surprised at the advantages that asymmetrical cryptography offers. It wants to introduce a key pair for each employee, with which the employee can encrypt and sign. This requires the following:

• Each employee should have only one key pair, not several.

• All public keys should be centrally registered.

• Each employee must use a key of adequate length.

- Each key pair ought to be changed after a given period (say every two years).

- If an employee leaves the company, his or her public key should be revoked automatically.

- All these requirements can only be met by Crypt & Co. if there is a way of enforcing certain procedures. These working procedures can be grouped under the collective name **local policy**.

The problem is that the prosecution of a local policy for the application of asymmetric algorithms is not possible without additional measures.

16.1.2 Trust model

To cut a long story short, we can say that when using asymmetrical algorithms without additional infrastructures, it is not easy to establish to whom a public key belongs. Even revoking a key cannot be reliably undertaken. The holder of a public key can deny ownership of the key and a local policy cannot be carried through.

Trust relationships are important

Since the four problems just described cannot be solved with the means that we have dealt with in this book so far, we now want to try this using an additional infrastructure. There are three popular ways of doing this, which all solve the first of the four above-named problems in a different way (authenticity of the public key). Trust relationships are important here. One therefore also speaks of **trust models**.

In the following, we assume that Alice sends an e-mail to Bob (whom she knows personally and trusts) or to Zacharias (whom she does not know and therefore does not trust). For this she uses their respective public keys. She has the problem, however, that she does not know if the keys are genuine. When it is a case of non-repudiation, we assume that Bob signs a message to Alice with his private key.

Direct trust

Direct trust is the simplest trust model

The simplest trust model (called **direct trust**) requires that Bob himself confirms the authenticity of his public key to Alice. Since Alice trusts Bob, this is surely enough. If Bob himself hands his key to Alice on a floppy disk, this is a form of direct trust. He can also send his key to Alice by e-mail. To prevent a man-in-the-middle attack by Mallory, he subsequently compares a cryptographic hash value of the key with Alice over the telephone. If the values agree, they can begin exchanging messages.

The infrastructure needed for direct trust is negligible. Direct trust is regarded as the null solution in PKI matters. In this book, therefore, I shall refrain from using the term PKI in connection with the direct trust model.

You already know how Alice checks the authenticity of Bob's key with direct trust. Let us now look at how the three remaining problems can be solved with direct trust:

With direct trust, revocation can be time-consuming

- Revocation of a key with direct trust can be achieved as follows: if Bob no longer wants Alice to use his key, he simply tells her so. If Bob has many communication partners, revoking in this manner can be rather tiresome.

- Non-repudiation is difficult to achieve with direct trust. Bob can deny at any time that a given public key belongs to him.

- The pursuit of a local policy with a non-participating authority (say the board of Crypt & Co.) is next to impossible with direct trust.

Direct trust is only suited to less demanding applications

Direct trust is the simplest trust model. Since Alice and Bob know each other it works well for them. But if Alice wants to send an e-mail to Zacharias (whom she knows only by name), things are a little more complicated because, in this case, she must first get in touch with Zacharias. If Alice wants to exchange encrypted e-mails with many other people as well as Zacharias, the direct trust option ultimately becomes too much trouble. Direct trust is only suitable for less demanding applications.

Web of trust

Web of trust is a further trust model

Alice wants to send an e-mail to Zacharias without using the long-winded direct trust approach. As it happens, Bob already knows Zacharias' public key and has verified this by direct trust. Because Alice trusts Bob, she can obtain Zacharias' key from him, then in turn verify this by direct trust. Because Alice knows Bob's public key (likewise by direct trust), there is a more elegant solution: Bob signs Zacharias' public key before sending it to Alice. Alice then checks Bob's signature and can therefore assure herself of the authenticity of Zacharias' key.

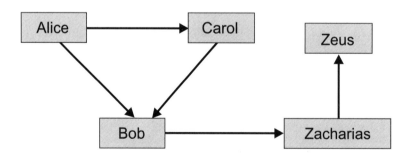

Figure 16.1 In a web of trust anyone can issue certificates for anyone else.

If Zacharias now signs the key of his friend Zeus, Alice can be assured of the authenticity of Zeus' key. In this way random trust chains can be built up to produce a network of signed keys (Figure 16.1). This arrangement is called a **web of trust**.

A web of trust involves digital certificates

So that no mistakes occur, in the web of trust, Bob sensibly not only signs Zacharias' key, but a data structure that contains Zacharias' name as well as his key. This kind of signed data structure is known as a **digital certificate**, or simply a **certificate**. As well as a name and key, a certificate can contain other details, of course, such as validity period, serial number and details about what the public key is used for (for instance, for a signature or for public key encryption). The signature on a digital certificate, of course, always refers to all the details it contains.

Even in a web of trust, the necessary additional infrastructure is not particularly extensive. However, it might be sensible to set up a server from which digital certificates can be called up. Despite these attempts at an infrastructure, the phrase public key infrastructure is not normally used in connection with a web of trust. We will leave it so in this book.

How can the three remaining problems now be solved with a web of trust?

Revocation is difficult with a web of trust

- In a web of trust, revocation is even more laborious than it is for direct trust. If Bob wants to revoke his key, he must tell everyone might possibly have it. This could be a lot of people, and thus many users will continue to use Bob's revoked public key.

- Non-repudiation in a web of trust is easier to accomplish than in the case of direct trust, because a certificate in each case gives a guarantee that attests to the ownership of a key. However, looking at things from a legal perspective, this is hardly sufficient proof in a court of law.

- The enforcement of a local policy is difficult in a web of trust.

A web of trust is more efficient than direct trust

A web of trust is therefore more efficient than direct trust. Unfortunately, it does not work very well in practice, or at least not in the worldwide Internet, for which it was actually envisaged. The Internet, with its approximately 100 million users, is simply too big for a web of trust to be established, in which people can verify each other's certificates via a chain of trust. If Alice wants to send a message to Zacharias, whom she does not know, then she must, where possible, follow a chain across umpteen stations to verify his certificate. If only one member of the chain is untrustworthy, it is worthless. Therefore, if possible, Alice will have to search several trust chains in order to be really sure after multiple checks.

However, a web of trust can work well within a company. The fact that the web of trust is so popular, despite its drawbacks, can be put down to pragmatism: it is quite simple.

Hierarchical trust

Hierarchical trust is another trust model

Because a web of trust is often inadequate in practice, we have to search for alternatives. One possibility would be to set up an independent authority to take over the task of signing the digital certificates. Such an authority is known, not surprisingly, as a **Certification Authority (CA)**. The term 'Trust Centre' is sometimes also used for an arrangement of this kind, although normally the definition for this is cast rather wider (see Section 17.1). The name of the trust model in which a CA issues digital certificates is **hierarchical trust**. So that Alice can verify the CA's signature on Bob's digital certificate, the latter must make his public key known. Alice must then obtain the public key of the CA and make sure that it is genuine. It doesn't matter if this costs a phone call to the CA, or entails some other expense, because Alice only needs to do it once. As soon as she has the CA's key, she can verify all digital keys signed by that authority.

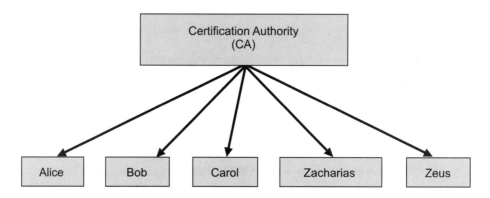

Figure 16.2   In a hierarchical trust, certificates are issued by a Certification Authority.

An infrastructure is needed for the operation of a CA

An extensive infrastructure is needed in order for a CA to work. The CA must therefore be run by a trustworthy orgasnisation. Alice must have the opportunity to register with the CA and obtain her certificate from it, which of course also requires infrastructural measures. For its part, the CA must make the issued certificate accessible. The term 'public key infrastructure' is therefore used mainly in connection with the hierarchical trust model. This is also the case in this book.

Let us now look at the question of how the three remaining problems of public key algorithms can be solved with the hierarchical trust model.

- Revoking a public key can be carried out very well with a CA. There are various ways of doing this, which will be looked at in more detail in Section 19.3.

- Because a CA issues digital certificates for all users, in the case of hierarchical trust, non-repudiation is much easier to guarantee. If Bob registers with a CA and is officially given a key pair, he can hardly dispute his ownership at a later date.

The pursuit of a local policy is easiest in a hierarchical trust

- The enforcement of a local policy is also much more possible in a hierarchical trust than in a direct trust or web of trust. Key changes at regular intervals, key lengths, centrally controlled revocation and much more can be supervised and controlled by the CA.

Hierarchical trust is thus the most complex, but also the most efficient trust model.

```
Owner's name:
Bob Offline

CA:
Certification Authority of Cryptoland

Public Key of the CA:
Ak0j6VcEFaj6Uja6sdaHAa8NaLak0MaSjdSfhK4HdD

Owner's public key:
qSdwsLSkdeAk0j6VcEFaj6Uja6sdaHAa8Nas4as4dL

Certificate Serial Number:
182374635254

Period of Validity:
01.09.01-31.08.2005

CA Signature:
0j6VcjdSfhK4HsEdF0sJk7d3wd3Saljad6sdas43Ls9a
```

Figure 16.3 Example of a certificate. Among other things, this includes the name of the owner and his public key.

16.1.3 So what is a PKI?

The term PKI is used mainly in connection with hierarchical trusts

With these three trust models, we now have various tools available for the application of public key procedures. In practice, all three are used extensively. In this book, however, we should limit ourselves mainly to the most professional variant. By public key infrastructure, therefore, I mean the sum total of the components necessary for the application of public key methods using a hierarchical trust model. Digital certificates are an essential part of a PKI. The other necessary components will be described in Section 17.1.

16.1.4 Authentication using digital certificates

Digital certificates can be used for authentication

A digital certificate confirms that a particular public key belongs to a particular user. Digital certificates (and hence a PKI) can be used to good effect for authentication with a challenge–response method. How this process actually looks will depend on whether the certificate is to be used for a key exchange or for a digital signature. In the following, we assume that Alice authenticates herself to a server.

Authentication with a digital signature

In the following protocol, Alice's certificate is used for the verification of a digital signature:

A challenge-response method is feasible

1. The server sends a random value (challenge).

2. Alice signs the challenge and sends the signature back to the server (response). She can send her certificate along with it.

3. The server verifies the signature with the help of Alice's certificate (if Alice has not sent it, the server can obtain it from a certificate server, see Chapter 19). If the signature is genuine, Alice is authenticated.

In order to prevent a chosen-plaintext attack, the protocol can also provide a transformation of the challenge before Alice signs it (see Section 11.2). This protocol is then particularly suitable if the purpose of the certificate is limited to digital signatures (see Section 18.4.2). The drawback is that, this way, there is no exchange of keys in the process.

Authentication by exchanging keys

In the following authentication protocol, Alice's certificate is used for the exchange of keys (we assume in this first instance that it is an RSA key exchange):

Encryption can also be used

1. The server encrypts a random generated secret key using Alice's public RSA key. It can take these public keys from Alice's certificate, which it can obtain from a certificate server. It sends the encrypted key to Alice (challenge).

2. Alice decrypts the challenge with her private key and by doing so acquires the secret key. With this, she encrypts an agreed value and sends this back to the server (response).

3. The server decrypts the response and verifies the result. If it is correct, the authentication was successful.

If the Diffie–Hellman procedure was used instead of RSA, the secret key in the first step would not be generated by a random generator, but in the way that is normal for the Diffie–Hellman method. The second step is changed accordingly.

The secret key can be used afterwards

The advantage of this protocol lies in the fact that the secret key can later be used either for encryption or for a cryptographic hash function. Because of this, the problem of a man-in-the-middle attack during key exchange is automatically solved.

Mutual authentication

Mutual authentication is also possible

In the two protocols just described, Alice authenticates herself to a server. If the server is supposed to authenticate itself to Alice at the same time, an additional challenge and a further response can be added (in this case Alice sends the challenge).

16.2 Variants of hierarchical PKIs

The hierarchical trust model allows for several variants. A hierarchical PKI can therefore be implemented in different ways. The four most important variants are described in the following.

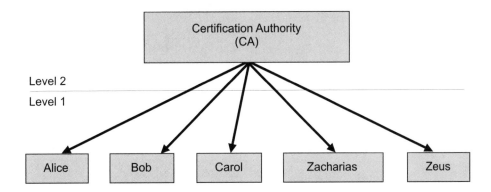

Figure 16.4 A two-level hierarchy is the simplest case of a hierarchy based on the hierarchical trust model.

16.2.1 Two-level hierarchy

The simplest implementation form of a hierarchical PKI consists in there being a Trust Centre that issues digital certificates for all users. In this case, this is called a **two-level hierarchy**. The first and lowest level consists of the users. The second and upper level consists of the CA. In this case, user Alice needs only one public CA key. She can use this to verify any certificate she likes.

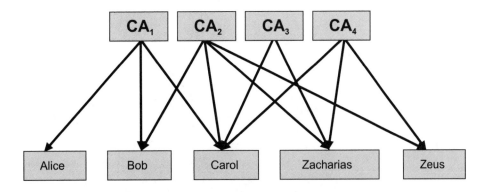

Figure 16.5 There are several CAs in the web model that make up certificates. A user can have several certificates from various CAs.

16.2.2 Web model

In the web model there are several CAs

In practice, there are often several competing CA operators, who woo customers top obtain their business. This results in certificates from different CAs being in circulation. In this case, Alice needs more than just one public Certification Authority key. She had much better invest in a list in which the public keys of all staple Certification Authority keys are detailed. If she wants to verify Bob's certificate, she first establishes which Certification Authority has issued it. Then she can check the signature on the certificate using the appropriate key.

This form of hierarchical trust, in which there are many independent CAs, is usually called a **web model**. The name stems from the fact that the situation that has been described is exemplary on the World Wide Web. There are very many independent CAs that offer certificates for Web browsers. The popular Web browsers come already supplied with a number of saved CA certificates.

It is very difficult to enforce a policy in the case of a web model

The drawback with the web model is that it is almost impossible to enforce a policy. If Bob does not want to accept the policy of a CA, he simply gets his certificate from another one. Because Alice accepts several CAs, it makes no difference to her which of them has issued Bob's certificate.

16.2.3 Cross-certification

The web model is used mainly when different CAs compete with each other. However, frequently there is the situation where several CAs are available whose circles of users do not overlap. In this case so-called **cross-certification** is available. This allows two CAs to exchange certificates with one another. Certification Authority CA_1 issues a certificate for Certification Authority CA_2 and thus authenticates the public key of CA_2. CA_2 does the same using the key of CA_1.

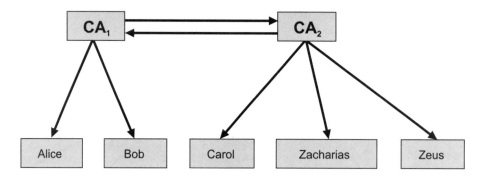

Figure 16.6 In a cross-certification two CAs issue mutual certificates.

In cross-certification, CAs issue mutual certificates

Alice, a client of CA_1, knows the CA_1 public key but not the public key of any other Certification Authority. Carol, a client of CA_2, knows the public key of CA_2 but of no other CA. If Alice gets hold of Carol's certificate (say from a certificate server, see Chapter 19), then she also obtains the certificate of CA_2. Subsequently, she first verifies the certificate of CA_2 using the public key of CA_1. She then verifies Bob's certificate using the public key of CA_2. By means of cross-certification, the catchment area of one CA is thus extended to that of another. One drawback is, of course, that a certificate must always be accompanied by the certificate of the corresponding CA.

16.2.4 CA hierarchies

If other CAs that serve different users are active as well as CA_1 and CA_2, mutual cross-certification can be too complicated. In such a case, a top-level CA is set up that issues certificates for the others. If there are several superordinate CAs, these in turn can also receive certificates from a further superordinate CA. This is what is known as a **CA hierarchy**. The CA at the very top of the hierarchy is known as the **root CA**.

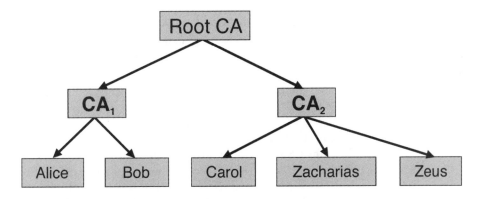

Figure 16.7   Example of a three-level CA hierarchy.

For user Alice, it is enough in this case to know the public key of the root CA. With this she can verify the certificate of the subordinate CAs and work her way down the hierarchy to user Bob. The certificates of the CAs that come between the user and the root CA must also accompany each certificate in this case.

16.3 PKI standards

Now that you know what a PKI is, you can imagine that within a PKI there is a great need for standards. After all, Bob and Alice not only communicate with each other within a PKI, they also communicate with the CA. So that this can work, numerous protocols and formats must be determined. The most important standards that achieve this will now be introduced.

16.3.1 X.509

There is a need for PKI standards One of the most important, and also one of the oldest, relevant standards of the PKI world is known under the name **X.509**. Its full name is CCITT X.509. After the name of the standardisation committee CCITT was changed to ITU-T, however (see Section 10.1), its official name changed to ITU-T X.509.

X.509 is one of the
most important PKI
standards
The standard itself is as circumstantial as the nomenclature. Much of what is contained in the standard is not of much interest today. The most important components were not always optimally disentangled. This failing is due to the fact that X.509 emerged at a time when the construction of public key infrastructures was still in its infancy (the first version appeared in 1988). The first revision of this standard occurred in 1993, the next in 1997. However, it is only possible to resolve some of the shortcomings by means of these revisions.

Contents of X.509

X.509 is a component of the X.500 standard, which will be looked at in Section 19.1. X.509 is actually an authentication standard for communication networks that have arisen from the collaboration of the ISO and the ITU-T (then CCITT).

X.509 has three parts
X.509 has three parts. Parts 1 and 2 – in which protocols for authentication with and without a trusted third party are specified – are of no interest to us, since they are only rough outlines and have no practical relevance. However, we are interested in the third part of X.509, which describes formats for digital certificates that are signed by a CA (see Section 19.3.2). These formats – despite some shortcomings – have established themselves and are used in practically every PKI.

16.3.2 PKIX

The most important PKI standard in existence from the point of view of the Internet is called the **Public Key Infrastructure X.509**, better known under the abbreviation **PKIX**. PKIX is the handiwork of the Internet Engineering Task Force (IETF)(see Section 10.1.1) and simply standardises everything that is of importance for setting up a PKI on the Internet. Up to now, around 10 RFCs and 20 Internet Drafts have emanated from the PKIX working group. Others will follow. PKIX is hence one of the most comprehensive crypto standards available.

PKIX is a standard of the IETF
The PKIX working group of the IETF started its work in 1995. The basic trust model of the PKIX is hierarchical trust. As indicated by the 'X' in the name, PKIX uses the certificate format and the revocation lists of the X.509 standard. On top of this, PKIX specifies protocols for managing digital certificates as well as protocols for their use. Further components are standard specifications for drawing up local policies.

16.3.3 ISIS and the German signature law

German signature law will be discussed in Section 29.2. Of interest at this point is the fact that the signature law and the affiliated signature regulations make numerous demands on a PKI. A PKI must be hierarchical. If a PKI meets all legal and regulatory requirements, then a digital signature that has been produced within this PKI complies with the signature law.

There are high legal and regulatory requirements
The signature law and the signature regulations make very high demands. One consequence is that numerous formats, processes and protocols in the PKIX standard cannot be reconciled. In order to combat this problem, various German Trust Centre operators, together with the BSI (in Berlin) and Teletrust, developed

their own standard, which is known as **ISIS, Industrial Signature Interoperability Specification**. Similarly to PKIX, ISIS standardises all relevant parts of a PKI. In contrast to PKIX, ISIS is almost exclusively oriented to digital signatures. Although ISIS uses numerous PKIX components, it differs from it in many respects. Because ISIS could be important in Europe in future, I shall be returning to it in the chapters that follow. In particular, I shall point out the differences between PKIX and ISIS.

16.3.4 Identrus

Identrus is a New York based enterprise, which was founded by eight banks in 1999. The aim of the enterprise is to create a worldwide hierarchy of Trust Centres, run by banks. Because Identrus lays down precise guidelines for the operation of a Trust Centre and its integration into the Identrus hierarchy, it is actually another PKI standard. Unfortunately, the details of this standard are secret and are only accessible to those banks that build up an Identrus CA. Despite all this secrecy, Identrus has developed into a worldwide success: over 40 banks have a share in Identrus.

Over 40 banks have a share in Identrus

The PKI provided by Identrus has four levels. At the top there is a root CA operated by Identrus itself. Below this there are so-called Level 1 CAs, which are run by member banks. In addition, there are also two Level 2 CAs, whose certificates are issued by Level 1 CAs (all Identrus CAs up to now belong to Level 1, however). Both Level 1 and Level 2 CAs issue certificates for bank customers. For Identrus, the aim is for interoperable Identrus certificates issued by banks to become established worldwide.

The Identrus certificates are, of course, particularly suitable for use in the area of e-commerce.

Identrus-conforming Trust Centres offer a high standard of security. Additionally we can assume that Identrus certificates will be readily accepted if they are appropriately marketed by the banks. For this reason, Identrus is currently a competitor to ISIS.

16.3.5 SPKI

SPKI is simpler than PKIX

As stated in Section 16.3.2, PKIX is a very complex standard. Many experts are of the opinion that it is too complex. Within the IETF a working group has therefore formed, which is in the process of building a standard in competition with PKIX. This is called **Simple Public Key Infrastructure (SPKI)** and is – as the name suggests – a lot simpler than PKIX.

Local names in a PKI

One of the big differences between PKIX and SPKI has to do with names that are detailed in the certificates. On this subject I would like to state the following: if Alice has a certificate, it bears Alice's name, or some other User-ID. But is anyone actually interested in Alice's name? The answer is often no, as in reality, only certain properties of the name are of interest. If Alice opens a bank account, the bank is not really interested in Alice's name. The bank merely wants to be sure that the person

Names are a problem on the Internet

who wants to withdraw money is the same person that paid it in. When Bob sends an e-mail to Alice, he is not interested in Alice's name. He simply wants to be sure that the the mail can only be read by the person he knows as Alice. Looking at things in this way, names are only labels that can be changed. The assignment of a name to its owner can also be a difficult task in a worldwide computer network: it is possible that there are two people called Alice Onliner, and a User-ID like 'aonliner' need not necessarily be Bob's friend Alice. If Zacharias – who is a stranger to Alice – requires Alice's certificate, he has a problem. He may not know her surname, or it may be that Mallory has told him that Alice's User-ID is 'mallory.cracker'. As a rule, Zacharias is not even interested in Alice as a person, but only in one or more of her particular properties. In other words: the term 'identity' has lost a lot of its meaning on the Internet.

Globally meaningful names are often impractical

With all these problems arising in connection with names, some cryptographers feel that globally meaningful names as a component of a digital certificate – as required in X.509 – are impractical. Instead, according to these arguments, each user should associate the public key of another user with a name or property (**local name**) of their choice. If Alice meets Zacharias at a crypto conference, and takes this opportunity to get hold of his public key, she can save this under the name 'Zacharias'. Perhaps she might also choose 'Crypto expert', 'friendly' or 'can access my Website' as local names, if such properties applied when she got to know Zacharias. Of course, she can also sign this kind of name–key pair, thus creating a **certificate with local names**. Certificates with local names are defined in SPKI and form a fundamental basis of this standard. The format used in SPKI for digital certificates is compatible with neither X.509 nor OpenPGP.

SDSI was the basis for SPKI

The idea of a certificate with local names goes back to Ron Rivest (a name with which you should already be familiar). Rivest described this principle in the context of a specification called **Simple Distributed Security Infrastructure**, SDSI (pronounced 'sadsi') [LamRiv]. SDSI forms the basis of SPKI, which was developed in a task force of the IETF security working area. This task force has produced a number of Internet Drafts, but no RFC as yet.

SPKI in practice

A certificate can also have a local name

If Alice has issued an SPKI certificate with local names, she can of course use it herself. Logically, however, a certificate is only of real use if others also use it. If Alice has acquaintances who trust her, they can use Alice's signed certificate with local names and even set up a certificate with a local name for Alice. This gives rise to a web of trust with local names. In principle, it is also possible to have a key with local names signed by a Trust Centre, but this is normally rather complicated, and rather contradicts the simplicity of this approach.

In Germany, the use of certificates with local names propagated by SPKI has played only a minor role up to now. In the USA also, the conventional approach is much more widespread. However, cryptographers such as Carl Ellison believe that many users will find certificates with local names to be more practical, which in the long run could help it along the road to success.

16.3.6 OpenPGP

OpenPGP is an alternative to PKIX

In addition to PKIX, ISIS and SPKI there is a fourth comprehensive PKI standard called **OpenPGP**. OpenPGP, which originates from the IETF, comes from PGP (Pretty Good Privacy) software, which appears in several places in this book.

Originally PGP was fully proprietary crypto software, aimed principally at e-mails. PGP provided certificates and supported the web of trust model (fundamentally, this trust model was the invention of PGP developer Phil Zimmermann). OpenPGP is an attempt to build a standard for a PKI from formats defined in PGP. In the best PGP tradition, OpenPGP also supports the web of trust model.

OpenPGP is of interest for private users

One effect of OpenPGP is that there is now other PGP-compatible software as well as PGP. However, at the moment it looks as though OpenPGP will remain popular among private users, but that PKIX will dominate the commercial sphere.

How a PKI works

In our opinion provable security is nothing more than a phantom, similar to the perpetuum mobile in thermodynamics.
JOAN DAEMEN

Key experience no. 17
In 1986, three Israeli cryptographers, Uriel Feige, Amos Fiat and Adi Shamir, submitted an application to patent a crypto method in the USA. To their surprise, they received a demand from the US patents office to keep the method secret in the interests of national security. Were they to violate this demand, they were threatened with a fine of 10,000 US dollars and two years in prison. But the US authorities were unlucky: the method had already been published several times and was known throughout the cryptography world. Two days later, the injunction was withdrawn.

In this chapter you will discover how a PKI is built up, which processes operate within it, and how these are standardised. We shall use the PKIX standard and, in parts, the signature law and ISIS standard as a guideline.

17.1 Components of a PKI

A PKI is built up from different components

First, let us look at the various components that make up a PKI. For the sake of simplicity, we will start off with a PKI in which there is only one CA. We can regard this kind of PKI as a client–server system and can divide its components into two areas: there are server components that are operated centrally, and client components that are used peripherally.

The central components of a PKI are collectively grouped under the term **Trust Centre**. Of course, one component of a Trust Centre is a CA. A Trust Centre is an entity that plays an important part in a PKI. Therefore, Trust Centres will find frequent mention in this book, especially because many Trust Centres offer their services on the market.

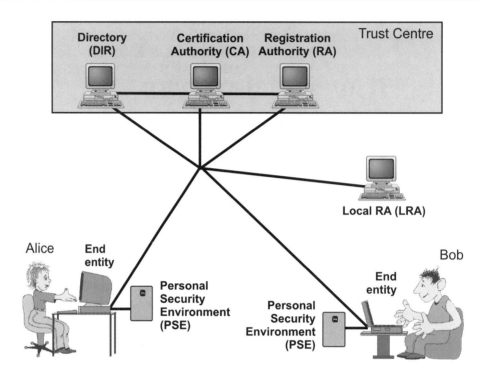

Figure 17.1   Structure of a PKI: the central components are located in the Trust Centre. Alice's and Bob's PCs are examples of end entities. Private keys are stored in PSEs, which can be in the form of smart cards.

Interestingly enough, the term 'Trust Centre' is not used in the Anglo-Saxon world – so don't be surprised if you cannot find anything about it written in English. Instead, the expression 'Certification Authority' is used internationally, although it is often not clear whether a whole Trust Centre or only a Certification Authority is meant by it. In this book we shall continue to use both terms as precisely as possible.

17.1.1   The components of a Trust Centre

Some PKI components belong to the Trust Centre   Let us now look at the components of a PKI that belong in the Trust Centre (see also Figure 17.1). As you will see, the arrangement is not always completely clear-cut and depends greatly on the form in which it is implemented.

Certification Authority (CA)

The CA is the most important part of a Trust Centre. By definition, a Trust Centre without a CA is impossible. As you already know, a CA has the task of generating digital certificates. This means that a data packet containing all the information of a certificate is accepted by the CA and then signed digitally.

The CA must be operated in a secure environment
Logically, the CA is a very security-critical component. If Mallory tries to access the CA's private key and use it to forge certificates, this is the worst thing that could happen within a PKI. The CA must therefore run in a secure environment, with special emphasis on the protection of the CA's private key (see Section 15.3.1). However, a Trust Centre is usually run in a high-security computer centre with thick walls and controlled access. As a rule, the computer running the CA software is not connected to the Internet, so as to avoid attacks from the network.

The signature law and corollary regulations place particularly high demands on the security of a CA. As well as structural measures (for instance, double doors at the entrances), ITsec evaluation for the software is mandatory.

Registration Authority (RA)

The RA accepts registrations
The **Registration Authority (RA)** is the administrative centre where Alice can apply for her certificate. An RA can be a part of the Trust Centre (**central RA**). It is also possible to locate the RA elsewhere, i.e. decentralised.

The RA feeds the CA with data accepted from Alice and the CA thereupon generates a signed certificate from it. The PKIX standard contains no stringent requirements regarding the operation of an RA within a PKI. In theory, Alice can communicate directly with the CA. However, almost all PKI implementations provide for an RA, and do not allow any direct communication between Alice and the CA. An RA can therefore be regarded as a necessary component of a hierarchical PKI.

How an RA is implemented in practice depends not only on whether it is a central RA, but also on whether the RA is to be laid out as a registration office, or as a virtual RA on the network. The form of implementation depends very much on the registration process to be used (see Section 17.3).

Certificate Server (DIR)

The Certificate Server holds certificates ready for calling up
When Alice's certificate has been generated by the CA, it must then be available for retrieval by other PKI users. For this purpose, every hierarchical PKI has a **Certificate Server** (sometimes the abbreviation **DIR** for Directory is also used). The Certificate Server contains all certificates created by the CA and keeps them until they are retrieved. The Certificate Server is also involved in key revocation. Whether a Certificate Server is installed in a Trust Centre or implemented elsewhere is optional. Certificate Servers are discussed in Chapter 19.

Time Stamping Service (TSS)

A Time Stamping Service is a component of some PKIs
A **Time Stamping Service** is a possible further component of a PKI. The abbreviation **Timestamping Server (TSS)** is also used. A Time Stamping Service is normally included as a component of a Trust Centre.

What the Time Stamping Service is used for is demonstrated in the following fraudulent scenario, which applies even if Alice's public signature key has been certified by an absolutely trustworthy CA: Alice signs a document, deliberately 'loses' her private key, and then has her certificate revoked by the CA. She now maintains that the said document is not from her, but has been signed by Mallory, who must have found her key. Alice can also refute signatures in a similar way if Mallory has broken into the CA, or if a new attack on the signature procedure has become apparent. In each case there is a question as to when the document was signed – before or after the revocation, before or after the break-in, before or after the attack became known. Since you cannot tell from a signature when it was formed, you have to find another way of getting round this: establishing a trustworthy authority to sign documents forwarded to it with the current date and time (a so-called **timestamp**). This can be used to good effect to provide Alice's signature with a reliable date. This allows Alice's business associate, for example, to insist that digitally signed contracts are time stamped before he or she accepts them. Should Alice's certificate be compromised at any time, she can no longer talk her way out of it.

Time Stamps strengthen the provability of a signature

The above makes clear what a Time Stamping Service is: it is a trustworthy authority that issues digitally signed timestamps. A Time Stamping Service is often offered as an additional service by Trust Centres. As well as its use in connection with digital signatures, which has just been mentioned, a Time Stamping Service is also useful if there is a question about the authorship of documents. For example, if Bob is afraid that Mallory could pretend to be the author of his new novel, then he provides it with a timestamp prior to its being published. By doing so, Bob can prove that the novel was written before Mallory claimed to be the author. Of course, things can work the other way round: if Bob forgets to have his novel stamped, then Mallory can do so – and Bob now suddenly finds difficulties in proving that he is the author.

A Time Stamping Service uses a key pair

A Time Stamping Service uses a key pair and a digital certificate. If a Time Stamping Service is run as an ancillary service of a Trust Centre, the certificate will normally be issued by the CA of this Trust Centre.

The PKIX standard contains a sub-standard for Time Stamping Services. This sub-standard currently has the status of an Internet Draft. It contains a format for a protocol message with which Alice can submit data to the Time Stamping Service to be time stamped. It also specifies a format for timestamps and for a protocol message that is returned with the timestamps. The respective protocol messages can be transmitted by e-mail, HTTP, FTP or directly over TCP.

Time Stamping Services are important in signature law

In connection with signature law, timestamps are very important. The law explicitly stipulates that a Trust Centre should operate a Time Stamping Service. A standard based on the PKIX TimeStamp Standard, which is supposed to be included in ISIS, was developed for this purpose by the Bundesamt für Sicherheit in der Informationstechnik (BSI), or in English, the Federal Office for Security in Information Technology.

17.1.2 The decentralised components of a PKI

Let us now look at the components of a PKI that do not belong to the Trust Centre.

Local Registration Authority (LRA)

An RA can also be operated outside the Centre

As well as an RA within the Trust Centrre, an RA can also be operated outside it, and then becomes known as a **local RA (LRA)**. It is also possible to have several RAs for one CA. If Crypt & Co. runs its own PKI, it can install an RA in every branch. The employees can then apply for their certificate from their RA administrator on-site.

Revocation Authority (REV)

Another component that is possible within a PKI is a **Revocation Authority (REV)**. The REV is the place for Alice to go when she wants to have her certificate revoked. An REV is usually implemented with the help of an existing hotline, whose phone number is already known to the users. The hotline employees, who take Alice's call, typically work with RA software dedicated solely to revocation.

Recovery Authority (REC)

A REC is responsible for key recovery

When key recovery is provided within a PKI, a separate **Recovery Authority (REC)** can be set up outside of the Trust Centre. According to the form in which it is implemented, REC can be accompanied by an LRA or an REV.

End entity

A PKI is only of interest, of course, if Alice and Bob can encrypt, and sign, and have an interface to the RA and to the certificate server. This is called a **PKI application**. A PKI component that embodies a PKI application is called an **end entity**. A typical end entity is, for example, a workstation with crypto software, a Web server or even a mobile phone that can process certificates. Examples of PKI applications can be found in Section 20.2.2.

Personal Security Environment (PSE)

Private keys are stored in the PSE

The environment in which Alice's private key is stored is called a **Personal Security Environment (PSE)**. Ideally, a PSE is a smart card that Alice can keep with her at all times. In practice, however, it is frequently an encrypted file saved on a hard disk or floppy – and is termed a **Software PSE**. The signature law does not specifically prescribe smart cards, but it does demand hardware PSEs in which the private key is encrypted.

Incidentally, the CA, RA and Time Stamping Service also use a PSE (they have private keys too). In practice, HSMs are frequently used for CA PSEs (see Section 15.3.1).

There are some standards that are of interest in connection with PSEs (they all belong to the PKCS family):

A PSE can be connected by means of PKCS#11

- The interface between smart card and end entity is usually governed by PKCS#11 (see Section 15.5.2).

- A smart card is a computer in miniature. In order to save the private key, the PIN and the certificate on the card, files must therefore be created on the chip. The structure of the files on the chip is standardised in PKCS#15.

The contents of a PSE must be exported at times

- There are instances in which the content of a PSE (usually the private key) must be exported or imported. With chip-card PSEs, this hardly ever happens because a private key should never leave the card. For software PSEs, importing and exporting can be appropriate, however. Formats for saving PSE items and similar personal data in an encrypted form are described in PKCS#12 [PKCS#12]. PKCS#12 specifies different modes. Usually a password-based encryption in line with a procedure similar to PKCS#5 is used. PKCS#12 is used primarily to transport the private key generated by the CA to the user in an encrypted form.

17.1.3 PKIs with several CAs

There can be several CAs in a PKI

To keep things simple, safer we have only looked at the components of a PKI containing just one CA. If we delve deeper, things naturally become a little more complex, but the basic principles remain the same. In a PKI there can, of course, be several Trust Centres, each having its own CA. It is also possible for a Trust Centre to run several CAs, which can be connected to each other in some way (for example, they can belong to the same hierarchy). Another possibility is that an RA could accept registrations for different CAs, or even different Trust Centres.

17.2 Certificate management

There is a protocol for certificate management

The purpose of a PKI, of course, is the creation, revocation and control of digital certificates, or in short, **certificate management**. So that a PKI can fulfil this purpose, the different PKI components must communicate with each other. The PKIX standard provides a number of protocols for this. These protocols are grouped together under the name **Certificate Management Protocols** and described in [RFC2510]. Although several protocols are involved, I shall treat Certificate Management Protocols as just one protocol under the abbreviation **CMP**. This simplification is justified because all CMP protocols are uniformly structured. CMP protocol messages are transmitted using another protocol. HTTP or FTP could be used. Direct TCP transmission is also possible. And last but not least, CMP protocol messages can also be sent by e-mail.

In the following sections, I shall introduce the most important processes that can be implemented with the help of a CMP. In places, I shall also consider ISIS and the signature law. The communication processes that can be realised with CMP can be divided into seven areas. I shall use these as headings for the descriptions.

17.2.1 CA initialisation

A CA must be initialised

Before a Trust Centre and its CAs can operate, several initialisation steps must be followed. The CA software must be started in controlled circumstances, and special attention has to be paid to the Trust Centre's private key. This must be generated using a good random generator, and while the CA is being set up, it must be protected against unauthorised copying by an administrator.

The ITsec evaluation stipulated in the signature law makes particularly high demands during initialisation. It must not be possible for any administrator alone to compromise the security of the CA. For this reason, the whole procedure must be executed by at least two administrators, who must check each other's work. Each step in the initialisation must be meticulously documented.

CMP leaves CA initialisation matters open

To a large extent, CMP leaves the sequence of the CA initialisation open. Only a few protocol messages are specified, such as for the distribution of initial revocation lists, and for the export of the public key.

17.2.2 Initialisation of end entities

End entities must also be initialised

The various PKI end entities must also be initialised. Although this process is not as complicated as for the CA, it is not entirely trivial. At this point, CMP provides a protocol message for the import of the Trust Centre's public key into the end entity. The registration of users with the Trust Centre and the generation of certificates do not belong in this area.

17.2.3 Generating certificates

There are various situations in which a new certificate is issued. Of course, this includes the case where a new user is to receive a certificate. But this area also covers the replacement of an existing certificate by a new one, and the issue of certificates to other CAs (for example, in the context of a cross-certification). CMP provides various protocol messages for this purpose. We are particularly interested in the generation of a certificate for a new user. This process, known as enrolment, is described in Section 17.3.

17.2.4 Publication of certificates and revocation lists

Messages must be exchanged by the CA and Certificate Server

Various pieces of information must be exchanged between the CA and Certificate Server. The CA must forward signed certificates and revocation lists to the Certificate Server. CMP specifies several protocol messages for this purpose.

17.2.5 Key recovery

Key recovery is a critical subject within a PKI. This is the process by which the Trust Centre 'recovers' a private key that is normally only accessible to the owner. In practice, recovery means that the private key is taken from a database in which it was stored after it had been generated. To enable key recovery, a Trust Centre must therefore operate a database in which all private keys are stored (this is only logically possible, of course, if the key pairs were generated in the Trust Centre).

Key recovery is often useful   Key recovery is often very useful. If Alice encrypts and stores some important data and then loses her smart card, all the data is lost – unless the Trust Centre has saved Alice's private key and carries out a key recovery. Key recovery can also be important for Alice's employer, Crypt & Co. Should Alice drive into a tree one day, or perhaps leave Crypt & Co. in a fit of temper, then at least her encrypted data can be rescued by means of a key recovery. Last but not least, key recovery can be used by the government. For instance, if the police need to recover the private key of a criminal, this makes life a lot easier for them.

Key recovery can also be a source of danger   Despite all its advantages, key recovery should be regarded with caution. It can very easily be misused. If Mallory gains access to the database in which the private keys are stored, PKI security breaks down completely. The fact that Alice is not happy that her employer can read all her encrypted files and messages should be obvious. In the hands of the government, key recovery would be a *1984* Orwellian nightmare.

The pros and cons of key recovery could be discussed ad infinitum. What cannot be disputed is that the following security measures should be undertaken if key recovery is practised:

Key recovery must be made secure
- The database used for storing the keys must be operated in a protected environment.

- Key recovery must only be permitted in specific, precisely defined circumstances.

- Key recovery must only be provided for private keys that are used for the encryption of data destined for long-term storage. If a private key is used only for signatures, no key recovery is necessary. This also applies to keys that are used only for the encryption of messages during transmission.

CMP supports key recovery   CMP provides several protocols to support key recovery. In the signature law and the associated ISIS standard, on the other hand, key recovery is not supported. Keys that are used for creating digital signatures may not in any event be stored in the Trust Centre.

17.2.6 Revocation

One of the greatest advantages of a hierarchical PKI is that revocation of certificates is easily executed and carried out. There are several reasons for the revoation of a certificate. The X.509 standard refers to the following as **revocation reasons**:

There are standard grounds for revocation
- Key compromise: Alice's certificate must, of course, be revoked if Mallory has possible access to Alice's private key. If Alice has lost her smart card or Mallory has copied her software PSE, the key is compromised.

- CA compromise: If there is a suspicion that Mallory has access to the CA key, this is also grounds for revoking certificates. In this case, all certificates that were signed with the key in question must be revoked.

- Alteration of the content of the certificate: If anything is changed in the contents of the certificate (for example, Alice's surname after she has married), the certificate must be revoked and a new one generated containing her new surname.

- New certificate available: If Alice's certificate is replaced by a new one, the old one must be revoked. This normally happens shortly before expiry of the validity period.

The end of an association is grounds for revocation

- Discontinuation of association: If Alice is no longer a client of the Trust Centre that issued her certificate, this is grounds for the Trust Centre to revoke the certificate. This reason for revocation arises, for example, when Crypt & Co. operates a Trust Centre for its employees and an employee leaves the firm.

- Suspension: A suspension is a temporary revocation, which is lifted after a short period provided a final revocation has not been received in the meantime. A suspension is mainly intended to prevent denial-of-service attacks: if a revocation can be cancelled after a short period, Mallory can cause less damage if he applies for a revocation of the certificates of other people.

Revocations are executed in the Trust Centre

Revocations are always performed by the Trust Centre. In the case of a key compromise, however, Alice must report the comprise and thus submit a revocation request. The CMP provides protocol messages for these kinds of revocation requests. Alice can send such a message to the Trust Centre herself if her private key has been compromised. It is also possible, however, that the Trust Centre operates a telephone revocation service that accepts revocation requests and then forwards them to the Trust Centre in digital form.

17.2.7 Communication with the PSE

CMP enables communication with the PSE

The exact form of the communication between PSE and application is not specified in CMP. However, there is a format for protocol messages that can be used to define a suitable protocol.

17.3 Enrolment

Alice would really like the Trust Centre to issue a certificate for her. The process by which Alice first registers and her certificate is then generated is called **enrolment**. There are various ways in which an enrolment proceeds. I will now introduce those which I feel to be the most important. The first three variants are supported by CMP. Then I shall talk about the signature law and a special enrolment protocol.

Enrolment with offline initialisation and decentralised key generation

These variants are suitable if the Trust Centre operates an RA that Alice can visit in person.

1. Alice generates a key pair and saves the private key in her PSE.

2. Alice takes the public key and gives it (say on a floppy disk) to an RA administrator. The RA administrator asks to see Alice's identity papers for authentication reasons.

PKCS#10 standardises a format for certification requests

3. The RA administrator generates a certification request, which he signs with the RA key. To do this he can use the **PKCS#10** standard, which specifies a format for certification requests [PKCS#10]. The PKIX standard specifies this kind of format, which is described in [RFC2511]. The certification request is sent to the CA.

4. The CA generates a certificate for Alice containing Alice's public key. The certificate is sent back to the RA and deposited in the directory service.

5. The RA administrator issues Alice with her certificate.

A good random generator is needed for this variant

Because Alice has to authenticate herself to the RA administrator in person with her identification papers, Mallory cannot pretend to be Alice. This method does, of course, require that Alice can generate proper random numbers (unfortunately, this is not the most natural thing in the world, as you saw in Chapter 9). Also, it has to be presupposed that Alice does not do anything silly with her private key (such as copying it and lending Bob a copy). As a result, this variant has the advantage that the CA never gets hold of Alice's private key.

Enrolment with online initialisation and decentralised key generation

Another variant of enrolment is normally used by companies. Let us therefore assume that Crypt & Co. operates a Trust Centre that issues certificates for its employees (including Alice). The process proceeds as follows:

In this case a PIN is sent by letter post

1. The CA administrator of Crypt & Co. sends a letter with a password by post to Alice (PIN letter).

2. Alice generates a key pair and stores the private key in her PSE.

3. Alice connects with the CA over the Crypt & Co. network (or via an RA intermediary). Alice sends the password and her public key to the CA.

4. The CA verifies the password and generates a certificate.

5. The certificate is sent back to Alice by the CA and put in the directory service.

Because Alice does not have to visit an RA in person, with this enrolment method Mallory will find it easier to pass himself off as Alice.

Enrolment with offline initialisation and central key generation

This variant is very secure

From the perspective of the CA, the following enrolment variant is the safest:

1. Alice fills out a written application for a certificate and submits this to the RA administrator.

2. The application is forwarded to the CA from the RA.

3. The CA generates a key pair. In addition, a certificate is generated that contains the public key. The certificate and the private key are sent back to the RA, and the certificate is also handed over to the directory service.

4. The RA generates a PSE for Alice that contains the private key.

5. The RA hands the PSE and certificate over to Alice.

If a smart card is used as the PSE, the CA stores the private key on this directly. Alice is then provided with her private key on the smart card, and has thus no possibility of accessing it herself.

Enrolment according to German signature law

German signature law affects enrolment German signature law and the associated regulations stipulate that Alice must visit an RA in person if she wants a certificate. She must identify herself to the RA administrator with her passport or some other form of documentary identification. The key generation must proceed in a such way that Alice has no opportunity to copy her private key.

CEP enrolment

CEP stems from the firm Cisco In addition to the function-rich CMP, there is yet another protocol that specifies protocol messages for communication with a CA: the **Certificate Enrolment Protocol (CEP)**. CEP was developed by the company Cisco, and is not compatible with CMP. As the name suggests, CEP is only suitable for enrolment and for changing certificates. Other processes are therefore not possible. CEP enrolment provides decentralised key generation and online initialisation.

Other forms of enrolment

Of course, there are other ways in which Alice can obtain her certificate. However, the most important questions are always where the key pair is generated, and whether Alice must appear somewhere in person.

17.4 Certificate policy and CPS

In a PKI many things must be specified When a PKI is established, a number of things must be specified. For example, which components are to be used, how the various processes will be organised, and which personnel will be involved. All these details must be documented and made available in part to the clients – after all, Alice will want to find out what to expect from her Trust Centre. The makeup of such documentation is described in

[RFC2527], which is part of the PKIX standard. This RFC provides two types of document: the **Certificate Policy** and the **Certification Practice Statement (CPS)**.

17.4.1 What is a certificate policy and a CPS?

A certificate policy and a CPS are issued by a Trust Centre Both a certificate policy and a CPS are issued by a Trust Centre. A certificate policy is defined as a number of guidelines that a Trust Centre is obliged to follow for a specific certificate. A certificate policy is published by a Trust Centre so that the clients know what confidence they can place in a certificate from that Trust Centre. If a Trust Centre issues certificates for different purposes, it should give each type of certificate its own certificate policy. This means that several Trust Centres can use the same certificate policy. This makes it easier for the clients to assess the quality of a certificate. RFC2527 assumes that a certificate policy contains a name in the form of an OID. This OID can be recorded in the certificates of the Trust Centre (see Section 18.4).

A CPS does not relate to specific certificates In contrast to the certificate policy, a CPS does not refer to a specific type of certificate, but to a whole Trust Centre. In the CPS of a Trust Centre, there are specifications regarding the structure of a PKI, the running processes, and other properties of the PKI. The different certificate policies of a Trust Centre are thus a component of a CPS. On top of this, the CPS also contains data that does not just relate to individual certificates. In contrast to a certificate policy, a CPS is assigned to a specific Trust Centre and is not intended for adoption by another. A CPS ought not to be published in its entirety, as not all Trust Centre proceedings should be detailed for all to see.

17.4.2 What does a certificate policy and a CPS contain?

RFC2527 contains certificate policy and CPS details RFC 2527 is not a standard that prescribes something. It is a document that lists the possible contents of a certificate policy and of a CPS. From this list, the author of a certificate policy or of a CPS can choose the points that are of most interest to him. It is up to the author as to what content is actually included in a certificate policy or CPS and how this is done. The eight points regarding content that are given in RFC 2527 are described in the following.

Introduction

Each certificate policy and each CPS should have an introduction. This can give the purpose of the document, the uses of it, the author and a possible OID.

General provisions

RFC 2527 gives a breakdown This part of a certificate policy or CPS is concerned with legal matters, such as intellectual property rights, limited liability, guarantees, and contractual liability. RFC 2527 also names such matters as fees, confidentiality, compliance audit, publication and repositories, interpretation and enforcement, etc.

Identification and authentication

The third part is concerned with identification and authentication

The third part of RFC 2527 deals with the important question of how the potential users of a Trust Centre are identified and authenticated, before they are given a certificate. In the simplest case, an e-mail will suffice for identification, although a passport or other document may also be required. The authentication required depends, of course, on whether it is a question of an enrolment or simply the renewal of a certificate. As well as authentication, the question of which names are used in a certificate (real names or pseudonyms) also plays an important part here.

Operational requirements

This part of a certificate policy, or a CPS, gives a description of the processes that run in a Trust Centre, and the associated PKI. These include enrolment, revocation, security checks, the archiving of data, key exchange, the reaction to critical situations and much more.

General security measures

RFC 2527 includes general security measures

This area includes the security measures for the operation of a PKI. Security in this connection means not only security, but also safety (see Section 2.1) – computer technical security is ignored and is dealt with in the next chapter. The chapter that deals with certificate policy or a CPS and the Trust Centre access control faculty should therefore also deal with topics like fire protection and power supply. Specifications that cover the responsibility for certain matters, and training for the Trust Centre staff, are also listed under security measures.

Technical security measures

Of course, a certificate policy or a CPS must also cover computer technical security. This is dealt with in this section. For instance, it needs to be clear whether the communication is encrypted in the Trust Centre, and whether log data is signed or not. The connection of the Trust Centre to the Internet or some other network is also dealt with here.

Format of the certificates and revocation lists

Certificate formats must be specified

As you will learn later, there are several standards and profiles for certificates and revocation lists. Suitable formats must therefore be selected for a certificate policy or a CPS.

Administration of the document

At some point, each certificate policy and each CPS will have to be changed and adapted to a new situation. Who can undertake such changes, and under what circumstances, is, according to RFC 2527, specified in the final section of such a document.

Digital certificates

Only the paranoid survive.
ANDY GROVE

Key experience no. 18
Rivest, Shamir and Adleman are known as the inventors of the RSA method. Since then, it has became known that the British mathematician Clifford Cocks had already discovered this algorithm as early as 1973 – some four years prior to the three well-known cryptographers. Cocks produced this invention under the orders of a British secret agency and was therefore sworn to secrecy. This amazing story was only made public in 1997.

The nature of a digital certificate was described in Chapter 16. As you may imagine, digital certificates must be standardised, otherwise Alice might not be able to read the certificate Bob sent to her. This chapter deals with the standards for digital certificates (if you want to find out more about digital certificates, I can recommend [FeFeWi]).

The most important standard for digital certificates is X.509

The measure for everything to do with certificate standards is the aforementioned X.509 standard (or more precisely, the third part of it). There are X.509 certificates in several versions, and many profiles, as you will learn in this chapter. X.509 certificates also use the PKIX and ISIS standards and specify a profile for each. The description of an X.509 profile made up the content of the first of the RFCs [RFC 2459] published by the PKIX working group. In comparison, OpenPGP and SPKI use their own formats for digital certificates.

X.509 is one of the oldest relevant crypto standards (the first version appeared in 1988). Unfortunately, it soon became apparent that the original version had many shortcomings, which have only been remedied spasmodically, and not always entirely successfully. As a result of this evolution, the subject of X.509 certificates has become quickly unnecessarily complicated. In the following sections I hope to throw a little light on the matter.

18.1 X.509v1 certificates

X.509v1 appeared in 1988 The first version of X.509 appeared in 1988. Certificates that conform to the specified format are called **X.509v1 certificates**. In accordance with X.509v1, a certificate has the following seven parts (fields):

1. Certificate Version Number: For X.509v1 this is the number 0 for version 1 (this follows the IT custom of counting from zero). In later versions, this number is changed accordingly to 1 or 2.

2. Certificate Serial Number: This is a number that must be unique among all certificates issued by a Trust Centre.

3. OID of the signature method with which the certificate is signed: Usually this is RSA, sometimes DSA or more recently a method based on elliptic curves.

4. Name of the CA which signed the certificate: Here is anticipated a name that corresponds to X.500 naming practice (see Chapter 19).

X.509v1 prescribes various fields 5. Name of the CA that has signed the certificate: A name that corresponds to the X.500 nomenclature is expected here.

6. Public key of the certificate holder: This public key is the actual reason for the existence of a certificate. Using this certificate, it should be possible to assign the public key to the owner.

7. Validity period of the certificate: This is given by means of a start and end date.

The seven fields of the X.509v1 certificate are the absolute minimum that a certificate must contain in order to find practical application. Unfortunately, it soon became apparent that this minimum was not enough in most cases.

18.2 X.509v2 certificates

X.509v2 appeared in 1993 A second version of X.509 was published in 1993. This added two new fields to the existing seven. However, this did not achieve a great deal. To this day, the new fields are hardly ever used, which proved that the additional fields that were actually needed were still not available.

18.2.1 The new fields in X.509v2 certificates

The two additional fields contained in the X.509v2 certificate have the following content:

- A unique identifier of the certificate holder: This identifier should be different for each certificate holder and should make it possible to distinguish between two certificate holders with the same name.

- A unique identifier of the CA: This identifier should identify each CA explicitly. This means that if several CAs have the same name, they can be distinguished from one another.

X.509v2 is little used   Most X.509 implementations do not use these two new fields. In the X.509 profiles of PKIX and ISIS it is also recommended that the fields are left empty. Instead, it is ensured that there are no identical names. For this reason, X.509v2 certificates are hardly used in practice.

18.2.2 The shortcomings of X.509v1 and X.509v2

The additonal fields of X.509v2 did not solve the problems of X.509v1. The fields that were actually missing in X.509v1 became apparent during the development of the PEM standard (Section 26.2). This was the first standard to put X.509 into practice, whereby the following X.509v1 deficiencies came to light, among others (this applies for X.509v2 also, of course).

X.509v1 and X.509v2 have drawbacks
- X.509v1 expects X.500 names for the holder and CA names, in a certain format. Because X.509 certificates are usually used independently of X.500, this restriction is pointless. For example, X.509v1 does not allow the use of an e-mail address as a name, although on the Internet this can be very apposite.

- X.509v1 certificates allow no inferences to be drawn about the intended use of the certificated public key. There is no field that gives this kind of evidence. It would be very useful, for example, to differentiate between keys that are used for encryption and those used for the verification of signatures.

- X.509v1 certificates do not give any information about the certificate policy on which they are based. For example, from Alice's certificate it cannot be ascertained whether Alice ordered it from the Trust Centre by e-mail without substantial authentication, or collected it in person after presenting her identification documents.

Because the X.509v1 certificate turned out to have so many shortcomings, which were not remedied by X.509v2, there was a need for some improvements.

18.3 PKCS#6 certificates

PKCS#6 sets a format for digital certificates   PKCS standards have already been discussed in many places in this book (see Section 10.4, for example). The PKCS developers took the shortcomings of the X.509v1 format that could not be remedied with X.509v2 as a cause for action. At the start of the 1990s, the **PKCS#6** standard therefore appeared, which specified a format for digital certificates [PKCS#6]. At first glance the format is quite complex: for a start, PKCS#6 simply leaves the X.509 format untouched. Instead of changing this format, PKCS#6 provides for new fields, including a signature field, to be appended to an X.509 certificate. The X.509 certificate and the new fields are then signed again by the CA. A PKCS#6 certificate is thus signed twice by the same CA. The reason for this seemingly curious approach to the problem is that the unchanged X.509 format means that there is still full compatibility.

Because the X.509 format was extended in subsequent years, PKCS#6 quickly became superfluous. It is rarely used today.

18.4 X.509v3 certificates

X.509v3 appeared in 1996 The third version of the X.509 standard appeared in 1996. The certificate format (X.509v3) it specified solved several problems, and made PKCS#6 superfluous. It did, however, create new difficulties instead.

18.4.1 The X.509v3 extension syntax

X.509v3 provides extensions X.509v3 did not immediately provide new fields for X.509 certificates, but specified a syntax with which new fields (**extensions**) can be defined. Each extension contains a subfield that indicates whether the extension is **critical** or **non-critical**. If a software application discovers a critical X.509v3 extension, which it does not support, the certificate is seen as invalid. A non-critical extension, on the other hand, will be ignored by the software.

18.4.2 The X.509 standard extensions

The X.509v3 extension syntax has the advantage that it finally puts an end to missing fields. No matter what kind of additional field is needed in an X.509 certificate, X.509v3 offers an opportunity to define it. This flexibility creates a new problem, however: an X.509v3 certificate is not automatically readable by every application that supports X.509v3 certificates. Whenever an extension is included that an application does not know, incompatibilities arise.

Several amendments were made to X.509v3 To avoid uncontrolled growth in the area of certificate extensions, X.509v3 was extended again in 1997 (through so-called amendments). As a result, some extensions were specified using the extension syntax specified in X.509v3. These extensions are now a fixed component of the standard. The extensions are listed in the following:

- Authority key identifier: If a Trust Centre uses several keys for signing, the key used for this certificate can be specified here. For example, the use of more than one key by a CA can happen during a routine key exchange. The PKIX protocol prescribes the use of this extension, as does ISIS.

- Key holder identifier: If Alice's public key is contained in more than one digital certificate, this can be quickly determined here. For instance, Alice may have more than one certificate for the same key if the validity period is coming to an end, and Alice has had a renewal issued for the same key. Alice can also have the same key certified by different CAs. The PKIX profile states that this extension must be used; ISIS leaves it up to the individual.

The purpose of use can be determined in the certificate

- Purpose of the key: What the public key contained in the certificate may be used for can be determined in this field. Examples of this are signature, encryption and certificate signing. The PKIX profile does not prescribe the use of this field. With ISIS, however, it is obligatory.

- Private key usage period: A digital signature must often still be verified, even though the owner no longer uses the associated key pair. It is therefore advisable to specify a different validity period for the private key than for the certificate itself. This is possible with this extension. The PKIX profile does not prescribe the use of this field. ISIS even recommends that it be dispensed with.

A certificate policy can be fixed in the certificate

- Certificate policy: In this field, a certificate policy that was used by the CA during the generation of the certificate can be referred to using an OID. The PKIX profile does not insist on the use of this extension, but ISIS requires its use.

- Policy mappings: This extension is only present in CA certificates. The CA that has issued a certificate indicates hereby that a certain certificate policy of a certificated CA is accepted as equivalent to one of its own. The policies are identified by OIDs. The PKIX profile does not prescribe the use of this extension, and neither does ISIS.

- Additional holder name: X.509v1 allows for an X.500 name in the name field for the holder of the certificate. An additional name of the certificate holder can also be stored in this field in an arbitrary form (for instance, in the form of an e-mail address, an IP address or a uniform resource identifier). The PKIX profile provides for this field to be used and its own name field to be left empty. ISIS leaves the use of this field up to the individual.

An additional name can be declared

- An additional CA name: This extension is used to associate Internet-style identities with the issuer. X.509 also requires an X.500 name for this CA name field. A further name can also be entered in this field. In this case also, the PKIX profile allows the X.500 name to be dispensed with, and the name in this field to be used on its own instead. ISIS leaves this up to the individual.

- Subject directory attributes: X.500 directory attributes of the owner can be given in this extension (see Section 19.1). PKIX recommends that this field is dispensed with. ISIS permits details to be entered either in this field or, alternatively, in the ISIS extension.

There are extensions that only apply to CA certificates

- Basic constraints: This extension is only of importance in CA certificates. In this extension, the number of levels that may appear in the certification tree below this CA is determined. The PKIX profile prescribes the use of this extension, as does ISIS.

- Name constraints: This field is only used for CA certificates. It specifies constraints for the names that can be used in the certificates issued by this CA. PKIX enables the use of this extension, ISIS forbids it.

```
Version: v3
Serial Number: 17
Signature Alg: dsa-with-sha (1.2.840.10040.4.3)
      Issuer: C=US, O=gov, OU=nist
    Validity: from 970630000000Z
          to 971231000000Z
    Subject: OU=nist, O=gov, C=US
SubjectPKInfo: dsa (1.2.840.10040.4.1)
    params:
      02 81 80 d4 38 02 c5 35 7b d5 0b a1 7e 5d 72 59
      63 55 d3 45 56 ea e2 25 1a 6b c5 a4 ab aa 0b d4
      62 b4 d2 21 b1 95 a2 c6 01 c9 c3 fa 01 6f 79 86
      83 3d 03 61 e1 f1 92 ac bc 03 4e 89 a3 c9 53 4a
      f7 e2 a6 48 cf 42 1e 21 b1 5c 2b 3a 7f ba be 6b
      5a f7 0a 26 d8 8e 1b eb ec bf 1e 5a 3f 45 c0 bd
      8a 0a 58 86 40 84 e3 a1 22 0d 88 ca 90 88 57 64
      9f 01 21 e0 15 05 94 24 82 e2 10 90 d9 e1 4e 10
      5c e7 54 6b d4 0c 2b 1b 59 0a a0 b5 a1 7d b5 07
      e3 65 7c ea 90 d8 8e 30 42 e4 85 bb ac fa 4e 76
      4b 78 0e df 6c e5 a6 e1 bd 59 77 7d a6 97 59 c5
      29 a7 b3 3f 95 3e 9d f1 59 2d f7 42 87 62 3f f1
      b8 6f c7 3d 4b b8 8d 74 c4 ca 44 90 cf 67 db de
      14 60 97 4a d1 f7 6d 9e 09 94 c4 0d
    Public Key:
      00 02 81 80 aa 98 ea 13 94 a2 db f1 5b 7f 98 2f
      78 e7 d8 e3 b9 71 86 f6 80 2f 40 39 c3 da 3b 4b
      cf 59 d4 6e da 44 99 3c 21 64 e4 78 54 9d d0 7b
      ba 4e f5 18 4d 5e 39 30 bf e0 d1 f6 f4 83 25 4f
      14 aa 71 e1
    issuerUID:
    subjectUID:
  1 extensions:
    Exten  1:   basicConstraints (2.5.29.19)
      30 00
Signature Alg: dsa-with-sha (1.2.840.10040.4.3)
    Sig Value: 368 bits:
      30 2c 02 14 a0 66 c1 76 33 99 13 51 8d 93 64 2f
      ca 13 73 de 79 1a 7d 33 02 14 5d 90 f6 ce 92 4a
      bf 29 11 24 80 28 a6 5a 8e 73 b6 76 02 68

------- extensions ----------

printber -s 616 pkix-ex1.ber
get 0, len=46 (662 bytes in file)
0000 30 2c     44: SEQUENCE
0000 02 14     20: . INTEGER
          : 9d 2d 0c 75 ec ce 01 79 25 4c cd 7b dc fc 17 0e
          : 0f 2a 22 ef
0024 02 14     20: . INTEGER
          : 80 61 6f fb dc 71 cf 3f 09 62 b4 aa ad 4b 8c 28
          : 68 d7 60 fe
```

Figure 18.1 Example of an X.509v3 certificate. The representation format has been altered to make it readable.

- Policy constraints: The policy constraints extension can be used in certificates issued to CAs. It constrains path validation in two ways. It can be used to prevent policy mapping, or it can demand that there is policy mapping in each level of a certification path. PKIX permits the use of this extension. ISIS does not.

- Additional purpose: This field defines one or more purposes for which the certified public key may be used in addition to, or in place of, the basic purposes indicated in the key purpose extension field. For instance, the PKIX profile names e-mail protection and TLS authentication as additional purposes (see Chapter 24 for TLS). ISIS prescribes the use of this field in certain cases.

Revocation list   - CRL distribution points: This extension specifies the location of a revocation list
distribution points   on the network in order to check whether of the certificate is revoked (see
can appear in the   Chapter 19). The PKIX profile recommends the use of this extension. ISIS leaves
certificate   it up to the individual.

Undoubtedly, these certificate extension fields should be enough for all standard needs. However, there are even more extensions that are used by certain implementations.

18.5 The PKIX and ISIS X.509v3 extensions

PKIX and ISIS   The profiles described in PKIX and ISIS not only give clues about how the standard
provide extensions   fields and extensions of X.509v3 certificates are used, but also describe some
additional extensions.

18.5.1 The PKIX extension

PKIX is content with one X.509v3 extension:

- Access to information: This extension gives a list of where information on the CA is available. This is usually in the form of a Web address. ISIS has adopted this extension, but does not insist on its use.

18.5.2 ISIS extensions

ISIS describes   In contrast to PKIX, ISIS defines a range of additional extensions. These extensions
extensions   are all significant for the German signature law:
pertaining to
signature law

- Constraints of usage: This extension can be used to indicate that certificate holder Alices may not use her signing key for certain cases.

- Date of creation: This field can be used to indicate when a certificate was created. The date of creation does not have to be the same as the date that is given to indicate the start of validity.

- Power of proxy: Alice's power of proxy for a third person (say Bob) is shown here.

- Licence: With this field, a CA can attest certificate holder Alice's licence to practise as a doctor, notary, solicitor ... etc.

Cash limits are a factor to consider for the signature law

- Cash limit: This defines a limit to the amount of cash Alice must guarantee with her certificate.

- Coming of age: This extension can be used to state whether the certificate holder is of age or not.

- Smart-card serial number: Signature law requires private keys to be stored on a smart card or some other hardware module. The serial number of the user's smart card can be stored here.

- Smart-card public key reference: This field can be used to store the public keys of other Trust Centres.

- Other constraints: further constraints on the use of the certificate can be listed here.

Additional extensions can be introduced

The X.509v3 fields, standard extensions and the ISIS extensions should meet most application requirements. If a Trust Centre needs additional extensions, they can be introduced in accordance with ISIS. The precondition is that a proposal has to be put to Teletrust (see Section 30.3.10).

18.6 Attribute certificates

As well as a name and key, the X.509 standard, with the above PKIX and ISIS extensions, allows much additional information to be saved in digital certificates. In most cases it is useful to move some of this additional information (and certificate fields) into an additional data structure. This additional data structure is signed by the same Trust Centre, and therefore resembles a digital certificate but does not contain a public key.

Attribute certificates do not contain a key

Data structures that resemble certificates, but do not contain public keys, are known as **attribute certificates**. To distinguish attribute certificates from 'normal' certificates, the latter may be called **key certificates**. The X.509 standard contains a format for attribute certificates. This format is largely the same as for any X.509 certificate, except that the public key is omitted.

18.6.1 Uses of attribute certificates

An attribute certificate is normally – albeit not necessarily – an addition to a key certificate. The attribute certificate contains fields transferred from the key certificate. Fields may be transferred for the following reasons:

Standard certificates often become too large

- A key certificate with a lot of fields often becomes too large. This can be a drawback, particularly when the certificate is to be stored on a smart card. By transferring fields to an attribute certificate, the size of the key certificate can be kept to a reasonable size.

- The validity of an attribute certificate is independent of the associated key certificate. For example, an attribute certificate can have a different (usually shorter) validity period. It can also be revoked independently of the key certificate. New attribute certificates can be generated as required, without changing the associated key certificate.

- An attribute certificate can be kept under lock and key, while the associated key certificate is published (this often makes sense with regard to data protection).

Attribute certificates have been used sparingly up to now

Despite these advantages, attribute certificates are still rarely used. However, this could change in the course of time, as in principle they make good sense.

18.6.2 Attribute certificates in the PKIX standard

The modest role played by attribute certificates is reflected in the PKIX standard. In RFC 2459, which describes an X.509 profile, attribute certificates are left aside.

There are, however, two drafts (i.e. possible future RFCs) that deal with attribute certificates:

Attribute certificates play a role in PKIX

- One draft specifies a format for attribute certificates that can be used for authentication purposes.

- Another draft suggests a CMP-based protocol called LAAP (Limited Attribute Certificate Acquisition Protocol). LAAP is a protocol that has deliberately been kept simple and is used for calling up attribute certificates from a server. A consequence of this is that the server has to generate the attribute certificate dynamically.

In the PKIX profile, attribute certificates can be issued under the guise of an **Attribute Authority (AA)**. As a rule, the two are identical.

18.6.3 Attribute certificates in ISIS and the signature law

Attribute certificates are interesting in connection with signature law

Attribute certificates are more important in the ISIS standard than in PKIX. They even receive special mention in the signature law, which is normally kept very general. As a result, there are no attribute certificates without an associated key certificate.

In accordance with ISIS, an attribute certificate can adopt virtually the same form as a key certificate (but without a key). The subject name, version number, serial number and CA name must be included in every attribute certificate. There is also a field that corresponds to the directory service attributes field of X.509v3. Attribute certificates are particularly well suited for alternative storage of key certificate extensions such as majority, power of proxy and usage constraints.

18.7 X.509 summary

X.509 contains elementary mistakes

X.509 is not exactly a shining light among crypto standards. The first version was not practical, and the second brought little improvement. The alternatives laid out in PKCS#6 were not exactly the best. The third version of X.509 attempted rather too much and had to be improved. All three versions leave too much room for interpretation, which means that there are scarcely two X.509 implementations that are actually compatible. Numerous profiles have done little to improve the situation.

The numerous deficiencies of X.509 have two plausible causes: firstly, X.509 was one of the very first crypto-standards. Therefore it is hardly surprising that many elementary mistakes were made. Secondly, X.509 was initially only intended for use as an authentication standard for X.500. To use X.509 for Internet applications is basically a misuse of the original standard.

Seen in this light, X.509 is just a legacy that we must live with. Everything would be a lot simpler if the standard could be redeveloped, starting from scratch. However, in view of the many existing implementations this is out of the question.

X.509 certificates are very useful

Despite all of its drawbacks, X.509 is one of the most important crypto standards available today. X.509 certificates will therefore crop up in this book every now and again.

18.8 PGP certificates

PGP certificates do not conform to X.509

As already mentioned, OpenPGP is seen as a competitor to PKIX. This is also apparent in digital certificates. Instead of X.509 certificate format, OpenPGP uses the PGP certificate format (**PGP certificate**), which is not compatible with X.509.

18.8.1 PGP certificate fields

There are now several versions of PGP certificates. The current version is number 4. The fields of PGP certificates are distributed in several packets. If we assume that we are talking about Bob's certificate, then a PGP certificate has the following packets:

PGP certificates have fewer fields than X.509 certificates

- Public Key Packet: This packet contains Bob's public key, the version number of the packet format and the date of origin.

- User ID Packet: This packet contains an identifier that identifies Bob. This is usually Bob's e-mail address.

- Other User ID Packets (optional): Further identifiers can be listed here; for instance, more e-mail addresses for Bob.

- For every User ID Packet there are none or more signature packets: Each signature packet contains a digital signature. These signatures are used to confirm that Bob's public key belongs to the respective identifier (and hence to Bob himself). This kind of signature can be prepared by anyone (by Alice, for instance). If there are several signature packets belonging to one identifier, these are normally from different people.

- Subkey Packets (optional): These can contain other public keys belonging to Bob.

- One Signature Packet per Subkey Packet: This signature refers to the respective subkey packet and has been prepared by Bob himself. To do this he has used the private key that belongs to the public key in the Public Key Packet.

18.8.2 Differences from X.509

There are some differences between PGP and X.509

Let us now look at the differences between X.509 and PGP certificates.

Number of keys and signatures

A substantial difference is that for X.509 certificates one public key is linked to a user name by one CA signature. With PGP certificates, on the other hand, there can be any number of public keys and any number of signatures. This difference is based on the web of trust model. As a consequence, for each key pair there are often many PGP certificates in circulation, all bearing different signatures.

PGP and policy

The is no policy field in PGP certificates

Many of the X.509v3 extension fields have no corresponding PGP certificate field. For example, in PGP certificates there is no field in which a policy is referenced. On the other hand, there are different types of signatures that can be defined in a signature packet. As a result, different levels can be defined for a certification (we assume Alice signs a certificate with Bob's key):

- Generic certification: At this level Alice reveals nothing at all about whether, or how, she has ascertained that Bob is the actual owner of the key.

- Personal certification: At this level Alice has not checked whether Bob is the owner of the key.

- Casual certification: At this level Alice has actually checked that Bob is the owner of the key. However, she has only performed a perfunctory, fleeting check (what this means exactly is not defined).

- Positive certification: At this level Alice has checked properly whether Bob is the owner of the key.

The individual levels are rather vaguely defined, and confirm that PGP is not particularly well suited to enforcing a specific policy.

Certificate management

Working with PGP certificates can be complex

PGP certificates may well have fewer fields than X.509 certificates, but managing them is often more complex. Because a PGP certificate can contain several keys and signatures, user Bob must always think about which signature he can trust in what situation.

In practice, however, PGP certificates are frequently used with the hierarchical trust model. This then means that a PGP certificate carries only one signature, which has been issued by one CA. Due to this 'misuse', part of the PGP principle is of course lost. However, the typical advantages of hierarchical trust, such as the enforcement of a policy, or a high degree of connectivity, are gained.

Certificate servers

If you write in an amusing manner, even the bitter truth will be consumed and digested.
MARTIN LUTHER

Key experience no. 19
The expression 'snake oil' became a secret star of the first edition of this book. Many readers apparently came across it in the list of contents and wondered what was behind it. I have received more questions on the subject of snake oil than on any other subject.

The certificate server holds certificates and information about the revocation of certificates, ready to be retrieved by users such as Alice and Bob. In this chapter we shall concern ourselves with certificate servers.

19.1 Directory service

Directory services are not only available in PKIs

It is the task of a certificate server to hold a large number of data sets (in this case, certificates and revocation lists) ready for retrieval over the Internet. Components that perform a similar function are also available outside of public key infrastructures. Many companies operate a server, for example, which holds data such as e-mail addresses, telephone numbers etc., ready for retrieval by the employees of the company. This kind of server is known as a **directory service**. For the construction of directory services there are standards and products that actually have nothing to do with public key infrastructures, but can nevertheless be used as certificate servers. So instead of reinventing the wheel, traditional directory service functions are used almost exclusively as certificate servers. In this chapter, we therefore take a detour around the topic of directory services. If you want to know more about them, I recommend you have a look at [SheShe].

19.1.1 What is a directory service?

In this context, a directory service is a database that is reachable via a network and is designed principally for reading data. It also provides suitable search functions that can be used to do so.

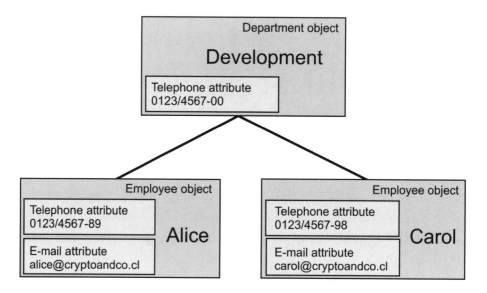

Figure 19.1   A directory service provides various objects arranged in hierarchical order.

Concepts

The information that can be retrieved from a directory service is divided into **objects**. An object is a data structure that stands for a thing, a person, or some other entity. For example, Crypt & Co. can store an object for each employee in their directory service. Each object has **attributes**. An attribute stands for a property of the relevant object. In the case of Crypt & Co., each employee object could contain an attribute in which a telephone number is stored.

A directory service is built to a specific schema   Of course, there must be rules regarding the creation of objects and attributes. These rules are assembled into a **schema**. A schema can, for example, specify that objects of the type 'Employee' must each have two attributes called 'Telephone No.' and 'E-mail Address'.

Structure of directory services

Directory services are normally hierarchical in structure. This means that various objects are assigned to a superordinate object. For example, in Crypt & Co. several employee objects are assigned to a department object, which in turn is assigned along with other department objects to a company branch object. The hierarchy so created is called a **directory information tree**.

The various objects of a directory tree must never all be stored on the same computer. It is more usual and easier to split up directory services. Thus, for example, a department object of Crypt & Co. can be located in a branch company, while the superior branch object is located in the company HQ.

Names are fixed in a namespace   So that a targeted search is possible in a (possibly divided) directory service, the names of the individual objects must meet certain specifications. These default specifications are fixed in the **namespace**. The namespace is a part of the schema.

19.1.2 X.500

The best-known standard for directory services is ITU-T X.500, **X.500** for short. X.500 is a typical ISO standard (see Section 10.1.1): it provides many functions, but is consequently very complex. In contrast to some other ISO standards, X.500 has gained acceptance to a certain degree.

X.500 includes several part standards X.500 has nine sub-standards, called X.501, X.509, X.511, X.518, X.519, X.520, X.521, X.525 and X.530. In X.509 authentication is dealt with, as you already know from Chapter 18. Since X.500 is a much more extensive standard, in this context I can only go into the most important rudiments here.

Structure of X.500

X.500 is a standard that is designed to form a distributed, global directory with a structure such as that shown in Figure 19.2. It has hierarchically distributed objects, each object having specific attributes. A schema specifies the rules to be followed for generating objects.

Taking a rather simplified view of X.500 (which is advisable in view of its complexity), there are two types of object:

Leaf objects are the lowest entries in the directory tree
• **Leaf objects** are at the bottom of the directory tree and have no subordinate objects (children). In accordance with X.500, leaf objects can be divided into approximately 15 categories (e.g. person, device, process, ...)

• **Container objects** are objects that have subordinate objects (children). In this simplified model all **non-leaf objects** are container objects. X.500 has four categories of non-leaf objects: Country (C), Locality (L), Organisation (O) and Organisational Unit (OU).

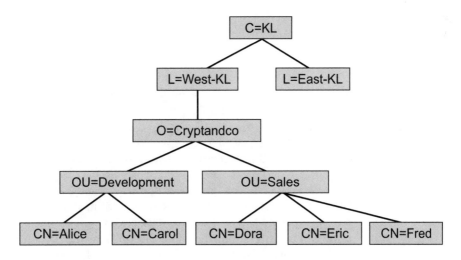

Figure 19.2 Example of an X.500 directory tree. A company's structure, for example, can be depicted in this way.

An X.500 directory tree in the most descriptive case has a country object at the root. Below this are several locality objects. Below each locality object there are several organisation objects, below which the organisational unit objects are located. Several leaf objects are located at the bottom, below each organisational unit object.

The Distinguished Name clearly identifies an object

There are other ways to build an X.500 directory tree, but these are beside the point here. What is interesting, however, is the X.500 namespace. Each leaf object, according to X.500, has a name that is known as its **Common Name (CN)**. When a person-type leaf object is created, the Common Name could be 'Alice', for example. More important than the Common Name, however, is the **Distinguished Name (DN)**. Each object in a directory tree has this kind of name. The Distinguished Name is an important feature of directory trees and specifies where an object is located within its directory tree. A Distinguished Name is built up by the concatenation of the name of the object and the names of the objects above it. Distinguished Names are written in the following format (we assume that the object is a leaf object):

```
C=CL,L=West-CL,O=Cryptandco,OU=Development,CN=Alice
```

This naming process is rather complex, but it means that an object can be quickly located in the directory tree using its Distinguished Name.

DAP

A directory service can be queried using the DAP protocol

X.500 not only describes a model for the structure of a directory service, but also specifies a protocol that can be used to call up information from the service. This protocol is called **DAP (Directory Access Protocol)**. Using DAP, the user, Alice, can search for objects in a directory service and request their contents. It is also possible to change objects if Alice has received permission to do so from the administrator. For Alice, the operation of a DAP client resembles that of a file manager.

19.1.3 LDAP

Like so many OSI protocols, DAP is quite complex. In addition, it is not designed for TCP/IP or Internet addresses. To circumvent these drawbacks, the **Lightweight Directory Access Protocol (LDAP)** was developed in the IETF. This has largely the same aim as DAP, but is much less complex. It is based on TCP/IP and uses Internet addresses. The current third version of LDAP is described in RFCs 2251 to 2267 (see [RFC2251], [RFC2252], [RFC2253], [RFC2254], [RFC2255] and [RFC2256]).

LDAP is simpler than DAP

LDAP is first and foremost a protocol that resembles DAP, but is much simpler and is different in several ways. The consequence of its limitations is that, from an LDAP user viewpoint, X.500 directory services are presented in a form that is simpler, and can be differentiated as such. For this reason, LDAP has since mutated from a protocol to a full standard for directory services. On this basis, LDAP is very successful: today there are many more LDAP than X.500 directory services.

19.1.4 DNS

DNS is another directory service

In addition to X.500 and LDAP, which specify all-purpose directory services, there is a directory service standard for a quite specific purpose. This is the DNS standard already mentioned in Section 3.2. DNS stands for Domain Name System. DNS is a directory service that provides the associated IP address (for instance, 119.19.34.155) with a text address (say www.cryptandco.cl).

19.1.5 Other directory services

NDS and Active Directory are further directory services

As well as X.500, LDAP and DNS there are two other types of directory services: **NDS** and **Active Directory**. NDS stands for **Novell Directory Services** and was developed by the company Novell. Active Directory is a Microsoft product. Since the main subject of this book is cryptography, and not directory services, I will not go into the details of NDS and Active Directory. It is enough at this point to know that NDS and Active Directory resemble X.500 and LDAP, but are not compatible in many respects.

19.2 Certificate servers and directory services

The standards for directory services that have been described can also be used for certificate servers. This will be investigated in the following.

19.2.1 X.500 as a certificate server

X.500 can be used for a certificate server

An X.500 directory service is the classical means for building a certificate server. This has historical reasons: the X.509 format for digital certificates was originally devised to link a public key to an X.500 object. For this reason, the X.509 format provides for one distinguished name in the name field. A second name field that could hold another name only appeared with the X.509v3 standard.

Certificates can be downloaded using X.500 or LDAP

Since then, X.509 has also been used independently of X.500; however, X.500 directory services continue to be used as certificate servers. With suitable crypto software, Alice can download a certificate she needs via LDAP or DAP. If Crypt & Co. operates an X.500 directory service, in which there is an entry for each employee, this can also be used for the PKI. Each certificate is then stored with its associated object. However, it is often the case that an X.500 directory service is specially built for a PKI. In this case an object must be set up for each user, whose distinguished name then appears in the certificate.

19.2.2 LDAP as a certificate server

If one regards LDAP not only as a protocol but also as a directory service standard, then compared with X.500 it does, of course, have limitations. These do not make any difference in the use of a PKI, however. Therefore, LDAP is currently the most important standard for certificate servers. As with X.500, an existing directory service can be used, or a new one can be built for a PKI.

19.2.3 DNS as a certificate server

DNS can also be used as a certificate server

To use a Domain Name System as a certificate server is a very obvious idea. At the start of the 1990s, an IETF working group was set up to develop extensions for the DNS standard to facilitate its use as a certificate server. These extensions were termed **DNSSec** [Martiu].

Since then, the DNSSec working group has published a number of RFCs (for example, [RFC2535] and [RFC2931]). These standards allow for public keys and digital signatures also to be transported in DNS messages. This implies the definition of a separate certificate format, which is not compatible with X.509. An advantage of DNSSec is that DNS spoofing is also prevented (see Section 3.2), because in accordance with DNSSec, the IP address can become a part of the certificate.

DNSSec has not asserted itself

Although the DNS protocol is more commonly used than LDAP or X.500, and although the use of DNS as a certificate server is a rather obvious application, DNSSec has not yet broken through. Owing to the popularity of the X.509 standard, and its links with D.500 and LDAP, DNSSec has never really got going.

19.2.4 Other directory services

NDS and Active Directory can also be used as certificate servers. Although Active Directory is becoming more popular, most certificate servers are still based on LDAP.

19.3 Requesting certificate revocation information

Certificate revocation information must also be distributed

As already described in Section 16.1, a Trust Centre must be able to declare certificates as invalid (i.e. revoke them). This is necessary, for example, if Bob loses his smart card with his private signature key. If an employee of Crypt & Co. leaves the company, his or her certificate must also be revoked. The revocation of certificates by a Trust Centre is only useful if user Alice can find out the current revocation status of a certificate. Further to this, Alice must not, of course, carry on using a certificate after she knows it has been revoked.

Certificate revocation lists can be distributed via a certificate server

So that Alice has easy access to information regarding certificate revocations, this is appropiately made accessible via the Trust Centre certificate server. This means, of course, that the Trust Centre must immediately inform the certificate server about any revocations. There are several ways for Alice to get hold of information about revocations via the certificate server.

19.3.1 Online revocation status checking

Ideally, revocation status checking can be done online

At first glance, the simplest way in which Alice can get hold of information regarding the revocation status of a certificate is by means of **online revocation status checking**. Conceivably it could be this simple: if Alice wants to know if a certificate has been revoked, she sends a message with the serial number of the certificate to the certificate server. The certificate server then checks the revocation status of the certificate with that serial number and sends a signed message to Alice, stating the current revocation status. This can also give the reasons for any revocation (see Section 17.2.6).

Pros and cons of online revocation status checking

The main advantage of online revocation status checking is obvious: the revocation of a certificate is executed very quickly. As soon as the Trust Centre has informed the certificate server about the revocation of a certificate, the latter answers all subsequent queries about the certificate revocation status accordingly.

Online revocation status checking is costly

Unfortunately, online revocation status checking also has drawbacks. For example, it is expensive (and often impossible) for Alice to set up an online connection to the certificate server just to check a revocation status. On top of this, every answer must be signed, which also requires a considerable amount of effort.

Standards for online revocation status checking

For online revocation status checking, there must be a protocol that operates between Alice and the certificate server. For this purpose, the Internet standardisation body IETF has created a protocol called **OCSP (Online Certificate Status Protocol)**, which is standardisd in [RFC2560]. In the terminology of Chapter 12, this is a finely detailed protocol, which is implemented without states. It belongs in Layer 7 of the OSI model (see Chapter 21).

OCSP is a simple protocol

OCSP is a simple protocol. It anticipates that Alice sends a protocol message to a server (OCSP responder), which answers this with another protocol message. In Alice's message to the OSCP responder there is a list of certificate serial numbers (the list often has only one entry). The message can be signed by Alice. The answer from the OCSP responder is usually signed and contains information about the revocation status of the certificate with the given serial number. In each case, a reason for revocation is included in the message.

The OCSP specification does not give any evidence about the OCSP responder itself. Normally, however, this can be imagined as a certificate server, or a device attached to it. It is also possible that the OCSP responder does not access the certificate server directly, in which case the O in OCSP becomes meaningless.

SCVP is more productive than OCSP

With OCSP, only the revocation status of a certificate can be checked. Therefore, a further protocol is being developed within the IETF, which has a similar aim but offers rather more functionality. Confusingly, this protocol is called **Simple Certificate Validation Protocol (SCVP)**. Confusing because the term 'Simple' gives the impression that SCVP is a simpler version of OCSP – but in reality, this is the complete opposite. Alice can use SCVP for other purposes than online revocation status checking:

• Alice can hand over the checking of a certificate to a server. The server checks which CA has issued the certificate and where this CA comes in a hierarchy. The server also determines whether the CA can be trusted, in that, for example, the path leads up the hierarchy to a trustworthy root CA. This SCVP function of course requires Alice to trust the server.

- If Alice does not trust the server, she can have the necessary information (above all, CA certificates that are contained in a hierarchy) sent to her via SCVP, so that she can carry out the checking herself.

Alice can use SCVP to download certificate revocation lists

- Via SCVP, Alice can also download certificate revocation lists (see Section 19.3.2).

Like OCSP, SCVP is also a comparably simple, stateless protocol, which is classed as Level 7 of the OSI model. For example, HTTP can be used as the transport protocol. The protocol messages can also be sent by e-mail.

19.3.2 Certificate revocation lists

Certificate revocation lists do not need online connections

An online revocation request has the obvious drawback that it always requires an online connection. It is also costly for the certificate server to sign each answer to every request. In practice, revocation information is therefore usually downloaded to stock, which means that a signature always relates to a whole list of revoked certificates. This usage requires the use of **revocation lists**, which are also called **Certificate Revocation Lists (CRLs)**.

A revocation list is a signed list (usually signed by a CA), in which the serial numbers of revoked certificates are detailed. If Alice downloads the current revocation list at regular intervals (say once a day), then she knows which certificates she may no longer use. An online revocation status request is then not needed. The advantage here is that online connections and computation time for digital signatures are saved – this is also the reason why, in comparison to online revocation status requests, the use of revocation lists is the older and, as yet, more practical approach. The drawback of revocation lists is that revocations are not effected so speedily: Alice only finds out about a revocation when she downloads a new list – by which time the certificate may already have been revoked for some time.

A revocation list must be updated

A revocation list is replaced by an updated version from the Trust Centre at regular intervals, or as necessary. The validity period must be determined by the Trust Centre – usually this is one day. Revocation lists are not intended for retrieval on demand. Instead, it is anticipated that user Alice will routinely obtain and store the current revocation list for herself. Of course, a certificate revocation list can be distributed by e-mail, or made accessible via a WWW page. There are many varieties of revocation list, as we shall now discover.

Complete revocation lists

A complete revocation list is the simplest variation

The simplest form of revocation list is the **complete certificate revocation list**. In a complete revocation list, a Trust Centre publishes the serial numbers of all revoked certificates. This can become very unmanageable in a large PKI, of course. A complete revocation list file might exceed several megabytes. If all PKI users have to download such an amount of data onto their computers once a day, it is time to look for an alternative.

Distributed revocation lists

A part revocation list does not detail every revoked certificate

One obvious way to avoid complete revocation lists is to distribute the serial numbers of the revoked certificates between several revocation lists. These are called **partitioned revocation lists**. At first glance, nothing is gained with partitioned revocation lists, because the data quantity does not decrease if Alice has to download several partitioned lists instead of a complete list. There is a trick, however, with which Alice can usually dispense with certain partitioned revocation lists: X.509 offers the possibility of specifying a **CRL Distribution Point** (CDP) in certificates. This is usually the network address (URL) of a directory service and the distinguished name of the object in which the revocation list is stored. A WWW address can also be specified if the revocation list can be called up over a WWW interface. Each partitioned revocation list contains its own CRL Distribution Point and is thereby distinguished from the others that are accessible to Alice.

The CDP states where a CRL can be referenced

If Alice wants to obtain the most up-to-date revocation lists, she looks first at the certificates of her communication partners and the CDPs specified in them. Then she can obtain the precise partitioned revocation lists she needs via the respective CDPs. Because one can assume that Alice only communicates with a small fraction of the other PKI users, the use of partitioned revocation lists and CRL Distribution Points can markedly reduce the data download. Of course, CRL Distribution Points have the additional advantage that the various partitioned revocation lists can be downloaded from different locations on the network.

Delta revocation lists

Delta revocation lists reduce the quantity of data

Another way of reducing the quantity of data in revocation lists is offered by **Delta CRLs**. A Delta CRL contains only those certificates that have been revoked since the issue of the last revocation list (**base CRL**). Delta CRLs can also be used in conjunction with partitioned revocation lists. Delta CRLs are not that widely used as yet, because most PKI applications do not support them. It is fairly safe to assume that this situation will change over the coming years, however.

Certificate revocation trees

Revocation lists are always transferred as a whole

By means of partitioned revocation lists and Delta CRLs, the amount of data that is called up can be markedly reduced. Nevertheless, user Alice must always download a whole CRL (or Delta CRL, or partitioned revocation list) – if she only downloads part of one, she cannot check the signature on the list.

However, there is a way for Alice to download a single entry from a CRL-type structure without having to dispense with a signature that can be checked. This becomes possible if the revocation list is replaced by a **Certificate Revocation Tree** (**CRT**). A revocation tree is a data structure that basically contains the same information as one or more revocation lists, and is also signed. In the procedure described below, Alice can download a single, isolated entry and check the signature, without any knowledge of the whole tree.

A revocation tree can be used for several *CAs* that issue certificates. Each *CA* is identified by a number (*CA* number) which, for example, can be a hash result of the public *CA* key. As an example, let us assume that there are five *CAs* with the numbers 1, 3, 6, 8 and 9. As usual, the certificates are identified by their serial numbers. In our example we assume that the five aforementioned *CAs* have each revoked the certificates with the following serial numbers (in practice, *CA* numbers and serial numbers are larger, of course):

CA number	Serial no. of revoked certificate
1	12, 48, 72
3	14, 15
6	35
8	42, 43, 44
9	9

Now let's assume that *CSN* is a variable that stands for the serial number of the certificate whose revocation Alice wants to query. Let's suppose that the variable *CA* stands for the number of the CA. We can transfer the data from the above table into the following statements using the variables *CSN* and *CA*:

```
 1.  IF CA<1 THEN unknown CA

 2.  IF CA=1 AND CSN<12 THEN not revoked

 3.  IF CA=1 AND 12<=CSN<48 THEN revoked, case CSN=12

 4.  IF CA=1 AND 48<=CSN<72 THEN revoked, case CSN=48

 5.  IF CA=1 AND 72<=CSN THEN revoked, case CSN=72

 6.  IF 1<CA<3 THEN unknown CA

 7.  IF CA=3 AND CSN<14 THEN not revoked

 8.  IF CA=3 AND 14<=CSN<15 THEN revoked, case CSN=14

 9.  IF CA=3 AND 15<=CSN THEN revoked, case CSN=15

10.  IF 3<CA<6 THEN unknown CA

11.  IF CA=6 AND CSN<35 THEN not revoked

12.  IF CA=6 AND 35<=CSN THEN revoked, case CSN=35

13.  IF 6<CA<8 THEN unknown CA

14.  IF CA=8 AND CSN<42 THEN not revoked
```

```
15.  IF CA=8 AND 42<=CSN<43 THEN revoked, case CSN=42

16.  IF CA=8 AND 43<=CSN<44 THEN revoked, case CSN=43

17.  IF CA=8 AND 44<=CSN THEN revoked, case CSN=44

18.  IF 8<CA<9 THEN unknown CA

19.  IF CA=9 AND CSN<9 THEN not revoked

20.  IF CA=9 AND 9<=CSN THEN revoked, case CSN=9

21.  IF 9<CA THEN unknown CA
```

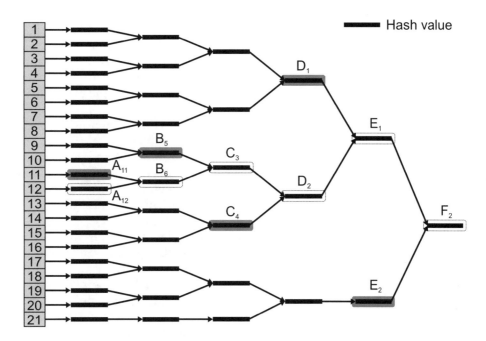

Figure 19.3 Example of a certification revocation tree: with statement 12 and the grey-shaded hash results Alice can calculate the specified hash results and then verify the signature.

Each certificate can be assigned to a statement
As is easy to understand, each certificate – regardless from which CA it is from and whether it has been revoked or not – can be assigned to just one statement. If we look, for instance, at the certificate with serial number 17, which has been issued from CA number 8, then statement no. 14 is correct. This statement tells us that it is a not-revoked certificate. On the other hand, if we consider the certificate with serial number 35 from CA number 6, then from statement 12 we determine that this certificate has been revoked.

With the aforementioned 21 statements, Alice can thus determine whether any given certificate has been revoked or not (provided the CA is not unknown). A Trust

Centre could therefore bring the 21 statements into a unified format, sign them, and publish them instead of a revocation list – but this would not gain anything.

A hash result is generated for each statement

The Trust Centre now generates a cryptographic hash result for each statement (see Figure 19.3). In our example we will label these as A_1, A_1, ..., A_{21}. The Trust Centre then reapplies a cryptographic hash function to each pair of hash results (A_1 and A_2, A_3 and A_4, ...), which gives rise to the hash results B_1, B_2, ..., B_{10} (because there is an odd number of statements, $B_{11}=A_{21}$). Similarly, from B_1, B_2, ..., B_{11} the Trust Centre then generates the hash results C_1, C_2, ..., C_6, which give rise to D_1, D_2 and D_3. These are in turn rehashed to E_1 and E_2 and finally the hash result F_1 is generated. This result is signed by the Trust Centre.

A statement, some hash results and the signature are enough to check a revocation

If Alice now wants to know whether a given certificate has been revoked or not (we assume it belongs to Bob, has the serial number 35 and originates from CA number 6), she need not retrieve the whole revocation tree. It will suffice if she downloads statement no. 12, the hash results A_{11}, B_5, C_4, D_1 and E_2 (these are shaded grey in the diagram) along with the signature. As you can easily see, from statement 12 and hash result A_{11} Alice can calculate the value of B_4. From B_4 and B_5 she calculates C_3. From C_3 and C_4 she calculates D_2. From D_2 and D_1 she calculates E_1. From E_1 and E_2 she calculates F_1. If she knows F_1, she can also verify the signature and hence find out whether Bob's certificate has been revoked. If the revocation tree is larger, the number of hash results needed to check an entry also increases. However, the increase bears only a logarithmic relationship to the number of revoked certificates – for a million revoked certificates, for example, only around 20 hash results are needed. The extra hash results that Alice must download are therefore only of minor importance.

Revocation trees are a temporary solution

Revocation trees can be used to provide a temporary solution between online revocation requests and CRLs. To achieve this, Alice never downloads a whole CRL – she always retrieves only the entry from a revocation tree that she needs (including the relevant hash results). Although this means that Alice gets a different answer message each time, the CA only needs to sign a new revocation tree once a day (or at some other time interval), and forward it to the certificate server. In this way the cost that arises from numerous signatures is prevented. On the other hand, revocation trees still have the same basic drawback as CRLs: they are never as up to the minute as an online revocation request.

Standards for certificate revocation lists

X.509 also standardises certificate revocation lists

The X.509 standard, which you already know from Section 16.3.1, not only describes a format for digital certificates, but also a format for certificate revocation lists. As with X.509 certificates, X.509 certificate revocation lists are also divided into fields. When the first version of X.509 appeared in 1988, the following CRL fields were provided:

- Version: In this field the version of the X.509 CRL format is specified. In the 1988 version, this was the number 0 (numbering started at zero).

- Signature: This field contains the OID of the signature algorithm used for signing the CRL.

- Issuer: This field contains the name (X.500 Distinguished Name) of the issuer of the CRL, say of a CA.

- This update: This field indicates the date that this CRL was issued.

- Next update: This field indicates the date by which the next CRL will be issued.

- Revoked certificates: This field contains the serial numbers of the revoked certificates.

X.509v1 CRLs had defects

As with X.509v1 certificates, X.509v1 CRLs proved to be underdeveloped. When the X.509v3 standard for certificates appeared in 1996, the standard also provided more flexibility for X.509 CRLs. X.509 CRLs corresponding to this standard were called X.509v2 CRLs. The fact that X.509v3 certificates are described in the same standard version as X.509v2 CRLs is rather confusing, of course, but logical. In the second X.509 version that appeared in 1993, the format for CRLs was left unaltered.

X.509v2 enabled extensions

The format for X.509v2 CRLs makes it possible to specify any number of extra fields (extensions). There are extensions that appear in just one CRL, and others that deliver additional information about revoked certificates and therefore provide one field per certificate. Each extension is marked as either critical or non-critical. If an implementation comes across a non-critical extension that it doesn't recognise, the extension is ignored – on the other hand, an unknown critical extension causes a CRL to be regarded as invalid. So that the situation doesn't become too unmanageable, several standard extensions were included in the X.509v2 standard. The following standard extensions relate to a complete CRL:

- Authority key identifier: This extension contains a unique identifier of the issuer's key, making it possible to differentiate between different keys of the same issuer. The PKIX and ISIS profiles both require this extension to be used and marked as critical (PKIX) or, in the case of ISIS, as non-critical.

Some extensions are fixed

- Issuer alternative name: In the CRL name field, an X.500 name must be given. An additional name or some other identifier of the issuer can be given in this field (for instance, an e-mail or IP address). PKIX requires the use of this extension if an alternative name is in use. It recommends that the extension be marked as non-critical. In accordance with ISIS, the extension can be used, but must then also be marked as non-critical.

- CRL number: This means a unique serial number for the CRL. PKIX prescribes the use of this extension as non-critical, as does ISIS.

- Issuing Distribution Point: In this always critical extension, a CDP (see Section 18.4.2) and, in some cases, some details about constraints in the use of the CRL are given. According to PKIX, this extension ought to be omitted, yet ISIS forbids it.

- Delta CRL Indicator: This always critical extension indicates that this CRL is a Delta CRL. In accordance with PKIX and ISIS, Delta CRLs and hence this extension can be used.

There are also extensions that relate to single entries

As well as the standard extensions for complete CRLs, there are other standard extensions that occur once in the list per certificate that is received. All of these are always non-critical and, according to PKIX, optional:

- Reason Code: This identifies the reason for the certificate revocation (see Section 18.4.2). PKIX recommends the use of this extension. ISIS states that it can be used.

- Certificate Issuer: This extension contains the name of the CA that has signed the respective revoked certificate. According to ISIS, this field can be used.

- Reason for Suspension: In the case of a suspension, this is a non-critical CRL entry extension that identifies the reason for the certificate suspension. Since ISIS does not allow suspensions, this extension may not be used.

- Invalidity Date: This is a non-critical extension that provides the date on which it is known or suspected that the private key was compromised, or that the certificate otherwise became invalid. ISIS forbids the use of this extension.

Both ISIS and PKIX dispense with extensions of their own. Altogether, the variety to be found in X.509 CRLs is nowhere near as large as is found in X.509 certificates.

Practical aspects of PKI construction

Few false ideas have more firmly gripped the minds of so many intelligent men than the one that, if they just tried, they could invent a cipher that no one could break.
DAVID KAHN

Key experience no. 20
In the middle of 1997, the Chaos Computer Club (a German hacker organisation) began a project whose aim was to crack DES [Spie97]. The point of attack was the short key length of DES. With 500 so-called ASICs (programmable computing units) it should have taken around two weeks to crack the key. Budgeted cost of the project: £170,000. This was just petty cash in comparison to the budget of a national secret service organisation, of course. For the Chaos Computer Club, however, it was too much – as a result, the project was abandoned.

In this final chapter on the subject of PKI, we shall concern ourselves with several practical questions relating to PKI construction. By doing so, we shall look mainly at the sequence of operations in the construction of a PKI, and the services and products on the market that can be used to do so. We shall assume that Crypt & Co. (Alice's employer) wants to construct a PKI and then run it.

20.1 The course of the construction of a PKI

PKI construction is a complex matter

The construction of a PKI is a complex matter. So that Crypt & Co. is successful, the components and commercial processes of the PKI must be built up in stages, and integrated into the existing infrastructure. A PKI is thus a computer system requiring comprehensive system integration (**PKI system integration**). An experienced PKI system integrator would probably recommend to Crypt & Co. a construction program that resembles the following:

A requirements analysis should come first

1. **Requirements analysis**: In this first step, the requirements that Crypt & Co. expect the system to meet are worked out. The four most important matters that are cleared up here are described in Section 20.2.

2. **Rough outline**: After Crypt & Co.'s requirements for the PKI have been established, the general architecture of the PKI can be determined. At this point the services and products available on the market must be examined (see Section 20.3). If the market cannot meet every requirement of Crypt & Co., additional in-house developments must be considered at this point.

3. **Test phase**: After it has been established which products and developments are needed for Crypt & Co.'s plans, these must be tested in the laboratory. This is necessary because many incompatibilities and other problems can be discovered during the testing.

A test phase is important

4. **Detailed specification**: After the test phase, the architecture of the PKI can be determined precisely. The individual components and commercial processes are defined at this point.

5. **Pilot**: In this phase, the PKI is put into operation with a small group of users. This involves issuing not much more than 100 certificates. The aim of this pilot scheme is to gather first impressions of how productive things are.

6. **Roll-out**: In this phase the PKI applications provided by the users are installed, and the actual working operation of the PKI begins.

System integration requires know-how

Of course, these are only rough suggestions for the course of a PKI construction. In practice, a PKI system integration is a very complex matter, and requires a high degree of expertise (see also Section 20.3.6).

20.2 Basic questions about PKI construction

Even in the first phase of a PKI project (requirements analysis), there are many questions that Crypt & Co. must ask itself and answer as quickly as possible. The four most important questions are introduced in the following:

20.2.1 Which commercial model?

The first question that Crypt & Co. should answer before anything else when constructing a PKI is which commercial model to use. In other words: how is the expenditure that Crypt & Co. lays out for a PKI to be recovered or justified?

PKIs as security measures

A PKI is often intended as a security measure

Crypt & Co. may very well want to construct a PKI in order to provide its employees and business partners with digital certificates. In this case, setting up a PKI is an infrastructure investment that brings no direct return. In this commercial model, the expenditure for a PKI would be repaid by the fact that Mallory's attacks would be prevented – which could otherwise cost Crypt & Co. a great deal of money. Because this commercial model of a PKI as a security measure appears most frequently at the moment, most considerations in this chapter are based on this.

A PKI as a source of revenue

A PKI can also be a source of income

The reason for Crypt & Co. to set up a PKI does not necessarily have to be worries about security. The company might be more inspired by the idea of selling digital certificates from its own Trust Centre. Clients could be private individuals, or companies that do not wish to operate their own Trust Centre and would rather use Crypt & Co. as an outsourcing partner. In this case, the expenditure for the PKI would be amortised by the revenue from the sale of certificates and possible ancillary services (e.g. encryption software).

To plan a PKI as a source of revenue is, of course, a risky undertaking. For this reason there are notably fewer PKIs working to this model than those set up as a security measure. Some of the organisations that offer Trust Centre services on the market, and hence were set up on a commercial model, will be introduced in Section 20.3.1.

A PKI as an ancillary service

A PKI service can also be set up as an ancillary service

Crypt & Co. might possibly set up a PKI for its customers' benefit, but give away the certificates as an ancillary service. For example, if Crypt & Co. is an active Internet provider, then a certificate with a PSE might well be part of the starting package received by every customer. Similarly, an online bank can also supply its account holders with certificates. In this case, the PKI costs are not amortised by direct cash payments from customers. Instead, the bank's main revenues provide the return on investment.

Combined models

Combined models are also possible

In practice, it is often the case that several commercial models are used when setting up a PKI. Thus, a PKI whose certificates are sold can also be used to meet the internal needs of the company. Any other combination is conceivable.

20.2.2 Which PKI applications?

Then there is the important question of which applications Crypt & Co. wants a PKI to serve. When all is said and done, a PKI is only an infrastructure, and as such, without suitable applications, completely useless. As you might expect, there are lots of applications – after all, there is practically no data that cannot be encrypted or signed. In the following sections, the ten most important PKI applications will be introduced.

1. E-mail encryption

E-mail encryption is a popular PKI application

Encrypting and signing e-mails is currently the killer application in the PKI field. Most PKIs I know of were set up, to a considerable extent, because it would facilitate the encryption of e-mails. This subject will be examined in detail in Chapter 26.

2. Protection of WWW connections with SSL

SSL is another PKI application

In addition to encryption of e-mail, encryption and authentication between Web browser and Web server is one of the most important PKI applications. The SSL protocol, which is described in Chapter 24, was developed to facilitate the protection of Web connections. Since all the usual Web browsers and Web servers support SSL, the protection of WWW connections can normally be introduced relatively easily.

3. Virtual private network (VPN)

In addition to cryptographic protection of e-mails and WWW connections, the operation of a virtual private network (VPN) is one of the most important applications of PKI. It will be looked at in more detail in Sections 22.4 and 23.6.

4. File encryption

There are two variations of file encryption

File encryption is seldom the reason for setting up a PKI, but in many cases constitutes an ancillary application. There are different ways to integrate file encryption in an operating system For **manual file encryption**, Alice starts the encryption process with a mouse click, or by calling up a command. For **transparent file encryption**, the encryption process is automatic if, for example, a file is saved in a specific directory.

5. SAP R/3 protection

The protection of SAP R/3 ports is another popular use of a PKI. Because sensitive data is processed in an R/3 system, it is obvious that PKI-based access protection is a must. More on this subject in Section 28.5.

6. Single Sign-on (SSO)

SSO is also a PKI application

By Single Sign-on (SSO, also Secure Single Sign-on), we understand the concept of providing just one authentication for several applications (see Section 13.7.1). Setting up an SSO system is an expensive matter, irrespective of a PKI. Because single authentication can take place in an SSO system that is PKI based, SSO is also an interesting application.

7. Form signing

With many PKIs, encryption has been at the forefront up to now. However, it also makes sense to use digital signatures. In addition to e-mails, signatures could also be used for forms displayed on a Web browser (this is known as **form signing**). This is discussed in Section 25.4.4.

8. Online banking

Online banking is a PKI application

Even online banking can be a very interesting PKI application, if a bank issues digital certificates to customers. This is discussed in Section 28.4.

9. SET

SET (see Section 27.2) is a protocol for the encrypted transfer of credit card data. Because digital certificates are used to do so, SET is another PKI application.

10. Code signing

Code signing is another PKI application

One of the most interesting applications for digital signatures is so-called code signing, which will be covered in Section 25.4.1. This involves signing program code in order to ensure that Mallory cannot alter it while it is being transported without being detected.

20.2.3 Outsourcing or own operation?

A crucial decision when setting up a PKI is to choose between outsourcing and self-operation. For **PKI self-operation**, Crypt & Co. sets up the PKI Trust Centre itself and operates it in its own computer centre. In the case of **PKI outsourcing**, on the other hand, Crypt & Co. uses an existing Trust Centre, which offers its services on the open market. The main arguments for self-operation or outsourcing will now be put forward.

For self-operation

From the viewpoint of Crypt & Co., the arguments in favour of self-operation of a PKI are as follows:

- With outsourcing, Crypt & Co. shifts responsibility for a critical security service outside of the company . This is not the case with self-operation – security thus remains in-house.

Self-operation is more flexible

- If resources (computer centre, administration personnel, ...) are already available, self-operation of a PKI can be the cheaper solution. This applies at least where demands on the PKI as regards performance and breakdown security are not particularly high.

- Most of the outsourcing organisations on the market are still quite new. There is a lot more experience available in the case of a self-operation solution.

- Self-operation is usually more flexible, because Crypt & Co. does not have to follow the guidelines of the outsourcing organisation.

Pro outsourcing

The following arguments are in favour of outsourcing:

- Outsourcing is the simpler and less nerve-racking solution. Crypt & Co. leaves the PKI operation to specialists and can concentrate on its own main business.

Outsourcing is usually less expensive

- As a rule, outsourcing is the less expensive choice (much depends, of course, on the exact circumstances). This applies above all if the demands made by Crypt & Co. as regards performance and breakdown security are particularly high.

Which is better – outsourcing or self-operation?

Both options have advantages

Whether outsourcing or self-operation of a PKI is the better choice is a matter of argument. It is generally true to say that self-operation would be more rewarding for a large than for a medium-sized organisation. Resources that are already available (a computer centre and administration staff, for example) must also be taken into consideration.

Since various outsourcing organisations have set themselves up on the German market, for example there is a general trend developing in favour of outsourcing. Many companies see no need to operate a Trust Centre under their own roof, and hope to keep costs down by outsourcing their PKI needs.

20.3 The most important PKI suppliers

The large demand for public key infrastructures has resulted in a wide range of PKI products and services. In my experience, suppliers on the PKI market are divided into the following six areas:

- Operators of Trust Centres

- Suppliers of CA and RA software

- Suppliers of PKI applications

- Suppliers of directory service products

- Suppliers of PKI ancillary products.

- System integration experts and consultants

We shall now examine these six areas in more detail.

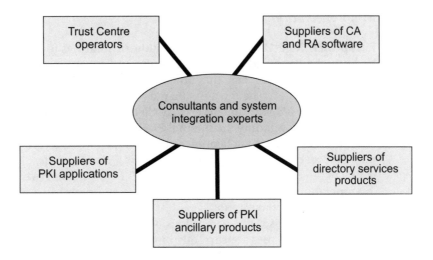

Figure 20.1 There are various suppliers in the market. In addition to Trust Centre operators and product suppliers, there are also companies offering consultation and system integration expertise.

20.3.1 Trust Centre operators

Among the most important large concerns on the PKI market are those that operate their own Trust Centre and sell certificates to their customers. Of course, individuals such as Bob count as customers – but very little money is to be made from such customers at the moment. Many Trust Centres therefore have concentrated their sales efforts on business customers who are looking for an outsourcing partner for their intra-organisational PKI.

There are many
Trust Centres
There are many Trust Centres that supply their services to the market. We can only take a look at the ten most important here.

1. A-Sign

A-Sign is currently the leading Trust Centre in Austria. It is operated by Datakom Austria, which is a subsidiary of Telekom Austria. A-Sign fulfils the requirements of Austrian signature law and, after the opening of the Austrian root CA (operated by state-owned company), will be the first Trust Centre in Austria conforming to legal requirements.

By their own account, A-Sign has already issued certificates in the tens of thousands for Austrian business customers. End users can currently only apply for certificates via the Web page (www.a-sign.datakom.at). In future, however, it should also be possible to purchase PSEs in post offices. A-Sign offers user-certificates in four different varieties (light, medium, strong and premium), whereby a different registration is provided for each. In addition, there is a different CA certificate for each type of certificate.

2. European Bridge-CA

European Bridge-CA connects company internal CAs

European Bridge-CA is a certification authority that was founded in October 2000 by Deutsche Bank and Deutsche Telekom, and began operating in January 2001. European Bridge-CA has the task of performing cross-certification in intra-organisation CAs. The idea is that a company-internal CA can establish a certification path with all other CAs that have also used Bridge-CA for cross-certification. As yet, only the internal PKIs of Deutsche Bank, Giesecke & Devrient and Deutsche Telekom are connected by European Bridge-CA. However, there are now over 20 other companies and authorities – for example, Siemens and BMW – who have already professed interest and for the most part have already carried out interoperability tests. European Bridge-CA is still mainly a German concern, but with an international outlook.

The need for a set-up such as European Bridge-CA is currently hard to ignore. Numerous companies are currently building internal PKIs, but do not want to be subordinate to a root CA. European Bridge-CA therefore provides mutual recognition without a large number of cross-certifications being necessary. For this reason, requirements imposed on European Bridge-CA clients are kept very realistic – although the aim is for a high level of security, no unnecessary demands are to be made on the companies participating.

European Bridge-CA ought to catch on

There is every indication that European Bridge-CA will establish itself as the connecting link between a large number of PKIs. In any event, it is praiseworthy that, by means of European Bridge-CA, enterprises are pulling in the same direction as government authorities. Further information on European Bridge-CA is available under www.bridge-ca.org.

3. Deutsche Post Signtrust

Deutsche Post Signtrust operates a Trust Centre

Deutsche Post Signtrust, a subsidiary of Deutsche Post AG, is the operator of a Trust Centre. Since this Trust Centre started operating early in 2000, Signtrust has been one of the most important large concerns on the German PKI market.

Of all German Trust Centre operators, Signtrust offers the most comprehensive choice in the area of German signature law. Thus, in addition to certificates conforming to the signature law, the undertaking also offers PKI applications conforming to the signature law (e.g. e-mail signing). Private keys are stored on E4/high-evaluated smart cards, and to register at an RA, you must appear in person.

Deutsche Post Signtrust obeys the signature law

Although Signtrust continues to implement the signature law, in the future the company will also offer reinforced solutions, which do not correspond to it. By this, Signtrust is reacting to the fact that many customers (especially large international undertakings) prefer solutions that do not conform to the signature law.

4. Deutsche Telekom (Telesec)

Deutsche Telekom (Telesec) is the leading pioneer in the German Trust Centre business. Since 1999, the Telesec Trust Centre has conformed to the German signature law, making it the first in the business to overcome that hurdle. In comparison to Deutsche Post Signtrust, however, Telesec is a lot less fixated on the signature law. Telesec now operates a second CA that does not conform to the signature law and thus offers more flexibility.

5. DFN-PCA

The Deutsche Forschungsnetz (German Research Network) operates a PCA

The **DFN-PCA** (Deutsches Forschungsnetz Policy Certification Authority) is a project of the Union for the Advancement of a German Research Network (Verein zur Förderung eines Deutschen Forschungsnetzes (DFN-Verein)). The DFN-PCA issues certificates for other CAs. Within the framework of this project, the DFN-User-CA and the DFN-Server-CA have also been created, which issue certificates for end entities. In these CAs, both OpenPGP and X.509 certificates are supported.

6. D-Trust

D-Trust is a subsidiary of the Bundesdruckerei (Federal Printers) that operates a Trust Centre. D-Trust operates on two tracks: for internationally-minded customers it offers certificates issued with Verisign software. In addition, there are certificates that follow the German signature law. So far, however, the D-Trust Trust Centre does not offer such certificates because the necessary evaluations have not yet been concluded.

7. RegTP

The RegTP operates the root Trust Centre in accordance with signature law

The Regulating Authority for Telecommunications and Post (**RegTP**) operates the root Trust Centre for German signature law. This Trust Centre only issues certificates for Trust Centres that conform to the signature law. It does not serve end users.

8. Swisskey

Swisskey is the leading Trust Centre in Switzerland. It is operated by Swisskey AG, which was founded in 1998 by, among others, the Swiss telecommunications concern Swisscom. Swisskey clients include several well-known Swiss companies.

9. TC Trustcenter

TC Trustcenter (see Section 30.2.8) is, after Deutsche Telekom and Deutsche Post, currently the third largest concern among commercial Trust Centre suppliers in Germany. In contrast to its two main competitors, TC Trustcenter was not born into a conglomerate. Instead, it was a spin-off from the Hamburg company MAZ, and has since been taken over by four large banks.

TC Trustcenter strives for signature law conformity

Although TC Trustcenter strives for signature law conformity, it has not yet achieved this (as at the end of 2000). As with Deutsche Telekom (but not Deutsche Post), the Hamburg company is following a strategy that is not fixated exclusively on signature law. Instead, TC Trustcenter takes care to make its offers to customers as diversified as possible, and they often contain special (and often more expensive, of course) adaptations.

10. Verisign

Verisign is the oldest in the business The US company Verisign is the operator of the oldest Trust Centre in the business. Verisign started in 1995 and has been able to maintain its position as the largest Trust Centre operator in the world up to now. There are now Verisign Trust Centres in many countries outside the USA. By its own reckoning, Verisign has issued around 400,000 certificates for Web servers and about 4 million certificates for end users. Test certificates are freely available for end users on the Verisign Web site.

20.3.2 Suppliers of CA and RA solutions

If Crypt & Co. decides on self-operation instead of PKI outsourcing, it needs the necessary software. The most important thing here is a software package to operate both CA and RA (CA and RA solutions are almost always offered in combination). Because such a software package lies at the heart of any PKI, I also use the terms **PKI solution** and **PKI software** for it. The suppliers of PKI solutions, as well as the operators of Trust Centres, play a central role in the PKI business.

There are more than 30 CA/RA solutions I know of more than 30 software products for operating CAs and RAs, and almost as many suppliers of such solutions. The ten most important are introduced in the following.

1. Baltimore Unicert

The Irish company Baltimore, with their PKI product **Unicert**, is Number Two (after Entrust) on the world market. For a start, Unicert stands out due to its very concise graphical user interface, on which a hierarchy of CAs with their respective RAs and other components can be well laid out. Policies can also be selected using drag-and-drop. Unicert is suitable for both intra-company and public PKIs.

2. Entrust/PKI

Entrust is the supplier of a successful PKI solution **Entrust/PKI**, from the Canadian company Entrust Technologies, is the current most successful PKI solution on the world market. Entrust follows the strategy of expanding its own CA/RA software by as many of its own PKI applications as possible, and by applications from other manufacturers that have been tested for interoperability (these applications are described as 'Entrust Ready').

The most important feature of Entrust/PKI is that 'Entrust Ready' applications do not access the PSE directly. Instead, there is an intermediary, a special client-component that user Alice must have installed in addition to the application. The interface to this extra client-component is proprietary, which is why there are also many applications that cannot address it. Among these applications (and the products which are not 'Entrust Ready') are the popular Web browsers (there are ancillary products that cure this failing, however).

Through its extra client-component, Entrust/PKI offers several interesting ancillary functions. It thus provides for automatic certificate renewals, and enables a smooth CA key change. In addition, the extra client-component enables preset configuration settings that are valid for all applications that work with the PSE.

Entrust/PKI is well suited for internal company PKIs

Entrust/PKI all very well suited for internal company PKIs, and is very successful in this market. For public PKIs, however, the compulsory client-component is more of a hindrance, and also, from my own experience, cross-certification and integration into a hierarchy are rather problematic with Entrust.

3. IBM Trust Authority

Through its subsidiary company Tivoli, IBM offers a PKI solution called **Trust Authority**. This can be considered as a serious alternative to the solutions from Entrust, Baltimore and RSA Security, but as yet is much less widely used.

4. Microsoft Windows 2000

Windows 2000 contains a CA

Within the folds of the Windows 2000 operating system is a simple software CA operator. This PKI software is a very inexpensive PKI solution, and is of special interest for companies that already work with Windows 2000 anyway.

Unfortunately, up to now, the Windows 2000 CA does not exactly offer the maximum as far as functionality is concerned. For example, there is no proper RA component. CA administration is inextricably linked with network administration, which causes security problems. Also, it is not possible to have certain types of certificate issued only by specific administrators, or to separate the CA configuration settings from the issue of certificates. Another drawback is this PKI solution's own proprietary components – the Windows 2000 CA – is only of interest in a Microsoft environment.

I assume that in future Microsoft will play an important part in the PKI market. The current PKI solution cannot yet compete with the proven products, especially since other manufacturers still have to adapt their products to the Microsoft PKI.

5. NAI PGP

PGP has been built up into a PKI solution

Over the past few years, NAI has built up the fairly well-known PGP software (see Section 26.3) from a simple crypto software into a PKI solution. PGP now offers the X.509 format as well as the OpenPGP format for digital certificates. As a result, PGP has developed more and more into professional PKI software, which is also suitable for larger companies. However, very little of the anarchic character of the one-time cult PGP software remains today, and many PGP fans even refuse to use the newer versions. Because NAI is less interested in nostalgic private users than in commercial customers, this trend is likely to continue.

6. Netscape CMS

Netscape offers a PKI solution with its **Certificate Management System (CMS)**. This product does not offer the comprehensive functions and ease of use of other products. However, for smaller PKIs (up to several thousand users), Netscape CMS is well suited. In this segment of the market, Netscape is very successful.

7. OpenCA

OpenCA is a freeware solution **OpenCA** is a PKI solution for the Linux operating system based on the open-source principle and hence freely available. Many PKI experts are involved in the development of OpenCA software on an honorary basis. OpenCA might one day become a PKI solution to be taken seriously, but that day might be a long way off. Up to now there have been only Beta versions, and it cannot yet be regarded in a practical light.

8. RSA Security Keon

Keon stems from RSA **Keon** is the PKI solution from RSA Security, which is of course one of the most important large concerns in the security business. Keon contains some code from Verisign, which is a spin-off company of RSA Security. Keon's architecture resembles that of Entrust/PKI, however: Keon also has an extra client-component, which fits between the application and PSE. The interface to this client-component is proprietary, but there are several self-manufactured RSA applications and some others that support this interface. Keon is mainly intended for company-internal PKI solutions.

9. SmartTrust Certificate Manager

Sonera SmartTrust is active in the PKI mobile phone network. In 2000, SmartTrust bought the Swedish company ID-2 and its **Certificate Manager** software. Certificate Manager is (together with several additional components) a PKI solution, which is aimed mainly at smart cards.

10. Verisign

Verisign also offers a CA/RA solution Verisign is primarily known as the operator of a Trust Centre. However, the US company also sells **PKI solutions**, which are designed especially for very big PKIs with several hundred thousand and more users (this software is, of course, also used by Verisign itself). In contrast to almost all other suppliers of PKI solutions, Verisign does not leave it up to the customer as to what he or she does with it. The operation of Verisign software is associated with numerous conditions – for example, security measures and connection to the Verisign hierarchy. Because of this, Verisign is a quasi franchise supplier.

20.3.3 Suppliers of PKI applications

There are innumerable application solutions

There are lots of possible applications for PKIs (the most important were looked at in Section 20.2.2). Therefore there are at long last innumerable products with which PKI applications can be implemented. For this reason, in addition to suppliers of PKI solutions and Trust Centre operators, suppliers of PKI applications are another established section of the PKI market.

I shall not attempt to list the most important PKI application products at this point. The most important examples have been named in the chapters in which the respective applications were looked at.

20.3.4 Suppliers of directory service solutions

The certificate server is normally part of a CA/RA solution

Software for the operation of a certificate server is not normally offered as a component of a PKI solution. This is due to the fact that there are many directory service solutions that were not fashioned specifically for the PKI field, but which can well be used as certificate servers. These are products for the operation of an X.500 or LDAP server. The most important suppliers include Microsoft, Siemens, Netscape, Critical Path and Novell. In addition to Trust Centre operators, PKI solution suppliers and PKI application suppliers, these companies play an important role in the PKI field.

Because in a PKI only a small part of the possible directory service functionality is used, the choice of suitable products is markedly less critical than for the other PKI components. And because this is not a book about directory services, I would like at this point to dispense with a more detailed account of directory service products.

20.3.5 Suppliers of PKI ancillary products

There are many ancillary products

As yet there are still no suitable software solutions for the operation of CA, RA, directory service and applications. As a rule, other products must be purchased in order to be able to operate a PKI. These might be a smart card solution, a PSE for the CA in the form of a hardware security module, as well as a special printer for printing out password letters. The suppliers of such PKI ancillary products are thus a further section of the PKI market that I do not propose to examine in detail.

20.3.6 PKI system integrators

As you learned in Section 20.1, a PKI is a system for which comprehensive system integration is necessary. In other words, building up a PKI is a complex business, which ought to be carried out in a structured and well-thought-out manner. Because such an undertaking is not that simple, there are numerous consultancy companies that offer PKI system integration. The companies establish the requirements a customer expects from a PKI, produce a plan, select suitable products, carry out tests, and provide support while putting the plan into practice.

PKI system integration is a business in itself

Along with Trust Centre and product suppliers, PKI system integrators represent one of the important sectors in the PKI market.

Part 5

Crypto protocols for the Internet

Coding machine H54 (with keyboard extension B63) 1960 model
(from the IT-Security Teaching & Study Collection of the BSI)

The Internet and the OSI model

Finally, although the IP and TCP protocols were carefully thought out and well implemented, many of the other protocols were ad hoc, generally produced by a couple of graduate students hacking away until they got tired... Some of them are a bit of an embarrassment now.
ANDREW S. TANENBAUM [TANENB]

21.1 The OSI model

With their diverse attributes, communication protocols have already been mentioned in Chapter 12. At this point, we wish to examine those finely detailed protocols that are used on the Internet. This can best be done using the so-called **ISO-OSI model** (a little shorter, but less euphoniously: **OSI model**). The OSI model is a standardised model of the ISO standardisation organisation (see Section 10.1.1) for the interaction of protocols, whose ideas are definitive for nearly all protocols of practical relevance. Detailed information on this is given in [PetDav].

The OSI model helps with the conception of protocols

The OSI model is not intended as a super protocol that regulates everything itself. Instead, several protocols are used. Each protocol falls into one of seven, strictly demarcated classes (called **layers**). The OSI model layers are numbered from 1 to 7 and mainly follow two axioms:

- The more a protocol has to do with the signal that flows through the transmission channel, the lower the layer it belongs to. The more a protocol has to do with an application program that initiates the communication, the higher the layer it belongs to.

- Each protocol in a given layer uses the protocol of the next lower layer exclusively. It does not use any other protocol. Thus, only the protocol of Layer 1 has anything to do with hardware directly, and only the protocol of Layer 7 has anything to do with the application program directly.

21.1.1 The layers of the OSI model

The OSI model has 7 layers

The seven layers of the ISO-OSI model have the following tasks:

- **Layer 1 (Physical layer)**. Governs hardware connections and byte-stream encoding for transmission. This layer changes the signals coming from the transmission channel into zeros and ones. This means that at the end of each line used for data transmission there must be a device that uses a Layer 1 protocol.

- **Layer 2 (Data link layer).** This layer takes the zeros and ones from Layer 1, uses checksums to search for errors, and assembles bits into groups (into ASCII characters, for example). Layer 2 protocols are used at the end of almost every transmission line.

Routing occurs in Layer 3

- **Layer 3 (Network layer).** Defines protocols for routing data between systems and decides where the characters received from Layer 2 should be sent. This routing is the task of the routers that have already been mentioned, which operate by Layer 3 protocols. Routers (and hence Layer 3 protocols) are used mainly at network nodes, where more than two transmission cables are connected together.

- **Layer 4 (Transport layer).** Controls the flow of data between systems, defines the structure of data in messages, and performs error checking. With the assistance of Layer 3, Layer 4 builds a connection between the data sender and receiver in which the intermediate routers are transparent. Level 4 protocols are mainly used by those network nodes that not only forward data, but also use it (the same applies for Layers 5–7 also).

- **Layer 5 (Session layer).** Controls the communication between endpoints. Layer 5 controls the communication over the connection created by Layer 4. It decides who transmits and who receives, for example.

Layer 6 is the Presentation layer

- **Layer 6 (Presentation layer).** On the sender's side, Layer 6 converts data into the format in which it is passed on to Layer 5. On the recipient's side, in Layer 6 the incoming data is converted into the format that he or she has chosen.

- **Layer 7 (Application layer).** This layer defines the way applications interact with the network and between systems. It creates the interface to the communication applications (e.g., a Web browser or e-mail program).

The advantage of using this kind of layer model for protocols is obvious: instead of constructing one giant protocol to handle every situation, you develop seven smaller protocols that are based on each other. If the interface between the protocols is standardised, then any one protocol can be changed without this affecting the others. In addition, the work of those developing application programs is made a lot easier because they only need to worry about the protocols of Layer 7, and, thanks to the lower layers, need not concern themselves with the data representation format, control of the data exchange, the routers, error correction etc.

Layer 7 (Application Layer)	HTTP, FTP, Telnet SMTP, SNMP
Layer 6 (Presentation Layer)	
Layer 5 (Session Layer)	
Layer 4 (Transport Layer)	TCP, UDP
Layer 3 (Network Layer)	IP
Layer 2 (Data link Layer)	PPP, SLIP
Layer 1 (Physical Layer)	

Figure 21.1 The TCP/IP suite protocols occupy Layers 3–4 and 7 of the OSI model, along with other protocols (except PPP and SLIP) not included in TCP/IP.

21.1.2 The OSI model and the Internet

TCP/IP fits into the OSI model

The ISO created protocols for each layer of the OSI model specially (the so-called **OSI protocols**). OSI protocols are both famous and infamous for being able to do everything, but they are frighteningly complex. Implementations of the OSI protocols are extravagant, and sometimes give rise to problems with compatibility between implementations from other manufacturers. Obviously, the OSI protocols tried to take on too much, which is why they never really caught on.

In contrast to the OSI protocols, the OSI model itself was thankfully taken up in order to fit in existing and newly created protocols. This has also shown several weaknesses of the model: in practice, Layer 2 normally has to be divided into two sub-layers. On the other hand, Layers 5 and 6 can be done away with, which is why there are hardly any equivalent protocols. And furthermore, some existing protocols do not fit into the OSI model quite so well. Nevertheless, this model remains a popular aid for describing protocols.

The TCP/IP suite is used on the Internet instead of OSI protocols

On the Internet, as is well known, instead of the OSI protocols, the less complicated (and less powerful) protocols of the TCP/IP family are used. This family now embraces several dozen different protocols, described in hundreds of RFCs. For an outline of these, I recommend [Lien00] and [Lien01], as I can only offer a short introduction to them here. In so doing, I shall try to fit the most important TCP/IP protocols into the OSI model.

- There are no Internet-specific protocols for Layer 1. Instead, any Layer 1 protocol can be used, such as ISDN, for example.

- There is a similar situation in Layer 2, which depends strongly on the hardware. There are, however, two TCP/IP protocols in this layer: the Serial Line Internet Protocol (SLIP) and the Point to Point Protocol (PPP). Both protocols are used for a stable connection between two points.

IP belongs in Layer 3
- IP belongs to Layer 3 of the OSI model. Also located here are protocols such as ARP, RARP, IMGP and IMCP, which do not play an important part in this book.

- In Layer 4, along with TCP and UDP, there are two protocols that use IP, and thereby create an end-to-end connection.

- Above Layer 4 there is a gaping hole on the Internet, as Layers 5 and 6 are empty.

- The gap is closed in Layer 7, where the widely known protocols HTTP, FTP, Telnet, DNS, NTP and others are to be found.

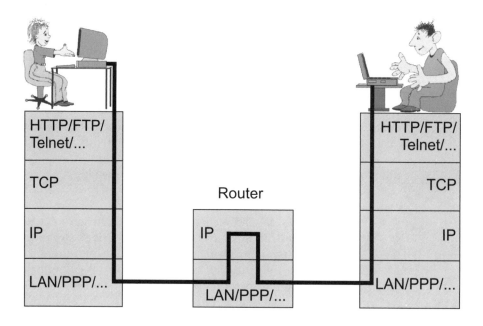

Figure 21.2 Internet communications travel over one or more routers. IP is the highest-level protocol in a router.

If Alice and Bob are communicating via the Internet, the simplest scenario is as follows: Alice and Bob each work at a computer on which an application protocol (HTTP, for example), TCP, IP and subordinate protocols are implemented. Among these there are several routers whose protocol stack only reaches to IP. On the IP layer, as we know, all transported data is packed in handy-sized packets. Routers have the task of forwarding these packets. Because a router is not concerned with the contents of a packet, routers do not need TCP or application protocols. Of course, communication between Alice and Bob is rather more complicated in practice than is represented here, if a firewall is inserted, for instance. However, for the time being Figure 21.2 is adequate for illustrating this idea.

Incidentally, the TCP/IP family of protocols did not just fall from heaven one night. For years they had to contend with protocols from the OSI and other families, which were still favoured by the experts at the start of the 1990s. Only since the World Wide Web caused the unforeseen Internet boom has TCP/IP come to the fore. A decisive factor in this victory was the simplicity of TCP/IP: the early protocols were very simple and sometimes not even particularly well thought through. However, on the plus side, they are easy to implement and cause comparatively few problems when products from different manufacturers are required to work together. The victory of TCP/IP over the OSI protocols is, without doubt, a victory of American pragmatism over European perfectionism.

21.2 In which layer can encryption be undertaken?

Cryptography can be implemented in any OSI layer

The older TCP/IP protocols are all quite simple, and many are now annoying anachronisms, as the quotation at the start of this chapter confirms. They lack the ability to handle real-time transmissions, as well as multicasting (transmission to more than one receiver), or a way of reserving transmission capacity. For us, the most important deficiency of the older TCP/IP protocols is that they provide no encryption or cryptography in any form. In view of the tremendous danger of eavesdropping and other security failings on the Internet, this is a great cause for concern. However, the IETF and several companies were, fortunately, not inactive. There are now dozens of standards for adding encryption to TCP/IP protocols retrospectively, and they continue to grow in number. You have already become acquainted with the cryptographic procedures used for this. In the following chapters you will discover how these procedures can work with TCP/IP.

There are different ways to marry cryptography and TCP/IP OSI layer

Perhaps you are now asking yourself why several dozen standards are needed just to operate a few encryption, signature and hash algorithms on the Internet. The answer is simple: there are different ways to connect cryptography and TCP/IP, and none of them is comprehensive enough to replace all the others. So there is nothing else for it but to try different approaches. The crucial question is: in which OSI layer should we apply the crypto procedures described in this book? There are several possibilities. However, in each case it is appropriate to keep to the OSI dogma: that the interfaces between the layers must not be touched, and that within a given layer only alterations which do not affect superordinate and subordinate layers (layer interface paradigm) are undertaken. Let us take a look at the pros and cons of introducing cryptology into the various layers of the OSI model. In this overview I will leave out Layers 5 and 6, which are not required in practice.

21.2.1 Layer 7 (Application Layer)

Applications operate in Layer 7

Integrating cryptographic procedures into Layer 7 means that an application program – a Web browser or an e-mail program, for example – takes on encryption, signing and authentication. Such programs must either take control of these procedures themselves, or achieve them by means of plug-ins, Java-Applets, CGI Scripts or via an interface. To apply all crypto procedures in Layer 7 is the best solution in many respects. If Alice is communicating with Bob, by using the appropriate features of their application software they can both apply cryptography to their hearts' content: for each message, Alice can decide how and whether it will be encrypted, and she can apply digital signatures and key-dependent hash functions. Bob can decrypt incoming data either straight away or later on. He can forward it while it is still encrypted, or he can save a digital document complete with signature. If Alice ever disputes having sent a message, Bob can use the signature to prove that this is not so (sometimes you can't even trust your best friend). Authentication measures are also most suitable in Level 7: layers lower than this cannot request a password from the user or ask for a smart card without calling on Level 7 for assistance, thereby contravening the layer interface paradigm. Looking at things like this, below Level 7 it is the computers that are authenticated rather than the users.

Cryptography in Level 7 requires application programs to be adapted

The substantial drawback to applying cryptography in Layer 7 is that Alice and Bob's application programs must support the procedures that are used. This means that the Web browser, e-mail program, Telnet clients and numerous other applications must be adapted. And this can be really expensive. Another drawback is that data that is relevant in the lower layers (e.g. the addresses of the sender and receiver) cannot be encrypted. This makes traffic analysis possible: by looking at the unencrypted addresses, Mallory can see where a message comes from and where it is going, even if he can't read the contents.

21.2.2 Layer 4 (Transport Layer)

Layer 4 is the Transport Layer

On the Internet, Layer 4 includes both the TCP (Transmission Control Protocol) and UDP (User Datagram Protocol) protocols. Some application layer protocols work via TCP, others via UDP, a few via both – but never both at the same time.

UDP is a connection-free protocol. It is less complex than TCP, but also less reliable because of it. Its job is basically to forward data from Layer 3 to the Application Layer without altering it, and vice versa. UDP comes into use when the higher-layer application protocol can administer the loss of a single packet. RADIUS and SNMP are examples of application layer protocols that use UDP.

Most Layer 7 protocols work via TCP

Most Layer 7 protocols work via TCP. TCP receives a so-called port number from Layer 7, using which it can be established to which application the data to be forwarded belongs. This also takes place in this layer.

Installing cryptographic procedures in Layer 4 means the creation of a secure tunnel between two application programs (e.g. Web server and Web browser). The application programs receive nothing from this tunnel, which is in practice the most important advantage of installing cryptography below the Application Layer:

instead of numerous application programs, only the program that implements the corresponding protocol needs to be altered. And from the port number in Layer 4 it is also known which application it is. Thus the application of cryptography can still be made independent from this. Because the port number can itself be encrypted with the data, it becomes impossible for Mallory to gain information about the type of the encrypted data, which in turn makes traffic analysis difficult.

Encryption in Layer 4 also has drawbacks

Using this layer for encryption also has its drawbacks, of course. It makes it more difficult for Alice to have any influence on the encryption: if the layer interface paradigm is not to be disregarded, then she can only switch the encryption of a given port number on or off using special software. She cannot use her application program to encrypt a given message. For the same reason, digital signatures cannot be used appropriately. With his application program, Bob would receive data that had not been signed anyway. The same goes for encryption: Bob's application receives unencrypted data, because it has already been decrypted in Level 4. Thus he can forward or store the unencrypted data, although it may not have been intended for his eyes at all. In short: cryptography below the application level creates a secure tunnel. However, once a message has left the tunnel, security disappears. This is most critical for e-mails, because e-mail gateways must always be implemented as application programs. Because of this, e-mails should be encrypted in the application layer if they are intended for the eyes of the addressee only. There are even more drawbacks: with TCP and UDP two protocols must be adapted if cryptography is used anyway. Of course, IP addresses cannot be encrypted in Layer 4 either, as these are needed for routing in Layer 3. The most important information for traffic analysis is thus also available to Mallory here.

21.2.3 Layer 3 (Network)

IP belongs to Layer 3

A secure tunnel between two users can also be created in Layer 3. The advantages and drawbacks to this are largely the same as for Layer 4. However, only the IP protocol needs to be adapted here if cryptographic procedures are used on the Internet. Port numbers are no longer known in Layer 3, however, which means that encryption can no longer reference the application without violating the layer interface paradigm. On the plus side, the port numbers are no longer available to Mallory either, which does not allow him to draw any conclusions about the type of data being transferred. Here again, however, IP addresses cannot be encrypted in Layer 3, because they are needed for routing.

IP spoofing is an attack at Layer 3

IP spoofing is a dangerous Layer 3 attack (see Section 3.2). In this attack, Mallory forges the sender address of IP packets and thus leads the receiver to believe the packets come from a trustworthy computer (e.g. a computer on the same company network). It is possible for Mallory to put the receiver out of action with a torrent of garbled data packets, without the attacked computer noticing anything untoward. Mallory can also falsify other data in the IP header and thus, for example, cause a router to send all packets via a given router which Mallory controls. Mallory can also cause mischief if he falsifies messages of the Internet Control Message Protocol (ICMP). This is also located in Layer 3 and uses IP packets to send control messages between routers. Thus, with spurious messages, Mallory can pretend to one router that the other is overloaded, or that a large number of packets have not arrived. Many kinds of denial-of-service attacks are conceivable here, of course. The above-named problems show that authentication and integrity checks are highly appropriate for IP packets. Of course, this cannot be carried out in higher layers.

A partial encryption can be carried out in Layer 3

Because an IP layer is available not only in applications, but also in routers, a partial encryption can be performed in Layer 3. Thus, if two routers are linked by a transmission medium that is very liable to eavesdropping, encryption at IP level is appropriate.

21.2.4 Layer 2 (Data-link interface)

Encryption can also be applied in Layer 2

Encryption can even be applied in Layer 2, but only from Layer 2 nodes to Layer 2 nodes (which includes practically all network nodes). This does not provide a secure tunnel between users, but only a secure stretch. This has mainly practical advantages: the Internet data transmission media (telephone network, long-distance networks, local networks) all have different owners. In Layer 2, any of these can take their own encryption measures, without the user being aware of this. The methods used can depend on the transmission medium: for a radio transmission stretch that can be easily eavesdropped on, it might be appropriate to encrypt all transmitted data, without informing the user. In Layer 2, IP addresses are not recognised and are included in the encryption.

The drawback of Layer 2 as compared to Layer 3 is that a secure tunnel from user to user is not created. Therefore, if Mallory attacks a Layer 3 node (i.e. a router), he will obtain the message unencrypted.

21.2.5 Layer 1 (Physical Layer)

Cryptography is rarely applied in Layer 1

For a start, encrypting data in Layer 1, rather than Layer 2, has no advantages. In Layer 2, checksums are normally used to detect errors, and it makes little sense to dispense with this error correction prior to encryption. A sole exception to this is when an important interface lies between Layers 1 and 2. This is the case for ISDN, for example, which counts as Layer 1: it makes a lot of sense to encrypt at ISDN level in order to leave the devices that are connected to this untouched. Otherwise, if needs be, in Layer 1 mechanical measures are used, which should prevent eavesdropping on the line. It is known, for example, that the military introduced transmission lines encased in pressurised, gas-filled cabling. If someone tries to tap the wire, the gas escapes and the falling pressure sets off an alarm.

21.2.6 Summary

The variants described have the aforementioned drawbacks and advantages. To summarise, there are three things that are worth remarking on:

The deeper the layer in which encryption is performed, the greater the encryption

• The deeper the layer in which encryption is performed, the better minimum disclosure can be implemented. Addresses, routing information and suchlike from a higher layer are always included in the encryption.

- The higher the layer in which encryption is performed, the more the user can influence what is encrypted, and how. Encrypting data in different ways cannot be controlled in lower layers.

- The higher the layer in which encryption is performed, the better intermediate stations can be bridged. In many cases it is not desirable, for example, that data being transmitted is decrypted by a router and then encrypted again.

After this analysis it may also be clear that there is no good or bad layer for cryptography. The layer in which encryption or similar mechanisms are applied depends on the individual case. Usually it is appropriate to combine different methods.

Crypto standards for OSI Layers 1 and 2

What's most interesting about these algorithms is how robustly lousy they are.
BRUCE SCHNEIER (on the GSM crypto algorithms)

Key experience no. 22
Phil Zimmermann was quoted by a British magazine as saying: 'I should be able to whisper something in your car, even if your ear is 1000 miles away, and government disagrees with that.' The reason for this quizzical non sequitur: due to a printing error, 'ear' became 'car'.

Now that you have learnt the advantages and drawbacks of the use of cryptography in certain OSI layers in the last chapter, we become more specific. We begin at the bottom of the OSI model (Layers 1 and 2) and consider the exertions necessary to equip the protocols in these layers with cryptographic mechanisms.

22.1 Crypto extensions for ISDN (Layer 1)

Encrypting ISDN communication is common sense

The versatile, multi-use data network, ISDN, was introduced in Section 3.2.4. You may recall the gaps in security which point to the need for important information to be encrypted when transmitted via ISDN.

22.1.1 Data encryption with ISDN

ISDN uses protocols, of course, which are located in different OSI layers. However, if ISDN is used as a means of transmission on the Internet, it is usually allotted to Layer 1. This is due to the fact that ISDN can be used as the bit-transport medium for protocols in the upper layers, which are only assigned a structure in the upper layers.

A Layer 2 protocol such as PPP, which can be missing, however, is sometimes used above ISDN on the Internet. Above this then comes, as usual, IP protocols in Layer 3, TCP or UDP protocols in Layer 4 and an application protocol in Layer 7 (see Figure 22.1).

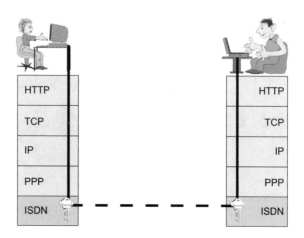

Figure 22.1   For the Internet, ISDN is a Layer 1 protocol. Cryptography can be used even at this low level.

Cryptography can be used at ISDN level

If ISDN is used as the transmission medium for the Internet, cryptography can even be used at the ISDN level. However, this is unusual, as cryptographic mechanisms are normally used in higher layers. On the one hand, this is due to the fact that the use of cryptology at ISDN level only ever secures one part of the connection. On the other hand, the fact that ISDN is hardly used in the USA and many other countries may also play a part. Crypto products for higher layers are therefore often available for use more cheaply, and in larger numbers, on the international market.

22.1.2 Speech encryption with ISDN

Of course, Alice and Bob can use ISDN not only for transmitting data, but also for telephoning. If they do not wish to be overheard by Mallory, they should encrypt the communication. However, they cannot look to a higher OSI layer for this, because in this case there isn't one. The ISDN telephone communication must be encrypted directly.

There are many ISDN encryption solutions

There are now many ISDN encryption solutions on the market. However, there is no standard for them as yet. So if Alice and Bob want to use ISDN encryption, they must buy two devices from the same manufacturer. Most ISDN encryption solutions are implemented as hardware, or more precisely, as crypto-boxes (see Section 15.3.3). Among the numerous manufacturers are German companies such as Siemens and Biodata. Most products use symmetric cryptography and therefore presuppose a manual key exchange. On the other hand, Deutsche Telekom offers an ISDN encryption solution with public key cryptography and PKI linkage at their Telesec product centre under the name Linecrypt. This uses digital certificates from the Trust Centre of Deutsche Telekom, whereby the private keys are stored on smart cards. RSA key exchange and IDEA encryption are used.

22.2 Cryptography in the GSM standard (Layer 1)

In this connection, GSM is a Layer 1 protocol
The GSM mobile phone standard behaves similarly to ISDN: if GSM is used as the transmission medium for the Internet, it must be considered as a Layer 1 protocol. It is certainly worthwhile encrypting the data transmitted with GSM. As a rule, however, this is left to the higher layers of the OSI model. A similar case is if GSM is used as the basis for WAP (see Section 24.5). On the other hand, if Alice and Bob use GSM for telephoning, there are no higher layers, which is why Alice and Bob should certainly give a thought to encrypting at GSM level.

22.2.1 GSM encryption

GSM provides cryptography
At first glance, thoughts about GSM encryption are completely unnecessary. GSM is actually one of the few telecommunication systems in which cryptography is a standard component. Each GSM mobile phone therefore encrypts automatically, and also performs authentication using a challenge–response procedure. Authentication is necessary so that Mallory cannot use his mobile phone to make calls at Alice's expense.

Unfortunately, GSM encryption does not apply over the whole connection between Alice and Bob, but only over the stretch from their phones to the respective nearest ground stations. This still has the advantage, at least, that Mallory cannot simply overhear their conversation using an antenna – eavesdropping is still possible over the remainder of the connection, however.

How GSM uses cryptography

GSM does not use public key cryptography
GSM does not use public key cryptography. Instead, GSM user Alice receives a smart card (**SIM card**) from her network operator, which she inserts into her mobile phone. The SIM card is protected by a PIN. A secret 128-bit key is stored on the SIM card, to which the network operator is also not privy. This secret key is used firstly for authentication and then for the generation of a 64-bit session key. This session key is used to encrypt communication between the mobile phone set and the ground station, using the A5 encryption algorithm described in Section 9.4.2.

Let us now examine authentication at the start of a GSM communication. This uses a challenge–response procedure:

A challenge–response procedure is used for authentication
1. The ground station sends a 128-bit value to Alice's mobile phone as the challenge.

2. The mobile phone forwards the challenge to the smart card.

3. From the challenge and the secret key, the smart card calculates a 32-bit response using an algorithm known as A3, and passes it back to the mobile phone.

4. The mobile phone sends the response to the ground station.

5. The ground station checks the correctness of the response using the secret key from Alice's smart card (this is actually known to the network operator).

6. The smart card uses the secret key and the challenge to calculate a session key using an algorithm known as A8. This session key is passed to the mobile phone.

7. The ground station also calculates a session key in the same way.

Encryption uses the
A5 algorithm

8. Alice's mobile phone and the ground station use the A5 encryption algorithm to encrypt their communications with the previously generated session key. For performance reasons, encryption is carried out in the mobile phone itself, rather than on the SIM card.

Only the SIM card and the ground station need to know the A3 and A8 algorithms. Because they are both controlled by the network operator, each network operator can determine the precise way in which both algorithms function. For this reason, only the sizes of the challenge, response, secret key and session key are fixed in the GSM standard. The functioning of A3 and A8 is left open. The most obvious way is to implement both A3 and A8 as key-dependent hash functions. For this, A3 uses the secret key to calculate a hash result from the challenge, which is used as the response. A further hash with the same key then produces the session key.

COMP128 uses A3
and A8

For A3 and A8, most GSM network operators use an implementation called COMP128. This takes a key and a challenge and returns a response and a session key. COMP128 thus implements both A3 and A8 at the same time. The way in which COMP128 functions was unfortunately secret in the beginning (as was the A5 algorithm itself). However, in 1998, a description of the function appeared on the Internet, blowing the secret. It is now known that COMP128 generates both response and session key using a previously unknown algorithm that – like DES – uses substitutions and permutations.

Security of the GSM crypto procedure

GSM is not secure

The security of the procedure used by GSM is unfortunately a tale of woe (see [JanLaa]). In Section 9.4.2 you learnt that the symmetric encryption algorithm A5 can be cracked. COMP128 is also anything but secure. In 1998, Ian Goldberg and David Wagner published an attack with which the secret key can be extracted from a SIM card. To do so, you need about 185,000 challenge values to be fed to the card, and the responses to be noted. The attack takes about 8 hours. If Mallory succeeds in extracting the secret key from Alice's SIM card in this way, he can transfer it onto another smart card (the process is known as **cloning**). The ground station cannot distinguish this card from the original. Mallory can thus make calls using this card at Alice's expense, without being detected. Of course, the secret key extracted from a SIM card is also a considerable aid for eavesdropping.

GSM encryption is
notably weak

Bruce Schneier made the following comments on the security of the A3, A5 and A8 procedures algorithms: 'What's most interesting about these algorithms is how robustly lousy they are.' In fact, it is impossible to prove out of hand that the GSM encryption procedure was intentionally constructed so weakly as to facilitate eavesdropping. Perhaps the secrecy that surrounded the way in which A5 and COMP128 works speaks for itself.

22.2.2 Crypto extensions for GSM

Up to now there are very few GSM extensions The blatant weaknesses of A5 and COMP128, as well as the fact that only the stretch between the mobile phone and the ground station is secured with it, naturally shout out for extra crypto mechanisms. A GSM crypto solution that enabled encryption from mobile to mobile using secure procedures would be very desirable. Unfortunately, scarcely any such solutions have been offered as yet. This is surely mainly due to the fact that GSM is to be replaced at some time by UMTS.

22.2.3 UMTS

Within a few years, the GSM standard should be replaced by the more powerful **UMTS (Universal Mobile Telecommunications System)**. UMTS is the embodiment of third-generation mobile telephones. In the summer of 2000, various companies forked out almost 100 billion DM for German UMTS licences, as was reported in great detail by the media. This almost unbelievable sum is a clear indication of the great expectations that the telecommunications companies have for this standard.

UMTS offers more security As well as a data transfer rate that is several times faster than GSM, UMTS should also offer much more security. In February 1999, a security working group was founded within the UMTS standardisation body 3GPP (third Generation Partnership Project). The aim of the group was to develop a security architecture for UTMS, which would avoid the numerous weaknesses of GSM. SIM cards were to continue in use, but with a greatly improved authentication process. The symmetric encryption is to be performed by a procedure named KASUMI that is based on MISTY (see Section 5.2.4).

22.3 Crypto extensions for PPP (Layer 2)

Most Layer 2 protocols are not from TCP/IP In Layer 2 of the OSI model, as in Layer 1, most of the protocols in use do not belong to the TCP/IP family. The reason is that the Internet is designed as a network that leaves the characteristic quirks of the different transmission media to other protocols that have been specially designed to cope with them.

There are two TCP/IP protocols, however, that are classed as Layer 2 of the OSI model: as well as the older Serial Line Internet Protocol (SLIP), first and foremost there is the **Point to Point Protocol** (PPP). Both are domiciled under IP. Because they operate between two points (routers, for example), they demonstrate the typical properties of a Layer 2 protocol. PPP and SLIP are used mainly in two situations: Bob can connect to the computer of his Internet provider (by modem, for example). The IP packets that Bob sends and receives then travel via this connection. Also, PPP and SLIP can be used to connect two local networks.

PPP is described in [RFC1661] and extended in several other RFCs. It describes a state-regimented protocol with the ability to negotiate (handshaking). The cryptographic extensions designed for PPP are linked into it via the so-called Link Control Protocol (LCP). LCP is the part of PPP that is executed at the start of communication, in order to facilitate the negotiation of protocol parameters between the two communication partners.

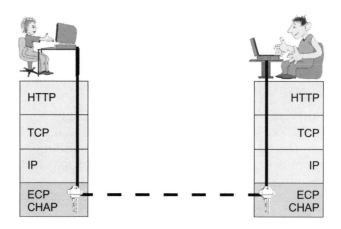

Figure 22.2   ECP (encryption) and CHAP (authentication) provide cryptographic security in Layer 2 of the OSI model.

22.3.1 CHAP

CHAP is an authentication mechanism for PPP

The **Challenge Handshake Protocol (CHAP)** is an authentication mechanism for PPP. CHAP is described in [RFC1994] (extension in [RFC2759]) and implements a simple challenge–response procedure. CHAP is executed during the establishment of a connection and can be repeated later as and when required. If Alice and Bob want to authenticate themselves using CHAP, they must agree on a common key beforehand. During authentication, Alice sends Bob a random value (challenge) that Bob processes with a key-dependent hash function. He sends the result (response) back to Alice, who can check it because she also knows the key.

CHAP is an authentication procedure for PPP

CHAP is a very simple procedure that operates without public key cryptography. It simply provides authentication, not encryption. Because Alice and Bob must use a secure channel to agree on a key, CHAP only works for a small number of potential communication partners. This is also the case with PPP, as it always works between two fixed network nodes.

22.3.2 EAP

EAP is an alternative to CHAP

In 1998, in the IETF, a PPP crypto extension for authentication was standardised, which was more powerful than CHAP. It was called **EAP (Extensible Authentication Protocol)**. EAP enables authentication by means of a challenge–response procedure (like CHAP), one-time passwords or smart tokens, or a combination of them. On top of this, EAP is extensible (as the name indicates). One extension was described in 1999 in [RFC2716]. This was an authentication protocol using key exchange, and was adopted by TLS protocols (see Chapter 24) and hardly changed at all.

22.3.3 ECP

ECP is an encryption add-on for PPP

The **Encryption Control Protocol (ECP)** takes care of the encryption of data being transmitted via PPP. ECP is defined in [RFC1968], and [RFC2419] and [RFC2420] describe extensions of it. Like CHAP, ECP assumes that when Alice and Bob use it, they have a common secret key – this key can be exchanged beforehand with EAP, for example. ECP gives Alice and Bob the opportunity to agree on an encryption procedure. [RFC2419] contains more information about the use of DES in connection with ECP.

22.4 Virtual private networks

VPNs are an important theme in IT security

So-called **virtual private networks (VPNs)** play an important role in connection with the use of cryptography in the lower layers of the OSI model. In the past few years, VPNs have become one of the most important topics of IT security, and market researchers and analysts prophesy continuing interest for years to come. This development is no accident, because VPN techniques permit a large measure of security to be achieved in a relatively simple manner. In many cases, they even save the operator of a network money.

As is so often the case with fashionable ideas, there is some confusion on the subject of VPN, in this case arising from the name itself. There is no agreement about just what a VPN actually is, so that not everything offered by the manufacturers as such is deserving of the name. The explanations given in this chapter can therefore contradict other sources of literature on the subject.

22.4.1 What is a VPN?

In order to understand what a VPN is, a little transformation is necessary. We therefore start with two problems that crop up in practice.

LAN-to-LAN VPN

VPNs can be used to connect two networks

Crypt & Co. operates a local TCP/IP network at two different locations (this can also be called an intranet). The company would like to connect these two networks together. Of course, Crypt & Co. could achieve this by simply connecting both networks to the Internet. There are, however, various reasons why this would be problematic:

• Without encryption, Mallory can snoop on company-internal data transmissions. To do this, Mallory only needs to eavesdrop on the Internet, and not on the Crypt & Co. intranet.

• Even if the transmitted data is encrypted, the IP addresses for sender and receiver are still readable on the Internet. From these, Mallory can infer how the Crypt & Co. intranet is structured. In addition to this, Mallory can forge messages and send them to a specific computer on the intranet (for this reason, internal IP addresses always represent interesting information to hackers).

- It is possible that the IP addresses used on the Crypt & Co. intranets might not be valid on the Internet.

LAN-to-LAN VPN
can connect two
local networks

For the reasons mentioned above, Crypt & Co will probably opt for another solution. This could run as follows: a router on one intranet is connected to a router on another intranet at Layer 2 via PPP. For example, ISDN, DSL or the analog telephone network can be used for this. A connection of this kind is known as a **LAN-to-LAN VPN**. LAN-to-LAN VPN makes no great demands on the computers in the two coupled networks. It simply adds some new potential communication partners.

The Tunnel Protocol
transports PPP
packets

Unfortunately, a LAN-to-LAN VPN via ISDN, ADSL or analog telephone is usually relatively expensive, especially if longer distances are to be bridged. An Internet connection over the same stretch is usually cheaper. The ideal solution here would be to implement a LAN-to-LAN VPN via the Internet. This means that a Level 7 protocol below PPP must be used between the two routers. Such a process is called a **tunnel** (although 'bridge' would surely be a better choice). The interaction between the different TCP/IP protocols can be seen in Figure 22.3 (the aforementioned Layer 7 protocol is called **Tunnel Protocol** in the diagram). The PPP packets are transported from one router to the other using the Tunnel Protocol. The Tunnel Protocol itself uses TCP or UDP (like other Layer 7 protocols), followed by IP. The special feature of a LAN-to-LAN VPN on the Internet is that some OSI layers come into play twice.

Connecting individual computers

Individual
computers can be
connected over a
VPN

Another practical example will now be looked at: Crypt & Co. wants to connect several home-workers to the company intranet. To open up the whole intranet and the home-workers' computers to the Internet makes just as little sense here as in the case of a LAN-to-LAN VPN. In this case also it is better to establish a PPP connection between each single computer and router pair on the intranet. For connecting individual computers at Layer 1, ISDN, DSL, analog telephone, or even the Internet could again be used (see Figure 22.3). Seen in this light, the connection of individual computers is similar to a LAN coupling.

What is a VPN?

Part connection
stretches are
connected with
tunnels in a VPN

With the transformation work out of the way, we can now finally define the term VPN: a VPN (virtual private network) is a computer network of manageable size (normally a company-internal network), in which connection stretches are bridged by tunnels on the Internet. These tunnels can be in the form of LAN-to-LAN VPNs, or the connection of individual computers. In the former case, we talk about an intranet VPN, and in the latter of a remote access VPN (a VPN can also be both simultaneously).

The bottom line of a VPN is that while the internet is used by the intranet, the Internet and intranet protocols are kept strictly isolated from each other. If the tunnel protocol also supports authentication and encryption, the danger of eavesdropping on the bridged stretches is thereby averted.

There are two methods for building a VPN
There are currently two different methods in use for constructing VPNs. One method provides a PPP tunnel (or another Layer 2 protocol) with a tunnel protocol in Layer 7, and thereby corresponds exactly to the implementations to date. This method is discussed in the following. There is another variation, which involves tunnelling IP via IP. This method uses IPSec and is described in Section 23.6.

22.4.2 Tunnel protocols for Layer 2

Let us now take a look at the protocols available for tunnelling PPP messages across the Internet (see also [Stende]). Three of these play a practical role. All three are protocols that could be used as tunnel protocols in the scenario described in Figure 22.3.

L2F

L2F is a protocol from Cisco
The **Layer 2 Forwarding Protocol (L2F)** was developed in the mid-1990s by Cisco. It is a quite simple protocol for tunnelling Layer 2 messages, which uses UDP as a protocol of the transport layer. L2F has since grown into L2TP and therefore is only important on grounds of compatibility.

L2F itself provides neither encryption nor authentication. Other protocols can be used to provide security, however. At first glance, SSL would be very suitable, because it could be inserted directly under L2F. However, SSL requires TCP in Layer 4, while L2F uses UDP. SSL is therefore out of the question. There are still two other crypto protocols, however:

- The crypto extensions of PPP can be inserted above L2F.

- IPSec an be inserted below L2F.

Both variants work in practice, where the lack of crypto functions in L2F does not matter too much.

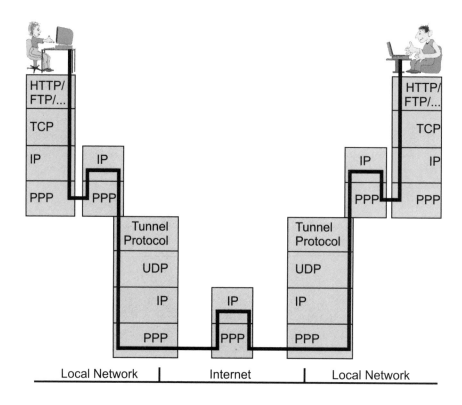

Figure 22.3 Example of a VPN: PPP packets are transported by a tunnel protocol across the Internet. The tunnel protocol belongs in Layer 7 of the OSI model.

PPTP

PPTP as a further tunnel protocol

Point-to-Point-Tunnelling Protocol (PPTP) is a Microsoft development. It fulfils the same purpose as L2F, but offers rather more functionality. PPTP provides two different sub-protocols: the tunnel protocol for the actual PPTP objective, and a control protocol for building and controlling the tunnel. The control protocol uses TCP in Layer 4, while the tunnel protocol is based on a protocol called GRE (Generic Routing Encapsulation). At this point, we can think of the latter as being a UDP-type protocol.

PPTP also leaves cryptographic measures to other protocol layers, which means that the same considerations as for L2F also apply here. The variant favoured by Microsoft itself allows the use of PPTP extensions. For this purpose, Microsoft has developed its own versions of CHAP and ECP. These are known as MS-CHAP and MPPE (Microsoft Point-to-Point Encryption).

L2TP

L2TP is the tunnel protocol of the IETF

L2TP (Layer 2 Tunnelling Protocol) is the youngest of the three tunnel protocols introduced here. It was developed in the IETF with the aim of replacing L2F and

PPTP by a protocol that would combine the advantages of both. L2TP, like PPTP, provides two sub-protocols for tunnel building and control. The control takes place via TCP, and for the tunnel, the usual UDP is used instead of the more exotic GRE. A feature of L2TP, however, is that it itself enables authentication: it supports a CHAP-type password request.

22.4.3 The VPN market

There are numerous VPN products

As is appropriate for such a booming topic, there have long been innumerable products and services in the VPN field (see [SchUng]). Some undertakings offer advice on constructing a VPN, which can become a steady business. Other firms limit themselves to the sale of VPN products.

For the LAN-to-LAN VPN, many manufacturers offer gateway products, with which both end points of a tunnel can be implemented. Such Gateway functions are also often integrated into routers, firewalls or operating systems. If large amounts of data are to be sent through a tunnel, it pays to use Gateway as a crypto-box (these types of solutions are offered on the market).

A VPN client is normally implemented in software

For connecting single computers there are equally many products on the market. Normally these consist of a client and a Gateway component. The client component is usually a piece of software, which is installed on the computer that is being connected. The Gateway component can here again be implemented as a crypto-box or as software. Some solutions now also support PKI functions, which means that each user of a connected computer receives his or her own digital certificate.

The administration of the client component is important in a VPN solution for the connection of single computers. Especially in the case of VPNs with many client components, a VPN solution should therefore include a powerful administration component.

IPSec (Layer 3)

IPSec was a great disappointment to us. Given the quality of the people that worked on it and the time that was spent on it, we expected a much better result.
BRUCE SCHNEIER, NIELS FERGUSON [FERSCH]

Key experience no. 23
Among the first people ever to think about the secure transportation of messages was the Persian Histiaios in the 6th century BC. He had a message tattooed on the shaven head of a slave. After the hair had grown back, the slave could travel to the intended receiver without being molested, and the latter could read the message after the hair was shaved off again.

In our stroll through the OSI layers and their crypto extensions, we now come to Layer 3 (Routing). Here we shall meet the protocol which gave the network of networks its name: IP (Internet Protocol).

An IP packet contains a payload and header

IP protocol messages are called packets. Each packet, which contains a header as well as a payload, is sent separately over the network. At the receiver end, IP protocols reassemble the packets into the original message. The header is divided into several fields, which contain details about the sender, the receiver, length of the payload, and many other matters.

23.1 IPSec and IKE

There are also extensions for IP, which are intended to guarantee confidentiality, authenticity and integrity. After several proprietary implementations of these appeared in the mid-1990s, in the past few years the **IPSec** standard, developed in the IETF, has come to the fore. IPSec is also a fixed component of the new IP generation, IP Version 6 (IPv6), which should replace the current IP within a few years. IPSec enables the encryption of IP packets, and guarantees their integrity by means of key-dependent hash functions. For communication, security associations (see Section 12.4.1) are used, and require Alice and Bob to have a common secret key.

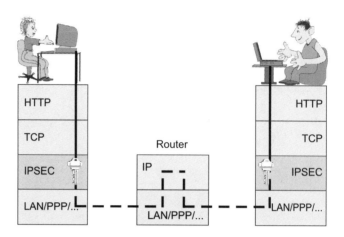

Figure 23.1   IPSec facilitates the application of cryptography in Layer 3 of the OSI model. With IPSec also, part of the connection stretch of the Internet can be secured cryptographically.

The construction and management of security associations, as well as key exchange, are not components of IPSec. These additional tasks are usually taken care of by a protocol called **IKE (Internet Key Exchange)**. Although IKE is not a component of IPSec, it is so closely linked with IPSec that it can be regarded as part of it. More detailed information on IPSec and IKE can be found in [KauNew] and [DorHar].

23.2 IPSec

IPSec has two component parts   Let us first consider IPSec without IKE. IPSec provides two components that are useful by themselves. One component takes care of the encryption of payloads, the other looks after the provision of integrity and authenticity using a key-dependent hash function. Logically, IPSec is a finely detailed protocol. It supports contexts and associations, whose administration is left to a protocol that is independent of IPSec, which also negotiates the procedure to be used and other parameters. In itself, IPSec is thus a stateless protocol that is not capable of negotiating.

23.2.1 ESP

ESP enables the encryption of payloads   The first component of IPSec is called **ESP (Encapsulated Security Payload)**, and is described in [RFC2406]. ESP enables the encryption of the payload of an IP packet, and in the newer version also provides the possibility of using a key-dependent hash function. Most of the fields in the header are not encrypted, so that they remain readable for the router. ESP adds additional header fields which, among other things, allow the communication partners to allocate a packet to a given context. If IPv6 is not used, the additional header fields are the last fields before the start of the payload, and are themselves partly encrypted.

ESP does not specify the procedures used

Which encryption procedure and key-dependent hash function are used in ESP is not specified in the ESP description. [RFC2405] describes the use of DES in CBC mode as a possible encryption procedure. In [RFC2451] Triple-DES, RC5, CAST, IDEA and Blowfish are given as alternatives. According to [RFC2403], [RFC2404] and [RFC2857], either MD5, SHA-1 or RIPEMD-160 respectively can be used as the cryptographic hash function. If Alice is not happy with these procedures, she can use others – provided communication partner Bob supports them.

Transport mode

ESP has two modes. The first is **transport mode**. In this method, the payload of an IP packet is encrypted and is left unchanged. This means that it is encrypted just as it is, after it has been handed down by TCP or UDP and split into smaller parts.

Tunnel mode

In tunnel mode, a whole packet is encrypted

In **tunnel mode**, on the other hand, the whole IP packet is encrypted and then packed into the payload section of a further IP packet. Because of this, the header of the first IP packet is no longer readable, which facilitates minimum disclosure (see Section 12.4.2). Tunnel mode can be used if information such as sender or receiver addresses should be unreadable over part of an Internet stretch. Tunnel mode is mainly of interest in connection with virtual private networks (see Section 23.6).

23.2.2 AH

AH is the second component part of IPSec

Authentication Header (AH) is the second component of IPSec. AH is described in [RFC2402]. AH provides an extra header field for the assignment to a context, and also adds another header field in which the result of a key-dependent hash function is transferred. This key-dependent hash function is used on the payload and on the header fields of the IP packet. This explains the purpose of AH: if Alice communicates with Bob via IP, then without being detected, Mallory can alter the IP packets. Because AH does not provide encryption of any kind, it does not prevent Mallory from reading an IP packet.

The header fields in an IP packet that can alter during transmission (for example, the counter for the stations covered) are not included in the hash function. The unalterable fields are covered by the key-dependent hash function, however. This includes the sender and receiver addresses, of course.

AH provides for the application of a key-dependent hash function

If Bob sends an IP packet to Alice, he calculates the result of the key-dependent hash function and writes it in the AH header. Alice also calculates the key-dependent hash function and compares it with the result received from Bob. Provided that only Alice and Bob know the key they are using, Mallory has no chance of changing the packet without being detected.

The AH specification does not specify which cryptographic hash function is used. The RFCs that deal with the use of cryptographic hash functions in ESP stipulate the same procedures for AH as for ESP. Of course, Alice and Bob can use other functions, if they can both support them. In principle, instead of a key-dependent hash function, a digital signature procedure can be used. Because digital signatures are relatively very slow, however, and are scarcely appropriate for use below the application layer, this is not usual.

AH also can be used in two modes

Just like ESP, AH can be used in transport or in tunnel mode. The method of working corresponds to that of ESP: in transport mode an existing IP packet is expanded, in tunnel mode a whole IP packet is packed into the payload section of a new IP packet.

23.3 IKE

IPSec supports contexts and associations, of course, but cannot administer these and is in itself unable to negotiate, nor does it have states. Added to which, IPSec presupposes that Alice and Bob own a common secret key – key exchanges are ruled out in IPSec. A powerful protocol using IPSec can therefore only result from cooperation with another protocol that can supply the missing factors. The protocol provided for this by IETF is called **IKE (Internet Key Exchange)**.

23.3.1 The emergence of IKE

While harmony was largely the order of the day during the development of IPSec, IKE was the cause of weighty discussions within the IETF. Basically there were two camps. One wanted to make IKE the most flexible and function-rich protocol operating in Layer 7. They produced an outline for this that was based on three existing protocols (ISAKMP, Oakley and SKEME). For the other camp, this proposal was too complicated. They preferred the markedly less complicated **Simple Key Management Protocol (SKIP)**, which is used in Layer 3 of the OSI model and offers less functionality. After lengthy discussions, the ISAKMP–Oakley–SKEME faction won the argument. And that is why IKE is a very complex protocol, but offers a multitude of possibilities.

23.3.2 ISAKMP

ISAKMP is the basis for IKE

In order to understand IKE, one must first be conversant with **ISAKMP**. ISAKMP stands for **Internet Security Association and Key Management Protocol**. It was – wait for it – developed by the NSA and is now standardised in [RFC2408].

ISAKMP protocol messages

ISAKMP is not a protocol, strictly speaking, but a meccano set with which a crypto protocol can be compiled. For this purpose, ISAKMP defines a format for protocol messages that can be used to specify a protocol. ISAKMP protocol messages are always transported in Layer 7 (Application) of the OSI model, while UDP comes into use in the Transport Layer beneath it. The use of ISAKMP in conjunction with IPSec (Layer 3) is thus a clear infringement of the layer interface paradigm, which is nevertheless accepted. While ISAKMP utilises UDP as its transport mechanism, it doesn't rely on any UDP information (e.g. checksum, length) for its processing.

ISAKMP protocol messages consist – as is common – of a header and a payload. For the payload the ISAKMP specification defines a total of 13 different types. Any type of cryptographic data can be transported from a hash value via a signature to a digital certificate in an ISAKMP protocol message in place of another payload type.

ISAKMP uses cookies

There are no addresses in the header of an ISAKMP protocol message – senders and receivers are handled by the underlying UDP. For this, each ISAKMP header has two fields for a sender cookie and one receiver cookie. A **cookie** in this case is a 32-bit value. To communicate by means of ISAKMP protocol messages, Alice selects an arbitrary value as a cookie for Bob, while conversely Bob chooses a random cookie for Alice. If Alice sends a protocol message to Bob, she inserts the cookie intended for Bob as the receiver cookie. If she has herself already received an ISAKMP message from Bob, then she is aware of the cookie that Bob selected for her. She inserts this in the message as the sender cookie. A cookie permits Alice and Bob to allocate a message to a specific security association. In addition, brute denial-of-service attacks can be prevented by cookies: if Mallory tries to flood Alice with false ISAKMP messages, Alice can immediately filter out all messages with a false cookie before she starts any kind of time-consuming public key operations. Of course, this cookie trick only works if Mallory does not intercept communications between Alice and Bob (in which case he could capture the cookies being used), but simply sends false ISAMKP messages to Alice out of the blue.

The two phases of ISAKMP

ISAKMP has two phases

ISAKMP has two phases. In the first, a security association is established, which means that normally asymmetric algorithms come into play. This security association is called **ISAKMP-SA**. In the second phase, the ISAKMP-SA is used to establish any number of further security associations (for IPSec, for example). In the second step, asymmetric algorithms can normally be dispensed with (asymmetric algorithms are very heavy on overhead, of course).

This two-phase operation sounds rather elaborate, but it has some advantages. The first phase can be taken care of by the operating systems of Alice's and Bob's computers, for instance. In the second phase, Alice and Bob can then quickly, and without the use of costly asymmetrical algorithms, establish communication connections or close them down.

23.3.3 How IKE uses ISAKMP

IKE is assembled from ISAKMP messages

The coherence between IKE and ISAKMP is easy to explain: IKE is a protocol assembled completely from ISAKMP protocol messages. Even the two-phase approach of ISAKMP is taken care of by IKE: in the first phase, an ISAKMP-SA is established (in this connection this is called **IKE-SA**), and in the second phase, on the basis of these, one or more security associations for IPSec (**IPSecSAs**) are established. The exact operation of IKE is supervised by the two above-mentioned protocols, Oakley and SKEME, which I do not propose to go into. An important component of IKE is the Diffie–Hellman key exchange – this is used to generate a common secret key for Alice and Bob (from which further secret keys are derived). IKE uses a total of five Diffie–Hellman variants: Alice and Bob can either use the classic procedure (Section 6.4) with a 768-, 1,024- or 1,680-bit key length, or alternatively it is possible to use two ECDH variants with 155- or 185-bit keys.

IKE Phase 1

IKE has two modes

In phase 1 of the IKE protocol, Alice and Bob exchange cookies, negotiate procedures and parameters, mutually authenticate themselves, perform a Diffie–Hellman key exchange, and on this basis establish an IKE-SA. IKE offers two ways of achieving this. The first is known as **main mode**.

In main mode, Alice and Bob take turns in sending each other a total of six protocol messages each:

Main mode uses six protocol messages

- In the first two messages, cookies and the parameters are transferred and there are negotiations about the procedure to be used.

- Messages three and four are used to carry out a Diffie–Hellman key exchange.

- With the fifth and sixth messages, the authenticity and integrity of the Diffie–Hellman public key that has been forwarded previously is ensured. If Alice and Bob already have a common secret key, then the authentication is achieved using a key-dependent hash function, which is used on the Diffie–Hellman key. If they do not have a common secret key, then instead of a hash value they can also send each other a digital signature, which is linked to their own Diffie–Hellman public keys. A digital certificate can also be sent with each signature, which allows the signature to be checked. Another method that can be used for authentication might be a special challenge–response procedure. If Alice and Bob use this, then in messages three and four they send each other a random value (**nonce**), which they then encrypt with each other's public key. This public key is usually an RSA key and can be a component of a digital certificate that can be obtained from a certificate server. In the fifth and sixth messages they send each other the hash value of the nonce they received.

Of course, it would also be possible to send the Diffie–Hellman key immediately in the form of a certificate – this is not done, however, so as to achieve Perfect Forward Secrecy (see Section 12.4.2).

The second mode is aggressive mode

For IKE Phase 1, as well as main mode, there is also **aggressive mode**, which is somewhat simpler but less efficient. In aggressive mode, in the first message Alice sends Bob a cookie, her suggested procedure and parameters, the encrypted nonce where applicable, and her Diffie–Hellman public key. Bob answers her with a message containing the cookie he intends for Alice, the procedure he accepts, and his Diffie–Hellman public key with hash value or signature. Finally Alice sends Bob a third and last Phase 1 message containing her hash value or her signature.

At the end of Phase 1, Alice and Bob have a common, secret key

At the end of Phase 1, Alice and Bob have a security association and a common secret key, which they can use as the basis for IPSec communication. As a result of the authentication, they also know that their partner is genuine.

IKE Phase 2

In Phase 2, using the ISAKMP-SA that was constructed in Phase 1, and their resulting common secret key, Alice and Bob can establish further security associations (IPSecSAs) and use these for IPSec. In addition to the two modes used in Phase 1 (main and aggressive modes), the IKE specification has a further mode called **quick mode**. In quick mode, Alice first sends a protocol message to Bob, receives one back from him and then sends him another – there are therefore three messages in total.

In Phase 2 Alice and Bob can establish further security associations

In quick mode, Alice and Bob do not have to bother with costly authentication and a key exchange using an assymetrical algorithm, because these have already been performed in Phase 1. If perfect forwarding secrecy is desired, however, a further Diffie–Hellman key exchange can be carried out.

Further protocol messages

There are other IKE protocol messages

In addition to the protocol messages of main mode, aggressive mode and quick mode, IKE provides another two types of protocol message. These are not used to establish security associations. One of them enables error and status messages to be sent. Using the other, Alice and Bob can negotiate new parameters for the Diffie–Hellman key exchange.

23.4 SKIP

SKIP is the protocol that lost out to ISAMKP, Oakley and SKEME in the IETF. Because of this, SKIP has become less important in the past few years. But because implementations of this are still around, I will go into it briefly here.

SKIP was developed by Sun

SKIP is a protocol developed by Sun Microsystems. Like IKE, it enables a Diffie–Hellman key exchange, but is based on another approach. SKIP does not provide for the execution of comprehensive protocols. Instead, in accordance with SKIP, each IP packet has special header extensions containing all the information the receiver needs for encryption, or for checking the hash value. Because all relevant information is contained in the data packet, security associations are not needed. SKIP is therefore a stateless protocol, while IKE is an implementation that contains many states. IKE uses Layer 7 of the OSI model, while SKIP works completely within Layer 3.

In comparison to ISAKMP and Oakley, SKIP is clearly a less taxing protocol. At IP level, where packages can go missing, renouncing associations also makes good sense. SKIP also has the advantage that Bob can also forward the packets he receives to Carol, provided Carol has the same Diffie–Hellman key as Bob. This also makes sense at IP level, because overloaded routers, for example, are not unheard of.

SKIP is a simple protocol The very simplicity of SKIP also has its drawbacks. Perfect forward secrecy is not provided, nor is negotiation of encryption procedures. Of course, when sending, Alice can choose which procedure she uses, and convey this information to Bob in the IP header. On the downside, however, she does not know whether Bob also supports this procedure.

23.5 Critical assessment of IPSec

IPSec and the associated IKE have not found universal favour for some time now. An interesting critical examination of IPSec and IKE was published in 1999 by Bruce Schneier and Niels Ferguson [FerSCh]. The document is available on the Internet. Even in the introduction, the two authors leave no doubt that they do not think much of IPSec. Because Schneier and Ferguson go into the diverse component parts in great detail, I will only give a summary of the most important criticisms here:

IPSec and IKE are complex • According to Schneir and Ferguson, IPSec and IKE are much too complex. The many variants, modes and types ensure that hardly anyone can find their way around. This is the main criticism that the two authors express. They even hold the view that it is practically impossible to implement IPSec and IKE without there being too many errors. However, they do not blame the developers of the two standards for this, but their development process. Because IPSec and IKE were developed by a group of people with completely different interests, the final result was a scarcely comprehensible hodgepodge of compromises and variants. Schneier and Ferguson therefore suggest that important standards should no longer be developed by a panel or board, but should be the product of a competition, as in the case of AES.

IPSec and IKE are poorly documented • IPSec and IKE are badly documented. Indeed, the relevant RFCs are not exactly an easy read, containing, as they do, errors, omissions and even contradictions. Schneier and Ferguson complain, with justification, that the design aims of IPSec and IKE are hardly mentioned in these documents. As a reader you therefore have to make your own assessment of the importance of the different functionalities.

• There are several variants of IPSec, all with very similar functionality. IPSec is available in ESP and AH variants, where tunnel mode and transport mode can be used respectively. ESP thereby includes the functionality of AH. To make life easier, the authors suggest that you don't bother with AH and the transport mode. To promote further simplification, encryption should be optional, while a key-dependent hash value is always used.

Much about IPSec and IKE cannot be checked • IPSec and IKE contain many illogical or incomprehensible aspects. For instance, if encryption and key-dependent hash values are used in IPSec, the hash values are applied to the encrypted text – it would make more sense if encryption was applied to the hashed text.

I do not propose to examine the numerous other, sometimes very technical points of criticism at this point. It is clear that Schneier and Ferguson – quite rightly in my opinion – have a low opinion of IPSec and IKE. However, in their document they both stress that there is currently no alternative. We shall have to go on living with IPSec, and admit that it is at least better than no encryption at all.

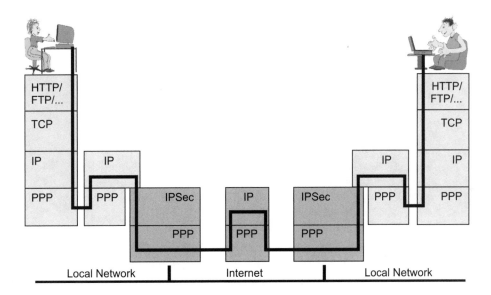

Figure 23.2 IPSec can also be used as a tunnel for a VPN. IP packets would then be transported inside IP packets.

23.6 Virtual private networks with IPSec

In Section 22.4 we were concerned with virtual private networks (VPNs). This involved Layer 2 protocol tunnelling (usually PPP) via an Internet protocol of the Application Layer (L2F, PPTP or L2TP). Using this kind of tunnel, a local network (intranet) can be connected with another network or single computer over the Internet, while still maintaining the strict boundary between intranet and Internet.

VPNs can be set up with IPSec Using IPSec, a similar effect can be achieved as if the methods described in Section 22.4 were used, but this has the effect that other OSI layers are affected by the tunnel. For this reason, VPNs can also be established using IPSec, without using L2F, PPTP or L2TP. How the establishment of a VPN works with IPSec is illustrated in Figure 23.2. IPSec in tunnel mode is used as the tunnel protocol. This operates between the two connected networks (in a LAN coupling) or between an individual computer and a network (for connecting the individual computers). The protocol being tunnelled in this case is not a Layer 2 protocol, but IP (or possibly IPSec, of course). Logically, the intranet and the Internet are – as is usual with a VPN – kept strictly separate here.

IPSec supports cryptography by design   One advantage of using IPSec as the tunnel protocol is that it supports encryption and authentication by design. Last but not least, IPSec has therefore become established as the alternative to the protocols specially designed for tunnelling, PPTP and L2TP. In the field of VPN, we shall therefore have to live with several standards in the future. Further details on building a VPN with IPSec can be found in [TilTil].

SSL, TLS and WTLS
(Layer 4)

With PCs 1,000 times more powerful than they used to be, our encryption keys can and should be 1,000 times bigger too. This means cryptokeys of at least 56,000 bits.
FROM THE DEVELOPER.COM NEWSGROUP

Key experience no. 24
Steffi Graf is one of those people who worry about the security of their e-mails. In an interview for German news magazine Focus, she said of her mail exchange with Andre Agassi: 'A personal security coding program for e-mails would certainly provide impetus to our communication on the Internet.'

After having examined the Layer 3 protocol IPSec in the last chapter, we shall now climb one layer higher in the OSI model. There, in Layer 4 (Transport), there are two protocols on the Internet: the connection-oriented TCP and the connectionless UDP (see Section 21.2.2). Like all early Internet protocols, TCP and UDP do not contain any kind of cryptography. Without appropriate extensions, TCP and UDP are therefore manna from heaven for an eavesdropper like Mallory.

SSL is a cryptographic protocol for Layer 4
    To my knowledge, as yet no one has developed a crypto extension for UDP. There is, however, a very successful crypto extension for TCP called **SSL (Secure Socket Layer)**. SSL is a cryptographic protocol that offers encryption, authentication and integrity controls for TCP. Apart from this, SSL also supports data compression, which is of no further interest to us in this context.

    While IPSec was being patched together from existing components in a long-winded process within the IETF, SSL was being developed solely by the company Netscape. The consequence of this is that SSL is far less complex than IPSec. It was also faster available in products and penetrated the market more quickly. Since then, SSL has been standardised, with some small changes, by the IETF [RFC2246] under the name **TLS (Transport Layer Security)**. However, TLS is still less widely distributed, which is why we shall only talk about SSL in this book. If the following description of SSL is not sufficiently detailed for you, you can find more details in [Thomas] and [Rescor].

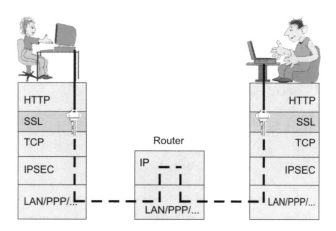

Figure 24.1   SSL is located between TCP and an application protocol such as HTTP or FTP. The application protocol and applications software must not be modified.

24.1 SSL working method

SSL only works together with TCP
While IPSec effects changes in IP packets, SSL does not act directly on TCP communications. Instead, SSL inserts an extra layer between TCP and the Application Layer above this (Figure 24.1). All crypto operations take place in this layer, without the TCP layer underneath being affected by them. Even the Application Layer above is left alone (largely). Although SSL builds its own layer above TCP, as a rule it is still always counted as Layer 4 (Transport) of the OSI model.

Like all protocols located below the Application Layer, SSL can be operated independently from the current application. It has established itself as an all-purpose protocol. For example, SSL is operated beneath Telnet or FTP and can also be used to enable the cryptographic security of SAP R/3, X-Windows, POP, IMAP, IIOP or Lotus Notes. This makes it very popular in the intranet field.

The name 'Secure Socket Layer' is derived from the interface between the transport protocol TCP and the Application Layer above it, which is known as the **socket**. SSL puts a further layer on this socket and provides the application with its own socket, which the application cannot differentiate from the real interface. As a result, the layer interface paradigm is not violated, because as far as the application is concerned, nothing has changed.

24.1.1 Protocol attributes

SSL is state-regimented
SSL is a connection-oriented protocol and only works with the equally connection-oriented TCP, not with the connectionless UDP. Because SSL is a protocol that has states, there are therefore contexts and security associations.

Like most other protocols, SSI does not tie itself down to specific crypto procedures. Instead, client and server have the possibility, using OIDs, to agree on the procedures to be used. SSL thus has the ability to negotiate (see Section 12.2.2). The TLS specification allows, for example, the symmetrical procedures RC2, RC4, DES, Triple-DES and IDEA, and SHA and MD5 can be selected as cryptographic has functions. RSA and Diffie–Hellman are named for key exchanges, and RSA and DSA as signature procedures. At this point you should be aware that digital signatures in a protocol that works below the Application Layer, like SSL, are only appropriate for authentication. As a rule, but not necessarily, the certificates used by SSL correspond to the X.509v3 standard.

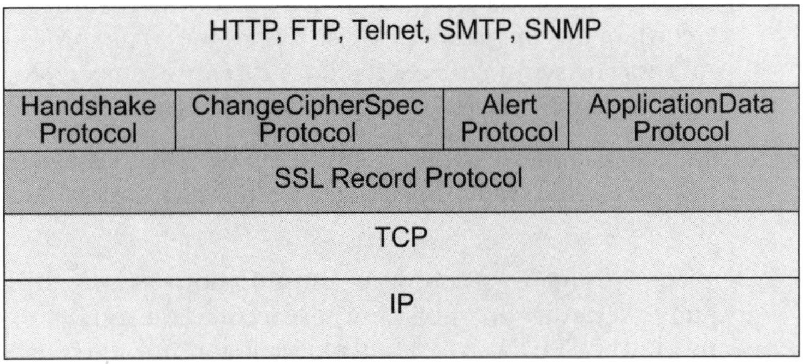

HTTP, FTP, Telnet, SMTP, SNMP			
Handshake Protocol	ChangeCipherSpec Protocol	Alert Protocol	ApplicationData Protocol
SSL Record Protocol			
TCP			
IP			

Figure 24.2   SSL splits into two layers. The upper layer is responsible for negotiating procedures and error messages. The lower layer handles the encryption process.

24.1.2 SSL sub-protocols

Internally the SSL layer is split into five sub-protocols, which form two sub-layers, one on top of the other (Figure 24.2). In the lower layer, the **Record protocol** is executed, while the four other protocols operate in the upper layer. The Record protocol has the task of using a key-dependent hash procedure on the data from the upper layer, and of appling symmetric encryption to that data together with the hash value. In principle, all the procedures introduced in this book (DES, IDEA, RSA, ...) can be used for this. The procedures that are actually in use are called current hash algorithms and current encryption algorithms respectively. Determination of the current procedures is carried out in the upper sub-layer. At the start of a communication, both current procedures are set to null, which means that, at the start, a hash procedure is not applied and encryption is not performed. Because it often makes no sense to apply encryption and a key-dependent hash function at the same time, one of the two values can remain null (it is possible for both values to remain null, but that case is of no interest).

24.2 SSL protocol operation

SSL is based on the premise that a client (a Web browser, for example) communicates with a server (a Web server, for example).

24.2.1 The Handshake protocol

SSL divides into several sub-protocols

The first sub-protocol, which operates at the upper SSL layer, is the **Handshake protocol**. This is used to authenticate the client (Alice in our case) and server (Bob in our case), to agree on the crypto procedures to be used, and to exchange a symmetrical key (from which a key can be calculated in the upper SSL layer, which is used for encryption and for the hash function). The exact operation is dependent on various options. Typically, the handshaking protocol works in the following way:

1. Alice sends a message to Bob, which shows him that she wants to use SSL (Client Hello). In this message, Alice also names the crypto procedure that she supports. At least one symmetric encryption procedure, one cryptographic hash function and one key exchange procedure must be named here.

SSL can negotiate

2. Bob sends a message back (Server Hello). The message states which procedure he has selected from Alice's suggestions. The message also contains Bob's digital certificate.

3. Alice sends her own certificate and a session key, which is encrypted with Bob's public key. Alice and Bob now have a common secret key, which they can use in the lower SSL layer for encryption, and for integrity control with a key-dependent hash function.

The sequence of operations that has been described is only one example, because communication can operate in other ways. For example, if an interrupted communication is restarted, the key exchange is omitted. If digital signatures are to be used for authentication, additional messages are needed. It is also possible that only the server owns a certificate, or that neither side bothers with certificates and just uses unsigned public keys. Another possibility is to use Kerberos, as described in [RFC2712].

24.2.2 The ChangeCipherSpec protocol

The ChangeCipherSpec protocol follows the Handshake protocol

After completion of the Handshake protocol, the **ChangeCipherSpec protocol** is used to inform the Record protocol of the agreed procedure. This makes it the current procedure. This sub-protocol only comes into use if something about the current procedure is to be changed. Only if the ChangeCipherSpec protocol – which ony consists of one message – has finished operating does the Record protocol change the procedure being used until that point.

24.2.3 The Alert protocol

Another SSL sub-protocol, which operates in the upper layer, is the **Alert protocol**. This is only needed if the exchange of data does not go to plan. Its task is to send error messages and warnings.

24.2.4 The ApplicationData protocol

The ApplicationData protocol can be adapted to the application

The fourth and last sub-protocol of the upper SSL layer is the **ApplicationData protocol**. This is responsible for the transfer of application data from above to the Record protocol. As a result, the ApplicationData protocol is the protocol that is normally used in the upper layer. The other protocols are only used for initialisation, for changing the procedure that is used, and in that case of faults, and therefore are the exception to the rule. The ApplicationData protocol can also be produced so that it is dependent on the application above it. This is, of course, a breach of the layer interface paradigm, but allows special requirements of the protocol above it to be taken into account at this point.

24.3 Successful SSL

SSL is a very successful protocol

Apart from PGP, SSL may well be the most commonly used encryption protocol on the Internet at present. As it is, the location of SSL between the Application Layer and TCP is ideal in many cases: SSL can be integrated into existing structures without (or with very few) application changes. At the same time, however, it is so close to the application that (with a minor breach of the layer interface paradigm) it can still be influenced by the application. A drawback is that SSL can only be applied above TCP, and not above UDP. Because of this, services such as TFTP, DNS, and especially Internet telephony cannot be protected with SSL, as these use UDP.

SSL is easy to integrate

If security measures had been incorporated in the TCP/IP suite from the beginning, a protocol such as SSL would surely not have succeeded. After all, it is not as powerful as a protocol at application level. Due to the negligence of earlier Internet councils, however, SSL has developed into a successful model among the crypto- protocols. It is easily integrated into existing structures, enables a speedy, cheap migration, and requires only minimal software changes. It is mainly intranet operators who are quickly convinced by these advantages of SSL. It is ideal for adding cryptographic security to complex TCT/IP networks, like those that occur in many large and medium-sized companies.

Other factors also contributed to the success of SSL: it is clearly less flamboyant and less complicated than the complex IPSec, with which it competes in many areas. On top of this, as early as 1994 it was already on the market as a component of Netscape Navigator. Of course, the great success of Netscape Navigator has strongly increased the popularity of SSL.

24.4 Technical comparison between IPSec and SSL

SSL and IPSec produce similar results

At first glance, they ways in which IPSec and SSL work are very similar. Both provide a secure tunnel between two computers connected to the Internet with similar functions below application level. Nevertheless, there are some differences:

- SSL only allows an end-to-end connection. IPSec, on the other hand, can also encrypt parts of the connection between two routers.

- SSL is closer to the application and, depending on the data transported, can select the procedure to be applied in a simpler manner. However, IPSec can only access the corresponding application by severely violating the layer interface paradigm.

- SSL does not work with UDP-based Level 7 protocols such as TFTP, DNS, L2TP and PPTP. Because the last two form the basis for many VPNs, SSL is not a suitable protocol for VPNs. Internet telephony also uses UDP and cannot therefore be protected using SSL.

SSL is more easily integrated
- SSL is more easily integrated into existing networks because it is located between two layers. However, IPSec requires existing protocols to be changed.

- For key management, IPSec uses a Layer 7 protocol (IKE). SSL only operates in the one layer (or more precisely in two sub-layers).

- IPSec is made up of several components (ESP, AH, IKE), which are partly of different origin and were patched together within the IETF. By comparison, SSL is a homogeneous protocol, which was developed by just one company (Netscape). Their different formations also help to explain why IPSec is the more complex, but also more efficient. This circumstance also led to the standardisation of SSL proceeding more quickly and less spectacularly than in the case of IPSec.

While SSL was in front for a long time, IPSec has clearly caught up. I believe that the two protocols will continue to coexist.

24.5 WTLS

To end this chapter, let us make an excursion into the world of mobile phones. The data services in mobile phone networks do not use TCP/IP protocols, but their own family of protocols called **WAP (Wireless Application Protocol)**. How WAP can be integrated into the OSI model is shown in Figure 24.3.

24.5.1 The WTLS protocol

WTLS protects WAP
As you can gather from Figure 24.3, the WAP architecture also has a layer that is dedicated to the protection of WAP communication with cryptography. The protocol used in this layer is called **WTLS (Wireless Transport Layer Security)**[BunPfa].

In WAP architecture, the WTLS layer sits on top of the Layer 4 protocol WDP, and is also classed in Layer 4. As the name suggests, WTLS is very similar to the TLS protocol (and hence to SSL). You could even say that WTLS is the WAP version of TLS.

Layer 7 (Application Layer)	Application Layer (WAE)
Layer 6 (Presentation Layer)	Session Layer (WSP)
Layer 5 (Session Layer)	Transaction Layer (WTP)
Layer 4 (Transport Layer)	Security Layer (WTLS) Transport Layer (WDP)
Layer 3 (Network Layer)	GSM, UMTS
Layer 2 (Data link Layer)	
Layer 1 (Physical Layer)	

Figure 24.3 WAP protocols use the mobile phone protocols GSM and UMTs. In contrast to TCP/IP, WAP also provides protocols in Layers 5 and 6.

24.5.2 WTLS operation

Like SSL, WTLS comprises two sub-layers. The Record protocol runs in the lower half, while the Handshake, ChangeCipherSpec and Alert protocols run in the upper half. How these protocols operate is largely the same as in SSL. In contrast to SSL, however, in WTLS there is no ApplicationData protocol (which takes care of the adaptation to the protocol in the layer above) – this is due to the fact that the same protocol is always used above WTLS, while numerous different application protocols can be used above SSL.

WTLS does not specify a crypto procedure Like SSL, WTLS does not specify any specific crypto procedure. Instead, different procedures are offered to suit each purpose: for example, RSA, Diffie–Hellman or ECDH is used for key exchange. Symmetric encryption uses DES, Triple-DES, RC5 or IDEA (each in CBC mode). MD5 and SHA-1 are available as cryptographic hash functions.

24.5.3 Differences between WTLS and SSL

WTLS is similar to SSL The architectures of SSL and WTLS are very similar. However, there are several differences. On the one hand, these can be traced back to the fact that the protocols above and below WTLS differ from those of SSL. On the other, WTLS protocols must take into consideration the fact that the computing power of mobile phones and the bandwidth of the communication lines are limited. The following list gives some of the main differences:

WTLS is rather simpler than SSL
- While SSL can only be integrated above the reliable, connection-oriented TCP, WTLS also supports connectionless protocols.

- The WTLS handshake protocol is somewhat simpler than the protocol used in SSL.

- Some fields in the protocol messages of WTLS are somewhat shorter than those in SSL.

- WTLS also supports a format for very simple digital certificates. This format corresponds largely to the X.509v1 format, but does not contain a serial number, for instance.

Cryptographic standards for the World Wide Web (Layer 7)

Web-site security is like anti-lock brakes on your car – you don't appreciate its value until you need it.
LARRY LOEB [LOEB]

Key experience no. 25
On of the most peculiar stories in recent Crpytography history is what happened to the Swiss Hans Bühler is told, who sold encryption devices for a Swiss company. In 1992, Bühler was unexpectedly arrested in Iran. The probable reason: the Iranian government suspected Bühler's employer of rigging the encryption devices delivered to Iran.

If there were no World Wide Web, this book would probably never have been written. And even if I had written it, you probably wouldn't want to read it. The reason for this is simple: the World Wide Web is the main reason for the downright incredible Internet boom that has taken place over the past few years.

HTTP is the protocol of the World Wide Web
On the World Wide Web, the leading protocol is HTTP (Hypertext Transfer Protocol). This brings us to Layer 7 (Application Layer) in our journey through the OSI layers. HTTP is a quite simple protocol, whose typical operation is easy to explain: Alice sends a request to a server, which contains the identifier (URL) of a file. In response, she receives this file (or an error message). The file requested by Alice can contain anything – however, it is usually the description of a Web page, which is then displayed by Alice's Web browser. Web pages are usually described in HTML format.

HTTP is, of course, a finely detailed protocol (see Section 12.1.3). In version 1.0 it is implemented completely without states. In version 1.1 it is at least possible to download files one after the other, without having to establish a new connection each time.

HTTP 1.0 does not provide cryptography
As you might have imagined, cryptography is completely missing in HTTP 1.0. This makes encryption and digital signatures very appropriate on the Web: if Crypt & Co., for example, wants to make its current pricelist available to home-worker Alice, but not to the competition, it can put this list on a Web page on which Alice must authenticate herself. If Bob orders his new washing machine on the Internet,

he wants his credit card number to be encrypted before it is transmitted to the server. These and similar applications lead us to think about how HTTP might be extended with cryptographic procedures. In this context, a whole ranger of sometimes completely different crypto extensions for HTTP appeared.

Figure 25.1 Basic authentication is a simple request for a password, which is supported by all browsers. Unfortunately, this does not use cryptography.

25.1 Basic Authentication

Basic Authentication is a password check

HTTP 1.0 contains no cryptography of any type – however, authentication can still be achieved by the request for a password. The HTTP component that supports this protection mechanism is called **Basic Authentication**. Basic Authentication is password authentication of the simplest type: a userID and a password are included in the request that Alice sends to the server. Only if the password is correct does the server then return the file that Alice wants. If you frequently surf the Web, you must have come across pages that will only load after you have entered a password – this means that you have already had a taste of Basic Authentication.

Of course, the password used in basic authentication is transported in a format that cannot be read by humans. This does not involve cryptography, however. Consequently, Basic Authentication is not particularly safe, but it is not useless: if it is not a question of keeping a Web page secret from the Mafia, but only from a young novice hacker, then Basic Authentication is still the method of choice. However, for applications such as Internet banking or payment over the Internet, stronger procedures should be used.

25.2 Digest Access Authentication

Digest Access Authentication embodies a challenge-response procedure

Because the Basic Authentication contained in HTTP version 1.0 hardly gives Mallory cause for concern, a further authentication mechanism was added to version 1.1. This is called **Digest Access Authentication** and is described in [RFC2617]. This is a challenge–response procedure (see Section 13.4.2).

The way in which Digest Access Authentication works is quite simple: if Bob wants to make his Web page accessible to Alice only, and not to all and sundry, then he agrees with her on a password (as in the case of Basic Authentication). If Alice wants to load this page into her Web browser, then Bob's Web server sends a random number (challenge) to Alice. Alice applies a cryptographic hash function to this random number, to the agreed password, the Web address and a part of the HTTP header, and sends the result back to Bob's server. This checks the result and, if correct, sends the Web page. Digest Access Authentication uses MD5 as the hash function, although other functions can be used.

Digest Access Authentication is a compromise
As is noted in [RFC2617], Digest Access Authentication is 'not a complete answer to the security needs of the World Wide Web'. Digest Access Authentication is more of a compromise. If SSL is too costly, and Basic Authentication too insecure, Digest Access Authentication is the correct choice.

25.3 HTTP on top of SSL (HTTPS)

HTTP is often used on top of SSL
Digest Access Authentication does provide HTTP 1.1 with a cryptographic protection mechanism. However, this only provides authentication, and not encryption. If confidentiality is required as well as authenticity, then SSL often comes into play on the World Wide Web. SSL as a crypto protocol for the Transport Layer has already been examined in Chapter 24. Because of its location between TCP and a protocol of the Application Layer, SSL can work very well together with HTTP. All current Web browsers and Web servers not only support HTTP, but also provide SSL in the layer immediately below as well. The advantage with this is that with the ApplicationData protocol, SSL has a component that can be adapted to the protocol in the layer above it (in this case HTTP).

If HTTP is used together with SSL, this protocol pairing is known as **HTTPS**. Looking at this historically, the insecurity of HTTP was the main reason for the development of SSL. The first product to support HTTPS, and simultaneously the first SSL product ever, was Netscape Navigator in 1994.

The use of HTTPS is indicated in the browser display
If Alice wants to use HTTPS, she enters an address in the browser beginning with 'https'. The browser then attempts to establish an SSL connection. If the server also supports SSL, the subsequent communication can be protected using SSL. In current browsers this is indicated by a closed lock symbol (if SSL is not in use, the lock is shown as open).

HTTPS offers authentication that is markedly more secure than Digest Access or Basic Authentication. In addition, with HTTPS the communication is encrypted. HTTPS, however, shares all the drawbacks of a crypto protocol below the Application Layer (see Section 21.2). In particular, digital signatures for signing Web pages cannot be used with HTTPS.

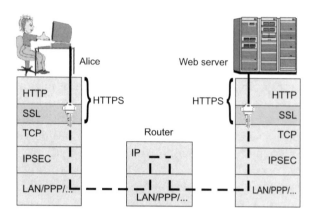

Figure 25.2 If HTTP is set above SSL, the arrangement is called HTTPS.

25.4 Digital signatures on the World Wide Web

SSL is not suitable for digital signatures

Because SSL or HTTPS protocols are situated below the Application Layer, they are not suitable for adding digital signatures to data transported on the Web. Because the use of digital signatures on the Web makes perfect sense, however, in the past few years several standards and products for the use of digital signatures on the World Wide Web have appeared. These are all intended for operation in OSI model Layer 7 (anything else would hardly make any sense).

25.4.1 Code signing

With her Web browser, and the HTTP protocol that supports this, Alice can of course not only download Web pages, but can, more excitingly, also access executable program code. Examples of this are Java applets, ActiveX controls, and other installation files. From a security point of view, it is of course very risky if Alice executes on her computer software about whose origin and operation she knows virtually nothing – it might after all have been programmed or manipulated by Mallory, and could cause untold mischief on her PC (erase all her files, or format her hard disk, for example). It could even hide a computer virus.

Code signing affords protection against corrupt software

Protection against corrupt software is an important topic in computer security. It is also a difficult subject, because it is not possible, on the face of it, to tell whether a program has malign intentions or not. There are, however, two approaches that enable Alice to use unknown software safely:

- The downloaded software is operated by Alice in an environment in which it can do no damage (sandbox principle). This approach is taken by Java, for example.

- Alice only uses software that comes from a trustworthy developer and has not been changed since being developed. To guarantee this, the developer signs his software digitally and sends the signature together with the program file (**code signing**). Before Alice uses the software, she checks the signature and can thus be sure that she has not received software that has been developed or manipulated by Mallory.

Code signing soon became established

The sandbox principle is of no interest to us at this point. Code signing, on the other hand, is an important matter for cryptologists. Because it solved an everyday, urgent problem, code signing is looked upon historically as the first application for digital signatures that became established on a wide base. The popularity of code signing is due, not least, to its having been quickly adopted by popular Web browsers.

There are many code signing applications

Unfortunately, there are many approaches of code signing, but as yet no recognised standard. The two most important procedures are introduced below.

Microsoft Authenticode

Authenticode is the code signing system from Microsoft. It uses X.509 certificates and some proprietary components. Authenticode can be used to add digital signatures to executable files for the Windows operating system. Microsoft's Internet Explorer supports Authenticode. It can store the certificates of those developers or companies that Alice trusts. If a downloaded software file is false or not even signed, Internet Explorer blocks this using an appropriate configuration.

Netscape Object Signing

Object Signing uses PKCS#7

Netscape has also developed a system for code signing. This is known as **Object Signing**. Object Signing uses the PKCS#7 format and X.509 certificates to sign programm files. It packs both signature and signed data into the Java archive format, JAR. Object Signing is intended mainly for Java and JavaScript files, but it can be applied to other data. Naturally, Object Signing is supported by Netscape Navigator.

25.4.2 The DSig Initiative

Authenticode and Object Signing are two different approaches that are aimed mainly at executable software. It is thus an obvious move to replace these two systems by a unified standard that is independent of the manufacturer. This would have more general aims, and not be intended only for executable programs. Such a standard was developed by the World Wide Web Consortium under the name **Digital Signature Initiative (DSig)**.

DSig enables signed labels

DSig builds on the PICS specification (Platform for Internet Content Selection) that was also developed by the WWW Consortium, which permits labels to be attached to Web pages. This should make it possible, for example, for a Web page developer to attach additional information such as 'for age 18 and over', 'top secret' or 'Author: Alice Onliner'. When configured appropriately, a browser can react to these labels. DSig adds a digital signature to the label, which tells the browser that the data being downloaded is original and unaltered.

25.4.3 XML-DSig

XML-Dsig is a comprehensive application

At present, the IETF and World Wide Web Consortium are working together to develop the most comprehensive application for digital signatures to date in the form of the standard **XML Digital Signatures (XML-DSig)**. XML-DSig describes a format for digitally signed data, and stipulates how this format is processed.

XML

XML-DSig is an HTML generalisation

XML-DSig is based on the XML language (Extensible Markup Language). XML can be regarded as a generalisation of HTML. Like HTML, XML uses so-called tags, with which a document is structured. A tag always has the form <xxx> or </xxx>, where xxx stands for any string of characters. You might already know tags such as <html>, </html>, <header> or </header> from HTML. A tag in the form of <xxx> marks the start, a tag in the form of </xxx> the end of a unit. This kind of unit is called an **XML element** (or simply just element). Elements can contain other elements. The following example borrowed from HTML comprises the element ('html'), which contains two other elements ('header' and 'body'):

```
<html>
    <header>
    This is the heading
    </header>
    <body>
    This is a text.
    </body>
</html>
```

XML makes no assertions about semantics

In contrast to HTML, XML only makes assertions about the syntax, but not the meaning of tags. XML can thus be used to describe HTML.

The XML-DSig format

The XML-DSig standard describes a format based on XML for digitally signed data. It defines a signature element, marked with the tags <signature> and </signature>. The name signature element is a rather unfortunate choice, because a signature element also contains additional information and, in some cases, the data to which the signature refers, as well as the digital signature itself.

A signature element comprises several elements

A signature element comprises several elements, which themselves contain further elements. Thus there is an element that stands for the date to which the signature refers. In addition, there are elements for the signature itself and for the public key belonging to the signature (which can also be in the form of a digital certificate).

In an XML-DSig document, the procedures that are used (signature procedure, hash function etc.) are always specified. These procedures are not identified by an

OID, but by a WWW address (URI), under which a description of the respective procedure is stored.

The data to which the digital signature actually refers does not itself have to be present in the signature element. It can also be referenced by a WWW address. Of course, this data is included in the hash value calculation.

25.4.4 Form signing

Form signing is an interesting use

The standards and formats that have been shown for digital signatures on the World Wide Web all relate to data that Alice downloads with her browser. However, HTTP offers the possibility for Alice to send not only a Web address but also additional information in her request to the server. To enable Alice to enter such information, HTML supports forms. This enables the browser to display a form in which Alice enters data and then sends by HTTP.

It is of course an advantage that Alice can sign the data that is entered in a form. This principle is called **form signing**. Although form signing is a very useful application, there is no related standard. Instead, there are several incompatible solutions, some in the form of Java applets and browser plug-ins. I hope that a standard will be developed for this as quickly as possible.

25.5 Sundries

There are many other crypto standards that apply to the Web, especially those used for transferring cash over the Net. But because these can also be used outside the Web, I shall treat them separately in Chapter 27.

Not all applications have become established

Several other crypto applications from the early days of the Web did not gain a foothold. For example, the Layer 7 protocol S-HTTP (not to be confused with HTTPS), which I shall look at briefly in Section 32.1.10. A similar fate was shared by the SSL object PCT from Microsoft.

E-mail encryption standards (Layer 7)

Pretty Good Piracy.
JIM BIDZOS (RSA SECURITY) on PGP

Key experience no. 26
There were many inventors of encoding machines. The only one of these that made his fortune from his invention was the Swede Boris Hagelin: he sold his first machine in the 1920s and by 1959 he had 170 employees working for him.

Despite the enormous success of the World Wide Web, the most widely used Internet service is still e-mail. E-mail is exactly the kind of service to be of interest to an eavesdropper like Mallory: while most of the information available on the Web would be generally available anyway, e-mail is very frequently used to transfer important information in business circles – a veritable feast for secret services and industrial spies. Despite this danger, encryption of e-mails was not provided on the Internet to begin with. However, e-mail took on a leading role in the implementation of cryptography, and e-mail became the first Internet service in which cryptographic mechanisms were integrated.

There are many e-mail encryption standards

Unfortunately, the situation in the field of e-mail encryption is very fuzzy, because there are several e-mail encryption standards, all trying to win over Internet users. All fulfil more or less the same purpose with more or less similar means, and are more or less compatible. Several e-mail encryption standards have now become PKI standards, while others are limited to describing suitable formats. Choosing the wrong standard can prove to be a poor investment with grave consequences. As you will discover in this chapter, however, choosing the right standard is less difficult than it might seem at first.

26.1 E-mails on the Internet

On the Internet, e-mails are mainly transported using SMTP (Simple Mail Transfer Protocol), but in some cases POP and IMAP are also used (see Section 26.7). If the e-mail destination is outside the Internet (even this is possible), other protocols can be used. All feasible protocols belong in Layer 7 of the OSI model.

26.1.1 The format of an e-mail

RFC822 describes
an e-mail format

The format of an e-mail itself is described in [RFC822]. If Alice sends an e-mail to Bob, then this can be regarded as the execution of a simple, stateless protocol, in which the e-mail itself is the protocol message. This protocol message comprises – as usual – a header and a payload. The header in turn comprises several fields, say, one for the address of the e-mail sender, and one for the address of the recipient of the e-mail.

The RFC822 format

RFC822 provides
only for simple text

In [RFC822], only written, English-language text can be transmitted by e-mail. Therefore, only 7-Bit ASCII characters were supported to begin with, and the header did not contain a field describing the e-mail format. The 7-bit limitation is still with us, as many mail servers still only support 7-bit characters and therefore, for example, all accented characters are lost.

MIME

Internet mail was a
very simple service
originally

The MIME (Multipurpose Internet Mail Extension) standard was a marked improvement, which is specified in [RFC1521]. MIME makes it possible for an e-mail to be split into any number of blocks. Each block contains its own header, in which the content type of the data can be specified. Examples of content types are ASCII text and binary data. The header can also contain additional fields (attributes), in which further properties of the data in the associated block can be given. Some important content types and associated attributes are described in the MIME standard, but the idea of MIME is that further MIME content types and attributes are specified in other standards.

MIME has several
advantages

The advantage of MIME is obvious: using MIME, in an e-mail to Bob, Alice can send an ASCII text, a picture and a software program. Each of these three message components is transported in its own block, and each of these contains its own header with corresponding attributes. If Bob's mail program supports MIME, then it knows that the ASCII text should be displayed on the screen, that the picture should be sent on to a corresponding application, and that the program should be saved. If, in a given block, a transformation into 7-bit ASCII has been applied, this is noted in an attribute of the header and can be taken into account by a mail program. Without MIME, Alice would be presented with a giant e-mail, and would have to decide herself which part is text, which is a picture, and which is a program.

26.1.2 Cryptography for e-mails

At the start, Internet
mail did not allow
for cryptography

It is hardly worth mentioning that the use of cryptography was not intended for e-mail on the Internet to begin with. Nevertheless, the need for more secure mail was recognised long before the great Internet boom. At first, only simple e-mail encryption with a hybrid procedure was in demand, but the need for signed e-mails was soon recognised. Of course, the use of cryptographic hash functions in e-mails is also possible – but because for an e-mail a short delay can usually be expected, at this point the use of digital signatures makes more sense, even if these are less effective.

An e-mail corresponds to a protocol message

Because an e-mail is the same as a stateless protocol, an encrypted or signed e-mail must always carry all the information that the recipient needs to process it. This means, in particular, that the key exchange and negotiation of crypto procedures must also take place without additional protocol messages. If RSA is used for the key exchange, the e-mail that Alice sends to Bob must contain the encrypted secret key. If the standard that is being used supports several procedures, Alice must list the OIDs of the procedures she uses in the e-mail.

The standards mentioned in this chapter for e-mail encryption and signing each describe a format that can be used for any type of file as well as for e-mails. For simplicity's sake, I shall always assume that we are talking about e-mails and not files.

26.2 PEM

PEM was the first crypto extension for an Internet service

By the middle of the 1980s, the first standard for the cryptographic protection of e-mails had already appeared. This standard bears the name **PEM** (**Privacy Enhancement for Internet Electronic Mail**). PEM is described in [RFC1421], [RFC1422], [RFC1423] and [RFC1424]. These RFCs were the very first to deal with the subject of cryptography. In one sense, PEM fulfilled a pioneer role, but on the other hand contained errors that could be put down to a lack of experience in the development of crypto standards.

26.2.1 PEM working method

PEM offers exactly what is expected of an e-mail crypto standard: with the support of digital certificates, it enables the digital signing and encryption of e-mails. For encryption using PEM, Alice and Bob can use a hybrid procedure, but they can also work with a secret key that they have agreed on previously in some other way. However, the latter variant is hardly ever used, and will therefore not be considered here.

PEM supports the DES

PEM allows the use of any given crypto procedure, provided the OIDs of the procedures used are listed in the respective mail. The procedures that any PEM implementation must support include DES in CBC mode for symmetric encryption, and the RSA procedure with a key length between 512 and 1,024 bits for the key exchange. As well as this, the cryptographic hash functions MD2 and MD5, and digital certificates and certificate revocation lists are mandatory.

A PEM message is always signed

In accordance with PEM, a message is always signed, but need not necessarily be encrypted. The components of a typical PEM message include the message (encrypted or not), the signature, a symmetrical key encrypted with the public key of the recipient, and the sender's digital certificate. The signature is not included in the encryption; the certificate is used for the verification of the signature by the recipient.

PEM messages are sent in the payload section of an e-mail. The use of PEM does not alter the header of an e-mail or a MIME block, which is why PEM messages can be sent over any given mail system. PEM is the basis for the antiquated idea that only text is sent by e-mail. Therefore, before encryption, all data is changed into a uniform 7-bit ASCII format (**canonicalisation**). Another conversion takes place after encryption: the created binary data is changed into 7-bit ASCII format once again.

PEM is compatible with PKCS#7 to a certain degree: PKCS#7 messages with the content type 'Signed data' and 'Signed and Enveloped data' can be converted into PEM messages, without cryptographic operations being necessary (digital signatures in particular remain valid).

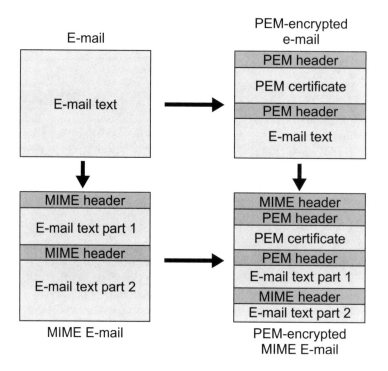

Figure 26.1   The e-mail encryption standard PEM structures e-mails in a way that is not compatible with the MIME e-mail structure standard.

26.2.2 PEM drawbacks

PEM is getting old   At more than 10 years old, it is little wonder that PEM has some drawbacks. Compatibility with MIME, for example: PEM is older than MIME, and the components of a PEM message are not divided up into blocks, each with its own header. Instead, PEM defines its own syntax for dividing up a message. The consequence of this is that a mail program, as well as parsing MIME blocks, must also take care of sorting out PEM components. Not exactly what one would call efficient.

PEM provides data conversion

The data conversions performed by PEM also create difficulties. The 7-bit limitation affects non-English text, and for other data the canonicalisation almost inevitably leads to chaos. Even the conversion after encryption is often unnecessary these days, as many mail gateways are no longer limited to 7-bit ASCII characters.

Even the crypto procedures supported by PEM are not that impressive nowadays. For a critical security application like e-mail encryption, DES should only be used as Triple-DES. MD5 also is no longer regarded as secure. Also, the lower limit for the key length of RSA is now 768 bits, and 1024 bits is no longer the upper limit.

Another problem with PEM is that only X.509v1 certificates and revocation lists are provided, which has the consequences described in Section 18.2.2. In particular, the fact that X.509v1 only accepts unwieldy X.500 names – and not e-mail addresses, for instance, which would make more sense in an e-mail standard – does not necessarily give rise to enthusiasm.

26.2.3 Summary

PEM is old

PEM is a crypto standard from the early days, whose drawbacks can be summed up in three words: PEM is old.

26.3 OpenPGP

Phil Zimmermann's cult PGP software (Pretty Good Privacy) has been mentioned several times in this book already. In this section, PGP software itself is not the theme, but the format it uses for e-mail encryption. PGP is based on many proprietary formats, which over the course of time have developed into a de facto standard. Nowadays, we can even officially talk about PGP as a standard, because within the IETF a working group has formed, which is developing a standard based on the PGP formats. This standard is called OpenPGP.

OpenPGP is a PKI standard

In Section 16.3.6 I have already considered OpenPGP as a PKI standard. At this point, however, we are only interested in its role as a standard for e-mail encryption.

26.3.1 PGP

The part that OpenPGP plays in e-mail encryption can only be understood in the light of the history of PGP. Here is a brief account.

Unique PGP

PGP is unique

PGP is unique among crypto software. It was developed by Phil Zimmermann shortly after the emergence of the PEM standard and largely fulfils the same purpose. Zimmermann knew nothing about PEM, however, and therefore did not adjust PGP to suit it. In any case, he did not think much of standards and was not a stickler for patents either. But the unexpected happened: PGP, the one-man show that did not stick to any standard, won through against all the implementations of the PEM official standard – a modern David and Goliath story. In a non-commercial environment, PGP is still without competition, even today.

PGP and PEM fulfil a similar aim

In principle, the formats used by PGP and PEM offer the same functions and use similar means. PGP offers digital signatures and encryption with a hybrid procedure, and supports digital certificates. The main difference between PGP and PEM lies in key management. PEM uses X.509 certificates, which of course form the basis of the hierarchical trust model. In contrast, PGP uses the web of trust model, which is a Phil Zimmermann quasi discovery.

Why PGP was a success

In retrospect, it is obvious why PGP won through against PEM. The following decisive factors were involved:

- PGP was superior to the early PEM implementations, despite a less edifying command line user interface.

PGP is more consistent

- PGP is built up on a more consistent basis: for example, PGP does not use DES. Instead, it uses one of the following more secure procedures, IDEA, CAST, Triple-DES, and other new ones. In addition, with PGP all data that is not needed for transmission is encrypted, thus maintaining minimum disclosure. With PEM, on the other hand, the digital signature and other information remain visible, even after encryption.

- PGP uses the web of trust trust model. The advantage of the web of trust, of course, is that it does not need a special infrastructure. PEM on the other hand, uses a hierarchy of CAs, which did not exist until just a few years ago.

PGP matches the Internet ethos

- PGP is better suited to the Internet ethos than PEM: while PEM was at first only a comprehensive specification, PGP was already in general use. The PGP source code was publicly available and could be viewed by anyone.

- The most important reason for the success of PGP was probably the stir that PGP caused among the general public. Because PGP became available in countries outside the USA, Zimmermann was charged with breaking US export regulations (the export of cryptography from the USA was strictly controlled at the time). Thanks to his unbending attitude when threatened by imprisonment, he soon became a folk hero in Internet circles. As an advertising campaign it could hardly have been bettered. The charges against Zimmermann were later dropped.

PGP profited from the US export embargo

- It could be seen as one of fate's little ironies that PGP profited indirectly from the US export regulations, while the distribution of PEM foundered precisely because of them. Because all early PEM implementations originated from the USA, their export was prohibited, just like PGP. Of course, PEM software also managed to reach other countries despite everything, but this caused much less of a stir than PGP had. Instead, little interest in PEM was shown outside of the USA because the American manufacturers could not deliver support for their products. For PGP, on the other hand, even without manufacturers' support, there was sufficient support from experts in the field.

26.3.2 Content of OpenPGP

After our excursion into the history of PGP, let us return to the formats that Zimmermann introduced and which are now standardised in OpenPGP. In OpenPGP, the RSA or DSA procedures are used for signing, and the RSA or Diffie–Hellman algorithms for key exchange. Procedures based on elliptic curves are in the process of being developed for OpenPGP.

PGP does not support the DES
Because Zimmermann did not trust DES, PGP first used IDEA as a symmetrical procedure, and others were added later. The OpenPGP specification now also offers Triple-DES, Safer, Blowfish and CAST. The cryptographic hash functions supported are MD5, RIPEMD-160 and SHA-1. The sender's certificate is sent with the encrypted mail. This does not correspond to the X.509 format, as OpenPGP certificates are used instead.

26.3.3 Drawbacks of OpenPGP

Despite its popularity, OpenPGP has its weaknesses, of course. The main drawback is that OpenPGP still represents a completely insular solution. Other standards such as X.509 or PKCS are not supported in OpenPGP, which uses formats not found outside of the OpenPGP world.

The web of trust is a drawback for OpenPGP
The web of trust is a further drawback of OpenPGP. As you discovered in Section 16.1.2, this is hardly suited to professional applications. Of course, OpenPGP certificates also could be signed by a Trust Centre and a hierarchical trust model thus set up, but OpenPGP certificates are not designed for this purpose and do not have the certificate fields required for it. A further drawback: as yet, OpenPGP does not support smart cards.

26.3.4 Summary

OpenPGP will find its market
PGP is without doubt an interesting piece of software, and for non-commercial users is the preferred medium for e-mail encryption. Therefore, OpenPGP will also certainly find a market. I believe, however, that OpenPGP – just like PGP – will only succeed in the private user field.

26.4 S/MIME

S/MIME (Secure MIME) is an e-mail encryption standard from the laboratories of the US firm RSA Security, and has since been further developed by the IETF. In recent years, S/MIME has become the most important standard for e-mail encryption. There are now nine RFCs and numerous drafts on the subject of S/MIME.

S/MIME is another standard for e-mail encryption

S/MIME offers the same functions as PEM and OpenPGP. The purpose of the standard is to encrypt e-mails with a hybrid procedure and add digital signatures to them, while supporting digital certificates. On top of this, S/MIME offers additional features.

26.4.1 Standards used by S/MIME

In contrast to PEM and PGP, S/MIME is based on other crypto standards (including some developed after PEM was published). In particular, S/MIME is based on various PKCS standards, which of course also come from RSA Security. The S/MIME message format was adopted from PKCS#7, and supports most of the content types it describes. Because PEM also supports two of these content types, S/MIME is partially compatible with PEM.

S/MIME is based on MIME

As the name suggests, S/MIME uses the MIME format for structuring messages. For this, content types from PKCS#7 are used as MIME content types, and the attributes can hold statements about the applied procedures. Because of this support for MIME, the processing of an S/MIME message is clearly simpler for an e-mail program than a PEM or PGP message.

S/MIME supports X.509v3 certificates and X.509v2 revocation lists in accordance with the PKIX standard. In contrast to PEM, MIME can also process unsigned, encrypted messages, while it can be seen from an encrypted message whether it is signed or not. A password-based encryption based on S/MIME is described in the most recent draft.

26.4.2 The procedures used by S/MIME

S/MIME supports several crypto procedures

S/MIME version 3 is described in [RFC2632], [RFC2633] and [RFC2634]. These prescribe support for Triple-DES (for symmetric encryption), DSA (for digital signatures), SHA-1 (as the cryptographic hash function) and Diffie–Hellman (for key exchange). To be compatible with S/MIME version 2, support for MD5, RSA and RC2 (with 40-bit key length) is recommended. Other procedures can be used if desired. There are already drafts and RFCs for the use of IDEA, CAST, Skipjack and various procedures based on elliptic curves.

26.4.3 S/MIME extensions

S/MIME supports ancillary services

Unlike PEM and PGP, S/MIME offers four ancillary services for e-mail encryption. These are described in [RFC2634]:

- Signed receipts: by means of this extension, Alice can request a digital signed receipt for the e-mail she sends to Bob. This is the e-mail equivalent of a registered letter.

- Security labels: by means of this extension, an e-mail from Alice can contain additional data comprising details about the properties of the contents relevant to security. A security label can state such things as 'for Bob Onliner only' or 'for internal use only' or 'strictly secret'. Security labels only make sense if receiver Bob takes note of, and follows, the inscription.

- Secure mailing lists: this extension provides some S/MIME additional features for the use of encryption in connection with mailing lists.

- Signing certificates: with the signed-data content type, S/MIME does not provide for the certificate sent by the receiver to be signed. This allows various attacks, which can be prevented by using some of the extensions described here.

The first three extension features are of particular interest. They offer logical extensions that make S/MIME into a standard which is clearly more dynamic than PEM or PGP.

26.4.4 Summary

S/MIME is supported by well-known undertakings

S/MIME has long been supported by all well-known suppliers (Microsoft, Netscape, RSA Security etc.). There are already dozens of implementations. For example, Microsoft Outlook can work with S/MIME, and for the more demanding Outlook user there are also S/MIME plug-ins from other manufacturers. There are also several extension products for Lotus Notes that implement S/MIME. Several e-mail programs (Netscape Messenger, for example) already have excellent inbuilt S/MIME support.

S/MIME has therefore recently established itself as the most important standard for encrypting and signing e-mails.

26.5 Mailtrust

Mailtrust is a German standard

In addition to PEM, PGP and S/MIME, there is a fourth standard for the encryption and signing of e-mails. The standard bears the name **Mailtrust**. This standard was developed by the German industrial organisation Teletrust, and is mainly intended for use in connection with the German signature law. Mailtrust is therefore only used in Germany as yet.

26.5.1 Provisions of the Mailtrust standard

Mailtrust version 2 appeared in 1999

Mailtrust version 2 appeared in 1999. E-mail encryption and encryption procedures only make up around one-third of the standard. So Mailtrust is now rather more than just an e-mail encryption standard. It could well be better called a PKI standard for e-mail encryption. One Mailtrust design principle is that – wherever possible – existing standards are retained, which are then adapted to the requirements specified by Teletrust. Altogether, Mailtrust comprises six sub-standards, which we shall now examine more closely.

Overall concept, structure and components of a PKI

The first part of Mailtrust is like an introduction. In this part we learn how a PKI is constructed and what aims are pursued by the Mailtrust standard.

Certificate and revocation list profiles

Mailtrust describes profiles for certificates and revocation lists

The second part deals with profiles for certificates and revocation lists. Mailtrust uses X.509v3 certificates and defines its own profile for them. This profile is oriented towards the profiles of PKIX and ISIS, but is not fully compatible with them. Mailtrust provides several of its own extensions. For example, there is an extension in which biometric data (a photo of the owner, for instance) can be saved.

The certificate revocation lists supported by Mailtrust correspond to the X.509v2 format. A profile for these is also given in the second part of Mailtrust, which contains Mailtrust-specific extensions.

PKI management

Mailtrust describes a CMP profile

The third part of Mailtrust deals with protocol messages that can be exchanged between the individual PKI components in order to guarantee the operation of a PKI. Here again the Mailtrust developers did not reinvent the wheel, but used an existing standard in the form of the CMP described in [RFC2510] (see Section 17.2). The third sub-standard of Mailtrust thus describes a CMP profile, which keeps strictly to the model.

Exchange format

The fourth part of Mailtrust describes the format used for sending encrypted e-mails. This would represent almost the whole content of PEM, PGP or S/MIME, although it is only a fraction of the Mailtrust standard.

Mailtrust adopts the PEM format

Mailtrust also relies on proven standards for the formats that are used. In the first version, which appeared in 1996, the PEM format was adopted in its entirety and improved by extra message formats and more secure cryptographic procedures. It soon became apparent, however, that instead of PEM, S/MIME was winning the race. For this reason, a profile of the S/MIME format was adopted in the specification of Mailtrust version 2. The Mailtrust format thus comprises the combined content of two e-mail encryption standards, together with some add-ons. PEM is only included on grounds of compatibility, while for the future, S/MIME is clearly given preference.

Token

Mailtrust describes a PKCS#11 profile

Mailtrust is tailored for the German signature law, and this of course requires hardware PSEs. Therefore, an interface to a hardware module (usually a smart card) is described in this fifth part of the standard. Because there are already several standards for such interfaces, the Mailtrust developers once again relied on existing developments. As a template they used the PKCS#11 standard, which you already know from Section 15.5.2. The fifth Mailtrust sub-standard thus describes a PKCS#11 profile.

Algorithms

The final part of Mailtrust describes the crypto procedures used. The Mailtrust developers settled for old and trusted algorithms. Symmetric encryption is thus carried out with DES or Triple-DES, and signing is performed using the RSA algorithm. The latter is also used for key exchange. MD2, MD5, SHA-1 and RIPEMD-160 are available as cryptographic hash functions.

26.5.2 Summary

Mailtrust is a basic standard

The Mailtrust standard is without doubt a triumph of German thoroughness. In comparison with S/MIME, PGP or PEM, Mailtrust takes a more comprehensive approach and, in addition to a format for signed and encrypted e-mails, also standardises numerous other important matters. Because of its focus on German signature law and the numerous add-ons, it is highly unlikely that Mailtrust is to become an international standard. In Germany, however, the Federal administration is to adopt Mailtrust software. In a large-scale pilot scheme called **SPHINX**, several Mailtrust products from various manufacturers were tested with 600 users from governmental authorities.

Mailtrust has to prove itself against S/MIME and PGP

Despite its adoption by several authorities, Mailtrust will find it difficult to stand its ground against S/MIME and PGP. The big players in the software field such as Microsoft, Lotus and Netscape are not likely to make their products Mailtrust-compatible. Mailtrust will therefore have to rely mainly on plug-ins and ancillary products being compatible with the popular e-mail programs. Some German manufacturers already offer Mailtrust solutions of this type.

26.6 Which standard is standard?

There are four relevant e-mail encryption standards

Because of the four standards described for e-mail encryption, the situation is unfortunately rather confusing, but it is simpler than it seems: PEM is dated. PGP is, of course, enjoying its cult status and will hold its popularity for some time – in the commercial field, however, it is unlikely that it will gain a foothold. Mailtrust will probably be able to continue as an indigenous standard in Germany.

The most important e-mail encryption standard by far, however, was, and still is, S/MIME. This is supported by renowned American suppliers like Microsoft, Netscape and RSA Security, and is the clear leader, predominantly in the commercial field.

26.7 Retrieving e-mails: POP and IMAP

E-mails are not always delivered directly to the recipient

As a student, Bob would really like to read his e-mails at home. However, his computer is switched off most of the time and is only connected to the Internet when Bob connects to the university by using a modem or through an Internet provider. Because almost all students at Cryptoland University have the same problem, the university has set up a kind of electronic post box: all incoming e-mails are stored on a mail server until they are retrieved by the recipient (by modem, for example).

26.7.1 Operation

There are two special TCP/IP protocols that are used to retrieve e-mails: the older bears the name Post Office Protocol (POP); its current version POP3 is specified in [RFC1939]. As the successor to POP, IMAP (Internet Message Access Protocol) is becoming more and more popular. The exact way in which it works is described in [RFC2060].

POP is older than IMAP

POP is not only the older, it is also the simpler of the two protocols. In its simplest form, it works as follows: Bob connects with the university mail server, enters a password, and finally gets his mail delivered to his computer. The server then erases the e-mails sent to Bob. In addition to this simple operation, POP now supports several online functions, which permit Bob to download only some of his mail, or to use different directories.

These online functions are considerably better implemented in IMAP: with IMAP Bob can manage several post boxes, share a post box with Alice, and mark e-mails in various ways without having to download them onto his computer. IMAP is also not only suitable for collecting e-mail, it also serves to provide access to news groups and other collections of documents.

26.7.2 The dangers of e-mail retrieval

Collecting e-mail entails security risks

Alarm bells must be ringing for you by now, because collecting e-mails from a server is, of course, fraught with security risks: if Mallory manages to pass himself off to the server as Bob, he can load e-mails addressed to Bob onto his computer. Bob will never receive these e-mails and possibly not even know that that something is missing. Of course, Mallory can also be satisfied with just intercepting Bob's communications with the server, in order to read the mail in transit.

Many mails are not encrypted

If Bob only receives e-mails that are encrypted with PGP or Mailtrust, or in some other way, Mallory can do little with them, except that he knows who has sent post to Bob. In practice, however, most e-mails are still not encrypted. On top of this, Bob would prefer that Mallory does not even discover who is writing to him. Added to that, by collecting Bob's mail, Mallory can make certain that Bob never receives it, because it will then be erased by the server. The unauthorised retrieval of mail by Mallory is thus a denial-of-service attack par excellence. If Mallory is particularly cunning (which we assume), he only lets encrypted mail disappear. Bob might then think that the mail server at the university is not able to handle this new-fangled encryption claptrap, and ask Alice not to encrypt her e-mails to him any more.

26.7.3 Crypto add-ons for POP and IMAP

There are crypto extensions for POP and IMAP
Despite the obvious security risks, the original versions of POP and IMAP offered no form of cryptography – only a password request was supported. Fortunately, a few things have happened since then, and therefore today there are several (perhaps even too many) crypto extensions for IMAP and POP.

RFC 1731 and RFC 1734

[RFC1731] describes three IMAP extensions to provide secure authentication (and part encryption). [RFC1734] specifies a POP extension, with which the same mechanisms can also be used with POP. These extensions are the following:

- Kerberos (see Section 13.5): executes authentication by a trusted third party, followed by encryption.

- GSS-API (see Section 15.5.6): allows authentication and encryption with the means provided by GSS-API.

- S/Key (see Section 13.4.2): enables the application of S/Key for authentication. Encryption is not covered.

CRAM

CRAM is a challenge-response protocol
In [RFC1731] there is no description of a challenge–response procedure of the type Digest Access Authentication or CHAP. This is remedied in [RFC2195]. This contains a procedure specially developed for IMAP called **Challenge–Response Authentication Mechanism (CRAM)**. This is a simple challenge–response procedure, with which the server sends a random value, its name and a timestamp to Bob. Bob applies a key-dependent hash function to this data and sends the result back to the server. The hash function provided for this is a key-dependent MD5.

IMAP and POP via TLS

As typical client–server protocols which work via TCP, IMAP and POP can also be safeguarded using SSL (or TLS). IMAP–TLS and POP–TLS combinations are described in [RFC2595].

IMAP and SASL

IMAP can be used via SASL
Finally, SASL (see Section 28.2) can also be used to protect IMAP and POP. In fact, SASL was developed with IMAP in mind. The first three protection mechanisms defined for SASL are (as in [RFC1731]) Kerberos, GSS-API and S/Key.

Internet payment systems (Layer 7)

Money, it turned out, was exactly like sex. You thought of nothing else if you didn't have it and thought of other things if you did.
JAMES BALDWIN

Key experience no. 27
That the manufacturers of biometric solutions usually claim spurious acceptance rates is understandable. However, one US manufacturer who told me that his fingerprint reader would only be fooled once in a billion cases was particularly audacious. To prove this empirically, he would have to have invited at least a sixth of the world's population to be tested.

After umpteen chapters on the theory and practice of cryptography, we have finally come to an important subject, around which it is said the world keeps turning: money. The desire to transfer this very same thing over the Internet becomes ever more important, as the Internet is used more and more as a marketplace.

Online payment is an important subject

For procedures and systems with which cash can be sent over the Internet (or other networks), names like Cybermoney, Electronic Cash and Electronic Payment Systems have come to stay. In this book I shall also use the term **electronic payment system** as a generic term, as it seems most appropriate. All payment systems work in Layer 7 (Application Layer) of the OSI model.

The field of application for Internet payment systems is gigantic: everything bought on the Internet must be paid for in the end, whether the payment is for books, CDs, shares or investment bonds. And not least, Bob might even use an Internet payment system to repay Alice the five Crypto-dollars he borrowed from her.

27.1 Internet payment systems in general

The Internet is not actually designed for the transfer of cash

Unfortunately, the notoriously insecure Internet is completely unsuitable for the transfer of cash – as we know, there are cunning eavesdroppers like Mallory everywhere, just waiting to fill their own pockets with cash that is being transferred on the Net. A dip into the cryptographic box of tricks can be of assistance, however.

Therefore, and because cash is always interesting, Internet payment systems have always been fascinating for cryptographers. The requirements that an Internet payment system must fulfil are listed in the following (we assume that customer Alice wants to send a certain amount of cash over the Net to online shop owner Oliver):

- There must be no possibility that Alice has to pay for something more than once, or conversely that she can increase her cash, without being detected.

- There must be no way for online shop owner Oliver to gain more cash than he has actually received from Alice.

- Mallory, who as usual can hear and manipulate everything, must have no opportunity to steal cash that is in the process of being transferred on the Net, or to annihilate it. He should not even be able to learn how much cash Alice is sending to Oliver.

Payment systems are cryptographically demanding

You may well think that this list of requirements has its pitfalls. It can, of course, be solved with cryptographic means, but there is no trivial single protocol able to transfer cash and meet all the requirements. Instead, these tasks demand the ingenious application of cryptographic methods, sufficiently ingenious to keep even the most dedicated cryptographer happily occupied.

Payment systems need a trusted third party

One of the few things that all payment systems have in common is that they need a trusted third party (see Section 13.2). A trusted third party is a neutral third entity, without which the transfer of cash over the Net is not possible. Incidentally, such entities are not only found on the Internet: the Bank of England is a trusted third party that prints banknotes and mints coins. With a cash transfer, it is the bank that ensures that Alice is credited with the cash that Bob has sent to her.

Depending on the exact role of the trusted third party, Internet payment systems can be divided into three classes: credit card systems, account systems and cash systems. These are discussed in the following sections.

27.2 Credit card systems

Credit cards can be used on the Internet

In Germany alone there are currently over 40 million credit cards in circulation. Instead of reinventing the wheel (Internet payment system), on the Internet it would therefore pay to have recourse to the established forms of payment with their existing infrastructure. Internet payment systems based on credit cards are termed **credit card systems**.

27.2.1 Unencrypted transfer of credit card data

Credit card systems include the simplest of all Internet payment systems. This works as follows:

1. Alice sends her credit card number (and the validity expiry date, which in the following I will automatically regard as part of the number) to online shop owner Oliver by, for example, typing it into a form on a Web page.

2. Oliver passes the number, together with the amount, to the clearing house of the credit card company. The clearing house in this case is the trusted third party.

3. The clearing house charges the corresponding amount to Alice's account, and transfers it to Oliver's account.

The transfer of unencrypted credit card data is not secure

There is no need to mention that this method of working brings several problems with it. For example, Mallory can find out the credit card number and use it himself. Alice can argue about whether she has effected payment or not. And shop owner Oliver can alter the amount in Alice's payment order and thus encash more than specified. On top of this, he can take a note of Alice's credit card number and invent false payment orders at a later date.

Leaving aside all security problems, there are still other drawbacks: Alice can only send her money to a licensed dealer, because private individuals and non-licensed dealers cannot accept credit card payments. In addition, the transaction costs for credit card payments are quite high, which renders the payment of small amounts (under 5 euros) unprofitable. Not least, there is also the drawback that the credit card company can check exactly when and how much Alice has paid out – Big Brother sends his regards.

Payment with credit cards is not only insecure on the Internet

To a large extent, the above-mentioned problems are not problems with the Internet, but problems with credit cards in general: a cashier could also note Alice's credit card number when she pays at a filling station. In restaurants it is even normal to hand the card to the waiter who then disappears with it for some time. Nevertheless, many methods have been developed long since to make the processes just described more secure by using cryptography. We shall now examine the most important of these.

27.2.2 Transfer of encrypted credit card data

SSL can be used to encrypt credit card numbers

At least the first of the problems listed above can be eliminated using cryptography: if the transfer of the credit card number is encrypted, Mallory does not get a look in. It was precisely this fear of an eavesdropper like Mallory that was one of the main arguments for the development of the already mentioned SSL protocol (Chapter 24). With SSL, credit card numbers are encrypted during their transfer between Web browser and Web server, and are hence unreadable for Mallory. When you type in your credit card number on a Web page, your browser indicates whether this information will be protected by SSL during transfer (provided that it supports SSL): the address then reads https:// ... and a corresponding icon is displayed. The use of SSL in credit card payments is now a standard – you should not give out your credit card number without SSL or some other encryption solution.

27.2.3 SET

SET is a protocol specially for payment by credit card

SSL solved the first problem listed above (the problem of eavesdropping), but left all the others unsolved. To enable really secure payment by credit card over the Internet, a Layer 7 protocol is needed, which also supports digital signatures. Such a protocol was introduced in 1994 by the US firm Cybercash, and was offered in the form of a product. Following the example of the Cybercash system, a protocol called **SET** (**Secure Electronic Transactions**) appeared later, in whose development Cybercash, Microsoft, Netscape, IBM, Visa, MasterCard and others were involved.

SET operation

SET is a protocol of Level 7 (Application Layer) of the OSI model. It serves the one and only purpose of transferring cryptographically protected credit card numbers. Digital signatures are of particular use here, which is why SET supports PKI techniques. In contrast to most other finely detailed protocols described in this book, a SET communication involves three partners: customer Alice, online shop owner Oliver, and the clearing house. A SET payment typically takes place as follows:

1. Customer Alice looks for the goods she wants on the Web page of online shop owner Oliver. She then sends an initialisation message to Oliver.

2. Oliver sends a digitally signed answer back, which contains his digital certificate and the digital certificate of the clearing house (payment gateway).

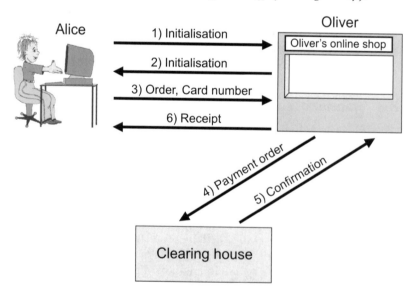

Figure 27.1 The SET protocol lets Alice send her encrypted credit card number and order to online shop owner Oliver who forwards it to the clearing house. The clearing house can decrypt the number, but Oliver cannot.

3. Alice now prepares a signed order and a signed payment instruction. The payment instruction contains the amount to be paid and Alice's credit card number. Alice encrypts the credit card number using DES and, in turn, then encrypts the key just used with the RSA procedure, for which she uses the public key contained in the certificate of the clearing house (hence this is a hybrid procedure). The order is not encrypted with SET so as not to contravene any laws. Alice sends the order and the encrypted payment instruction (including the RSA-encrypted DES key), together with her certificate, to Oliver.

Three participants are provided for in SET

4. Oliver receives the order and the encrypted payment instruction. He cannot decrypt the latter because he cannot decrypt the DES key that has been encrypted with the RSA procedure. Oliver now puts together a request message, which he signs and encrypts with DES. In addition, he also encloses the DES key encrypted with the clearing house's public RSA key. He sends this request message and the payment instruction received from Alice, together with his signature and encryption certificate, to the clearing house.

The capture token is needed for settlement

5. The clearing house decrypts the request message and the payment instruction with the help of the private RSA key and checks whether everything is correct with the payment. If everything is in order, it sends a confirmation message back to Oliver, which is signed digitally and DES-encrypted, and in which the RSA-encrypted DES key is enclosed. The confirmation message contains a so-called **capture token**, which is encrypted and can only be read by the clearing house. The capture token is needed later to invoice.

6. If Oliver has received a positive confirmation message, he sends a signed receipt message to Alice.

Oliver sends the capture tokens he has received to the clearing house at regular intervals. The latter can use them to calculate the amounts due and enact the necessary payment transfers.

Oliver does not get to see Alice's credit card number

It is a basic principle of SET that Oliver does not get to see customer Alice's credit card number. Added to this, all relevant messages are digitally signed, so that neither Alice, Oliver nor the clearing house can dispute or alter anything. This resolves three further problems in the above list.

SET procedures and formats

SET uses the RSA algorithm for digital signatures and for public key encryptions as a component of a hybrid procedure. DES is supported as the symmetrical procedure. In addition, shop owners, customers and clearing houses all have digital certificates, which correspond to the X.509v3 standard with some SET-specific extensions. Signature certificates and encryption certificates are differentiated.

27.2.4 Summary

The infrastructure for credit card numbers is already available

The advantage of credit card systems is that the infrastructure needed for payments is already there. The clearing houses of the credit card companies form the necessary trusted third parties, and the customers do not need any special hardware in order to type in their credit card numbers. These plus points have ensured that credit cards are still the no 1 means of payment on the Internet, which means that once more a pragmatic solution has, at least for the time being, prevailed against a better, at least in theory, competitor.

27.3 Account systems

Payments under the five-euro limit are called micropayments

If you think back to the problems listed in Section 27.1, you will notice that several points cannot be resolved with SET. In particular, the high cost associated with every credit card transaction must be taken into consideration. This is primarily of importance for amounts under the five-euro limit (so-called **micropayments**), because the transaction costs can quickly exceed the amount of the transaction itself.

Micropayments are very important, because even small amounts will change hands on the Internet. For example, the online edition of a magazine will hardly cost more than a few euros. The publisher might even cost each magazine article separately and charge a few cents for it. Micropayments are also of interest for the operators of search engines and other WWW information services, because what seems more natural than to charge a few cents for the retrieval of some information?

Private Internet users can also gain from micropayments

Because, with micropayments, both professional suppliers and especially hobbyist Internet users like Bob receive payments, credit card systems cannot be used, as only authorised dealers can accept credit card payments. From these considerations came the idea of replacing credit card payments by simple transfers. Transfers are not as expensive, and in contrast to credit card payments, can be accepted by anyone who has an account. Payment systems based on this concept are known as **account systems**. If Alice and Oliver want to use an account system, they must have an account with a trusted third party, who can move the amount to be transferred from one account to the other. Money can also be paid into this kind of account by credit card, for example.

With an account system, payment is made by cheque or transfer

With an account system, a payment can be made as if it were a cheque (Alice gives Oliver permission to debit her account) or a transfer (Alice instructs the central bank to transfer the cash). In both cases digital signatures can be used. In the following sections the main account systems available at present are introduced.

27.3.1 Paybox

Now that many account systems from the early years have disappeared from the scene (for instance, Netbill and Cybercoin), the German system **Paybox** is a promising newcomer. The special feature of this system is that a mobile phone is included in the payment process. Because of this, Paybox can also be used outside the Internet.

Paybox is a new German account system

If Alice wants to use Paybox, she must first register with the operator (who in this case is the trusted third party) and set up an account number complete with direct debit authorisation. She then receives a password (a PIN). A payment is then made in the following way:

1. Alice gives her mobile phone number to shop owner Oliver.

2. Oliver sends the transaction to the operator over a secure data connection.

3. The operator calls Alice on the number she has given.

4. Alice authorises the transaction by entering her PIN.

5. The operator withdraws the cash by debit entry and forwards it to Oliver.

Paybox is thus a very simple procedure, which largely dispenses with cryptography. Its appeal lies in its very simplicity, and could be instrumental in the system becoming accepted.

27.3.2 Millicent

Particularly small amounts are called picopayments

If Alice wants to buy a magazine article over the Internet, or if she needs some information over the telephone, she only wants to pay a few cents at most. For such a small amount, most micropayment systems are not particularly suitable. As well as the term micropayment, the term **picopayment** has now become established, and means a payment of a very small amount. The border between micro and pico is not precisely defined, but could well be set at about 40p. Picopayment systems are usually implemented as account systems. They stand out mainly because of their need to keep expenses down so as to keep transaction costs as low as possible. Thus public key operations are avoided and the payment process only requires a few messages to be sent. The trusted third party, which supervises the payments, does not usually get involved in the online operation. The fact that these savings are made at the expense of security need not give cause for concern – after all, even Mallory would not make much of an effort to rob Alice or Bob of a few pence. Once again, this confirms the fact that a sense of proportion has a role to play in cryptography – instead of absolute security, pragmatic solutions are often demanded.

How Millicent works

Millicent stems from DEC

The most well-known picopayment system was developed by Digital Equipment Corp. (DEC) in 1995, and carries the name **Millicent**. Millicent was designed for amounts from 10 dollars down to fractions of a cent. To the benefit of low overheads, Millicent does not bother with an online TTP and expensive communications. Instead, a so-called broker assumes the job of the central bank. If Alice wants to use Millicent, she first hands over a sum of money (say five dollars) to the broker, using another payment system. For her five dollars, Alice receives a so-called scrip, which can be seen as a digitally signed credit note. If Alice now goes shopping at Oliver's, she swaps part of her scrip with the broker for a trader-scrip which she can only use at Oliver's. She gives this to Oliver, who returns her updated trader-scrip. At regular intervals, Oliver exchanges scrip he has received for real money at the broker.

Millicent has very low transaction costs

Using Millicent, Oliver can of course swindle people very easily, but this is consciously taken into account, as only small sums are involved. Transaction costs are so low for Millicent that it is also worth while settling even the smallest amounts individually. Because of this, Bob can put some information on the Web for the price of a few Cryptocents.

Growth of Millicent

Millicent is now five years old, but it has not yet found widespread acceptance. In Japan it is already in use for making payments. According to the Millicent Web page, it should soon be available in Europe and the USA. Let us hope it proves to be more than just a proclamation.

27.4 Cash systems

In credit card and account systems, money can be traced

Credit card systems and account systems have one feature that can be regarded as an advantage or drawback, depending on your point of view: in principle, money can be traced back to its origin. The bank through which the transfer was routed, or the credit company knows how much money Alice sent to Bob. Of course, there is no central bank that oversees every payment, but the totally transparent consumer is nevertheless a good deal closer because of it. To avoid the possibility of such supervision, an electronic equivalent to cash is needed, which would enable the anonymous transfer of money. Payment systems that make that possible are usually called Electronic Cash or Cybermoney. I shall use the less evocative expression **cash system**.

Cash systems are easy to implement

Cash systems are not easy to implement: digital data has no material value and is easy to copy. How can this be used to create digital banknotes, whose path cannot be traced by a central bank? The solution, of course, is cryptography. This will prove to be a hard test for it, however: of course the central bank can issue digital banknotes that are digitally signed. However, this will not prevent anyone from copying a banknote, complete with signature, and issuing it several times (**double-spending problem**).

A cash system ought to solve the double-spending problem

There are two solutions to this problem: firstly, by means of a protocol that the central bank is party to online, it can be ensured that each coin is only spent once. However, this kind of process requires a few tricks to be used to make sure that the central bank cannot trace the money. There is more on this subject in the next section on Ecash. The second solution is to use hardware, smart cards in particular (see Section 15.2). Because a smart card is not easy to copy, it is an ideal storage medium for a digital banknote. But be warned: many payment systems that are based on smart cards take on the name electronic cash, although payments can be traced by the central bank.

27.4.1 Ecash

The best-known cash system is still Ecash, which was launched on the market by the Dutch company Digicash. Ecash is based on the ideas of the US cryptographer David Chaum, who founded Digicash. Ecash is without doubt one of the most interesting crypto solutions there is. Unfortunately, it was not a commercial success and Ecash has since disappeared from the market. In the hope that it is not yet quite dead, I shall describe it here regardless.

Ecash is the best-known cash system

Ecash is intended for amounts of from one to 20 euros, and hence is suitable for micropayments. Ecash is thus to be seen as an alternative to account systems like Paybox, rather than a competitor to credit card systems.

How Ecash works

Ecash is a payment system that simulates cash using digital data. To do this it mainly uses two protocols that operate in Layer 7 of the OSI model. The first protocol enables Alice to withdraw money from her bank online. The second is used to spend money.

Ecash simulates cash

Ecash simulates coins using digitally signed data sets. An online TTP takes care of the double-spending problem. This requires a few tricks: on the one hand, Ecash coins are signed with blind signatures (see Section 12.6). Blind signatures have the property, of course, that the person signing does not know what he or she is signing. This can be used in digital cash so that the central bank can sign a coin while the the serial number remains concealed.

If customer Alice wants to use Ecash, she needs some special software (Cyberwallet), with which she can withdraw digital coins from her bank account and save them on her hard disk. If Alice now wants to purchase and pay for some item from online shop owner Oliver, things proceed as follows:

Ecash uses a complex protocol for payments

1. Alice sends an order to Oliver.

2. Oliver sends a request for payment to Alice's Cyberwallet. This displays the payment details on Alice's screen, so that Alice can confirm the payment.

3. Alice's Cyberwallet sends the required number of digital coins to Oliver.

4. Oliver sends the digital coins to the central bank.

5. The central bank checks its own signature on the coins and then checks to see if coins with these serial numbers have already been used once. If not, it sends Oliver a report stating that everything is in order, and credits him with the corresponding amount. It also stores the serial numbers of the coins, which may not be used again. The central bank has no way of knowing, however, that the

coins come from Alice, because it signed them blind and cannot relate the serial numbers to Alice.

6. Oliver sends a confirmation to Alice and delivers the goods that have been ordered.

Ecash coins can only be spent once

The main difference between Ecash and real cash is that each Ecash coin can only be used once. The recipient of a coin can only take it to the bank.

The misfortunes of Ecash

Ecash offers one of the most important attributes of real cash: it is anonymous. The bank has no way of tracing cash. Because of this anonymity, Ecash is favoured by both cryptographers and those with interest in data protection alike.

Ecash has been a commercial flop up to now

Although Ecash is a technically elegant system, which offers great advantages for the user, commercially speaking it was a flop. Despite great effort, Digicash failed to establish their product on the market. There were only a few places where it gained acceptance, and therefore not many customers who wanted to use it (and vice versa). Without doubt it was the complexity of the system that led to it failing – who wants to trust his money to a system he cannot understand? Digicash has simply disappeared from the marketplace and has made Ecash one of the greatest flops for cryptography (see Section 32.1.3). I think it is a pity, because such a cryptologically advanced product should have had more success.

27.4.2 The cash card

Most cash systems use smart cards

While Ecash did not need special hardware, virtually all other cash systems operate on a different basis: they use smart cards.

Electronic purse

As already explained in Section 15.2, the chip on a smart card can be manufactured so that the information that is saved on it is very difficult to alter, extract, or copy. Smart cards are therefore the ideal medium for the implementation of digital cash. A sum of money is saved on the card in a file, which can only be altered after suitable authentication. Thus the bank is authorised, for example, to increase the amount on Alice's card if Alice has deposited a corresponding amount. On the other hand, a trader may deduct the amount from the card after Alice has purchased goods from him. The amount deducted is credited to the trader. A smart card that implements digital cash in this way is usually known as an **electronic purse**.

There are many different electronic purses

By my reckoning, there are dozens of projects that implement electronic purses. Almost all of them were designed for paying at the corner shop, rather than for Internet payments. However, those who have undertaken such projects have now discovered the giant market waiting for them on the Internet. Several electronic purses are therefore being adapted for the Internet at the present time. As is usual with smart cards, most of the impressive projects are European. However, it is a little early to talk about a united Europe: from the Danish Danmont to the British Mondex, in true European tradition, incompatibility rules.

How cash cards work

The cash card is an electronic purse made in Germany

There are also several electronic purse projects in Germany. The system that has become established is the **cash card**. Since the start of 1997, a cash card chip forms part of the Eurocheque card, which means that it can be used as an electronic purse. There is also a card with the original name **White Card**, which can only be used as a cash card.

The cash card specification specifies three types of terminals: bank terminals, where the cards can be charged with cash, dealer terminals, where payments are made, and special function terminals that banks can use for special operations (e.g. discharging a card, or checking its authenticity).

A bank that issues cash cards holds a so-called master key

A bank that issues cash cards has a so-called **master key**, which is stored in special hardware that the bank terminal can access. Before the bank issues a cash card to Alice, it generates a hash value from the master key and the card number, which is then stored on the card as the card key. A DES-based method is used as the cryptographic hash function. If Alice now wants to charge her card at the bank terminal, the card and bank terminal authenticate themselves mutually using the card key (with a challenge–response procedure based on DES). In addition, Alice must also enter a PIN, without which the card cannot be charged with cash. After successful authentication, Alice enters the desired amount, which is then deducted from her bank account and saved on the card.

With her cash card, Alice can even pay in the supermarket

Using her charged cash card, Alice can pay for a pack of diskettes in the supermarket, or for her bread rolls at the baker's on the corner – provided the cash card is accepted in those places. In order to pay, she inserts the card in the dealer terminal, whose card reader usually stands on the shop counter. Of course, authentication is also needed for the dealer terminal to deduct the amount. This is achieved with the help of another card key, which is generated from a dealer key. In turn, each dealer has a key stored on a special dealer card. To keep things as simple as possible, no PIN is needed to pay with a cash card. This also means, of course, that a lost card means lost cash.

To make things more efficient, and to avoid an expensive infrastructure, public key cryptography is not used with cash cards. Hence secure storage of the secret key on the smart card and in special hardware becomes very important.

The cash card on the Internet

The cash card can also be used on the Internet

Although the cash card was originally developed for the corner shop and not for the Internet, there are also ways of using cash cards on the network of networks. Thus the homebanking standard HBCI should support cash cards in future. The company Brokat is also developing a cash card solution for the Internet. However, it is still early days for the use of cash cards on the Internet.

27.5 The payment system crisis

When Internet payment systems surfaced around 1995, their multiplicity and the euphoria that surrounded them was immense. Numerous companies hoped to offer the means of payment that within a few years would be used by millions of Internet users. In favourable conditions, the business should amount to billions.

Payment systems are in crisis

Since then, the market for payment systems has become more settled, and the euphoria has subsided. Despite several online shops that are running well, we cannot overlook the fact that Internet payment systems are in crisis. According to [iX01], a whole 2 per cent of online shoppers made use of an Internet payment system in the year 2000 (in this respect the unencrypted or SSL-encrypted transfer of credit card numbers is not regarded as an Internet payment system). A truly successful Internet payment system is currently not envisaged. Ecash, although convincing in theory, has flopped, while SET, despite support from renowned companies, has hardly got onto its feet. Up to now, the cash card has not been a success on the Internet nor off it. Paybox gave cause for hope, but is still waiting to gain acceptance. Picopayments never got past the pilot stage. Shortly before this book went to press, it was announced that the company Cybercash, which specialises in payment systems, was withdrawing its micropayment system from the German market [iX01]. Even the banks have put the subject of payment systems on the back burner for the time being.

On the Internet, invoices, credit cards, and cash-on-delivery continue to be used

Because Internet payment systems have not gained acceptance, conventional means of payment will continue to be used in the 21st century: the transfer of credit card numbers without SET, payment on delivery, or by invoice. We can only wonder what will develop in the coming years.

Further Application Layer protocols

Historically, four groups of people have used and contributed to the art of cryptography: the military, the diplomatic corps, diarists, and lovers.
ANDREW S. TANENBAUM [TANENB]

Key experience no. 28
Whenever an eavesdropper succeeds in decrypting an intercepted message with explosive content, he is confronted with a difficult choice: on the one hand, something must be done about the message. On the other hand, the other party should not be given cause to suspect that their coding process has been broken. In the Second World War, Winston Churchill is supposed to have desisted, on these very grounds, from ordering the evacuation of Coventry before the night of the German blitz. An evacuation might have raised German suspicions about the security of their encoded radio transmissions.

Most crypto protocols in the Application Layer are used to protect e-mail, the World Wide Web, and Internet payments. There are, however, many more crypto protocols that Layer 7 has to offer on the Internet. In this chapter we shall examine the most important of these.

Many Internet services can be protected with SSL

At this point I would like to remind you that many Internet services can be cryptographically protected simply by using SSL (or TLS) underneath the Application Layer. Such services include Telnet, FTP, Lotus Notes, SAP R/3, Oracle databases, and many others. In this chapter, however, we are interested only in the 'genuine' Layer 7 crypto protocols, which means to say those that apply directly to the Application layer.

28.1 Secure Shell (SecSH)

Telnet is a Layer 7 protocol

In the world of Unix, the commands rlogin, rsh and rcp are often used to access one computer from another and initiate some action or other. Using these commands, Bob can work from home on the computer at his university, or access its files, as though he was sitting in front of it. Behind each of these three commands is hidden a Layer 7 protocol. The Telnet protocol has a similar function, and likewise runs in

Layer 7. All four of these protocols work on the principle of a dumb terminal accessing an intelligent server. Although Telnet & Co. have become dated in the meantime, they are still often used.

The three r-protocols are not secure

The danger inherent in the use of rlogin, rcopy, rsh and Telnet is obvious: Mallory can use these protocols to access a computer under Bob's name and create mischief to his heart's content. It is even possible to eavesdrop on or hijack a communication between Bob and the computer at the university. And this is made easy for Mallory because, of course, neither Telnet nor the three r-protocols support cryptography. The only authentication measure is an unencrypted password request, which doesn't exactly unnerve Mallory. Little wonder that it is precisely this weak spot that is favoured by hackers.

As a secure alternative to Telnet, rlogin, rcp and rsh, the Finn Tatu Ylönen developed a piece of software that he called **Secure Shell (SSH)**. Like the above four commands, Secure Shell enables access to a remote computer over the Internet – but this access is protected using cryptographic means. Secure Shell uses a protocol developed by Ylönen himself, which operates in Layer 7 of the OSI model.

28.1.1 Secure Shell versions

There are two versions of Secure Shell

In many ways, the development of Secure Shell resembled that of PGP: the comparatively high quality of the implementation, good documentation and free availability for non-commercial purposes all contributed to a speedy distribution of the software. Allegedly, there are now over two million SSH users worldwide.

Unfortunately, there are currently two different versions of SSH in circulation, which are not compatible: the original version developed in 1996 was called **SSH1**. In 1998, Ylönen brought out SSH2, in which an improved protocol was used. The changes in the protocol meant that SSH2 and SSH1 were incompatible. However, SSH1 is still being used in many places.

Secure Shell is now a standard

As with PGP, SSH software led to the creation of a standard: in 1997 an IETF working group was set up, with the aim if turning the Secure Shell protocol into an Internet standard. To differentiate the SSH software from the SSH standard, the latter is called **SecSH**. In the beginning, the SecSH working group used SSH1 as a base, but SSH2 is now used as the basis for the standard. Several drafts have appeared (but no RFC as yet).

28.1.2 How Secure Shell works

In both versions, Secure Shell uses a protocol with which a client (in our case, Bob) can access a remote computer (in our case, the computer at the university) over the Internet. This access is protected using cryptography: a key is exchanged using an asymmetrical procedure, and the associated communication encrypted with a symmetrical procedure. A feature of the protocol is that the computer to which Bob logs-on has two RSA keys, one of which is changed every hour (this key is also different for every user). This ensures that, if the keys are compromised, Mallory will subsequently only be able to decrypt data encrypted with the current second RSA key, and not the whole of the data exchange between Bob and the computer.

SSH1 uses RSA SSH1 uses RSA for the key exchange, but SecSH uses Diffie–Hellman (RSA and other algorithms are optional). Both versions support Triple-DES as the symmetric encryption algorithm, and SecSH also recommends Blowfish and Twofish. SecSH supports SHA-1 as the cryptographic hash function, while SSH1 uses MD5.

SSH1 does not use digital certificates. This deficiency was remedied in the SecSH specification. In the latter, not only X.509v3 certificates conforming to PKIX, but also OpenPGP and even SPKI certificates are supported. However, this support does not extend to SSH2.

28.1.3 Implementations

The two current implementations of Secure Shell, SSH1 and SSH2, are incompatible. Also, there is a further difference between the two versions: SSH1 is available for free, and can be used without charge even in the commercial field. With the publication of SSH2, Ylönen and his company SSH Communications Security changed the licence conditions, which means that licence fees are charged if SSH2 is used commercially. For this reason, SSH1 is still more widely distributed than SSH2.

There are now many SSH implementations As well as Ylönen's products, there are at least ten other implementations, covering all current operating systems. One project is particularly interesting in that its aim is to develop a freely available Secure Shell implementation: this is called **OpenSSH**. OpenSSH supports both old and new SSH protocols and should eventually implement the complete SecSH standard.

28.1.4 Secure Shell as a substitute for SSL

Secure Shell can be used instead of SSL One interesting aspect of Secure Shell is that it can not only be used as a substitute for Telnet and similar protocols, but can even protect other protocols like FTP or HTTP. This is because all these protocols provide for the exchange of ASCII texts only. Since Secure Shell works with ASCII data, it can fit between TCP and the protocol immediately above it. Because of this, Secure Shell plays a similar role to SSL.

28.2 SASL

SASL enables authentication **Simple Authentication and Security Layer (SASL)** is a Layer 7 protocol, which enables the authentication of a client to a server (and vice versa in some cases). It is described in [RFC2222]. SASL can be integrated with any other Layer 7 protocol that can be adapted to suit. With SASL, both communications partners can also agree on the encryption of the subsequent communication. This encryption is not described in the RFC. SASL was developed mainly for IMAP (see Section 26.7), but can be used for other protocols.

SASL enables authentication using Kerberos, GSS-API and S/Key. Other authentication mechanisms can be specified. For example, the use of SecurID cards with SASL is described in [RFC2808].

28.3 Crypto extensions for SNMP

SNMP enables component servicing

As in any computer network, including the Internet, the networked components must be maintained. Network nodes of all kinds must be configured, and settings must be altered. In short: the Internet has to be managed. Ideally it should be possible to manage network components over the network, otherwise an administrator would be constantly on his or her way to fulfil some local management task or other. For network management, the TCP/IP family provides a special protocol, the **Simple Network Management Protocol (SNMP)**. SNMP is a Layer 7 application protocol. It enables different attributes of a network component to be tested and changed.

It speaks for itself that SNMP is one of the most critical Internet protocols when it comes to security. Just querying the attributes of a network node can provide interesting information for an intruder such as Mallory. If Mallory should succeed in manipulating network components using SNMP, this could lead to enormous damage. For example, Mallory could divert packets to a router that he has control of, or cause a noticeable drop in performance. Therefore, as with FTP and Telnet, SNMP included a password request procedure from the beginning – although without encryption as usual, which made things considerably easier for password hackers.

Security risks originate in SNMP

The great dangers for the Internet arising from an insecure SNMP quickly prompted security developments [Stalli]. Three RFCs appeared as early as 1992, and resulted in the belated addition of cryptography to SNMP. These proposals did not succeed, however, because a new version of SNMP (SNMPv2) was on the horizon, which already contained security extensions. But SNMPv2 was seen as too complex and found little application in practice. The IETF working group responsible therefore reconvened, but still could not finalise a unified new version. Instead, the situation became rather involved and finally resulted in two proposals: USEC (User Based Security) and SNMPv2*. Both proposals were based on the same ideas, but USEC was less complex while SNMPv2 was more powerful. Fortunately, the two camps were then able to agree on a common standard. For SNMPv3, which now exists, a procedure for providing SNMP message-level security was defined in [RFC2274]. This is called the **User Security Model (USM)**. USM provides several appropriate crypto mechanisms:

SNMP offers security mechanisms

- SNMP communication can be encrypted using DES.

- To ensure the authenticity and integrity of management data, a key-dependent hash function can be used. MD5 is mandatory, SHA-1 is optional.

- Timestamps can also be used to prevent replay attacks.

USM makes no statements about a key exchange for DES, or the key-dependent hash function. There is the obvious proviso that the number of network components being managed by a network administrator using SNMP is practical, and that keys can be configured by hand. USM is therefore much simpler and faster than SSL, which could of course be used instead.

28.4 Online banking with HBCI

Online banking has advantages

Online banking has advantages for banks and bank customers alike: if customer Alice can take care of her banking at home, she need not run to the bank for every transfer, and need not wait for the post to deliver her bank statement. Opening times no longer apply. Alice's bank (the often-mentioned Cryptobank) saves on personnel and can service a large number of clients without a dense network of branches.

Cryptobank can offer online banking in various ways: it can arrange for Alice to access her account using a Web browser, or special software, or access software of an online service. In each case, a Layer 7 protocol is needed to control communications between Alice and Cryptobank. Obviously, these Layer 7 protocols must be protected against attack by Mallory. If Mallory should gain access to Alice's account, it might soon be empty. If he should succeed in eavesdropping on communications between Alice and the bank, he might discover her bank balance. Therefore: authentication and encryption are de rigueur.

There are several protocols for online banking

There are several protocols for online banking, some of them proprietary. SSL is usually used for cryptographic protection, normally in conjunction with PINs and TANs. Because SSL does not support digital signatures for application data, and because PINs and TANs do not remedy all authentication problems, this is certainly not an ideal solution. An attempt to replace the various protocols with a single protocol, and hence to increase security, is a standard called **Home-Banking Computer Interface (HBCI)**. HBCI was developed by the central credit committee (Zentral Kreditausschuss, ZKA) for the German credit industry. HBCI is a German standard and as yet is only of domestic interest.

28.4.1 The HBCI standard

HBCI is intended as a unified standard for online banking

The aim of HBCI is obvious: it is supposed to create a unified standard for online banking, which ideally would allow software to work with any bank. This means that HBCI should support all current banks. HBCI version 2.2 standardises communications between a customer (Alice in our case) and a bank (the Cryptobank in our case). To be ready for all eventualities, HBCI defines a larger number of financial operations, covering account balance enquiries, single transfers, standing orders, and so on. There are other financial operations which do not concern banks, and HBCI is of interest for other authorities and institutions. There is a special protocol message for each financial operation. Most financial operations are optional, however, in order not to make implementations too costly.

BPD and UPD enable configuration

Before bank customer Alice can begin conducting her bank transactions, Cryptobank must send bank parameter data (BPD) and user parameter data (UPD). The BPD inform Alice of the institute's name, operations supported and such like. UPD contains information such as Alice's account number or her personal limits. Alice's software can configure itself using BPD and UPD.

28.4.2 HBCI cryptographic functions

HBCI provides modern cryptographic procedures at the application level (Layer 7). In particular, digital signatures are supported, which is not the case with SSL. Up to now, HBCI has dispensed with PKI support, but this situation is expected to change.

HBCI is available with or without smart cards

Unfortunately, HBCI had to be developed by two different interests under one hat: private banks favoured encryption without ancillary hardware, while the German savings and Giro banks voted for an existing smart-card implementation (the ZKA smart card). At first therefore, there were two HBCI variants: with and without ZKA smart cards.

HBCI without a ZKA smart card

HBCI can be operated with a hybrid procedure

In the option without a ZKA smart card, HBCI uses a hybrid procedure comprising RSA and Triple-DES. In addition, digital signatures (as with the RSA procedure) are used. Alice's private RSA keys are not normally saved on special hardware, but on a floppy disk or hard disk instead (smart cards are sometimes used, but not ZKA smart cards). Using the RSA procedure, a Triple-DES key (112-bit) is exchanged, and then used for encrypting the subsequent HBCI communication.

Up to now, authentication has not entailed digital certificates. Instead, both Alice and Cryptobank must send an 'initiation letter' by post, in which a checksum for the relevant RSA key is specified. The RSA procedure is also used for signing messages exchanged before encryption.

HBCI with a ZKA smart card

HBCI can also be operated without public key procedures

In the variant with a ZKA smart card – it is optional – public key cryptography is not used, because the ZKA smart card does not have sufficient storage capacity. Instead, customer Alice receives a smart card (the ZKA smart card) on which a 112-bit key is saved. This key is used for a Triple-DES encryption of the whole communication. Before the encryption, each message is provided with a key-dependent hash value, for which a DES-based hash function is used. Of course, the authenticity and integrity of the message are already largely guaranteed by the encryption. The hash value is therefore only important if a message is to be saved or forwarded after encryption.

Comparison of the HBCI variants

Both HBCI variants are a compromise

Both HBCI variants represent a compromise: on the one hand, public key cryptography is dispensed with so that ZKA smart cards can be used. On the other, the ZKA smart card is dispensed with so that public key cryptography can be used. There are plans afoot to replace both variants with an RSA-based smart-card solution soon, when a new generation of ZKA smart cards becomes available.

Will HBCI become established?

HBCI is slowly being adopted

The early euphoria surrounding HBCI has now subsided. With the transition to the euro and the end of the millennium, the banks have had matters other than the speedy implementation of HBCI to worry about. Slowly but surely, however, the standard seems to be spreading. HBCI is still not supported by the majority of German banks, but its growing acceptance cannot be overlooked. Possibly HBCI could serve as the basis for a European standard, but this must first be developed.

28.5 Crypto extensions for SAP R/3

R/3 from SAP is, of course, the leading software for enterprise resource planning. In our view, R/3 is first and foremost a system of clients and servers, where the clients communicate with servers using a proprietary Layer 7 protocol. TCP is used underneath this proprietary protocol.

An SAP R/3 system is a rewarding target for Mallory

It might be obvious that Mallory could cause damage inside an R/3 system. If he should succeed in accessing the server in place of authorised R/3-user Alice, he can cause a lot of mischief. Even the interception of protocol messages is a danger.

R/3 supported passwords from the beginning, but – like so many systems – no cryptography originally. Of course, SAP recognised the danger and developed several countermeasures. SAP did not opt for the immediate implementation of cryptography, but made two interfaces available to allow cryptography to be added later instead.

28.5.1 Secure Network Communication (SNC)

SNC is a cryptographic interface for SAP R/3

The first crypto interface for R/3 is called **Secure Network Communication (SNC)**. SNC has the job of encrypting data before transport over the Internet, or of decrypting it after arrival. Instead of starting from scratch, SAP relied on proven developments: SNC was based on the GSS-API, which you remember from Section 15.5.6.

R/3 can be configured so that data to be transmitted is first sent to the SNC interface. Attached to this interface there must be a module that encrypts the data (or processes it cryptographically in some way). The encrypted data is then sent back from the module via the SNC interface to R/3.

Once R/3 user Alice has processed her data via the SNC interface, she sends it off. At the server, the whole process is repeated in reverse order: the received data is sent to a module via the SNC interface, which decrypts it and sends it back. The server can then process the decrypted data in the usual way. If the server sends a message to Alice, the process runs in reverse order.

28.5.2 Secure Store and Forward (SSF)

SSF is the second crypto interface of R/3

Secure Store and Forward (SSF) is the name of the second R/3 crypto interface. Over this interface, however, data is cryptologically prepared not for transmission, but for storage on a data bank server. A module attached to the interface encrypts or signs the data for this, and sends it back in PkCS#7 format (see Section 10.4.2). It can then be stored in this form. When the data is read, the process operates in reverse.

28.5.3 Implementations

R/3 crypto products that can be addressed via SNC and SSF are now offered by several manufacturers. In addition to Deutsche Telekom (Telesec Product Centre), these include Secude, RSA Security, Entrust and Utimaco Safeware.

Part 6

More about cryptography

The Hagelin Crypto C-52 cipher machine, manufactured in 1952
(from the IT-Security Teaching & Study Collection of the BSI)

Political aspects of cryptography

You cannot compare me to Bill Gates. He is worth 80 billion, I may be worth only half of that.
JIM BIDZOS

Key experience no. 29
Almost all the encryption methods used in the Second World War were cracked. One of the few exceptions was an amazingly simple system used by the US army for encrypting radio messages. Navajo Indians translated messages into their mother tongue and read them out into the transceiver. At the other end, a fellow tribesman retranslated the message: this was the decryption.

Cryptography would not be as exciting without its close links with politics. Therefore, this book can certainly not ignore this aspect, which means that we will now include a chapter on the political aspects of cryptography (or on the cryptographical aspects of politics).

There are numerous points of contact between cryptography and politics
At the core of the political debate on cryptography is one fundamental question: should effective encryption be accessible to everyone, or should there be policies to restrict its use? Unfortunately, this debate is not always objective. There are far too many interest groups that wish to steer the discussion in a certain direction: practical economic interests mean that companies are against restrictions, while services responsible for security and investigation fear that whole departments may be put at risk if the State does not regulate the widespread use of encryption. Politicians, who try to please everybody and do not want to upset anyone, take a stand somewhere between these two extremes. Taking all this into account, I have made a special effort in this chapter to introduce the most important facts and arguments related to possible restrictions for cryptography as objectively as possible, but without ignoring my own standpoint.

Fortunately, we have the intermediate topic of digital signatures, which is a sort of interface between cryptography and politics. Discussion of this topic is somewhat more objective, and not quite so controversial. Even so, there is no agreement at all in terms of how this should be regulated, as you will see in Section 29.2.

29.1 How governments control encryption

Encryption was withheld from the general public for a long time

For thousands of years, cryptography was a privilege afforded only to secret services, governments and the military. Over the past few years, things have changed radically. Since then, not least thanks to the Internet boom, secure encryption products have also been available for private individuals – I have already introduced some of these in this book. For secret services and investigative authorities, the fact that encryption was being made accessible to the public obviously set off some alarm bells: since listening-in to communication networks had been child's play for a long time, PGP and Co. could now knock governmental eavesdroppers' plans on the head. Most countries where the new technique has become widespread show a certain unease and uncertainty in terms of how to legislate for it. The government has therefore found ways of stopping encryption from taking off in a big way. As a result, it is interesting to note that controlling encryption is States' main concern – digital signatures and other crypto applications do not appear to bother governments as much, since these do not impinge on monitoring activities. When people talk about crypto regulation, it is therefore the control of encryption to which they are referring.

29.1.1 Legal restrictions

The use of cryptography can be legally restricted

The easiest way of controlling the use of cryptography politically is through laws. However, there's law and there's law. There are a number of variations on the theme.

Bans, restrictions of use

Encryption, or the use of certain methods of encryption, can be legally banned. There may be exceptions to this kind of law, for instance for financial data. France is the most well-known example of a country where the use of encryption has been restricted by law for quite some time. In France, companies were allowed to obtain a licence for encryption; however, licences were not issued to private individuals. In theory, it was a punishable offence to use software such as PGP in France. Fortunately, since the beginning of 2000, this stance has loosened up considerably.

Export bans, export restrictions

In the USA there was a ban on the export of powerful encryption

Instead of controlling the distribution of cryptography in its own country, a government can also try to do this abroad. Indeed, in the USA, there was an export ban on powerful encryption techniques, which has already been mentioned several times in this book.

Key recovery

There is a compromise solution between crypto bans and crypto freedom which consists of allowing data to be encrypted, but the key that is used to do so has to be deposited at a government location (Key recovery, see Section 17.2.5). As a rule, the government location can only hand over the key if judicial permission has been granted. It is also possible for the key to be distributed to several depositories for security reasons. Key recovery is also the main topic of dicussion in the USA.

29.1.2 For and against crypto restrictions

There are arguments for and against crypto restrictions
There is often intense discussion about whether restriction in the use of encryption makes sense. Let's look first at the parties involved in this discussion and their arguments.

Disadvantages of crypto restriction

The opponents of crypto restriction include data protection authorities, civil rights campaigners, consumer rights authorities, liberals, and practically the entire computer and telecommunication industry. Here are the arguments that are put forward by them:

- Cryptography offers protection against government intervention: if effective encrpyion is not allowed, the floodgates are opened to snooping by the government.

- Cryptography makes industrial espionage more difficult: if no effective encryption measures are used, industrial espionage is on the agenda – a massive disadvantage for the companies affected.

- In Germany and other states, there are constitutional doubts about crypto restrictions: regulations that prohibit citizens from using encryption are possibly unconstitutional. They could violate the individual's right to decide on information management, confidentiality of communication, and freedom of development.

Crypto laws are easy to evade
- Crypto laws are easy to evade and are therefore useless: a criminal is hardly going to take any notice of a ban. On the other hand, commercial users in particular would have to stick to the regulations whether they liked it or not, and this would mean that the objectives of a crypto restriction would be defeated.

- Crypto laws weaken confidence in products that are available on the market: today, American companies suffered huge losses because, for a long time, they were not allowed to export their powerful crypto software. A general crypto restriction would have similar consequences. Regulations for key recovery would weaken the confidence of users at home and abroad enormously.

- The police have other means of fighting crime: even if the use of cryptography spreads further afield, this will not be the end of all police investigations. Even without means of bugging, perpetrators will still be caught.

- You must allow others to do what you do yourself: if a democratic country such as Germany controls encryption, people cannot complain if other countries do the same – even if these are totalitarian goverments.

Advantages of crypto restriction

Crypto restriction also has its advantages

The opposite standpoint is mainly taken by conservative groups and government authorities that are responsible for internal security. Their plea for crypto restriction might go as follows:

- Without crypto restriction, the fight against crime loses an effective tool: eavesdropping on telephone conversations and other kinds of communication is an effective weapon against criminals. It would be reckless to give this up without a struggle.

- The secrecy of telecommunications and post is not sacrosanct: however, by using cryptography, legal forms of eavesdropping are also lost.

- Although crypto laws can be evaded, this does not normally happen: users are lazy, and so are criminals. In most cases, they are too lazy to get hold of illegal software that encrypts their data, even though this is still so easy. Steganography (the hiding of information in inconspicuous data) is not used either for the same reasons. The police benefits from the mistakes that criminals make. Therefore, if encryption were to become a standard component of e-mail and word processing applications, everyone would encrypt automatically, without ever having to think about it. With crypto restrictions, on the other hand, commercially available applications do not offer any secure encryption. There is no doubt that, this being the case, most criminals make the mistake of not using special encryption software.

Key recovery could be a compromise

- By carefully regulating key recovery, governmental misuse can be avoided to a large extent, even when using secure methods: in the eyes of many advocates, this is a sensible compromise. We have to trust our governments in many things, so why not trust them to look after our keys?

Summary

Supporters' arguments are not completely absurd

Although I am happy to admit that I am against legal crypto restrictions, I do not believe that the arguments of those in favour are completely absurd. Most notably, the supporters quite rightly do not accept the argument that crypto bans are useless because they can be evaded. After all, the fact that something can be easily evaded does not mean that everyone does it. A crypto regulation simply makes sure that all standard programs do not use any effective cryptography, and as long as this does not happen, only a minority will take the trouble to evade the bans.

29.1.3 Governmental crypto restriction without law

A State can also prevent encryption from being established

A State can prevent good encryption methods from being applied completely independently of a legal crypto restriction. This has been done for centuries using a simple system: knowledge about encryption was withheld from the public. In principle, this also happens today: the NSA and other secret organisations are supposedly always one step ahead of academic cryptography. They guard their knowledge as if it were hidden treasure. However, now that academic cryptography has gained ground over the past 20 years, the policy of secrecy in secret organisations is no longer sufficient. They have therefore come up with other methods.

The NSA influences standards

For example, the NSA now has a main role in the development of standards. DES, the Data Signature Standard (DSS), the Secure Hash Algorithm and Skipjack are all methods that were co-developed by the NSA. In all cases, the design criteria were initially kept secret, and in the case of Skipjack, even the functionality was kept secret at first. I feel that it is nothing short of scandalous that the cards were not laid on the table when these types of standards were introduced. It is nevertheless fair to say that, until now, no hidden weaknesses have been discovered in any of the methods that have been mentioned. However, there is more to this than meets the eye: the 56 key bits of DES are clearly too short, which is something the NSA wanted. IBM had originally provided a 128-bit key length. The stinginess of the NSA as regards key bits was markedly sucessful. To this day, DES is still used on a grand scale, although the key length of 56 bits is becoming increasingly less secure.

Bugs were inserted in secret

If the influence of the State on standards is still obvious to some extent, the insertion of bugs in hardware and software is done almost completely in secret. But not only the NSA knows: instead of cracking an algorithm, it is easier to make sure that it is not applied correctly – for instance, by means of a targeted manipulation of the crypto implementation, whereby a key is used that is not actually random. There are many rumours about this kind of activity: as is reported in [Spie96], during the Cold War, Western secret services are supposed to have installed bugs in computers that were bought in the East. There was also speculation about equipment from the Swiss company Crypto AG, which was used in several States for military purposes: 'Up to the end of the 1980s, German and American services are suspected to have manipulated Crypto's security equipment so that their codes could be cracked in no time at all', wrote *Der Spiegel* [Spie96]. Such cases are, of course only the tip of the iceberg, and no one really knows who had a hand in which crypto solution. Against this background, products such as PGP are a blessing, as their source code is open and can be seen by everyone.

29.1.4 Summary

The government still eavesdrops on a grand scale

The fact that governments of numerous countries fight against the use of cryptography, and use so many tricks, is an impressive indication that the State is eavesdropping on a grand scale. The 'big brother' of today is not looking at us directly, but is simply observing what information about ourselves we give over the Net, and what is sent to us. The transparent human is out, the networked human is in. If, on the other hand, you want to protect yourself, your last resort is to use cryptography. It is hoped that there will not be a law to prevent this.

29.2 The German signature law

When we discuss digital signatures, the following question always comes up: is a digital signature accepted by courts in case of a lawsuit?

Digital signatures are also valid without a special law

The answer to this question is as follows: in principle, yes. Since the principle of free assessment of evidence applies in most states, a judge can accept a digital signature if the given circumstances make this plausible. There are exceptions to this in some special cases, when a handwritten signature is required by law (for instance, on a will or when purchasing real estate).

29.2.1 What is the use of a signature law?

In Germany, digital signatures were already legally valid before any laws were discussed, thanks to the unrestricted assessment of evidence. Nevertheless, in the mid-1990s, it was decided to have a special signature law, which officially established digital signatures as an alternative to handwritten ones. The advocates of this kind of signature law had high hopes of increased legal security and a higher acceptance of digital signatures.

Unfortunately, there were different views as to what a signature law should state. The hardliners demanded a strict law that established a high standard of security for working with digital signatures – Trust Centre operators in particular were supposed to have been encouraged by the law to take security measures. However, some experts turned down such a strict law. They preferred to leave questions of security to the marketplace – by means of appropriate liability provisions, the Trust Centre operators were to be encouraged to provide a high degree of security without any explicit regulations to that effect.

29.2.2 The signature law of 1997

The first signature law came into force in 1997

One of the main opponents of a strict signature law was consumer rights organisations. They were of the opinion that this kind of signature law would provide the manufacturers of signature solutions with a tool with which they could protect themselves against claims from consumers.

Despite this objection, the signature law hardliners kept the upper hand. On 1 August, 1997 the time had come: the German **signature law** came into effect as part of the **Federal Act Establishing the General Conditions for Information and**

Communication Services (IuKDG). As a result, Germany was the first country in the world to adopt a signature law. In the meantime, others – for example, the USA [Miedbr] – have followed suit.

The law

The hardliners have won recognition

Since the hardliners won recognition, the signature law of 1997 essentially consists of a description of basic conditions that have to be met for a digital signature to be said to 'conform to the signature law'.

Incidentally, there is no compulsion to use a signature that conforms to the signature law. It is up to Trust Centres whether they abide by the law or not. Alice can choose whether to obtain her certificate from a Trust Centre that conforms to the signature law or not. The signature law can therefore be seen as an offer that is made by the legislator. There are various incentives to take up this offer and strive for conformity to the signature law: since the basic conditions in the signature law are not strict, Alice can, as a rule, rely on a signature that conforms to the law as having standing in a court of law (she cannot, however, be 100% certain, as the unrestricted assessment of evidence is not overridden by the signature law). Also, there may be future cases in which signatures that conform to the signature law are explicitly stipulated – for instance, in the case of communication with authorities. Before this case arises, however, a number of other legal regulations must be brought into line with the signature law.

Of course, there are also cases when conformity to the signature law can be ignored. This applies particularly to closed systems that are based on voluntary arrangements between the participants. Within these systems, the participants can, to a large extent, agree freely upon the conditions under which signatures are accepted.

Ordinance, motivation, technical catalogues

The signature law is very general

The signature law itself consists of 16 paragraphs, and is kept quite abstract. It contains definitions of terms such as 'digital signature', 'timestamp', and 'certifying body' (official term for Trust Centre). Moreover, it is stipulated that a Trust Centre that conforms to the signature law must be approved by the 'responsible authority' (this is the regulatory authority for telecommunication and post, see Section 30.3.9).

More concrete details were taken from the signature law and put into the 19-paragraph **signature ordinance**, which was decided on, and can be changed by, the Federal Government. The signature ordinance also contains details regarding the operation of Trust Centres, licensing procedures, aspects of security, and fees for licences.

The law includes technical catalogues and motivations

The sphere of influence surrounding the signature law includes, as well as law and order, the **motivation for signature ordinance** and the two **technical catalogues** at §12 and §16 of the signature ordinance. The technical catalogues that were produced by the BSI, the German equivalent of the NSA, also give further technical details regarding the signature infrastructure.

The crypto methods that may be used in connection with the signature law are published in the Federal Bulletin. These are currently (and not surprisingly) the RSA, DSA and three ECDSA variants. The cryptographic hash functions that are mentioned are RIPEMD-160 and SHA-1. The final topic in the publication is that of random number generation: a genuine random number generator is required. Its output should then be treated cryptographically.

ISIS specifies the requirements of the signature law

The standard that is supposed to convert the requirements of the signature law into practical formats and procedures is the ISIS standard mentioned in Section 16.3.3. Therefore, anyone wanting to operate a Trust Centre that conforms to the signature law has to struggle through a lot of paperwork: law, ordinance, motivation, technical catalogues, Federal Bulletin publications, and the ISIS specification – German thoroughness leaves nothing to chance.

Criticisms of the signature law

Not everyone was happy with the signature law

With so much thoroughness, it is hardly astonishing that not everyone was happy with the signature law [Schm98/2]. To many, one of the requirements in the signature ordinance appeared particularly harsh. This was the one that, in accordance with ITSEC, required an E4-level evaluation for 'Components for creating signature keys or for saving or using private signature keys' (see Section 15.7.1). Other components have to be evaluated to the level of E2, in accordance with the signature ordinance. Since an E4 evaluation quickly eats up a few hundred thousand euros, smaller providers who did not have an appropriate financial cover were excluded from the lucrative market of signature law from the outset. Even larger providers feared that, because of these requirements, the price for products that conformed to the signature law would climb to astronomical heights.

Some requirements were removed

The E4 level of evaluation remained unchanged, but fortunately some other requirements were removed and the technical catalogues reduced. Nevertheless, it took until 1999 for the first Trust Centre conforming to the signature law to open, the Trust Centre of Deutsche Telekom (the German telecommunications service). The second came into being at the beginning of 2000 (Deutsche Post Signtrust), and this was followed by the third, established by the Federal Association of Notaries. Other Trust Centres conforming to the signature law were set up shortly before this book was completed.

After a few teething problems, the German signature law, which was without a doubt an experimental law in its previous version, secured its place in the PKI world. There have been reports on possible perspectives for further development in this area [Belke].

29.2.3 The European signature directive

Since digital signatures play a role in more than one country, people were also dealing with this subject matter on the level of the European Union at the end of the 1990s. The goal that those in Brussels clearly had in mind with regard to this topic was an EU guideline for digital signatures that should be implemented as part of the laws of individual member states.

Origin of the signature directive

The European signature directive came into force in 1999

Of course, on the EU level, there were also different views on how a signature directive should look. With its signature law, Germany had already forged ahead, and demanded a guideline that enforced the strict German regulations at a European level. Some of the other EU states supported this, others preferred a less strict version. After heavy discussions, a compromise was finally found, and so in December 1999 (therefore two years after the German signature law) the **European signature directive** came into effect [BreWel].

Content of the signature directive

Terms such as 'certification service provider' (which means a Trust Centre), 'certificate', 'electronic signature' (a generalisation of the digital signature), and 'signature creation device' are introduced in the European signature directive. In the guideline, there are gradations for all of the terms that have been mentioned. In accordance with [BreWel], there are no fewer than 42 forms of possible implementations, which are produced by combining the different gradations, and from which the legislators of the EU states can choose the variant that is suitable for them.

The European signature law defines advanced signatures

At this point, we are only interested in the gradations that are available for electronic signatures. An electronic signature is defined as arbitrary information that can be assigned to a person (so, their name in ASCII format, for example). The **advanced electronic signature**, on the other hand, describes a digital signature in the normal sense. When using certificates, a choice has to be made between simple and **qualified certificates**. An advanced electronic signature with a qualified certificate in accordance with the EU guideline, for example, is equivalent to a signature that conforms to the signature law of 1997 (whereby the requirements on the EU guideline are defined less precisely).

An important difference between the European signature directive and the German signature law is that the former does not require any official authorisation for Trust Centres – a Trust Centre that does not follow the signature law, on the other hand, requires the authorisation of the regulatory authorities for post and telecommunication. Only a voluntary accreditation system is allowed.

29.2.4 The German signature modification law

The signature modifcation law came into effect in 2001

The European signature directive meant that all EU member states had 18 months to adapt their national laws to bring them into line with it. Austria was the first state to approve a signature law in accordance with the EU guideline. This took place in 2000 [MenSch]. At the start of that year, the **signature modification law** was tackled in Germany, which pursued precisely this goal. This came into effect in 2001 (see [Reimer] and [Welsch]).

The qualified electronic signature is in the signature modification law

The signature modification law includes the concept of the **qualified electronic signature**. This is equivalent to the advanced electronic signature with a qualified certificate from the EU guideline, and takes the place of the signature that has previously been described as conforming to the signature law. Until now, it has not been clear how high the requirements will be for a qualified signature in Germany, as there is still no new signature ordinance – however, we can assume that the very rigorous requirements that have existed up until now will remain in place. It is already clear, though, that Trust Centres no longer require a licence from the regulatory authorities, since this has been stipulated in the European signature law. There will, however, be a voluntary accreditation system in Germany, which is to protect the investments of the Trust Centres that already have a licence. In the signature modification law, as well as the qualified electronic signatures, normal signatures are also given legal status. Although this is an increase in value, they will probably not be given the same evidential value as qualified signatures.

29.2.5 Summary

The signature law activities of recent years have not exactly produced a clear situation. On the one hand, those who are not from a legal background find it almost impossible to see through the confusion of law, guideline and modification. On the other, it is still unclear as to how the future looks, legally speaking. Since there is no compulsion to stick to a legal requirement, it is primarily the market that has to decide whether and how signatures that conform to the signature law (or qualified signatures) are enforced.

There are many arguments in favour of the use of the qualified signature by government authorities and management. In large enterprises, however, there is a tendency at present to use solutions that do not conform to the signature law. This trend could be reversed, though, as soon as solutions that do not conform to the signature law are not accepted in a lawsuit. Therefore, as yet, there is no certainty in terms of the legal dimension.

29.3 Cryptography and policy in the USA

The crypto policies of the USA are met with great interest

The United States of America is the country that has the greatest influence in the computer world. Since cryptography is no exception to this rule, the crypto policies of the USA are met with great interest in other countries.

29.3.1 The export restrictions

In this book, I have already stated several times that in the USA the export of crypto products was strictly regulated until recently. Although these US export restrictions now belong in the past, they have nevertheless left their mark on cryptography.

The US export regulations originated during the Cold War

The export restrictions for cryptography in the USA originated from the time of the Cold War. At that time, encryption consisted almost only of devices that were used together with radio and telephone equipment. Even though the products that were commercially available then were not particularly secure, compared with today's standards, they nevertheless found a number of buyers in the military field of various countries. Against this background, it is quite understandable that, in the USA, encryption devices were perceived as weapons, and to a large extent their export was banned. At that time, the relevant ordinance was the International Traffic and Arms Regulation (ITAR), which actually regulated the export of weapons used for war. Devices which could only be used for decoding (for example, pay-TV decoders and products that could only be used for authentication or for digital signatures) were excluded from the ban.

The US export regulations led to a loss in turnover

In the 1990s, when the Internet – and consequently also cryptography – was becoming increasingly popular, the situation changed. Encryption (particularly encryption software) was now being ever more used by private individuals and in companies. The fact that encryption programs such as PGP were put on a par with war weapons in the USA was certainly acceptable to an increasingly sensitive public. The computing industry in the USA was not enthusiastic about the export regulations, which led to a serious loss in sales. Moreover, the export regulations lost their credibility since smuggling crypto software out of the USA was a relatively simple exercise. In spite of this, more and more good crypto implementations were being developed in other countries, which meant that these countries became less dependent on products from the USA.

For a long time, only 40 bits were allowed

It took the US government a long time to react to this. Different manufacturers were given authorisation to export encryption with a key length of up to 40 bits for symmetrical keys – even then, this was seen, at best, as third-rate. Both Netscape and Microsoft had to stick to this regulation with their Web browsers. Later on, the limit was increased to 56 bits, and then, in 1997, the export of symmetric cryptography with key lengths of up to 128 bits was permitted – but only if it was ensured, by means of technical measures, that this was only used for the transfer of financial data.

At the end of 1999, the US government finally saw sense. In September 1999, it announced that the export regulations were to be relaxed extensively. This came into effect in January 2000. In July 2000, there was a further liberalisation, whereby the US export restrictions for cryptography were as good as abolished. There are only seven countries – Cuba, Iran, Iraq, Libya, North Korea, Sudan and Syria – which are still affected by the export ban.

The US export regulations have had a number of repercussions on cryptography. Without these, PGP would not have become the most popular crypto software. Not least, numerous German companies have also profited from the US export policy, and were able to establish themselves on the market with their crypto solutions thanks to a lack of competition from the USA.

29.3.2 The crypto home policies of the USA

The use of cryptography is not restricted in the USA

While the export of cryptography outside the USA was a punishable offence for a long time, the use of cryptography in the USA was not – and is not – restricted by law. However, this does not mean that government authorities in the USA stand by and do nothing while cryptography grows.

As long ago as the 1970s, during the development of DES, the NSA successfully prevented longer key lengths. Allegedly, even the method was supposed to have been kept secret and only be available in hardware, which was not the case because of a mistake (see Section 5.1). The fact that the design criteria of DES were not initially published is another piece of evidence for the blocking tactics of the NSA.

The Clipper chip caused a big sensation
Moreover, the almost legendary Clipper chip with its brother Capstone (see also Section 32.1.2) caused a particularly big sensation. Using this encryption chip, which contains a pre-installed bug, the US government wanted to make sure that there was 'security' for digital communication. Although the plan was a flop, this shows how crypto policies can be created even without any bans.

29.3.3 Signature laws in the USA

There are also signature laws in the USA
The development of signature laws in the USA shows some parallels to development in Europe. In the USA, it was the various Federal states which adopted the legal regulations before the government in Washington became active. Of course – without exception – there were also different views expressed concerning the nature of a signature law. Today, the result of this is that signature laws vary from state to state. Throughout the US, the **Electronic Signatures in Global and National Commerce Act (E-SIGN)** came into effect on 1 October, 2000. This contains some basic conditions in connection with digital signatures. The Federal states are still solely responsible for all details.

People who play a role in cryptography

What does NSA stand for? No Such Agency.
ANON

Key experience no. 30
Most experts on cryptography who are not in the civil service are against the regulation of cryptography. The book author Rudolf Kippenhahn is an exception. In [Kippen] he writes (loose translation): 'Altogether, I have lived for ten years under two dictators and I value democracy. I would therefore grant it the right to control encrypted communication in well-founded cases.'

Now that you know the most important methods, standards and products, I wish to introduce the most important people, businesses, and non-commercial organisations that are currently involved in the Internet crypto scene. Of course, this kind of compilation cannot be exhaustive; in any case, Murphy's Law tells me that the ones I have forgotten are probably precisely the ones I certainly needed to mention.

30.1 The ten most important people

The ten most important people are introduced here

As is the case with every field, the cryptography scene is also formed by the people who are active within it. You have already come across some of the names that have made an impact on cryptography. In this section, I will introduce the ten most important people in more detail. When people who have carried out important work in the field of cryptography are discussed, you should remember that many clever cryptographers work for the NSA or other secret organisations, without anything ever becoming publicly known about the outcomes of their research. Therefore, the list introduced here inevitably includes only these whose work has become publicly known in the form of products or publications.

The top-ten list not only includes cryptographers

As you will see, not only cryptographers feature in my top-ten list. After all, my book deals with the practical side of cryptography and therefore, in my opinion, a business person, a book author and a software developer all belong to the top ten. Naturally, the list is not definitive. A completely different list of people may appear in the next edition. If you have any favourites, please send me an e-mail. If you yourself want to be included in this list, then have a go – after all, nothing is impossible.

30.1.1 Jim Bidzos

Jim Bidzos is one of the most significant business people in the field

Jim Bidzos is not a cryptographer, but he has left his mark on the crypto scene as a businessman. Jim Bidzos is an American of Greek descent, born in 1954. In 1989 he took over the controls of the company RSA Data Security, which was bobbing along unsuccessfully, and established it as a leading reference in the area of cryptography. In 1995, he founded Verisign as a spin-off business venture of RSA Data Security, and also had a hand in the formation of the companies Cybercash and Netscape. After the takeover of RSA Data Security by Security Dynamics, Jim Bidzos became the vice chairman of this enterprise. In addition to his successes as a businessman, Bidzos also consistently appeared on the media as an opponent of crypto restrictions. He also had some verbal slanging matches with PGP developer Phil Zimmermann. You can read an interview with Jim Bidzos in [Schu99].

30.1.2 David Chaum

David Chaum is the founder of Ecash

The American **David Chaum** made his name as a cryptographer in the 1980s. His primary concern was with the different variants of digital signatures and their uses in different scenarios. Chaum gave particular attention to blind signatures, and the simulation of cash with these. There are five patents from Chaum that fall into this area.

In contrast to many other cryptographers, Chaum dared to utilise his ideas commercially. In the mid-1990s, he founded the company Digicash in Amsterdam, which launched the payment system Ecash on the market (see Section 27.4.1). Thanks to its sophisticated concept, which was based on Chaum's patents, Ecash was quickly able to establish itself as one of the most important of the countless payment systems. Unfortunately, however, Digicash also had to recognise that, as yet, Internet payment systems were not ready to be fully accepted. As a result, Ecash ultimately foundered (see Section 32.1.3). Despite this, in my opinion, Chaum has earned a place of honour amonge the most important cryptographers.

30.1.3 Don Coppersmith

Don Coppersmith is one of the developers of DES

Don Coppersmith has been employed by IBM for more than 30 years, and has rendered outstanding services to cryptography thanks to his numerous contributions. Don Coppersmith is one of the crypto pioneers per se: as far back as the start of the 1970s, while working for IBM, he was involved in the development of a symmetric encryption algorithm. The result of this was an algorithm called Lucifer. When the American standardisation authority, NIST, was looking for a standard for the encryption of data, Coppersmith, along with some of his colleagues, developed Lucifer further, which generated DES. As we know today, the DES developers achieved first-class work.

In subsequent years, Don Coppersmith continued to be active in cryptography, which is verified by numerous specialist publications. In 1994, together with a colleague at IBM, he developed the stream cipher, SEAL. MARS, a development from IBM, was also one of the candidate ciphers for AES, which was largely formed by Don Coppersmith.

30.1.4 Whitfield Diffie

Whitfield Diffie is one of the founders of Diffie–Hellman

Whitfield Diffie, together with Martin Hellman and Ralph Merkle, is one of the founders of public key cryptography. Diffie, who was born in 1944, studied at the Massachusetts Institute of Technology (MIT), and, at the start of the 1970s, got involved with computer security and cryptography. During this time, it became clear to him that solving the key exchange problem would be a big step for cryptography. In 1974, he found out that Martin Hellman was also working on the problem of key exchange. Diffie contacted Hellman, and the rest is history: after researching together for two years, Hellman discovered that the power function in a Galois field could be used to exchange keys – and the Diffie–Hellman method was born.

30.1.5 Martin Hellman

Martin Hellman was born in 1946 in the Bronx district of New York. At the start of the 1970s, he researched the area of cryptography at the University of Stanford in California. He was particularly fascinated by the yet unsolved key exchange problem. To begin with, Hellman worked as a lone figure, until 1974, when he received a call from a colleague called Whitfield Diffie. Diffie was also working on the key exchange problem, and was looking to Hellman as an ally. The two met up with one another, and decided to work together from that moment on.

Martin Hellman is the second founder of Diffie–Hellman

After two years of research with Diffie, Martin Hellman finally made a breakthrough: he discovered the method that we know today as the Diffie–Hellman key exchange (see Section 6.4). Diffie and Hellman published their method in an American professional journal under the title 'New directions in cryptography' [DifHel]. This article remains the most well-known scientific work in the history of cryptography.

30.1.6 Ralph Merkle

Ralph Merkle, an American of Swiss descent and the grandnephew of a famous baseball player, is without a doubt one of the greatest cryptographers alive. However, the methods that he developed were usually unsuccessful. Nevertheless, his ideas often gained recognition and it was not rare for him to be ahead of his time.

Ralph Merkle is the co-founder of public key cryptography

One of Ralph Merkle's greatest achievements occurred in 1974 when – still a student at the University of Berkeley – he invented a method that can be described as the first public key method. This method appeared later in the crypto story as **Merkle's Puzzles** – in those days, Merkle was able to convince neither his professor nor the publishers of professional journals of the merits of his idea. Merkle's achievement was only finally acknowledged after Diffie and Hellman gained credit as founders of the public key method, which was named after them in 1976. Compared with RSA and Diffie–Hellman, Merkle's puzzles offer only modest security, but, nevertheless, Merkle is quite rightly described today as the co-founder of public key cryptography.

In 1978, Merkle was already involved in the development of another public key method. Together with his colleague, Martin Hellman, he founded the so-called knapsack method, which was able to be used as the first public key method for encryption (Merkle's puzzles and Diffie–Hellman can only be used for key exchange). Unfortunately, gaps in the security of the knapsack method soon appeared, and in 1982 it was scrapped. Several proposals for improvement suffered the same fate, and so the knapsack method is only of historic interest today.

Merkle developed several methods

Ralph Merkle was also active in the area of symmetric cryptography. In 1990, he published two encryption methods: **Khufu** and **Khafre** (named after Egyptian pharaohs). The two algorithms, which differed only in the way they process keys, were one of the first DES alternatives that could be taken seriously. However, at that time, differential and linear cryptanalysis were still unknown, and Khufu and Khafre proved to be susceptible to these attacks.

The design principle, in accordance with which all current popular cryptographic hash functions are constructed, can be traced back to Merkle (in particular, the compression function is one of Merkle's inventions). In contrast, his own development, **Snefru**, was not able to gain acceptance.

Since then, Ralph Merkle has unfortunately no longer been active in cryptography, but now carries out research in other areas of computer science. However, his ideas and methods have had an incalculable impact on cryptography.

30.1.7 Ron Rivest

Ronald Rivest is the greatest living cryptographer

In my opinion, **Ronald Rivest** is the greatest living cryptographer. The professor completed his studies in mathematics at the exclusive university of MIT (Massachusetts Institute of Technology) in 1969, and in 1974 obtained his PhD in computer science.

Rivest succeeded with his greatest invention in 1978, when, together with Abi Shamir and Leonard Adleman, he invented the RSA method. At that time, cryptography was still quite a new academic discipline, and Ron Rivest's career was also in its infancy. With the RSA method, he had invented one of the first asymmetrical methods, and as we have found out since then, it is also one of the most practical. In subsequent years, RSA developed into the most important crypto method around. Of the numerous products that can be used for asymmetrical encryption or digital signatures, there is hardly one that does not support the RSA method. This situation will not change much, because, as we know from Section 6.6, there are not many alternatives to RSA.

After his ingenious invention, Rivest did not manage to produce any more successes of this magnitude. Nevertheless, he demonstrated his abilities as a brilliant cryptographer often enough. Among other things, he developed the symmetric encryption methods RC2, RC4, RC5 and RC6, as well as the cryptographic hash functions MD2, MD4 and MD5. Of these, RC4 and MD5 are particularly widely used. It is unique for someone to have developed so many successful crypto methods. Moreover, Rivest is also active in other branches of cryptography. He has also produced publications on the topic of payment systems, information hiding, PKI, and much more. Rivest is therefore one of the most versatile and most productive cryptographers.

30.1.8 Bruce Schneier

Bruce Schneier became well known due to his book

Bruce Schneier is the manager of a company (Counterpane Systems), the founder of the symmetric encryption algorithm Blowfish, and co-founder of the successor to Blowfish, which is called Twofish. However, first and foremost, he became well known from his book '*Applied Cryptography*' (see Section 31.2.6). This work is today seen as the bible of cryptography, and is the book that every cryptographer must have on his or her bookshelf.

As a researcher, Schneier does not quite belong to the greatest of the cryptographers' guild. However, as a result of his exceptional book, he became a star in the field. His numerous lectures at congresses are always well attended; his Web page is also visited frequently. Unfortunately, according to his own statements, Schneier does not plan a revised edition of his book, which is getting on a bit now. However, in the meantime, Schneier has published '*Secrets and Lies*', which is already seen as one of the classics [Schn00]. In this book, he points out that, despite cryptography and other security measures, plenty of gaps in security still remain (for example, because of mistakes in the implementation and human error). As well as this, Schneier published a book on his encryption algorithm, Twofish, in 1999 – another achievement [SKWHFW].

30.1.9 Adi Shamir

Shamir is the 'S' in RSA

Adi Shamir is a professor at the Israeli Weizman Institute, and is the 'S' in RSA. Even without his involvement in the invention of the RSA method, Adi Shamir would still be one of the most important cryptographers. He is the co-founder of differential cryptanalysis, and also probably the most successful cryptanalyst on the crypto scene. Furthermore, he developed several methods, which we have not looked at in detail in this book.

30.1.10 Phil Zimmermann

Phil Zimmermann has not invented any crypto methods worth mentioning, has not cracked anything, and has not written any remarkable books. Nevertheless, for some years, Zimmermann has been the most well-known personality on the cryptography scene. His popularity is inextricably linked with the PGP software that he developed, which can be described as his life's work.

Figure 30.1 Phil Zimmermann is the founder of PGP.

Phil Zimmermann developed PGP

Zimmermann studied physics and computer science in Florida. In the 1980s, he became increasingly involved in the peace movement. He demonstrated against armament and atomic testing, and even being arrested at a rally could not put a stop to his commitment. As the danger of an atomic attack became more and more unlikely at the end of the 1980s, Zimmermann transferred his commitment to another area. He got involved in cryptography, and saw how this could be used by average citizens to protect themselves from the government, which Zimmermann still did not trust. He decided to develop software that made modern cryptography usable for PC users – and Pretty Good Privacy (PGP) was born.

Zimmermann did not make any compromises with PGP. Ignoring the patent situation, he used RSA for key exchange and for digital signatures. He did not feel that DES was secure enough, and therefore used IDEA. However, he did not have a less powerful version for export in mind. He also avoided the hierarchical trust model of the X.509 standards, and instead used a web of trust. In 1991, Zimmermann made PGP freely available to download from the Internet.

PGP became an overwhelming success

PGP was distributed quickly, and, as this happened, Zimmermann faced some difficulties. The company RSA Data Security (today RSA Security), and in particular, Jim Bidzos, reproached Zimmermann for violating the RSA patent. Also Zimmermann was accused of an alleged violation of the US export regulations. These quarrels led to vibrant press coverage and quickly made Zimmermann a national hero. As a result, the popularity of PGP increased considerably. In 1996, the proceedings against Zimmermann were discontinued, and the dispute regarding the patent was also reconciled. For a long time, PGP was the most popular cryptography software around.

In recent years, Zimmermann has tried successfully to convert his development into hard cash. He has given well-paid lectures at various congresses, and formed a company (PGP Inc.) which was taken over in 1997 by Network Associates Inc. (NAI). NAI extended PGP into a user-friendly PKI solution, which no longer had anything to do with the primitive crypto tool from the early days. Phil Zimmermann is reputed to be still involved in the further development of PGP, and also still actively contributes to, and is often booked for, cryptography events.

30.2 The ten most important companies

Quite some time ago, cryptography became a business that shifts billions. The United States of America is still the biggest player, and this is where most of the buyers and providers have their headquarters. However, with their export restrictions, the US government made sure that the US crypto industry was only allowed to export its products in toned-down form, and European enterprises in particular profited from this situation.

Cryptography has been an international business for a long time. The tiger states in South-east Asia are just as interested in encryption as the countries in the Far East, or the formerly communist countries in Eastern Europe. Obviously, people in countries that were formerly ruled by a dictator are particularly aware of the dangers of eavesdropping. It must not be forgotten that the military and secret service both have a great need for encryption. While large countries have their own crypto experts, there are small, internationally isolated countries that have to help themselves to the free market. The story told in [Strehl] impressively shows how closely the trade in encryption technology is connected to that of arms.

Although the demand for cryptography comes from all corners of the world, commercial providers concentrate on just a few countries. Most of these have their headquarters in the USA. At the same time, Germany, Israel, Finland and Switzerland are also particularly active in the crypto market. The most important protagonists on the market are introduced in the following list.

30.2.1 Baltimore Technologies

Baltimore consistently backs standards

The Irish company Baltimore Technologies is active worldwide, and provides products and advice in the area of information security. As well as crypto hardware and content security solutions, Baltimore also offers some particularly successful PKI products. The main item in the PKI product range is the software package Unicert, with which a CA and an RA can be run. On top of this, Baltimore also provides some PKI applications, for example a plug-in for e-mail encryption and a form-signing solution.

In contrast to their arch rival, Entrust, Baltimore backs standards more consistently. On the one hand, this leads to a large degree of interoperability; however, on the other, some interesting functions can only be implemented badly on the basis of existing standards. At the beginning of 2000, Baltimore took over the US company GTE Cybertrust, which also provided a CA/RA solution. In so doing, Baltimore secured its position as number two on the PKI market, behind Entrust. We may now be curious as to whether Baltimore will be successful in reconciling the product line of GTE Cybertrust with Unicert.

30.2.2 Computer Associates

Computer Associates (CA), which was founded in 1976 in New York, is the third largest software manufacturer in the world (measured by sales) after Microsoft and Oracle. The company offers over 1000 software products, which normally run behind the scenes and are mainly of interest to large enterprises. The company does not offer products for private users.

Among the numerous CA products, those of the eTrust family are the most interesting to us. As well as solutions for virus protection, access control and central user management, these also include a VPN and a PKI solution which both include a directory service. The topic of PKI was tackled relatively late by Computer Associates, and the company did not bring an appropriate software package onto the market until the spring of 2001. One may be curious as to whether the market-strong generalist Computer Associates is winning through against the PKI specialists Entrust and Baltimore.

30.2.3 Cylink

Cylink, a Californian company with its headquarters in Santa Clara, specialises in crypto products, and is one of the leading providers in this area. From the smart card to crypto software and crypto toolkits to PKI solutions, Cylink provides almost everything that a cryptographer could ever desire. In 1997, Cylink bought out the Israeli company Algorithmic Research, and supplemented its program, which mainly consisted of crypto hardware, with various software solutions.

30.2.4 Entrust Technologies

Entrust is active in the PKI market

Entrust is a Canadian company that is exclusively active in the area of PKI. The most important product is Entrust/PKI, a software solution for the operation of CAs and RAs. Entrust also offers a range of PKI applications, from an e-mail encryption solution to an SAP-R/3 security solution. Although Entrust backs proprietary formats in some places, it offers interfaces at which other manufacturers (especially manufacturers of PKI applications) can dock. Products that use these interfaces are certified by Entrust as 'Entrust Ready'.

Entrust therefore follows the strategy of supplementing its own CA/RA solution with as many of its own PKI applications as possible (or certified applications from other manufacturers). In so doing, Entrust/PKI offers some interesting additional functions, but at the price of proprietary components. So far, this strategy has worked well, and Entrust is a clear market leader on the worldwide PKI market.

30.2.5 F-Secure

Several interesting crypto companies have settled in Finland. The most important
of these is **F-Secure**, which has its main headquarters in Helsinki. F-Secure
exclusively provides software solutions for IT security, as well as, for example, a
piece of anti-virus software and a firewall product. For us, the product from F-
Secure that is of most interest is the VPN solution, which is one of the most-used
VPN solutions on the market. Moreover, F-Secure also provides a successful SSH
implementation as well as a PKI solution, but this is not one of the market-leading
products. Today, F-Secure, which was established in 1988, now has branch offices
in the USA, the UK, Germany, Sweden and Japan. As a result, the Finnish company
has established itself as one of the most successful European providers of crypto
software.

30.2.6 Microsoft

Microsoft, the largest software provider in the world, took some time to equip its
numerous products with cryptographic functions. Previously, those using
Windows, Outlook & co. often had to buy expensive additional products from
other providers if they wanted to encrypt and sign. However, this was not because
of a possible lack in crypto competence of Redmond's software giant, but because
of the US export regulations that were in force. This reduced the export of powerful
crypto products substantially, and thus forced Microsoft to deal with cryptography
carefully. It was only when these regulations ceased to apply at the start of 2000 that
cryptography became a fixed component of Microsoft products. As a result,
Microsoft developed almost instantaneously into one of the most important
providers of crypto software on the market.

Microsoft's most important crypto solutions include those that are installed in
the Windows 2000 operating system and have been clearly extended in its
successor, Windows XP. Windows 2000 provides functions such as file encryption,
Kerberos authentication and IPSec, as well as a CA that can be used as the basis for
a PKI. None of these solutions can keep up with the top products of the respective
market. Nevertheless, owing to their extremely low price (the mechanisms that
have been mentioned are already contained in the operating system), many
companies and end users have opted for solutions on the basis of Windows 2000.
In addition, we can assume that Microsoft will improve its crypto mechanisms with
each new operating system that it brings out.

The situation looks similar for other Microsoft products, for instance for the e-
mail and groupware solution, Outlook, which has also been equipped with proper
crypto functions. The Web browser, Internet Explorer, also provides several crypto
functions, which could be extended even further in the future. We can therefore
assume that Microsoft will gain a lot more importance in the area of cryptography.

30.2.7 Network Associates (NAI)

Network Associates Inc. (NAI) comes from the anti-virus specialist McAfee, and over the past few years has developed into one of the most important providers of security software. The company, which is listed on the NASDAQ and has its headquarters in Santa Clara (California), has an annual turnover of somewhere in the upper hundred million dollar bracket.

For us, it is particularly interesting that NAI bought out PGP Inc., which was established by Phil Zimmermann, the inventor of PGP, and since then has had the crypto software PGP in its portfolio. During to the further development of recent years, the cult software that once had anarchic tendencies has become a crypto solution that is oriented to the interests of the market. Many of the fans from the early days no longer use the newer versions. The success of NAI in the crypto market in future years depends strongly on whether it manages to establish the originally fully proprietary software PGP for business customers as well.

30.2.8 RSA Security

RSA Security is a well-known company

RSA Security, headquartered in the USA, is without doubt one of the leading companies in the area of cryptography in the world. The company was formerly called Security Dynamics. The company RSA Data Security, which is rich in tradition, has also contributed this name.

RSA Data Security was established in 1982, with the purpose of marketing the RSA method. Despite the quality and the monopoly of this method, it did not at first succeed in making RSA Data Security a profitable enterprise. Things changed when the wily businessman, Jim Bidzos (see Section 30.1.1), took over. He turned RSA Data Security into a profitable enterprise, and thus into one of the most influential crypto enterprises in the USA.

RSA Security was formerly called Security Dynamics

Security Dynamics had its headquarters in Bedfort (Massachusetts). The company was known particularly for its SecurID cards, which I have already introduced in Section 15.3.2. Although the SecurID card is a rather drab tool from the point of view of a cryptographer, this product was enormously successful because of its simplicity. The turnover of Security Dynamics exceeded that of RSA Data Security by several times, which yet again shows that pragmatic solutions often have the greatest success.

In 1996, Security Dynamics bought out RSA Data Security. Since the abbreviation RSA still has a good reputation in the crypto world, the company was renamed RSA Security in 1999. The SecurID card is still one of the best-selling products that RSA Security has. Furthermore, RSA Security is currently publicising the PKI solution, Keon, and is thus in competition with Entrust and Baltimore.

30.2.9 Utimaco

Utimaco Safeware is the most important German enterprise in the area of IT security. Utimaco was established in 1983 and, at first, specialised in PC-based security systems. Because of this, Utimaco was one of the pioneers of the IT security industry. Nowadays, the enterprise has its headquarters in Oberursel near

Frankfurt, and its main interest lies in the area of cryptography and firewalls. Its products include solutions for e-mail encryption, for the protection of PC access, and for virtual private networks, as well as smart-card solutions. Something that is quite interesting for end users is the encryption protocol, Privatecrypto, which can be downloaded from the enterprise's home page. Privatecrypto is one of the first AES implementations and can be used for the symmetric encryption of files.

30.2.10 Verisign

Verisign is a PKI provider

The US company Verisign was founded in 1995 as a spin-off from RSA Data Security (today RSA Security) and went public in 1998. Initially, the operation of a Trust Centre was the only business segment of Verisign. Verisign was the first company in this market, and is still a market leader.

Since then, Verisign has become active as a provider of a software solution for the operation of a CA and of RAs, which are sold under the name Onsite. Onsite is an excellent product for very large PKIs, which can deal with several thousand certificates without problems. In contrast to Entrust and Baltimore, Verisign has not as yet developed any PKI applications of its own.

30.3 The ten most important non-profit organisations

As well as commercial companies, various authorities, associations and organisations also play an important part in the crypto scene. I will now introduce the ten most important of these.

30.3.1 BSI

The BSI is the most important German authority in the area of cryptography

The **Bundesamt für Sicherheit in der Informationstechnik (BSI)** (the Federal Office for Security in Information Technology), which was founded in 1990, is based in the central office for the coding industry of the Federal Intelligence Service (BND). The tasks of the Federal Office, which is subordinate to the Federal Ministry of the Interior, are recorded in the so-called BSI law. These include, for example, the development of security precautions for Federal authorities and the testing and appraisal of security tools, as well as consultation with manufacturers, operators and users. For example, the BSI promoted the German signature law. The BSI was also one of the initiators of the SPHINX project, which dealt with the interoperability of German crypto products. Other BSI projects concern evaluation methods for biometric systems, and the safeguarding of official communication using VPN techniques.

Another of the BSI's tasks is the 'support of the police and law enforcement agencies' as well as 'defence authorities' (BSI law), which in practice means bugging communication. As in the case of the NSA, we have very little practical information about the activities of the BSI; we can, however, assume that in this area, which to a large extent escapes public control, there are no amateurs at work.

30.3.2 Chaos Computer Club

The CCC deals with the effects of new technologies on society

Perhaps you have already heard of the **Chaos Computer Club** (**CCC**), even if you are not an expert in computer security. After having been a permanent fixture in the media for years, at long last the registered organisation with its headquarters in Hamburg has acquired a reputation as the terror of the computer establishment.

The Chaos Computer Club began in 1981 as a loose association of computer and media experts wanting to discuss topics relevant to ways of communicating electronically. They see the 'communication platform for hackers' in use for 'the freedom of information and communication without censorship from the State and industry', as well as consideration of the 'effects of technology on society', as their mission. The Chaos Computer Club gained popularity mainly because of the vigour with which it pointed out gaps in security and other forms of abuse in our computer-dominated world, whereby the protection of the consumer is always paramount. Politics and industry are not always enthusiastic about this, in complete contrast to the press, which often reports this in great detail.

Some of the CCC's activities are also interesting for cryptographers

Many of the Chaos Computer Club's activities are also interesting for cryptographers. For example, members of the CCC succeeded in cloning smart cards of the mobile network system D2, and in proving that there were gaps in security in home-banking. It has also pointed out more than once that there was a lack of security in EC cards. The signature law (Section 29.2) is seen quite critically within the ranks of the club. Of course, it goes without saying that they reject a legal crypto regulation. To sum up: anyone interested in cryptography should take a look at the CCC Web site (www.ccc.de).

30.3.3 Cypherpunks

The cypherpunks are a group of people who are interested in cryptography

The **Cypherpunks** are a loose network of people interested in cryptography, whose members mainly come from the USA. As the name suggests, the Cypherpunks are not exactly the conservatives of the crypto industry. Instead, the aim of this organisation is the use of crypto software all over the country and the prevention of all kinds of crypto regulation. The mailing list of the Cypherpunks is particularly well known (see Section 31.1.4).

30.3.4 GMD research centre for information technology

The GMD research centre for information technology (normally shortened to **GMD**, which stands for 'Gesellschaft für Mathematik und Datenverarbeitung', or 'The Organisation for Mathematics and Data Processing') is an organisation that has devoted itself to research in various branches of information technology. We are interested in the Institute for Secure Telecooperation (SIT) which is part of the GMD. This is one of the most active research institutions in the area of cryptography in Germany. The company Secude has arisen as a spin-off of this branch of the GMD.

30.3.5 IACR

The IACR is an international association of cryptographers

The **International Association for Cryptologic Research (IACR)** is a non-commercial, international association of cryptographers. It is the most important organisation of this kind. It has become well known due to Crypto and Eurocrypto conferences, which are seen as the Mecca of scientific cryptography. However, the practical aspects of cryptography described in this book (and the market that these give rise to) play only a subordinate role in the IACR.

30.3.6 NSA

The NSA bugs all kinds of communication

The American secret authority **NSA (National Security Agency)** has already been mentioned so often in this book that a Section devoted to it is long overdue. This legendary organisation was founded in 1952 as a successor organisation of the AFSA (Armed Forces Security Agency) within the US Department of Defense. The most important task of the NSA is to bug all foreign channels of communication that are of interest for the security of the United States. The NSA is also active in the development of cryptographic methods.

In order to carry out its tasks, the NSA not only operates numerous ground stations for bugging radio links, but also uses satellites and reconnaissance aircraft. Compromising radiation is also part of the NSA's repertoire (see Section 3.2.8). Moreover, rumour has it that every telephone call between the USA and a foreign interlocutor is recorded by the NSA. Even in Europe, no telephone call and hardly any e-mails can be safe from the NSA. In Europe, data is collected in Menwith Hill in the UK and, from there, is sent by satellite to Fort Meade, Maryland.

The NSA has tens of thousands of employees

The number of people that the NSA employs is estimated at several tens of thousands – more than any other US secret service. Without suitable support, even this concentrated manpower would find itself overtaxed by the mass of data that is circulated around the world. Undoubtedly, the NSA is a world leader in the intelligent processing of large amounts of data. It is a known fact that the NSA is the largest purchaser of hardware. It is also a known fact that the NSA uses a voice recognition system called Oratory, which can analyse telephone conversations. A computer system called Echelon processes enormous amounts of information which are fed into a program called MEMEX that filters out any interesting data by means of artificial intelligence. The employees of the NSA then deal with this filtered data personally.

We are told truly marvellous things about the abilities of the NSA

Cryptographers are a lot less impressed by the amount of technology used by the NSA for its work than by the cryptographic know-how of the NSA, about which truly marvellous accounts are given. The NSA is the largest employer of mathematicians in the world. According to rumours, the NSA is ahead of public research by at least ten years with regard to cryptography. Presumably, the NSA knew about public key cryptography and symmetrical ciphers of the quality of DES long before they were discovered by civilian scientists. The NSA might also be ahead of academic research in the cryptanalysis of current methods. When cryptographers talk about the NSA, they normally do so not only with admiration, but also with contempt. The fact that DES was only equipped with 56 key bits is due to the influence of the NSA. The design criteria for the DES and the DSA (which came into being with the aid of the NSA) were not made public, or if they were, only much later on. The Skipjack method installed in the Clipper chip was initially not made public at all. It was also the NSA which had it out with Phil Zimmermann about the export of PGP, and even wanted to force the RSA inventors, Rivest, Shamir and Adleman, to keep their method secret. Not least, the former US export ban on powerful cryptography can also be put down to the influence of the NSA. It is therefore obvious that one of the most important aims of the NSA is to withhold cryptography from the public.

30.3.7 PKI Forum

The PKI forum should accelerate the acceptance of PKI

The **PKI Forum** is a non-profitable organisation of international companies, whose intention is to accelerate the acceptance and the use of public key infrastructures. The PKI forum advocates the cooperation of industries and market observation in order to make it possible for organisations to recognise the value of, and make use of, PKI for electronic connection between businesses.

The key aims of the PKI Forum are the acceptance and the use of PKI for e-commerce, stressing the value of PKI for customers and business partners, convincing customers and independent software dealers, and implementing PKI, as well as accelerating the increase in income for products and service capacities that are based on PKI.

30.3.8 Radicchio

Radicchio is a global initiative that aims to bring companies and customers together in order to make mobile e-commerce more secure [Engel]. It focuses on the use of cryptographic infrastructures based on the public key method. Radicchio has over 30 members from Europe, North America and Asia.

30.3.9 RegTP

RegTP is the successor of the Ministry of Post

The **Regulatory Authority for Telecommunication and Post (RegTP)** is the successor organisation of the Federal Ministry of Post in Germany. The latter became superfluous after the privatisation of post and Telekom (German telecommunications service). The RegTP (part of the Federal Department of Trade and Industry) therefore has the job of making sure that a certain amount of regulation exists in a market that is actually deregulated.

After the BSI, RegTP is the second most important German authority for cryptographers. It provides accreditation for Trust Centres that conform to the signature law. Also, the root Trust Centre of the German signature law is run by RegTP.

30.3.10 Teletrust

Teletrust is the industrial union of the security industry

Even though there is still so much competition on the market for the same things, opponents normally prefer to bury the hatchet and join forces. The forums that are responsible for this are normally industrial unions, who do lobby work and develop standards. The German crypto industry is no exception to this: despite all the competition, the German companies mentioned in Section 30.2 are united when it is a case of railing against legal regulations. Even in the case of the signature law, many joined forces, and with Mailtrust, the German crypto industry produced its own standard. The platform on which a lot of this kind of thing happens is the industrial union **Teletrust** (www.teletrust.de).

Teletrust was established in 1989

Teletrust was established in 1989. Most companies that are active in the German computer security industry belong to this union (therefore not only crypto providers). At present, there are about 40 members. Being an important sponsor of the signature law, one of Teletrust's current tasks is to create the appropriate conditions for the practical implementation of the law. At the same time, Teletrust continues to make powerful counter-plans against the legal restrictions of encryption that would naturally hit German crypto manufacturers where it hurts.

The managing director of Teletrust is Prof. Dr Reimer, who has repeatedly supported me in my journalistic enquiries and has also contributed to this book.

31

Where to find out more about cryptography

Knowing something is knowing where to find it.
ALBERT EINSTEIN

Key experience no. 31
While there are numerous novels, stories and films in which cryptography features, music remains largely unaffected by this science. The only exception to this that I know of is the song 'Sex Bomb' by Tom Jones. At the beginning of this song, he sings 'Spy on me Baby, use satellite' and later, 'You found the secret code I use'.

The previous chapters have given you a quite good overview of cryptography and its use on the Internet. However, at best, you have only covered the first stage on your way to becoming Internet cryptography experts. The rest of the way is paved with crypto methods, crypto protocols, crypto standards and crypto products. It leads into the infinite depths of mathematics, of which I have described only the bare minimum in my book.

It takes a long time to become a crypto expert
Naturally, the story of cryptography is continually unfolding, which is why you should stay on the ball after reading this book. To cut a long story short: it is worth while looking around for more sources of information on the topic of cryptography. In this chapter, you will learn where you can begin your search. I begin with the ten most important sources of information, followed by a top-ten list of books on cryptography and the ten most important Web sites.

31.1 The ten most important sources of information

The following top-ten list tells you where you can find information about cryptography.

31.1.1 Books

Hopefully, while reading this book, you will have noticed that books are a good source of information for those interested in cryptography. There are, of course, even more books that are worth reading on the market, which is why I look at books in more detail in Section 31.2.

31.1.2 Congresses and conferences

Congresses are expensive, but worth while

Anyone not wanting to learn about cryptography from just books and journals should attend a congress (or conference). At conferences such as those mentioned below, you have the opportunity to listen to lectures on cryptography from morning to night; often several take place at the same time. Normally, the lectures are not the most interesting thing: it is much more interesting to talk to like-minded cryptographers or even a famous cryptographer at lunch or to talk shop with like-minded people. At many congresses, there is an accompanying exhibition where manufacturers present their innovations. On your way out of a congress, you are normally offered piles of paper and a dozen calling cards.

Theorists meet up at Crypto

The most important congress for the theorists amongst cryptographers is the **Crypto** conference that takes place in August every year in Santa Barbara. The European counterpart to this is a series of conferences called **Eurocrypt**, which takes place somewhere different every year in spring. Asian cryptographers meet at the **Asiacrypt**. All three conferences are organised by the International Association of Cryptological Research (IACR), on whose Web site there is more information available (http://www.iacr.org).

The RSA conference is commercially oriented

My favourite event is the convention of the US company RSA Security, which is held every January (**RSA Conference**). In contrast to the IACR congresses, this is more commercially oriented.

31.1.3 Educational events

Cryptography is taught at universities

The universities that carry out research in this area are one of the main reasons for the increased level of interest in cryptography in recent years. To that effect, numerous lectures, seminars, and practical training courses on the topic of cryptography are available in universities today.

31.2.4 Mailing lists

There are interesing mailing lists on the topic of cryptography

There are many mailing lists covering cryptography, with the topics of PGP, S/MIME, e-commerce and much more. You can find more information about these on the Web sites given in section 31.3. Those who are feeling brave should take a look at the **mailing list of the Cypherpunks** (see Section 30.3.3). However, you must expect 70 or more mails per day if you subscribe.

31.1.5 Trade fairs

The most important European trade fair for cryptographers (and others) is, of course, **Cebit** in Hanover. Every year, most of the crypto providers rush down to Hall 18, which is reserved for the computer security industry. Crypto providers (Systems, Comdex, Banking Technology Fair) are also always represented in other trade fairs.

Trade fairs are also part of an RSA conference

The most important specialised trade fair takes place every year as part of the RSA conference.

31.2.6 Museums

There are museums with exhibits on the topic of cryptography. The most important of these is the **National Cryptologic Museum** of the NSA in Fort Meade, Maryland. A visit is worth while, even though you should not expect anything wonderful. Some of the rotor cipher machines (some of the Enigmas in particular) and a bombe are especially worth a look (see Section 4.4).

There are even cryptography museums

As well as the National Cryptologic Museum in the USA, there are also museums that are closer to home, such as the German Museum in Munich as well as the Heinz-Nixdorf-Museum in Paderborn, which both have interesting crypto exhibits to offer. A museum that is particularly recommended can be found in Bletchley Park in London, where the Enigma code was cracked during the Second World War.

31.1.7 News groups

sci.crypt is a crypto newsgroup

One of the routine tasks in the life of a cryptographer is to take a regular look at the newsgroups **sci.crypt** and **sci.crypt.research**. In the former, there are normally hundreds of messages to read in which all sorts of important and unimportant things on the topic of cryptography are discussed. As well as questions and announcements, sci.crypt also contains suggestions which appear again and again, and which can be classified as snake oil. Anyone who takes the pick of the bunch will also find interesting information here. Moreover, sci.crypt is an excellent way of finding answers to questions on cryptographic topics. When writing this book, I took advantage of this opportunity a number of times.

In contrast to sci.crypt, sci.crypt.research is a moderated newsgroup. This means that you can only read things that the censor has considered important enough to be shown. As a result, the level of sci.crypt.research is far higher than in sci.crypt. However, this means that there are normally only three or four messages to read (sometimes even none at all) that are neither relevant or intelligible for the average crypto consumer.

31.1.8 Software

Of course, the principle of 'learning by doing' also works in cryptography. If you want to get a feel for the functionality of encryption methods, I recommend that you use some suitable learning software.

The best crypto software for pedagogical purposes that I know of is Cryptool, which you can download freely on the Internet under www.cryptool.de. Using Cryptool, which was developed by the Deutsche Bank, the company Secude and the Forschungszentrum Informatik (Computer Science Research Centre) (FZI), it is possible to encrypt and then decrypt data using a number of modern and older methods (including DES, RSA and Caesar). It is also possible to generate hash values.

For those interested in Enigma, there is a simple Enigma simulation on the Web site of the book (www.dpunkt.de/buch/krypto.html), with which you can adapt the functionality of the most well-known encryption machine.

31.2.9 Web sites

There are interesting Web sites on the topic of cryptography

There are a lot of Web sites on the topic of cryptography, many of which are good. The ten best ones are listed in Section 31.3.

31.1.10 Journals

Yes, there are also journals that deal exclusively with the topic of cryptography. I know of three: *The Cryptogram* (not to be confused with Bruce Schneier's newsletter called Crypto-Gram, see Section 31.3.1) is a US journal that deals mainly with cryptographic puzzles. *Cryptologia* is also available in the USA and reports on historical aspects of cryptography. The journal that is still the easiest to get hold of for those of us in Europe is the demanding *Journal of Cryptology* from the International Association of Cryptologic Research (IACR), which is available in most scientific libraries. The *Journal of Cryptology* also contains research works.

Many computing periodicals sometimes contain reports on cryptography

For chip card fans, there is the **Card Forum**. Unfortunately, such periodicals are not available in shops, but can be subscribed to. However, you should be careful, as the price for this kind of technical magazine is quite high (for example, a year's subscription to the *Card Forum* costs over 400 euros).

31.2 The ten most important cryptography books

There is no shortage of books on the topic of cryptography

In the past few years, more and more books on the topic of cryptography have been published, so it is slowly becoming difficult even for experts to maintain an overview. In addition to a range of books that only cover the basics, there are at long last numerous books that just cover a sub-field of cryptography such as public key infrastructures, cryptography using Java [Lipp] or digital certificates [FeFeWi]. In the following sections, I will introduce ten books that I feel are the most important. If this selection is not sufficient for you, there are other interesting books such as [Kippen], [BeScWo] and [Bauer]. Anyone looking for a reasonably priced book should try [Selke] or [Beutel]. For a mathematical basis, [BaKeRu] is highly recommended.

Incidentally, gaps still exist in the crypto book market. Bruce Schneier's masterpiece is now out of date (*Applied Cryptography*), and as yet no other worthy successor has been found. This can also be said for the *Handbook of Applied Cryptography* by Menezes, van Oorschot and Vanstone. To my knowledge, no book on the topic of cryptanalysis that is worth mentioning has yet been published.

31.2.1 Adams, Lloyd: *Understanding Public Key Infrastructure*

One of the few books on PKI comes from Adams and Lloyd

Over the past few years, the topic of public key infrastructures has gained so much significance that a book about it was long overdue. In 2000, the time had come: Carlisle Adams and Steve Lloyd launched their book, *Understanding Public Key Infrastructure* on the market [AdaLlo]. This work provided a competent introduction to the topic, and is therefore a must for anyone interested in PKI. The book from Adams and Lloyd is still far from being a bible, but a start has been made. I hope that the book that you are now holding in your hands is a further enrichment to the literature on PKI.

31.2.2 Kahn: *The Codebreakers*

The Code-breakers is a book about the history of cryptography

If you want to be fully informed about the history of cryptography, the right for this is David Kahn's classic, **The Codebreakers** [Kahn]. On approximately 1000 pages, the historian Kahn has compiled almost everything that is known about the history of this fascinating science, although of necessity, modern cryptography does not get its fair share. In the revised edition that appeared in 1996, the history of the Enigma is also disclosed. Kahn's merit is that he was the first to show the enormous influence of cryptography on the history of man.

31.2.3 Menezes, van Oorschot, Vanstone: *Handbook of Applied Cryptography*

The Handbook of Applied Cryptography *is for those who wish to know the topic inside out*

The *Handbook of Applied Cryptography* is the book for those wanting to know the topic inside out [MeOoVa]. On over 700 pages, it describes the most important methods and protocols, backed up mathematically. The practical side of cryptography goes almost completely by the board, in favour of theorems and proofs. You should invest 75 euros in this book only if you have already worked though Schneier or if it is too unmathematical for you. Beginners should leave it well alone.

31.2.4 Nichols: *ICSA Guide to Cryptography*

The *ICSA Guide to Cryptography* by Randall K. Nichols is a book of more than 800 pages, which covers the fundamental principles and applications of cryptography [Nichol]. This extremely extensive piece of work cannot quite hold a candle to the archetypal *Applied Cryptography* by Bruce Schneier. It is, however, a lot more up to date (it was published in 1999) than Schneier's book, which was published in 1995 and has not been updated since. The *ICSA Guide to Cryptography*, which consists of over 500 pages, is the only reasonably up-to-date book covering the basics of cryptography.

Nichols looks at historical aspects

As regards content, Nichols goes into great detail about crypto systems that are interesting from a historical aspect. The topics of PKI, chip cards, and the implementation of cryptography are some of the other topics that are also dealt with. The *ICSA Guide to Cryptography* is without a doubt one of the benchmarks in the area of cryptography.

31.2.5 Schmeh: *Cryptography and Public Key Infrastucture on the Internet*

This book covers cryptography in practice

Cryptography and Public Key Infrastructure on the Internet is the book that you are now holding in your hands. I have already explained the special features of this book in Section 1.4: it was my aim to convey the uninspiring and sometimes downright complicated material clearly and in a way that is fun to read. As far as the content is concerned, this book is different from other books on cryptography primarily because it focuses consistently on the use of cryptography on the Internet.

It does not concentrate on the countless crypto methods, but on their practical use on the Internet. Even four years after the publication of the first edition, there is no other book that can come close to dealing with this important area so exhaustively.

31.2.6 Schneier: *Applied Cryptography*

Bruce Schneier's
Applied
Cryptography is
the absolute classic

Bruce Schneier's 800-page tome, **Applied Cryptography**, is the book to end all books in the field of cryptography [Schn96]. It is without a doubt one of the best books on this subject matter that I know of. It contains practically all the methods that are significant in cryptography (and many that are not), and irrespective of exceptions, everything is explained fairly well and is not only intelligible for crypto experts. Bruce Schneier's book is undoubtedly one of the things that I would take with me to a desert island.

With all this praise, I could not resist pointing out the weak points that the book naturally has. Therefore, here are some reasons why you are better off with another book (mine, for example):

- Schneier completed the work on his book at the end of 1995. As a result, this book is already out of date in many respects. No updating is envisaged though, as Schneier has himself stated that he is not planning a revised edition.

Schneier's book is
not for beginners

- Schneier's book is not suitable for beginners. It is simply so extensive that they would quickly lose the plot and would not see the wood for the trees. Furthermore, although the order in which topics are dealt with is logical, for a beginner it is rather confusing. For example, anyone wanting to work through a DES chapter of almost 40 pages first has to struggle through 265 other pages that deal with world-shaking topics such as mental poker or one-way accumulators. Before they finally meet the RSA topic, they will learn in detail how Khufu, LOKI, REDOC and numerous other more or less important symmetric encryption methods work before they finally meet the RSA method. As interesting as these things are – Schneier's book is not recommended for beginners.

- In Section 1.4, I gave you an outline of the merits of my book. Almost none of the points mentioned are looked at in any more detail by Schneier.

For the time being, Schneier's *Applied Cryptography* remains unsurpassed. It is a shame that no new edition is planned at present.

31.2.7 Singh: *The Codebook*

Singh's book
explains the history
of cryptography

The Codebook by Simon Singh is currently the most important popular scientific work about cryptography [Singh]. Singh, who has already found great success with *Fermat's Last Theorem*, tells the story of cryptography from the ancient Egyptians to today. A lot of emphasis is put on Enigma, and DES and RSA are given some attention. To a large extent, Singh is not strong on the mathematical and technical sides of cryptography. The ten cryptographic puzzles of increasing difficulty that the author puts at the end of the book are really interesting (www.4thestate.co.uk/ CipherChallenge). The last puzzle in particular has proved to be a tough one, and was only cracked for the first time one year after the book was published (you can read about this under www.codebook.org).

Without any hesitation, Singh's book can be recommended to people who are interested neither in cryptography nor in mathematics. The stories that it contains are fascinating for anyone interested in history or social topics. If you disregard a few sorry mistakes in the content – the author is quite clearly not a cryptographer – then it is also worth while for experts to read *The Codebook*. If you are not an expert cryptographer, Singh's book can be a lovely birthday present or can serve to provide topics of conversation at a party.

31.2.8 Smith: *Internet Cryptography*

Internet Cryptography is also rich in content

At present, **Internet Cryptography** by Richard E. Smith, which was published in 1997, is the book that comes closest to mine as regards content [Smith]. In this book, Smith describes the basics of cryptography and key management, as well as their incorporation into the TCP/IP protocols. No fewer than 80 pages are devoted to the topic of cryptography on the level of IP. Even SSL is dealt with adequately, and the discussion of the World Wide Web takes up 40 pages. On a more negative note, it could have gone into more depth with regard to the topic of e-mail encryption.

Internet Cryptography does not deal with many topics

Unfortunately, Smith does not say a word about almost any other area of cryptography. Crypto extensions for the protocols of DNS, SNMP and Telnet are conspicuous by their absence, and only a few sentences are devoted to PPP. Payment systems are also passed over, which is why SET and Ecash are not described. RADIUS, TACACS, Secure Shell, SecurID, Digest Authentication, PKIX and SPKI are other keywords that do not appear in the index. There is no chapter on applications, which is why even PGP – the most important crypto software there is – is only of minor importance here.

In short: the 350-page *Internet Cryptography* by Richard E. Smith is a good (again, in parts, this is out of date) book on the fundamentals of cryptography and their use in the protocols TCP and IP. However, the title, *Internet Cryptography* does not, deliver what it promises, as a large part of Internet cryptography is not dealt with.

31.2.9 Stinson: *Cryptography Theory and Practice*

Cryptography Theory and Practice is a sophisticated introduction

The title is deceiving. Stinson's work **Cryptography Theory and Practice** is undoubtedly a book on the theory, but not on the practice, of cryptography [Stinso]. In the style of a mathematical textbook, it contains records, proofs and exercises. *Cryptography Theory and Practice* is thus a sophisticated introduction for readers with a mathematical background. If you have worked through Schneier's book, then you should carry on with Stinson's book. But be careful: you will have to invest about 150 euros in this book.

31.2.10 Wobst: *Abenteuer Kryptologie*

Abenteuer Kryptologie is the best German book on the topic to date

Abenteuer Kryptologie by Reinhard Wobst is the best beginners' book on cryptography that has come out of Germany [Wobst]. In his book, Wobst gives a detailed introduction to cryptography, whereby he cannot deny that he has modelled it on Schneier's book. However, it is more up to date and cheaper than Schneier's book, and is certainly more suitable for beginners. Moreover, it is specific to the German market and also does not omit the history of cryptography. Nevertheless, as complete as it is, Wobst can still not hold a candle to *Applied Cryptography* by Schneier.

The points mentioned in Section 1.4 distinguish my book from Wobst's *Abenteuer Kryptologie*. While I tend to go into the practice of cryptography on the Internet and public key structures, Wobst focuses primarily on numerous cryptographic methods. Overlaps are therefore limited.

31.3 The ten most important Web sites

The Internet provides a wealth of information on cryptography

It is a known fact that one of the best sources of information on all topics related to the Internet is the Internet itself. Cryptography is no exception here: there are droves of crypto Web sites. So that you do not get lost in the complexity that is typical of the Internet, in the following I will introduce the ten crypto Web sites that I think are the most important.

31.3.1 Crypto-Gram

Crypto-Gram is a newsletter

If you always want to be on the ball about what is happening in the area of cryptography, then once a month you should take a look at the Web site of Bruce Schneier's company, Counterpane. On this site you will find the **Crypto-Gram**, a monthly newsletter which reports on what is happening in cryptography. As expected from Schneier, all the information is presented in a competent and critical way.

Address: `www.counterpane.com/crypto-gram.html`

31.3.2 Cryptography Research's Web site

Cryptography Research is the company owned by the well-known cryptographer Paul Kocher. On this company's Web site there are a number of interesting links on the topic of cryptography.

Address: `www.cryptography.com/resources/index.html`

31.3.3 IETF's Web site

The IETF provides interesting information

The Internet Engineering Task Force (IETF) plays a central role in the standardisation of cryptography on the Internet (see Section 10.1.2). The IETF's Web site is therefore an important source of information, as it provides a list of all standards, as well as standards that are planned. Since the IETF standards (RFCs) are normally quite readable, not only developers of the IETF site should pay a visit now and then. Most cryptography-relevant standards have, of course, arisen within the Security Working Area, to which you can easily click to from the start page.

> **Address**: `www.ietf.org`

31.3.4 Crypto Law Survey

Do you want to know where in the world cryptography is legally regulated and how? If so, then the Web site of the Dutchman Bert-Jaap Koops is the right place to go. This site has been up and running since 1996, and since then has accumulated quite a lot of information.

> **Address**: `cwis.kub.nl/~frw/people/koops/lawsurvy.htm`

31.3.5 PKI page

The best overview on the topic of PKI that is given on the Internet to date is provided by the **PKI page** by Stefan Kelm. From standards to products to Trust Centre services, this contains references to almost anything available is on the Internet on the topic of PKI – a must for anyone interested in PKI.

> **Address**: `www.pki-page.org`

31.3.6 Ron Rivest's Web site

Ron Rivest is not only one of the greatest living cryptographers, but also runs one of the best cryptographer sites on the Internet. Visually, it does not look much, and it contains hardly any content. But it does have a very extensive list of links. Whatever you are looking for on the topic of cryptography on the Net, you should start off on this site.

> **Address**: `theory.lcs.mit.edu/~rivest`

31.3.7 The Web site of RSA Laboratories

RSA Laboratories is the research centre of RSA Security. Its Web site contains information on some interesting topics and is therefore worth a visit. For example, there is detailed information on the PKCS standards, a cryptography FAQ, and the newsletter Cryptobytes.

> **Address**: `www.rsalabs.com`

31.3.8 Securityportal

The Securityportal is seen as the refuge for anyone interested in computer security. It contains up-to-date news, detailed technical contributions, and plenty of links. Cryptography is therefore only one of many topics; however, it is worth a visit for anyone interested in cryptography.

> **Address**: `www.securityportal.com`

The home page of Peter Centmann contains hundreds of intresting Cryptography and security links.

Address: www.cs.aukland.ac.nz/npgut001/

31.3.9 Security Server of the University of Siegen

The best general site on the topic of IT security in the German language is the Security Server of the University of Siegen. Here, you can also find many references to other German Web sites on the topic.

Address: www.uni-siegen.de/security

31.3.10 The Web site to this book

Of course, there is also a Web site to this book, which you should occasionally visit. As well as general information, it also contains a list of errata.

Address: www.dpunkt.de/buch/krypto.html

The last chapter

I hate quotations.
RALPH WALDO EMERSON

Key experience no. 32
There are some very interesting scenes for those interested in cryptography in the James Bond film, *Tomorrow Never Dies*: both facial recognition and fingerprint recognition make an appearance. In addition, the film also features a man-in-the-middle attack on the GPS system, which is carried out using a stolen encryption machine. Even an SSL encryption with 128 bits is mentioned and cracked. However, nothing is disclosed about how this attack actually works.

After several hundred pages on every conceivable aspect of cryptography, we finally come to the last chapter of the book. This chapter deals with the topics for which there was no space in the previous chapters, but which I do not want to withhold from you. In the course of this chapter, I will look at the greatest flops, the worst methods, the most popular misapprehensions, and the bitterest truths that cryptography has to offer. A good cryptographer also has to be informed about these.

32.1 The ten greatest crypto flops

There are also flops in cryptography Cryptographers take a lot of enjoyment from other people's misfortune. Therefore, let's first of all take a look at the numerous flops that have littered the path of cryptography in the past few years.

32.1.1 Weak GSM encryption

As one of the few original communication networks, the mobile radio communication system, GSM, supports encryption. To do so, the algorithms A3, A5 and A8 are used. As you have learnt in Sections 9.4.2 and 22.2, the quality of this method leaves a lot to be desired. If you consider the fact that because of the wide distribution of GSM, the A3, A5 and A8 algorithms are some of the most-used crypto algorithms avaiable, then unfortunately you have to count this as one of the greatest flops in crypto history.

32.1.2 Clipper

Clipper makes bugging possible

Clipper is a crypto chip that was developed in the mid-1990s for the encryption of telephone conversations (a comparable chip for computer data is called Capstone). The special thing about Clipper is that it uses an originally secret encryption algorithm called Skipjack. On the otherhand, the chip makes it possible to decrypt all messages that have been encrypted with this method by using an additional key (unit key). The unit key is different for every copy of the chip.

In accordance with the plans of the US government, Clipper was to become an everyday tool for telephone encryption in the USA. In the process, the unit key of a chip was to be broken down into two parts and kept by two independent authorities. With Clipper – as was envisaged by the US government – communication via the telephone in the USA would be secure from bugging. If bugging by a government authority should become necessary, this would still be possible using the unit key. Of course, the unit key should only be made available by the two independent authorities after an appropriate court decision.

Clipper did not win any confidence

So far, so good. Unfortunately, cryptographers, civil rights campaigners and a lot of other people did not think a lot of Clipper. An unfamiliar algorithm and a built-in government back door – nobody wanted to use something like this for secret data. A legal obligation for the use of Clipper was never planned, although an additional, secure encryption is also possible when Clipper is used. Nevertheless, the wide use of this chip would have meant a false sense of security, and would have prevented genuinely secure solutions from being distributed.

The opponents of Clipper obtained additional ammunition due to the fact that there was a weak point of the chip, discovered by the cryptographer, Matt Blaze. This means that there is a way that Alice and Bob can use the encryption function of Clipper without Uncle Sam being able to get anywhere with the unit key. All these failings finally persuaded the US government to back down. Today, Clipper is out of the question. The much-discussed chip has, however, effortlessly made it into the list of crypto flops.

32.1.3 Ecash

Ecash was supposed to realise cash

Unfortunately, the much-praised payment system Ecash (see Section 27.4.2) also has to be counted as one of the greatest flops in crypto history. Ecash was invented by the cryptographer David Chaum, and marketed by his company Digicash. Ecash was supposed to have been the most advanced crypto implementation on the market. The purpose of Ecash is to simulate cash by means of software alone. In contrast to almost every other payment system, Ecash is therefore completely anonymous and thus facilitates the perfect protection of data.

Unfortunately, Ecash was a flop in practice and the company has since disappeared from the market. Its failure was certainly due to the fact that so far, Internet payment systems have generally found it almost impossible to gain a foothold. In addition, despite its simple operation, Ecash proved to be too complicated in practice. Technical problems were reported constantly. In any case, hardly any of its customers understood how it works. So, yet again, a technically brilliant solution had to let its less advanced competitors go first. Shame.

32.1.4 The stolen Enigma

The Enigma theft was not an April fool's joke

On 1 April 2000, a burglar stole an Enigma from a display case in the museum in Bletchley Park near London (see Section 31.1.6). What at first seemed to be an April fool's joke turned out to be deadly serious, as it became clear that the thief was demanding a £25,000 ransom for the machine. The museum was prepared to pay this amount, but several ultimatums were involved. The kidnapping of the Enigma came to a surprising end when, in October 2000, a BBC presenter received the stolen machine by post. In November 2000, a suspect was finally arrested.

32.1.5 FEAL

FEAL was supposed to be a competitor of DES

In 1987, two Japanese cryptographers published an encryption algorithm called FEAL (Fast Encryption Algorithm). They intended FEAL to be an alternative to DES. The 56 key bits of DES were already seen as too few, and it bothered many people that as a software implementation, DES is quite slow. FEAL was supposed to overcome these weaknesses. The method is similar to DES, that it has only four rounds and uses operations that are particularly fast for a software realisation. Moreover, the FEAL key length is 64 bits.

Did this mean that, ten years after DES had been made public, an alternative had been found that could be taken seriously? The answer to this question is no, because while the cryptographers at DES still had their work cut out, they found some weak points in FEAL, just like holes in Swiss cheese. The first weaknesses were uncovered just a few months after the method had been made public. The developers induced other successful attacks, first increasing the number of rounds to eight, later to 16, and finally to a variable number (normally greater than 16). The best attack on FEAL using four rounds that is known to date is a known-plaintext attack with only five blocks of text [Schn96]. No other method from the crypto scene is quite so weak.

FEAL has a number of gaps in security

FEAL showed that flops can be made famous. In his book, Bruce Schneier made the following comment about FEAL: 'Whenever someone discovers a new cryptanalytic attack, he always seems to try it out on FEAL first.' In Menezes, van Oorschot und Vanstone's benchmark on cryptography, they even acknowledge the following: 'FEAL ... played a critical role in the development and refinement of various advanced cryptanalytic techniques.'

32.1.6 Magenta

Magenta was the most unsuccessful AES candidate

Magenta is not only the colour of Deutsche Telekom (Germany's telecommunications service), but also the name of a symmetric encryption algorithm that was developed by two of this company's employees. Being the only German method, Magenta was put forward as a candidate for the new encryption standard, AES (see Section 5.3). This was not a success: without exception, Magenta left a bad impression. Of all 15 methods, it showed the largest gaps in security, and was also one of the slowest algorithms. If there had been a ranking list, Magenta would certainly have been in the last place. But at least the developers still had the Olympic concept as a consolation: it is the taking part that counts.

32.1.7 PCT

PCT did not win through against SSL

In Chapter 24, you learnt that SSL (Secure Socket Layer) is one of the most successful crypto protocols. SSL was originally developed by Netscape and then standardised as TLS (Transport Layer Security) by the IETF. However, Microsoft wanted its own standard to catch on. It developed PCT (Private Communications Technology), which was not very different from SSL but was not compatible with it. PCT turned out to be a flop, though. While the whole world currently uses SSL, PCT has practically disappeared from the scene.

32.1.8 The Russian attack on McEliece

No one understood this attack

The McEliece method is a public key encryption algorithm that is rarely used. Nevertheless, the method, which came out in 1978, is quite fast and (in contrast to many others) has never been cracked. Therefore, it was seen as quite a sensation when, at Europcrypt 1991, two unknown Russians presented an attack with which they had apparently cracked the McEliece method [Schn96]. The only snag was that no one could make any sense of the lecture that was given by the two Russians, nor could anyone follow their reasoning. Anyone who wanted to obtain more detailed information had to struggle through the Russian texts. It slowly dawned on people that the supposed attack on McEliece was no more than hot air. The McEliece method is again seen as secure, and nothing more has been heard of the Russian cryptographers.

32.1.9 Skipjack

Skipjack contains a theoretical weakness

Skipjack is the symmetric encryption algorithm that is used by the encryption chip, Clipper (see Section 32.1.2). Clipper is already one of the greatest crypto flops, but Skipjack is a source of further irritation. When the functionality of the method was published in 1998, the cryptographers Biham, Biryukov and Shamir discovered a theoretical weak point in this method (see Section 5.2.4). For the first time, there was doubt about the competence of the NSA.

32.2.10 S-HTTP

S-HTTP has never caught on

S-HTTP is a crypto protocol that was supposed to facilitate the use of encryption on the World Wide Web on an application level. The data formats that were supported leave nothing to be desired: the format specified in PKCS#7 is supported in the same way as the formats of the standards PGP and PEM (which are normally used for e-mails). For symmetric encryption, DES, Triple DES, IDEA or RC4 can be used according to individual preference. Key management can be carried out either symmetrically over Kerebos or asymmetrically by RSA, whereby in addition to X.509 certificates, PKCS#6 certificates are also supported. Digital signatures are possible with RSA and DSA, whereby MD2, MD5 or SHA is available as a hash function.

So far, so good. Unfortunately, the cryptographic heavyweight called S-HTTP never caught on. Instead, SSL became the measure of all things to do with cryptography. Another example of an attempt that failed on account of its complexity.

32.2 Ten indications of snake oil

Cryptography looks easier than it is

In all sciences there are amateurs, charlatans and know-alls who regale the world with useless theories (for a critical analysis of such phenomena I recommend you visit the Web site of the CSIOP (Committee for the Scientific Investigation of Claims of the Paranormal), www.gwup.org). However, we can see from several examples that cryptography seems to attract a particularly large number of pseudo-scientific adventurers. The encryption of data simply fascinates many people, and also looks a lot easier than it actually is. Unfortunately, as well as a number of good methods and implementations, there is also a lot of cryptographic amateurishness.

Bad cryptography is described as snake oil

The term **snake oil** is often used for bad cryptography. This term comes from the USA where it was originally used to describe a miracle cure. These days, snake oil can confidently be seen as a cryptographic technical term, as there is enough opportunity to use it. Owing to the increasing popularity of scientific cryptography, the flow of snake oil has eased off considerably in recent years – however, an all-clear is still out of the question.

Fortunately, it is normally quite easy to 'smell' snake oil. The following section gives some typical 'smells'. The methods and implementations introduced in this book, such as PGP, DES, RC4 and IDEA, are, of course, not snake oil, but rather approved, or at least promising, methods. In Section 32.3 there are some good examples of snake oil.

32.2.1 Great promises

Snake oil stands out thanks to great promises

Snake oil developers are not usually economical with great promises. If a method of implementation is described as 'revolutionary', 'best method in the world' or 'uncrackable', snake oil is normally hidden behind these promises.

32.2.2 Secretiveness

In the military and secret services field, there are many completely secret crypto methods, but there are also a few exceptions: the functionality of a good method is known publicly. Otherwise, there is the suspicion of snake oil, since anyone who keeps a method secret usually has good reasons for doing so (because it is not secure).

32.2.3 Exaggerated key lengths

Key lengths in excess of 256 are unsuitable for symmetrical methods

As you know from Chapter 1, key lengths of 128 bits cannot be cracked by brute force key searches in the case of symmetrical methods. Anyone using 256 bits has to ward off the suspicion of paranoia. If, on the other hand, a method uses several thousand or even a million bits (these do exist), there is acute suspicion of snake oil – because obviously the developer does not understand much about cryptography. It goes without saying that a method with extreme key lengths need not necessarily be secure. Often enough, apparently exaggerated key lengths have a simple explanation anyway: the key length is, in fact, a lot shorter, but it was not at all clear to the developer what the key actually is.

32.2.4 Complexity

Complexity does not necessarily mean security

A good encryption algorithm is as simple as possible and as complicated as necessary. Methods such as DES, IDEA and RC4 therefore have such great success not least because they are comparatively simple. As a result, the possible targets for an attack are obvious, and the possible weak points are discovered more quickly. The implementation is also easier and less prone to faults because of this. On the other hand, those producing snake oil often tend to make their methods as complicated as possible – in the vain hope that complexity means security. In contrast, good cryptographers stick to the motto: 'keep it simple'.

32.2.5 A lack of discussion among experts

A good crypto method is tested rigorously

A crypto method is only a good crypto method if unbiased experts have tested it rigorously and have not run into any weaknesses that could be exploited. Snake oil producers, on the other hand, do not normally carry out this kind of testing, which can be done by publishing the method in professional journals or bringing them to attention during professional conferences. The powers that be have obviously decided that such methods are good.

32.2.6 Talking subjectively

Descriptions of snake oil often begin with some kind of subjective statement about the situation of cryptography. In these statements, people normally use false claims to write off existing methods as being unsuitable, and present their own solution as the new measure of all things. Even the description of the methods is approached subjectively: cryptographic terms are used incorrectly and new ones are introduced at will. As a reader of this book, you will no longer be taken in by such subjective talk.

32.2.7 Missing details on known attacks

A good method must be protected against known attacks

As you have learnt from reading this book, there are various attacks with which a cryptanalyst can work. These include differential and linear cryptanalysis, reaction attacks, and brute force key search. Many methods also have weak keys. The developer of a good crypto method knows of these possible attacks and secures his or her algorithms against them. Producers of snake oil, on the other hand, often know nothing about the attacks mentioned or implicitly assume that they will not work against their methods.

32.3.8 Quantum leaps

New methods are normally only slightly better than the existing ones

There are already many good crypto methods. Newcomers are therefore only slightly better than existing methods. On the other hand, if a new method is hailed as being a quantum leap from the methods that have existed up to now, there is a suspicion of snake oil. In particular, it is highly unlikely that a crypto newcomer will discover something that revolutionises cryptography.

32.2.9 A lack of practicality

A good method must be practical

A crypto method must be not only secure, but also practical. An encryption procedure should therefore not take too long, and, decryption should be as simple as encryption (which is precisely what is often forgotten in the case of snake oil). Since chip cards are often used for encryption, the program code of a method should take up as little memory as possible. A lack of practicality is a typical feature of snake oil.

32.2.10 Origin

Of course, small companies and individuals that are not known in the crypto scene can also develop good crypto products and methods. Nevertheless, it is becoming more and more apparent that there is a correlation between professionalism in the associated field and the quality of a crypto solution. Products that are offered by companies that are run from someone's garage, and displayed on Web sites that are obviously set up by people at home, or in primitive catalogues, normally (though not always) have to be handled with kid gloves. The same applies to methods that have been developed by an unknown person, who belongs neither to a larger company nor to a university.

32.3 Ten examples of snake oil

There are numerous examples of snake oil

The following sections show that the ten criteria for snake oil have not just been plucked out of thin air. I will introduce ten examples of crypto products and crypto methods that have earned the label of snake oil. I can recommend [Schn99] as a good source of information on this topic.

32.3.1 Encryption by non-existence

Cryptec is a classic example of snake oil

In November 1999, a company with its headquarters just outside Berlin produced a rare pearl of snake oil. In a report that I received via the German crypto mailing list, it announced a 'completely newly developed security product for the information society of the 21st century' called 'Cryptec'. Cryptec uses an 'encryption system ..., which completely protects man as an individual, as well as his work'. The function of this evolutionary encryption system is described as follows: 'The information is first encrypted using the new Cryptec technology and the amount of data is divided unequally. Part of this amount of data is sent directly to the addressee. After encryption, the other part of the information is compressed a million times and sent to a separate server. From here on, this second part of the information is sent to the desired addressee. Only this addressee can decode the information. Due to the Cryptec technology, the encrypted information does not show any surface structure. Unauthorised people can thus not infer anything about the original text.' Even with this pseudo-cryptographic drivel, the warning bells ring for every cryptographer. But the best is yet to come: 'The information is protected against access by a third party by the fact that it no longer exists.' The following note is also interesting: 'In the process, the authorised user does not even know where the information has gone.'

As a convincing – in their opinion – example, the manufacturer then shows off with a massive key length: this amounts to 57,000 bits and is larger than anything that is in use at the moment.

The whole Cryptec report smells so pungently of snake oil that it can only be a hoax. A call to the providing company did not confirm, this though. The lady who took my call tried to convince me that it was, in fact, a first-class product. However, she could not tell me anything about the technique that was behind it and promised me that one of her colleagues would call me back. To this day, I am still waiting.

32.3.2 A particularly bad RSA attack

Now and then, a seemingly ingenious method in cryptanalysis also turns out to be snake oil on closer inspection. In December 1998, someone who subscribed to the German crypto mailing list section pointed out a German Web site on which an attack on the RSA method was described. No more than a few lines were required to explain this attack. Had the author – a man who was unknown on the crypto scene – actually made the most important cryptographic discovery of the past two decades?

RSA by brute force was not a new thing   On closer inspection, you have to grant the described attack the following: it works. However, there is a catch: the attack means that you have to try every feasible key, one after the other. In other words, this means that the said attack is nothing more than a brute force key search. With the 1,024 key bits that are normally used for RSA at present, this attack has undoubtedly earned the gold star for particularly bad attacks.

32.3.3 Incremental base shift algorithms

Nobody knows the incremental base shift algorithms   Another typical example of snake oil is the family of incremental base shift algorithms. A member of this family is used by a product called 'Encryptor 4.0', whose manufacturing company, Comotex, invented this revolutionary form of encryption. It is just a shame that there are still no cryptographers who have ever heard about incremental base shift algorithms and that nothing is known about their exact functionality. Nevertheless, this does have an advantage: 'Due to this unique algorithm', boasts the manufacturer on the Web site, 'we are in the position to satisfy the US export regulations for crypto technology and at the same time give you the highest possible security.' The fact that it was only possible – at least when these lines were written – to satisfy the US export regulations with comparatively poor crypto products escaped the attention of the manufacturer.

32.3.4 The virtual encryption matrix

A truly classic example of snake oil comes from the company Meganet. In accordance with the details on the Web site, its encryption system, called VME, uses *A million key bits arouses suspicion*   a so-called virtual encryption matrix; so far no one knows what is hidden behind it. At any rate, the key length, which is somewhere in the region of one million bits, arouses suspicion – you should again note here that conventional systems work with around 40 to 160 bits. This will then still 'prove' that VME is just as secure as the one-time-pad. If you believe that, you'll believe anything.

32.3.5 Enigma instead of PGP

The Enigma was supposed to have made a comeback as crypto software

'Professional Cryptography Software' was the promise from the American company Enigma & Co., on their Web site in 1996. The company did not make any secret of the functionality of their encryption software. As the name suggests, this uses a rotor cipher based on the Enigma (see Section 4.4.2). Although this form of encryption had already become insecure 60 years before, Enigma & Co. extolled their product for security-relevant data (this would obviously have been a source for amusement for Enigma fans). Under these circumstances, the Enigma should also be described as snake oil.

32.3.6 The solved PNP problem

In theoretical computer science, the set of problems with which an algorithm can be solved in polynomial time is described as P. Since these kinds of algorithms are comparatively performant, it is also possible to describe P as the set of actually solvable problems. The set of problems with which an algorithm can be solved in non-polynomial time is, described as NP. Problems that lie in NP, but not in P, are not actually solvable.

The solution of the PNP problem would have a huge effect on asymmetrical cryptography

All the knowledge that has been gained in the past decade indicates that there are problems that lie in NP, but not in P. The factorisation problem and the discrete logarithm problem (both of which you know from Section 6.2) are candidates for this. However, no one has yet proved that there are NP problems that do not lie in P. Therefore, theoretical by $P=NP$ could be valid. This would then automatically mean that all crypto systems based on the factorisation problem or on the discrete logarithm problem would be broken – RSA, DSA and Diffie–Hellman would also be particularly affected by this.

The PNP solution proved to be snake oil

In October 2000, several Internet sites reported that a Ukrainian mathematician had proved $P=NP$. Did this mean that RSA, DSA and Diffie–Hellman were all suddenly cracked? And this by an unknown scientist who had no knowledge of cryptography? On closer examination, the 'proof' quickly turned out to be snake oil. In a newsgroup, a mathematician described the work of the Ukrainian as 'total chaos' and added: 'That is about as much proof of $P=NP$ as my telephone book would be.'

32.3.7 The L5 algorithm

L5 does not rely on tried and tested methods

The US company Jaws Technology achieved a certain notoriety on the snake oil scene. The encryption solution from this company is described on its own Web site using the words: 'The world's strongest commercially available software of its kind'. This uses an algorithm called L5, about which nothing is known. However, the key length of 4096 bits indicates that L5 has little in common with approved symmetric encryption methods.

32.3.8 A new age dawns

The snake oil contributions from Germany include a piece of software called Best Possible Privacy (BPP). What is particularly infuriating about this odd product is that even the otherwise respectable news magazine, *Der Spiegel*, was taken in by the completely subjective PR work of the manufacturer, Ciphers.de [Spie00].

Best Possible Privacy lacked any respectability

The first lines on the Web site of the manufacturers of BPP lacked any respectability. There the emergence of BPP was heralded as 'The dawning of a new age'. The method used by BPP is described in all seriousness as 'the first 10,240 bit cipher' (the final zero is not a printing error). These details are supplemented by the unavoidable reference to the usual methods of the present day that normally only use 128 bits. What follows is a completely subjective description of the supposed weak points in current crypto methods. According to this, it is 'probable that all the encryption methods that are supported by the NSA contain a type of short cut' – what methods are meant by this is not mentioned. It also says, with regard to the encryption methods that are normally used today: 'It is generally claimed that long keys excessively slow down encryption methods.' This is, of course, not so. With DES, for example, it is possible to use an independent 48-bit subkey for each of the rounds, which in fact accelerates the method a little (this is similar to what happens with other symmetrical methods).

'The dawning of a new age' is still to come

The answer to the oh-so-poor crypto methods of the past is, of course, Best Possible Privacy. And at least its functionality is described on the Web site (the method is, of course, quite complicated). According to my understanding, a pseudo-random sequence is created using a password, from which a program code is generated. This program code manipulates a data memory that is also filled pseudo-randomly on the basis of a password. Its content is XOR'ed with the plaintext, which produces the ciphertext. The program code is also dependent on previously installed program fragments (in the process, this can be existing methods such as DES and IDEA). The whole method is normally described as being a 'polymorphic algorithm'. Why this is referred to as 'The dawning of a new age' is still not entirely clear to me.

It is unnecessary to mention that the 'polymorphic algorithm' belongs to the world of snake oil. Thus it does not make any sense to talk about a 10,240-bit key if, in reality, the key is formed from two passwords. Also, the developers have obviously not considered it necessary to have their method scrutinised by experienced cryptographers – I would therefore not put any money on the security of BPP. It is also clear that the security of this method depends strongly on the program fragments – however, since these are completely variable, a general statement about the security of BPP is impossible.

BPP is not practical

Apart from this, the method does not seem to me to be particularly practical, because only after executing the randomly generated code can the encryption begin. Even if the method is supposed to be secure (which is still to be proved), I can see no reason to give it preference over approved algorithms.

As the icing on the cake, on the Web site we are led to believe that, thanks to its revolutionary high security, BBP has been implemented by the German authorities

(BPP is allegedly supposed to be classified as a state secret). Don't let anyone tell you that cryptography is no laughing matter.

32.3.9 World-class encryption

The company GenioUSA glorifies its product with the title 'world-class secret key encryption'. However, the explanations on the Web site tend to suggest world-class snake oil instead. GenioUSA rejects the use of asymmetrical cryptography, because this cracks faster than brute force key searches and therefore requires particularly long keys – a nice rationale, which can be worked out by those with little expertise.

32.3.10 The most secure algorithm in the world

SenCrypt from ION Marketing was described on the company's Web site as 'the most secure cryptographic algorithm known to mankind'. How the company reached this verdict remains a mystery.

32.4 Ten popular crypto misapprehensions

As in other in areas of knowledge, there are also numerous popular misapprehensions in cryptography that do not seem to have been eradicated. I will introduce the ten most important of these in the following sections.

32.4.1 Double DES is not twice as secure

Double DES is twice as secure In Section 5.2.2, you learnt that double DES is not as secure as you would first expect. Many junior cryptographers draw the wrong conclusion that double DES is not twice as secure as DES. This is not so. It is true that double DES is not 2^{56} times as secure as single DES – this is what you would initially expect, but it is not the case in the instance of a possible meet-in-the-middle attack. There is, nevertheless, double the security. Basically, this is a misapprehension in itself, because this double security only applies if attacker Mallory has an enormous memory capacity which he can access without any delay. Since this is not realistic, double DES offers far more than double security. Double DES is thus better than its reputation.

32.4.2 DES has a key length of 64 bits

In reality, the specification of the most well-known encryption algorithm, DES (Data Encryption Standard), prescribes a key length of 64 bits. As you have learnt from Section 5.1, eight of these 64 bits are used to form a checksum and cannot therefore be chosen freely. The actual key length of DES is therefore 56 bits.

32.4.3 The signature law is a must-regulation

Nobody has to adhere to the signature law The German signature law of 1997 is a genuine law (see Section 29.2). However, this does not mean that anyone has to adhere to it. The signature law is a pure can-regulation. Anyone wanting to stick to it can do so, and will possibly benefit from doing so. Anyone not sticking to it has nothing to fear, apart from not being able to make use of certain advantages. The signature law is thus primarily a standard that could have been developed in a similar form by a standardisation committee. In any case, in the current legal climate, nobody can be charged with violating the signature law.

32.4.4 A brute force key search is always possible

Sufficiently long keys cannot be cracked

'If only enough computers were connected over the Internet', you often hear, 'it would also be possible to crack the longest key by means of a brute force key search.' This is, of course, a classical misapprehension, due to the fact that many people have a false idea of large numbers. As you can easily check, the effort for a brute force key search doubles with every additional key bit. With a large amount of effort and by using thousands of computers, today it is possible to crack a 56-bit DES encryption in one day (see Section 5.1.5). This means that a 128-bit encryption would require 2^{72} days. This is approximately 10^{19} years and thus approximately 10^{10} times the amount the time since the big bang. Even if computer technology continues to improve, it will be a long time before we experience such a fast brute force key search on a 128-bit encryption. Not to mention 256 bits.

32.4.5 A digital signature is just a signature that has been scanned in

A digital signature is not just a signature that has been scanned in

As you learnt in Chapter 7, a digital signature is the result of an arithmetic procedure in which a private key is deployed. However, a digital signature does not have the slightest thing to do with a signature that has been scanned in. Digital signatures can replace handwritten signatures in many cases. However, they only do this if the copy of a signature is not required.

32.4.6 PGP is an encryption algorithm

You will sometimes read that 'the most well-known encryption methods are DES, RSA and PGP'. Of course, this is incorrect, as PGP is not a method but a piece of software (see Section 26.3). However, PGP uses encryption methods, for example RSA, IDEA and Triple DES.

32.4.7 Random numbers are easy to generate

Random numbers are difficult

Our life is so dedicated to chance that it is difficult to imagine that the generation of random numbers is a difficult thing to do. However, this is the case, especially in cryptography. As you read in Chapter 9, it is anything but easy to produce a sequence of numbers that cannot be guessed even with the greatest amount of effort. Under no circumstances should we leave chance to chance.

32.4.8 Asymmetric is better than symmetric

Asymmetric and symmetric complement one another

Cryptographic lay people often have the view that asymmetrical methods are 'better' than symmetrical ones. This view stems from the fact that asymmetrical methods were only discovered much later and are more mathematically advanced than symmetrical ones. At first glance, asymmetrical methods can also do everything that symmetrical ones can do. On closer examination, asymmetrical methods are neither 'better' nor 'worse' than symmetrical ones. They are simply different, and both have their own value. As you saw in Section 6.7, symmetrical and asymmetrical methods complement one another well.

32.4.9 RSA and DSA are related

RSA and DSA are not related
The two most important signature methods are called RSA and DSA. Time and time again, the two similar names lead to the assumption that the methods are in some way related to one another. This is not true: the two methods are very different from one another in the way that they function, and were also developed by different people. The fact that the similarity in the names has nothing to do with being related to one another is shown as soon as you write out the abbreviations. RSA stands for 'Rivest–Shamir–Adleman' (these are the names of the inventors), while DSA quite mundanely stands for 'Digital Signature Algorithm'. The similarity ends here.

32.4.10 Iris recognition is the same as retina recognition

Iris recognition and retina recognition are often mixed up
The most widespread misapprehension within biometries (see Section 13.3.2) is without a doubt the view that iris recognition and retina recognition are the same thing. Every biologist will confirm that this is not true: the iris is the coloured rim around the pupil of the human eye, while the retina is the back wall of the eye. Both the iris and the retina of a human are as invariable and as distinctive as a fingerprint and therefore can be used to identify a person. Iris and retina recognition conseqently play an important part in biometries. Despite this, the two techniques must be kept apart: iris recognition can be carried out using a sharp photograph. In the case of retina recognition, on the other hand, a photograph of the back wall of the eye is required, which can only be taken using a special device. However, since only a few people feel the inclination to look into a tube that bears a small resemblance to the barrel of a revolver in order to have a photo of their retina taken, I see the future for iris recognition looking a lot brighter. In any event, you should by no means confuse the two techniques – however, this does happen quite often.

32.5 Murphy's ten laws of cryptography

Murphy's laws tell the truth
To conclude, I would like to tell you the truth about the topic of cryptography. Nothing is more significant than Murphy's ten laws of cryptography.

32.5.1 Mallory is always cleverer than you think

Mallory is always cleverer than you think. All the following laws are special instances of this law, whose scope and application runs through the whole range of laws. Only Murphy's 10th law of cryptography is a strong as this one.

32.5.2 Crypto methods do not have to be kept secret

It is impossible to keep crypto methods secret

It is impossible to keep a crypto method secret. Consequently, you should not try to do so.

32.5.3 New crypto methods are always prone to errors

New crypto methods are always prone to errors. Therefore, only trust methods that have been well tested.

32.5.4 Self-developed methods are prone to errors

Self-developed methods are prone to errors

Self-developed crypto methods are always prone to errors. This is already shown in the third law, but is nevertheless disregarded time and time again.

32.5.5 Keys are compromised

An absolutely secure crypto system is cracked by compromised keys. The work of a cryptanalyst is made considerably easier if a user's key comes into his or her possession because of the user's carelessness.

32.5.6 Random numbers are not random

Random numbers are never as random as you think: nothing in this world really happens by chance, which is why there are no random numbers.

32.5.7 Trust nothing and nobody

You should not trust anyone

Trust nothing and nobody. This law is particularly harsh, since there is always somebody you have to trust in cryptography.

32.5.8 Users are lazy

Users are infinitely lazy. Users are basically too lazy to use a crypto system.

32.5.9 Cryptography is implemented erroneously

In principle, crypto programs are implemented erroneously. Even the most powerful algorithms do not faze Mallory if they are integrated into a faulty program.

32.5.10 Cryptography is pointless

Cryptography is a pointless science

Cryptography is a pointless science. It does not matter how securely a message is encrypted, there are always ways of getting round it. It is all just a question of effort, unscrupulousness, and bribes. On this note I want to conclude my book. I hope that you had fun reading it.

List of abbreviations

AES	Advanced Encryption Standard (symmetrical encryption method)
AH	Authentication Header (component of IPSec)
ARP	Address Resolution Protocol
BSI	Bundesamt für Sicherheit in der Informationstechnik (German equivalent of the NSA)
CA	Certification Authority (component of a PKI)
CAST	Carlisle Adams, Stafford Tavares (symmetrical encryption method)
CBC	Cipher Block Chaining Mode (operating mode for block ciphers)
CCC	Chaos Computer Club
CDP	CRL Distribution Point (distribution point for revocation lists in a PKI)
CDSA	Common Data Security Architecture (crypto interface)
CHAP	Challenge Handshake Protocol (authentication protocol)
CMP	Certificate Management Protocol
CPS	Certification Practice Statement
CRAM	Challenge Response Authentication Mechanism (authentication protocol)
CRL	Certificate Revocation List
CRT	Certificate Revocation Tree
CSMA/CD	Carrier-Sense Multiple Access/Collision Detection (functional principle e.g. in the case of Ethernet)
CSP	Cryptographic Service Provider
CSSM	Common Security Services Manager (part of CDSA)
DAP	Directory Access Protocol (protocol the access to directory services)
DES	Data Encryption Standard (symmetrical encryption method)
DFN-PCA	PCA of the German research network

DIR	Directory Service (component of a PKI)
DLSS	Discrete Logarithm Signature System (signature method based on elliptic curves)
DNS	Domain Name System (directory service for IP addresses)
DNSSec	Secure DNS
DSA	Digital Signature Algorithm (digital signature method)
DSS	Digital Signature Standard (standard for digital signatures)
EAP	Extensible Authentication Protocol (authentication method)
ECB	Electronic Codebook Mode (operating mode for block ciphers)
ECC	Elliptic Curve Cryptosystem (crypto system based on elliptic curves)
ECDH	Elliptic Curve Diffie–Hellman (Diffie–Hellman method based on elliptic curves)
ECDSA	Elliptic Curve DSA (DSA on the basis of elliptic curves)
ESP	Encapsulated Security Payload (component of IPSec)
FAR	False Acceptance Rate
FEAL	Fast Encryption Algorithm (symmetric encryption method)
FRR	False Rejection Rate
GSS-API	Generic Security Services API (crypto interface)
HBCI	Home-Banking Computer Interface (home-banking protocol)
HPC	Hasty Pudding Cipher (symmetric encryption method)
HSM	Hardware Security Module (hardware module for saving private keys)
HTTP	Hypertext Transfer Protocol (protocol of OSI Layer 7)
HTTPS	HTTP Secure (HTTP via SSL)
IACR	International Association for Cryptologic Research
IDEA	International Data Encryption Algorithm (encryption method)
IETF	Internet Engineering Task Force (Internet standardisation committee)
IKE	Internet Key Exchange (key exchange protocol for IPSec)
IMAP	Internet Message Access Protocol (protocol for the retrieval and control of messages)
IP	Internet Protocol (protocol of OSI Layer 3)
IPSec	Secure Internet Protocol (crypto protocol of OSI Layer 3)
IPv6	Internet Protocol Version 6 (new IP version)
ISAKMP	Internet Security Association and Key Management Protocol (management protocol for IPSec)

ISDN	Integrated Services Digital Network
ISIS	International Signature Interoperability Specification (PKI standard)
IuKDG	Information and communication services act
IV	Initialisation vector
LAN	Local Area Network (local network)
LDAP	Lightweight Directory Access Protocol (protocol for access to directory services)
LFSR	Linear Feedback Shift Register
LRA	Local Registration Authority (local registration component of a PKI)
L2F	Layer 2 Forwarding Protocol (tunnel protocol for layer 2)
L2TP	Layer 2 Tunneling Protocol (tunnel protocol for layer 2)
MAC	Message Authentity Check
MDC	Message Digest Code (cryptographic hash function)
MD4	Message Digest 4 (cryptographic hash function)
MD5	Message Digest 5 (cryptographic hash function)
MIC	Message Integrity Check
MIME	Multipurpose Internet Mail Enhancement
MS-CHAP	Microsoft Challenge-Handshake Protocol (authentication protocol)
NDS	Novell Directory Service (directory service product of the company Novell)
NSA	National Security Agency (US secret service authority)
OCSP	Online Certificate Status Protocol
OFB	Output Feedback Mode (operating mode for block ciphers)
OID	Object Identifier
OTP	One Time Password
PCA	Policy Certification Authority (primary certification authority, component of a PKI)
PCT	Private Communication Technology (crypto protocol for OSI Layer 4)
PEM	Privacy Enhancement for Internet Electronic Mail (e-mail encryption standard)
PFS	Perfect Forward Secrecy
PKCS	Public Key Cryptography Standard (family of crypto standards)
PKI	Public Key infrastructure
PKIX	Public Key Infrastructure X.509 (PKI standard)

POP	Post Office Protocol (protocol for the retrieval of e-mails)
POP	Point of Presence
PPP	Point-to-Point Protocol (protocol of OSI Layer 2)
PPTP	Point-to-Point Tunneling Protocol (tunnel protocol for Layer 2)
PSE	Personal Security Environment (storage entity for private keys)
RA	Registration Authority (registration authority, component of a PKI)
RADIUS	Remote Access Dial-in User Service (authentication protocol)
RC2/4/5/6	Rivest Cipher 2/4/5/6 (symmetrical encryption method)
REC	Recovery authority (component of a PKI)
RegTP	Regulation authority of telecommunication and post
REV	Revocation authority (component of a PKI)
RFC	Request for Comment (publication from the IETF, some RFCs are standards)
RSA	Rivest, Shamir, Adleman (asymmetrical encryption and signature method)
SASL	Simple Authentication and Security Layer (crypto protocol for OSI Layer 7)
SCVP	Simple Certificate Validation Protocol
SDSI	Simple Distributed Security Infrastructure
SET	Secure Electronic Transactions (protocol for the transfer of credit card data)
SHA-1	Secure Hash Algorithm (cryptographic hash function)
SKIP	Simple Key Management Protocol
SMTP	Simple Mail Transfer Protocol (e-mail protocol)
SNC	Secure Network Communication (SAP-R/3 security interface)
SNMP	Simple Network Management Protocol
SPI	Service Provider Interface
SPKI	Simple Public Key Infrastructure (PKI standard)
SSF	Secure Store and Forward (SAP-R/3 security interface)
SSH	Secure Shell (crypto protocol for OSI Layer 7)
SSL	Secure Socket Layer (crypto protocol for OSI Layer 4)
SSO	Single Sign-on
S/MIME	Secure MIME (e-mail encryption standard)
TAN	Transaction Number (one-time password)

TCP	Transmission Control Protocol (protocol of OSI Layer 4)
TLS	Transport Layer Security (crypto protocol for OSI Layer 4)
TSS	TimeStamp Service (component of a PKI)
TTP	Trusted Third Party
RIS	Reliable IT systems (IT security congress)
VPN	Virtual Private Network
WAN	Wide Area Network
WTLS	Wireless Transport Layer Security (crypto protocol for mobile telephone network)
W3C	World Wide Web Consortium

Bibliography

B

[AdaLlo] Carlisle Adams, Steve Lloyd: *Understanding Public Key Infrastructure.* Macmillan Technical Pub, London, 1999

[Anonym] Anonymous: *Hacker's Guide Sicherheit im Internet und im lokalen Netz.* Markt und Technik, Haar, 1999

[Ashbou] Julian Ashbourn: *Biometrics: Advanced Identify Verification: The Complete Guide.* Springer-Verlag, Berlin, 2000

[BaDeFW] Dirk Balfanz, Drew Dean, Edward W. Felten, Dan S. Wallach: *Web Spoofing: An Internet Con Game.* 20th National Information Systems Security Conference, Baltimore, 1997

[BaHaJK] Backslash, Hack-Tic, Jansen & Janssen, Keine Panik: *Der kleine Abhörratgeber.* Edition ID-Archiv, Berlin, 1994

[BaKeRu] Andreas Bartholome, Josef Rung, Hans Kern: *Zahlentheorie für Einsteiger.* Vieweg, Wiesbaden, 2001

[Bauer] Friedrich L. Bauer: *Kryptologie Methoden und Maximen.* Springer-Verlag, Berlin, 1994

[BelChe] Steven M. Bellovin, William R. Cheswick: *Firewall and Internet Security.* Addison-Wesley, New York, 1994

[Belke] Marcus Belke: *Die Digitale Signatur kurz vor dem Start.* Dat enschutz und Datensicherheit 2/2000

[BeScWo] Albrecht Beutelspacher, Jörg Schwenk, Klaus-Dieter Wolfenstetter: *Moderne Verfahren der Kryptographie.* Vieweg, Wiesbaden, 1999

[Beth] Thomas Beth: *Datensicherheitstechnik (Signale Codes und Chiffren II).* Institut für Algorithmen und Kognitive Systeme Universität Karlsruhe, 1990

[Beutel] Albrecht Beutelspacher: *Geheimsprachen Geschichte und Techniken.* C. H. Beck, München, 1997

[BiShWa] Alex Biryukov, Adi Shamir, David Wagner: *Real Time Cryp tanalysis of A5/1 on a PC.* Fast Software Encryption Work shop, New York, 2000

[Brands]   Stefan A. Brands: *Rethinking Public Key Infrastructures and Digital Certificates: Building in Privacy.*

[Brauer]   Eckart Brauer: *Durchgecheckt.* c't 8/1996

[Breite]   Marco Breitenstein: *Biometriesysteme.* Diplomarbeit Univer sität Clausthal, 1999

[BreSch]   Marco Breitenstein, Klaus Schmeh: *Punkt, Punkt, Komma, Strich.* c't 20/1999

[BreWel]   Kathrin Bremer, Günther Welsch: *Die europäische Signatur richtlinie in der Praxis.* Datenschutz und Datensicherheit 2/2000

[Buchma]   Johannes Buchmann: *Faktorisierung großer Zahlen.* Spektrum der Wissenschaft 9/1996

[BunPfa]   Michael Bungert, Oliver Pfaff: *Das WAP-Sicherheitspro tokoll WTLS.* Datenschutz und Datensicherheit 11/1999

[CamWie]   K. W. Campbell, M. J. Wiener: *Proof that DES Is Not a Group.* Advances in Cryptology, Crypto '92 Proceedings; Springer-Verlag, Berlin, 1993

[Certic]   Anonym: *The Elliptic Curve Cryptosystem.* Certicom White paper, 1997

[Damm]   Frank Damm: *Data Encryption Standard The User's View.* Europäisches Institut für Systemsicherheit Untiversität Karlsruhe 1992

[DifHel]   Whitfield Diffie, Martin E. Hellman: *New Directions in Cryptography.* IEEE Transactions on Information Theory v- IT 22 n. 6/1976

[DorHar]   Naganand Doraswamy, Dan Harkins: *IPSec.* Prentice Hall, Upper Saddle River, 1999

[EffRan]   Wolfgang Effing, Wolfgang Rankl: *Handbuch der Chip karten.* Carl Hanser Verlag, München, 1999

[EllSch]   Carl Ellison, Bruce Schneier: *Ten risks of PKI.* Computer Security Journal 1/2000

[Engel]   Stefan Engel-Flechsig: *Radicchio: a Global Initiative for Security in Wireless E-Commerce.* Datenschutz und Daten sicherheit 9/2000

[FeFeWi]   Jalal Feghhi, Jalil Fegghi, Peter Williams: *Digital Certifi cates.* Addison-Wesley, Reading, 1999

[FerSch]   Niels Ferguson, Bruce Schneier: *A Cryptographic Evaluation of IPSec.* Counterpane Internet Security, San Jose, 1998

[Fink]   Manfred Fink: *Lauschziel Wirtschaft.* Boorberg, Stuttgart, 1996

[Flanne]   Sarah Flannery: *An Investigation of a New Algorithm vs. the RSA.* White Paper, 1998

[Fox]   Dirk Fox: *Zu einem prinzipiellen Problem digitaler Signa turen.* Datenschutz und Datensicherheit 7/1998

[FoxRöh]   Dirk Fox, Alexander Röhm: *Effiziente Digitale Signatursys teme auf der Basis elliptischer Kurven*. In: Patrick Horster (Hrsg.): Digitale Signaturen DuD Fachbeiträge, 1996

[Frisch]   Markus Frisch: *Ein Überblick zum Thema RSA*. Europäisches Institut für Systemsicherheit Universität Karlsruhe 1991

[GeLuWe]   Werner Geyer, Stefan Luchs, Rüdiger Weis: *Stand der Fak torisierungsforschung*. Datenschutz und Datensicherheit 3/1999

[GolWag]   Ian Goldberg, David Wagner: *Randomness and the Netscape Browser*. Dr. Dobb's Journal 1/1996

[HaNiSS]   Uwe Hansmann, Martin S. Nicklous, Thomas Schäck, Frank Seliger: *Smart Card Application Development Using Java*. Springer-Verlag, Berlin, 1999

[Hühnle]   Detlef Hühnlein: *Effiziente Exponentiation und optimale Punktdarstellung für Signatursysteme auf Basis elliptischer Kurven*. In: Patrick Horster (Hrsg.): Digitale Signaturen DuD Fachbeiträge, 1996

[iX01]   Anonym: *Aus für CyberCash-Coins*. iX 2/2001

[JaBoPa]   Anil Jain, Ruud Bolle, Sharath Pankanti: *Biometrics: Personal Identification in Networked Society*. Kluwer Academic Publishers, Boston, 1999

[JohMat]   Don B. Johnson, Stephen M. Matyas: *Asymmetric Encryption: Evolution and Enhancements*. CryptoBytes 1/1996

[Johnso]   Don B. Johnson: *ECC, Future Resiliency and High Security Systems*. Certicom Whitepaper, 1999

[JuJaKo]   Benjamin Jun, Joshua Jaffe, Paul Kocher: *Introduction to Differential Power Analysis and Related Attacks*. Cryptography Research Technical White-Paper, 1998

[JanLaa]   Marcus Janke, Peter Laackmann: *GSM: Schwachstellen in der Verschlüsselung*. Card Forum 7/1998

[Kahn]   David Kahn: *The Codebreakers*. Simon & Schuster, New York, 1997

[Karkow]   Josef Karkowsky: *Wirtschaftsspionage, Deutschland als Selbstbedienungsladen*. KES 4/1997

[KauNew]   Elizabeth Kaufman, Andrew Newman: *Implementing IPSec*. John Wiley & Sons, New York, 1999

[Kippen]   Rudolf Kippenhahn: *Verschlüsselte Botschaften*. Rowohlt Taschenbuchverlag Reinbek, 1997

[Knuth]   Donald Knuth: *The Art of Computer Programming*. Vol. 2. Addison Wesley, 1981

[Koch95]   Paul Kocher: *Cryptanalysis of Diffie-Hellman, RSA, DSS and Other Systems Using Timing Attacks*. Cryptography Research Technical White-Paper, 1995

[Koch99]   Paul Kocher: *Breaking DES*. Cryptography Research Technical White-Paper, 1999

[LamRiv]   Butler Lampson, Ronald Rivest: *SDSI A Simple Distributed Security Infrastructure*. MIT, Cambridge, 1993

[Lemme]   Helmuth Lemme: *Chipkarten: Milliardengeschäft des 21.Jahrhunderts*. dreiteilige Serie, Elektronik 13,14,15/1996

[Lessig]   Lawrence Lessig: *The Future of Ideas: The Fate of the Commons in a Connected World*.

[Lien00]   Gerhard Lienemann: *TCP/IP-Grundlagen*. dpunkt.verlag, Heidelberg, 2000

[Lien01]   Gerhard Lienemann: *TCP/IP-Praxis*. dpunkt.verlag, Heidel berg, 2001

[Lipp]   Peter Lipp: *Sicherheit und Kryptographie in Java*. Addison-Wesley, München, 2000

[Loeb]   Larry Loeb: *Is your network safe*. Internet World (USA) 8/1997

[Luck96]   Norbert Luckhardt: *Horchideen*. c't 6/1996

[Luck97]   Norbert Luckhardt: *Auf dem Weg zum Standard?* c't Report Geld Online, 1997

[Luck99]   Norbert Luckhardt: *Schlüsselknacker aus Leuchtdioden*. c't11/1999

[LuWe99]   Stefan Lucks, Rüdiger Weis: *Advanced Encryption Standard*. Datenschutz und Datensicherheit 10/1999

[LuWeZe]   Stefan Lucks, Rüdiger Weis, Erik Zenner: *Sicherheit des GSM-Verschlüsselungsstandards A5*. Datenschutz und Daten sicherheit 7/2000

[LW00/1]   Stefan Lucks, Rüdiger Weis: *Die dritte AES-Konferenz in New York*. Datenschutz und Datensicherheit 7/2000

[LW00/2]   Stefan Lucks, Rüdiger Weis: *Der DES-Nachfolger Rijndael*. Datenschutz und Datensicherheit 12/2000

[Martiu]   Kai Martius: *Nachschlag*. iX 2/1999

[Matsui]   Mitsuru Matsui: *New Block Encryption Algorithm MISTY*. White Paper of Mitsubishi Electric Corporation, 1997

[MraWei]   Viktor Mraz, Klaus Weidner: *Falsch verbunden*. c't 10/1997

[MeOoVa]   Alfred J. Menezes, Paul C. van Oorschot, Scott A. Vanstone: *Handbook of Applied Cryptography*. CRC Press Boca Raton, 1997

[MenSch]   Thomas Menzel, Erich Schweighofer: *Das österreichische Signaturgesetz*. Datenschutz und Datensicherheit 9/1999

[Miedbr]   Anja Miedbrodt: *Das Signaturgesetz in den USA*. Datens chutz und Datensicherheit 9/2000

[Nichol]   Randall K. Nichols: *ICSA Guide to Cryptography*. McGraw-Hill, New York, 1999

[P1363]   Anonym: *IEEE P1363: Standard Specifications For Public Key Cryptography.*
            IEEE, 2000

[P1363a]   Anonym: IEEE P1363a: *Standard Specifications For Public Key Cryptography:
            Additional Techniques Version D7.* IEEE, 2001

[PetDav]   Larry L. Peterson, Bruce S. Davie: *Computernetze.* dpunkt.verlag,
            Heidelberg, 2000

[PKCS#1]   Anonym: *PKCS #1 v2.1: RSA Cryptography Standard.* RSA Laboratories, 1999

[PKCS#3]   Anonym: *PKCS #3: Diffie-Hellman Key-Agreement Standard Version 1.4.* RSA
            Laboratories Technical Note, 1993

[PKCS#5]   Anonym: *PKCS #5: Password-Based Encryption Standard Version 1.5.* RSA
            Laboratories Technical Note, 1993

[PKCS#6]   Anonym: *PKCS #6: Extended-Certificate Syntax Standard Version 1.5.* RSA
            Laboratories Technical Note, 1993

[PKCS#7]   Anonym: *PKCS #7: Cryptographic Message Syntax Standard Version 1.5.* RSA
            Laboratories Technical Note, 1993

[PKCS#8]   Anonym: *PKCS #8: Private-Key Information Syntax Standard 1.2.* RSA
            Laboratories Technical Note, 1993

[PKCS#9]   Anonym: *PKCS #9: Selected Attribute Types Version 1.1.* RSA Laboratories
            Technical Note, 1993

[PKCS#10]   Anonym: *PKCS #10 v1.7: Certification Request Syntax Standard.* RSA
            Laboratories, 2000

[PKCS#11]   Anonym: *PKCS #11 v2.10: Cryptographic Token Interface Standard.* RSA
            Laboratories, 1999

[PKCS#12]   Anonym: *PKCS 12 v1.0: Personal Information Exchange Syntax.* RSA
            Laboratories, 1999

[PKCS#13]   Burt Kaliski: *PKCS #13: Elliptic Curve Cryptography Standard.* Präsentation
            beim RSA Laboratories PKCS Workshop, 1998

[PKCS#14]   Robert W. Baldwin, James W. Gray: *PKCS #14: Pseudo-Random Number
            Generation.* Präsentation beim RSA Labo ratories PKCS Workshop, 1998

[PKCS#15]   Anonym: *PKCS #15 v1.1: Cryptographic Token Information Syntax Standard.*
            RSA Laboratories, 2000

[Pordes]   Ulrich Pordesch: *Der fehlende Nachweis der Präsentation signierter Daten.*
            Datenschutz und Datensicherheit 2/2000

[Rannen]   Kai Rannenberg: *Sicherheitszertifizierung.* Datenschutz und Datensicherheit
            4/1998

[Reimer]   Helmut Reimer: *Digitale Signatur: Update fürs Signaturges etz.* KES 4/2000

[Rescor]   Eric Rescorla: *SSL and TLS: Designing and Building Secure Systems*. Addison-Wesley, Reading, 2000

[RFC822]   D. Crocker: *Standard for the format of ARPA Internet text messages*. RFC 822, 1982

[RFC1321]   R. Rivest: *The MD5 Message-Digest Algorithm*. RFC 1321, 1992

[RFC1421]   J. Linn: *Privacy Enhancement for Internet Electronic Mail: Part I: Message Encryption and Authentication Procedures*. RFC 1421, 1993

[RFC1422]   S. Kent: *Privacy Enhancement for Internet Electronic Mail: Part II: Certificate-Based Key Management*. RFC 1422, 1993

[RFC1423]   D. Balenson: *Privacy Enhancement for Internet Electronic Mail: Part III: Algorithms, Modes, and Identifiers*. RFC 1423, 1993

[RFC1424]   B. Kaliski: *Privacy Enhancement for Internet Electronic Mail: Part IV: Key Certification and Related Services*. RFC 1424, 1993

[RFC1492]   C. Finseth: *An Access Control Protocol, Sometimes Called TACACS*. RFC 1492, 1993

[RFC1508]   J. Linn: *Generic Security Service Application Program Interface*. RFC 1508, 1993

[RFC1509]   J. Wray: *Generic Security Service API: C-bindings*. RFC 1509, 1993

[RFC1510]   J. Kohl, C. Neuman: *The Kerberos Network Authentication Service (V5)*. RFC 1510, 1993

[RFC1521]   N. Borenstein, N. Freed: *MIME (Multipurpose Internet Mail Extensions) Part One: Mechanisms for Specifying and Describing the Format of Internet Message Bodies*. RFC 1521, 1993

[RFC1661]   W. Simpson: *The Point to Point Protocol*. RFC 1661, 1994

[RFC1731]   J. Myers: *IMAP4 Authentication Mechanisms*. RFC 1731, 1994

[RFC1734]   J. Myers: *POP3 AUTHentication command*. RFC 1734, 1994

[RFC1750]   D. Eastlake, S. Crocker, J. Schiller: *Randomness Recommendations for Security*. RFC 1750, 1994

[RFC1938]   N. Haller, C. Metz: *A One-Time Password System*. RFC 1938, 1996

[RFC1939]   J. Myers, M. Rose: *Post Office Protocol Version 3*. RFC 1939, 1996

[RFC1964]   J. Linn: *The Kerberos Version 5 GSS-API Mechanism*. RFC 1964, 1996

[RFC1968]   G. Meyer: *The PPP Encryption Control Protocol (ECP)*. RFC 1968, 1996

[RFC1994]   W. Simpson: *PPP Challenge Handshake Authentication Protocol (CHAP)*. RFC 1994, 1996

[RFC2025]   C. Adams: *The Simple Public Key GSS-API Mechanism (SPKM)*. RFC 2025, 1996

[RFC2058]   C. Rigney, A. Rubens, W. Simpson, S. Willens: *Remote Authentication Dial In User Service (RADIUS)*. RFC 2058, 1997

[RFC2060]   M. Crispin: *Internet Message Access Protocol Version 4rev1*. RFC 2060, 1996

[RFC2078]   J. Linn: *Generic Security Service Application Program Interface, Version 2*. RFC 2078, 1997

[RFC2144]   C. Adams: *The CAST-128 Encryption Algorithm*. RFC 2144, 1997

[RFC2195]   J. Klensin, R. Catoe, P. Krumviede: *IMAP/POP AUTHorize Extension for Simple Challenge/Response*. RFC 2195, 1997

[RFC2222]   J. Myers: *Simple Authentication and Security Layer (SASL)*. RFC 2222, 1997

[RFC2246]   T. Dierks, C. Allen: *The TLS Protocol Version 1.0*. RFC 2246, 1999

[RFC2251]   M. Wahl, T. Howes, S. Kille: *Lightweight Directory Access Protocol (v3)*. RFC 2251, 1997

[RFC2252]   M. Wahl, A. Coulbeck, T. Howes, S. Kille: *Lightweight Directory Access Protocol (v3): Attribute Syntax Definitions*. RFC 2252, 1997

[RFC2253]   M. Wahl, S. Kille, T. Howes: *Lightweight Directory Access Protocol (v3): UTF-8 String Representation of Distinguished Names*. RFC 2253, 1997

[RFC2254]   T. Howes: *The String Representation of LDAP Search Filters*. RFC 2254, 1997

[RFC2255]   T. Howes, M. Smith: *The LDAP URL Format*. RFC 2255, 1997

[RFC2256]   M. Wahl: *A Summary of the X.500(96) User Schema for use with LDAPv3*. RFC 2256, 1997

[RFC2274]   U. Blumenthal, B. Wijnen: *User-based Security Model (USM) for version 3 of the Simple Network Management Pro tocol (SNMPv3)*. RFC 2274, 1998

[RFC2402]   S. Kent, R. Atkinson: *IP Authentication Header*. RFC 2402, 1998

[RFC2403]   C. Madson, R. Glenn: *The Use of HMAC-MD5-96 within ESP and AH*. RFC 2403, 1998

[RFC2404]   C. Madson, R. Glenn: *The Use of HMAC-SHA-1-96 within ESP and AH*. RFC 2404, 1998

[RFC2405]   C. Madson, N. Doraswamy: *The ESP DES-CBC Cipher Algorithm With Explicit IV*. RFC 2405, 1998

[RFC2406]   S. Kent, R. Atkinson: *IP Encapsulating Security Payload (ESP)*. RFC 2406, 1998

[RFC2408]   D. Maughan, M. Schertler, M. Schneider, J. Turner: *Internet Security Association and Key Management Protocol (ISAKMP)*. RFC 2408, 1998

[RFC2419]   K. Sklower, G. Meyer: *The PPP DES Encryption Protocol, Version 2 (DESE-bis)*. RFC 2419, 1998

[RFC2420]   H. Kummert: *The PPP Triple-DES Encryption Protocol (3DESE)*. RFC 2420, 1998

[RFC2451]   R. Pereira, R. Adams: *The ESP CBC-Mode Cipher Algorithms*. RFC 2451, 1998

[RFC2459]   R. Housley, W. Ford, W. Polk, D. Solo: *Internet X.509 Public Key Infrastructure Certificate and CRL Profile*. RFC 2459, 1999

[RFC2479]   C. Adams: *Independent Data Unit Protection Generic Security Service Application Program Interface (IDUP-GSS- API)*. RFC 2479, 1998

[RFC2510]   C. Adams, S. Farrell: *Internet X.509 Public Key Infrastructure Certificate Management Protocols*. RFC 2510, 1999

[RFC2511]   M. Myers, C. Adams, D. Solo, D. Kemp: *Internet X.509 Certificate Request Message Format*. RFC 2511, 1999

[RFC2527]   S. Chokhani, W. Ford: *Internet X.509 Public Key Infrastruc ture Certificate Policy and Certification Practices Frame work*. RFC 2527, 1999

[RFC2535]   D. Eastlake: *Domain Name System Security Extensions*. RFC 2535, 1999

[RFC2560]   M. Myers, R. Ankney, A. Malpani, S. Galperin, C. Adams: *X.509 Internet Public Key Infrastructure Online Certificate Status Protocol OCSP*. RFC 2560, 1999

[RFC2595]   C. Newman: *Using TLS with IMAP, POP3 and ACAP*. RFC 2595, 1999

[RFC2612]   C. Adams, J. Gilchrist: *The CAST-256 Encryption Algorithm*. RFC 2612, 1999

[RFC2617]   J. Franks, P. Hallam-Baker, J. Hostetler, S. Lawrence, P. Leach, A. Luotonen, L. Stewart: *HTTP Authentication: Basic and Digest Access Authentication*. RFC 2617, 1999

[RFC2632]   B. Ramsdell, Ed.: *S/MIME Version 3 Certificate Handling*. RFC 2632, 1999

[RFC2633]   B. Ramsdell, Ed.: *S/MIME Version 3 Message Specification*. RFC 2633, 1999

[RFC2634]   P. Hoffman, Ed.: *Enhanced Security Services for S/MIME*. RFC 2634, 1999

[RFC2661]   W. Townsley, A. Valencia, A. Rubens, G. Pall, G. Zorn, B. Palter: *Layer Two Tunneling Protocol "L2TP"*. RFC 2661, 1999

[RFC2712]   A. Medvinsky, M. Hur: *Addition of Kerberos Cipher Suites to Transport Layer Security (TLS)*. RFC 2712, 1999

[RFC2716]   B. Aboba, D. Simon: *PPP EAP TLS Authentication Protocol*. RFC 2716, 1999

[RFC2759]   G. Zorn: *Microsoft PPP CHAP Extensions, Version 2*. RFC 2759, 2000

[RFC2808]   M. Nystrom: *The SecurID(r) SASL Mechanism*. RFC 2808, 2000

[RFC2857]   A. Keromytis, N. Provos: *The Use of HMAC-RIPEMD-160-96 within ESP and AH*. RFC 2857, 2000

[RFC2931]   D. Eastlake: *DNS Request and Transaction Signatures (SIG(0)s)*. RFC 2931, 2000

[Rosing]   Michael Rosing: *Implementing Elliptic Curve Cryptography*. Manning Publications, Greenwich, 1998

[Schläg]   Uwe Schläger: *Datenschutz in Netzen.* Hamburger Datens chutzhefte 1995

[Schm98/1]   Klaus Schmeh: *Safer Net Kryptografie im Internet und intranet.* dpunkt.verlag, Heidelberg, 1998

[Schm98/2]   Klaus Schmeh: *Digitale Papiertiger.* Global Online 1-2/1998

[Schn96]   Bruce Schneier: *Applied Cryptography.* John Wiley & Sons, New York, 1996

[Schn99]   Bruce Schneier: *Snake Oil.* Crypto-Gram 2/1999

[Schn00]   Bruce Schneier: *Secrets and Lies.* John Wiley & Sons, New York, 2000

[Schu96]   Christiane Schulzki-Haddouti: *CIA schleust trojanisches Pferd in feindliche Geheimdienste ein.* Internet Aktuell 3/1996

[Schu99]   Christiane Schulzki-Haddouti: *Krypto-Invasion aus den USA Im Gespräch mit Jim Bidzos.* c't 25/1999

[Schu00]   Christiane Schulzki-Haddouti: *Elektriktrick.* c't 3/2000

[SchUng]   Isabell Schüßler, Bert Ungerer: *Verschlusssache.* iX 12/1999

[Selke]   Gisbert Selke: *Kryptographie Verfahren Ziele Einsatz möglichkeiten.* O'Reilly, Köln, 2000

[SheShe]   Beth Sheresh, Doug Sheresh: *Understanding Directory Serv ices.* New Riders, Indianapolis, 2000

[Singh]   Simon Singh: *Geheime Botschaften.* Carl Hanser Verlag, München, 1999

[SKWHFW]   Bruce Schneier, John Kelsey, David Wagner, Chris Hall, Niels Ferguson, Doug Whiting: *The Twofish Encryption Algorithm.* John Wiley & Sons, New York, 1999

[Smith]   Richard E. Smith: *Internet-Kryptographie.* Addison-Wesley, München, 1998

[Spie96]   Anonym: *Lauscher im Datenreich.* Der Spiegel 36/1996

[Spie97]   Anonym: *Gepflegtes Zwielicht.* Der Spiegel 27/1997

[Spie00]   Anonym: *Geheimpost im Internet.* Der Spiegel 18/2000

[Stalli]   William Stallings: *SNMPv3: Simple & Secure.* Information Security 1/1999

[Stende]   Arnold Stender: *Tunnel durchs Internet.* Gateway 7/1997

[Stinso]   Douglas R. Stinson: *Cryptography Theory and Practice.* CRC Press, Boca Raton, 1995

[STOA]   Anonym: *Development of Surveillance Technology and Risk of Abuse of Economic Information.* Europäische Union, Sci entific and Technological Options Assessment (STOA), 1999

[Strehl]   Res Strehle: *Verschlüsselt Der Fall Hans Bühler.* Werd Verlag, Zürich, 1994

[Tanenb]   Andrew S. Tanenbaum: *Computer Networks.* Prentice Hall, Upper Saddle River, 1996

[TegWün]   Frank Tegtmeyer, Veikko Wünsche: *Namensschutz.* iX 7/2000

[Thomas]   Stephen Thomas: *SSL and TLS Essentials*. John Wiley & Sons, New York, 2000

[TilTil]   Jim S. Tiller, James S. Tiller: *A Technical Guide to IPSec Virtual Private Networks*. CRC Press, Boca Raton, 2000

[Ulfkot]   Udo Ulfkotte: *Marktplatz der Diebe*. C. Bertelsmann, München, 1999

[Verste]   Gerhard Versteegen: *Knackpunkte Zertifizierung nach der ITSEC*. iX 2/1997

[Weck]   Gerhard Weck: *Bedrohungen in Netzen*. Dokumentation Fachseminar „Sicherheit in Netzen", Systems 96, München, 1996

[Welsch]   Günther Welsch: *Das Signaturänderungsgesetz*. Datenschutz und Datensicherheit 7/2000

[Wirtz]   Brigitte Wirtz: *Biometrische Verfahren*. Datenschutz und Datensicherheit 3/1999

[Wobst]   Reinhard Wobst: *Abenteuer Kryptologie*. Addison-Wesley, München, 1998

[X.509]   Anonym: *Information Technology Open Systems Interconnection The Directory: Authentication Framework*. 1993

[Zimmer]   Christian Zimmermann: *Der Hacker*. MVG-Verlag, Landsberg am Lech, 1996

Index